Crime in Canadian Society

Fourth Edition

ROBERT A. SILVERMAN
University of Alberta

JAMES J. TEEVAN, JR.
University of Western Ontario

VINCENT F. SACCO
Queen's University

D1445048

Butterworths
Toronto and Vancouver

Crime in Canadian Society
© 1991 Butterworths Canada Ltd.

Printed and bound in Canada by John Deyell Company

The Butterworth Group of Companies

Canada	Butterworths Canada Ltd., 75 Clegg Road, MARKHAM, Ontario, L6G 1A1 and 409 Granville St., Ste. 1455, VANCOUVER, B.C., V6C 1T2
Australia	Butterworths Pty Ltd., SYDNEY, MELBOURNE, BRISBANE, ADELAIDE, PERTH, CANBERRA and HOBART
Ireland	Butterworths (Ireland) Ltd., DUBLIN
New Zealand	Butterworths of New Zealand Ltd., WELLINGTON and AUCKLAND
Puerto Rico	Equity de Puerto Rico, Inc., HATO REY
Singapore	Malayan Law Journal Pte. Ltd., SINGAPORE
United Kingdom	Butterworth & Co. (Publishers) Ltd., LONDON and EDINBURGH
United States	Butterworth Legal Publishers, AUSTIN, Texas; BOSTON, Massachusetts; CLEARWATER, Florida (D & S Publishers); ORFORD, New Hampshire (Equity Publishing); ST. PAUL, Minnesota; and SEATTLE, Washington

Canadian Cataloguing in Publication Data

Main entry under title:

Crime in Canadian society

4th ed.
Includes bibliographical references
ISBN 0-409-89643-8

1. Crime – Canada. I. Silverman, Robert A., 1943–
II. Teevan, James J., 1942–   . III. Sacco,
Vincent F., 1948–   .

HV6807.C74 1991   364.971   C90-095749-2

Sponsoring Editor — Sandra Magico
Editor — Julia Keeler
Cover Design — Brant Cowie
Production — Kevin Skinner
Typesetting — McGraphics Desktop Publishing

This book is dedicated
to our wives and
to our teachers.

PREFACE

The first edition of *Crime in Canadian Society* was published in 1975. At that time, the materials available for a book of readings were limited and of uneven quality. In the more than fifteen years, and two subsequent editions, that have passed there have been vast improvements both in the quantity and the quality of criminological research in Canada. One of our most difficult tasks in editing this version was trying to decide which of the many very good pieces we considered could fill our limited space. We cannot overemphasize the quality of the articles available and hope that our choices will best enhance the learning experience for students.

The advent of the fourth edition marks some significant changes in the book and in Canadian criminology. Those who have used or seen earlier versions of the book will note the addition of a third editor. In joining us, Vincent F. Sacco brings new ideas and makes a major contribution to the writing of the introductory sections.

* * * * *

The fourth edition is designed to introduce students to the field of criminology. The organization of the book is more or less the same as that of the previous editions, but there have been major modifications both to the introductory essays and in the choice of articles included (about 90% are new since the last edition). In spite of the changes, the focus of the book remains sociological, and the book will probably work best in criminology courses in which that approach dominates.

The introductions to the sections familiarize students with the major topics in criminology: the law, criminal statistics, and theories of crime. These introductions have been rewritten and reflect changes to the academic discipline of criminology and to the criminal justice system that have occurred since the last edition. For instance, the federal government is in the process of changing the way in which crime in Canada is "officially" counted. Both the old and new systems are described in the introduction to Part Two. Also, since victim-centered theories have become popular explanations for crime, they are highlighted in the introduction to Part Three. Similarly, recent changes in the law itself are reflected in the introduction to Part One.

The readings are chosen to illustrate the points made in the introductions. Students are offered a chance to read the results of original Canadian research. The topics span the scope of crime as well as the boundaries of the country. There is research represented from the east coast to the west coast, running the gamut from arson in Nova Scotia to heroin use in Vancouver, robbery in Montreal, and juvenile delinquency in Toronto. As well, of course, many of the articles use the country as a whole as their data base.

Definitions of crime and delinquency are the subject of the first part of the book. Students will learn through the introduction and the readings that defining crime is not as easy as it seems. There are a variety of definitions of crime, and serious students should be aware of them all. There are controversy and conflict in attempts to define crime and criminality. The introduction and the readings illustrate how different orientations lead to different definitions. Examples of recent changes in the law are also discussed in this section.

Part Two is about measuring crime — trying to find out how many of which crimes are happening in Canada. This too is not as easy a task as it may first seem. Through the introduction and the readings, students are shown the problems inherent in current data-collection techniques, and are introduced to alternative measures and to a new system being initiated by Statistics Canada. The readings show how different measurement techniques produce the information and how behavioural changes can affect measured crime levels.

Part Three introduces the student to contemporary explanations of crime causation and presents the major theories currently being discussed by sociologists. The readings include overview articles (e.g., critical criminology) and some original theory generated in Canada (power-control theory), as well as research showing the application and testing of particular theories.

Part Four has been renamed "Crimes and Criminals: Selected Research." The name fits the array of research presented in this section. The articles explore criminal activities ranging from covert deviant sexual behaviour to armed robbery, arson, fraud, and corporate crime. The articles in Part Four, along with the others in the book, clearly illustrate the vast scope of criminological work being undertaken in Canada.

Our goal in putting this book together has been to update our overview of Canadian criminology. We present the major variants of mainstream criminology along with empirical work that is relevant to Canadian students. We hope they will benefit from the balance of orientations offered. It was serendipity more than design that we also have achieved greater geographical balance than was evident in earlier editions. It seems that there is good criminology being done throughout the country and we were fortunate enough to locate much of it.

Robert A. Silverman
James J. Teevan, Jr.
Vincent F. Sacco

ACKNOWLEDGEMENTS

Many people participated directly and indirectly in making this revision possible. As with the three earlier editions, we would like to thank our colleagues across the country for responding to our call for Canadian criminological research. Much of the book is composed of materials we received from that solicitation. We are sorry that space limitations made it impossible to use more of the excellent work we received. We would also like to thank those colleagues who provided comments and criticisms of the earlier editions.

The University of Alberta, Queen's University, and the University of Western Ontario provided the facilities and the environment needed for the completion of our tasks. Indirect support was obtained from the Contributions Grant of the Solicitor General of Canada through the Centre for Criminological Research at the University of Alberta.

The editors would like to thank the following people for their help and/or encouragement.

In Toronto: Catherine Matthews and her staff at the Centre of Criminology Library at the University of Toronto. We owe a special thanks to Sid and Rose Silverman who provided a place to work and nourishment while we made some of the tougher decisions regarding the selections.

In Ottawa: Bob Granger at the Canadian Centre for Justice Statistics provided important information concerning the new Uniform Crime Reporting system.

In Edmonton: Typing and collating tasks were admirably performed by Dorothy Burgess, Florence Avakame, and Frank Avakame. Jason and Michael Silverman and Melanie Marshall (with help from mother Charlene) did the never-ending photocopying without missing a page.

In Kingston: Joan Westenhaefer for her tireless assistance, and for meeting, and in some cases even beating, deadlines. Wilma Bauder for all that she did to facilitate the completion of the manuscript. Special thanks are owed from all of us to Katherin and Daniel Sacco, whose obsessions with New Kids on the Block and *Teenage Mutant Ninja Turtles* respectively allowed Vince Sacco the time to get some work done.

Our first contact at Butterworths for this edition was Gloria Vitale, who encouraged us and started the process. Sandra Magico took over and this became one of her first projects at Butterworths. She has done an admirable job. Our copy editor, Julia Keeler, is terrific — sharp-eyed and wise, she has kept us honest.

Our wives — Elaine, Bonnie, and Tiia — have provided support and encouragement throughout.

We are grateful to all of those who contributed directly or indirectly. Now that there are three editors, we can say that any error of omission or commission is someone else's fault.

Robert A. Silverman
James J. Teevan, Jr.
Vincent F. Sacco

LIST OF CONTRIBUTORS

Nicholas N. Bala
Queen's University Law School

Frederick J. Desroches
Department of Sociology
University of St. Jerome's College
University of Waterloo

Anthony N. Doob
Centre of Criminology
University of Toronto

Duncan Chappell
Australian Institute of Criminology

Karlene Faith
School of Criminology
Simon Fraser University

Thomas Gabor
Department of Criminology
University of Ottawa

A.R. Gillis
Department of Sociology
University of Toronto

John Hagan
Department of Sociology and Faculty of Law
University of Toronto

Timothy Hartnagel
Department of Sociology
University of Alberta

Alison J. Hatch
Criminology Research Centre
Simon Fraser University

Delbert Joe
Vancouver School District

Holly Johnson
Statistics Canada

Carl Keane
Department of Sociology
University of Western Ontario

Leslie W. Kennedy
Department of Sociology
University of Alberta

G. Won Lee
Department of Sociology
University of Alberta

Robyn Lincoln
Department of Anthropology and Sociology
University of Queensland, Australia

John L. McMullan
Department of Sociology
St. Mary's University

André Normandeau
School of Criminology
University of Montreal

Bill O'Grady
Department of Sociology
University of Toronto

Graham Parker
Osgoode Hall Law School
York University

Norman Robinson
Faculty of Education
Simon Fraser University

Vincent F. Sacco
Department of Sociology
Queen's University

Anton R. F. Schweighofer
Department of Psychology
Simon Fraser University

Robert A. Silverman
Department of Sociology
University of Alberta

Laureen Snider
Department of Sociology
Queen's University

Kenneth Stoddart
Department of Anthropology and Sociology
University of British Columbia

Peter D. Swan
Department of Law
Carleton University

James J. Teevan, Jr.
Department of Sociology
University of Western Ontario

Pierre Tremblay
Department of Sociology
McGill University

Paul R. Wilson
Department of Anthropology and Sociology
University of Queensland, Australia

TABLE OF CONTENTS

PART I

Definitions of Crime and Delinquency

Everyone knows what crime is, or so it seems. Crime is after all a "hot" topic. The mass media often report to us on the sorry state of our society by telling us how much crime and violence there is in Canada. People discuss their fears of becoming victims of crime, especially those who live in large cities, and then take protective measures against that possibility (cf. Fattah and Sacco, 1989; Sacco and Johnson, 1990). Crime is cocktail conversation. Crime is the subject of social surveys. Crime is a political issue. But what exactly is crime? Crime is in fact different things to different people. Trying to sort out the various definitions of crime — for there is no one perfect definition — is the subject of this portion of the book.

LAY DEFINITIONS

Generally the legal bureaucracy and the average citizen agree on the acts to be labelled crimes. Murder is a crime, as are shoplifting, arson, robbery, fraud, and break and enter. In some instances, however, citizens define acts as criminal when legally they are not (a practice criminologists call *inclusion*), while in other instances they refuse to define certain acts as criminal when legally they are (what criminologists call *exclusion*). [1] Inclusion is apparent in casual conversations in which individuals refer to general social ills as crimes. The price of housing, the change in the value of the dollar, the disrespect of youth, or a refusal to show deference to the mention of the Queen (none of these phenomena are legally defined crimes)

may thus be defined as crimes. Even the more serious examples of emotional neglect and psychological abuse of children, spouses, and the elderly are generally not criminal matters. For laypeople, this process of making crime roughly equal to what they consider bad in their society [2] is not an important error, and is certainly quite acceptable in an informal context. For a scientific study of crime, however, the inclusion of the merely bad or immoral would make the field of criminology almost limitless. In attempts to be precise, criminologists usually reject such popular definitions of crime.

On the other hand, there are many instances in which crimes legally have occurred but the individuals involved — victim, offender, or both — do not define the act as criminal. Until recently, much spousal abuse fell into this category. Such omissions are examples of exclusion. In practice, the definition of acts as crimes often depends on the perceptions of the actors involved, how they define the behaviours that have occurred. For example, when one individual strikes another, legally an assault may have occurred. But suppose it was in fun, as a result of a playful struggle? Most people experience an assault in fun at some time in their lives. The pushing and shoving of children, considered to be a normal part of growing up, is just one example. Among adults as well, and not only on hockey ice, one finds the equivalents of pushing and shoving matches, few of which are defined as criminal. Even if the force used is excessive and injures one of the participants, the injury is often defined as accidental. The injured party is given comfort and the perpetrator is warned to be more careful in the future. None of the actors involved feel that a crime has been committed.

Similarly, an assault that occurs during the course of an argument may be considered a part of daily life, and not a crime, by some segments of our society. Hitting an individual, for example, may be viewed as a legitimate way of settling a dispute in some subcultures in Canada today. If both parties agree to this solution, then neither will define the act involved as criminal. The control agencies will not be called to intervene, except perhaps by some observer, and the argument will be settled.

Suppose, however, that one of the participants does not believe that a fight is an acceptable way to solve a dispute. Or suppose an individual is hit, not by a friend or an acquaintance, but instead by a stranger, perhaps in a pub. In such a case, the individual may indeed define the event as a crime and call the police. In this instance an assault, as defined by the Criminal Code of Canada (section 265), may have been committed, not because the act was different, but because *it was defined differently*. The attacker may even be arrested and prosecuted. Thus, the same use of force may or may not be a crime depending upon the context and upon the actors', especially the victims', perceptions of the situation.

Another example may help to illustrate some of the problems in utilizing popular definitions of crime. The public and the mass media both refer to the crime of rape and assume that it occurs with some frequency in this country. The action involved, according to common knowledge, involves forcible sexual intercourse, a man forcing a woman or less frequently a man forcing another man to engage in sexual behaviour including penetration. The behaviour in question is apparently quite clear: it involves force and sexual relations. But "rape" is not a crime in Canada, the rape sections of the Criminal Code having been repealed and replaced in a process begun in 1980. The activities just described are now found under the general heading of *assault* and are specified as sexual assault (sec. 271), sexual assault with a weapon, threats to a third party, or causing bodily harm (sec. 272), or aggra-

vated sexual assault (sec. 273). The sexual aspect has been downplayed — even penetration is no longer a requirement in the definition of the crime — and the physical harm emphasized (cf. Hinch, 1988). Changing the crime to assault shifted the focus away from the end sought (sexual activity) to the force used, and thus sexual assault joined a punch to the face, a knife to the stomach, or a kick in the head as assaults to the body. [3] So extensive was the change in definition that in fact the term "rape" is now found only in the index of the Pocket Criminal Code (1989) and then only in relation to publication of the complainant's identity. Nowhere is "rape" listed, defined, or discussed as a crime. Thus, most Canadians (including the press) call the event previously described a rape, but legally, in Canada, no crime of rape exists.

Most criminologists avoid lay definitions, preferring more precise legal definitions of their subject matter. One of the major reasons for using the legal definition is a pragmatic one. As the reader will see in Part Two of this book, most crime data are based on legal definitions of crime and most theories (see Part Three) are in turn tested using these data. For consistency, therefore, in most instances we shall use legal definitions of crime.

DEFINITIONS MADE BY POLICE, PROSECUTORS, AND JUDGES

Not only the victims but also the agents of the Canadian criminal justice system, from police to crown prosecutors to judges, may exercise considerable discretion in deciding whether an act is a crime. For example, suppose one man attacks another and hurts him, and the victim calls the police. Under a strict and static notion of law enforcement and crime, section 267 (assault with a weapon or causing bodily harm) of the Criminal Code would be enforced by the police:

Every one who in committing an assault, ... causes bodily harm to the complainant, is guilty of an indictable offence and is liable to imprisonment for a term not exceeding ten years.

The Crown would then prosecute the defendant using the available evidence, the accused would be found guilty, and the convicted criminal would be given a sentence of up to ten years.

But there are alternatives to this scenario: (1) The police arrive and the victim indicates that while he did call the police, he is not willing to testify against the offender in court. His motives are private but could include an unwillingness to take time off from work to appear in court as a complainant, or an unwillingness to see the assaulter, often a friend or a relative, sent to trial. The police in most cases will not pursue the case, because they know that they will have insufficient evidence without the testimony of the victim. According to all public records, then, no crime of assault has taken place. The legal code does not indicate that the police have such discretion, but under these conditions it is in fact normal practice. (2) The *victim* is abusive to the police, and in anger they decide not to record the crime (Ericson, 1982:113). In fact, the police take many variables into consideration in deciding to write up a case. For example, property disputes involving losses to middle-class, white males are more frequently recorded than their counterparts, that is, personal offenses with victims different from the above (Ericson, 1982:113). (3) The police do arrest the alleged attacker and charge him with unlawfully causing bodily harm. The Crown is ready to proceed when the defence attorney suggests a deal. If the charge is reduced to *assault*, punishable by a summary (less serious) conviction (Criminal Code, section 266), the accused will plead guilty. Otherwise he will plead not guilty to the original charge and will insist on a trial. To speed things through the overburdened criminal justice process, the Crown agrees. The advantage to the defendant is the possibility of a shorter sentence and a less serious record, while the advantages to the criminal justice system are efficiency and economy. (4) The police arrest the individual and charge him with unlawfully causing bodily harm. The prosecutor proceeds with the case. The defendant pleads not guilty to the charge and is able to convince a judge that he in fact did not intend to injure the victim (see the discussion of *mens rea* later in this chapter).

The judge finds the defendant not guilty. Officially, then, no *crime* of assault took place.

The combinations of events in the criminal justice system that can occur to redefine an act, compared to the behaviours that actually happen, are thus numerous. The subject is introduced here to point out that agents of social control must interpret and enforce the law, and the way in which they do so is a part of the process of defining crime (Doob and Chan, 1982; Osborne, 1983).

A SOCIOLOGICAL DEFINITION

In a sociological sense, crimes involve the violation of *norms* — social rules that attempt to regulate behaviour and tell people what to do and what not to do in various situations. These rules range from the important and binding (thou shalt not kill) to the less important and optional (standing when an older person enters a room).

Norms or social rules are learned by individuals in the *socialization* process. This process, which begins in infancy, is the way in which people learn how society wishes them to behave. To oversimplify a complex process, individuals internalize norms, and then rarely have to think about them. People simply do what they have learned to be the right (or natural, or correct) thing to do. From a sociological point of view, the norms control behaviour. A personal example may help. Think of a simple activity, such as greeting someone you know. What are the "rules" you follow in completing this ritual? What do you say? How do you act? Shake hands? Kiss? Punch shoulders? Do the rules change depending on the individual met? Your behaviour in such situations is governed by social norms you learned long ago, probably without being aware that you were learning them. All will go well in the ritual as long as you follow the rules. You do not normally think about them; you follow them automatically. What would happen if you broke one of the rules? For instance, what if you as a male kissed another male in greeting (acceptable in some European and Middle Eastern societies, and even parts of Quebec)? What would happen? Again, it would depend on the specific individuals involved and the situation, but if you believed you were breaking a rule, you would probably be correct, and the violation would likely cause a negative reaction.

One measure of how strongly a society feels about its various norms is the punishment or sanction applied to those who violate them. Breaking even the weakest norm usually results in some type of reaction, although it may be insignificant in terms of punishment. For another personal example, walking down a street has many behavioural requirements that you rarely think of as norms. As you approach another individual coming toward you, you must avert your eyes at a certain point. You may not stare at the other person as you pass. If you stare, you violate a norm and the reaction to the violation may be anything — from nothing, to the other individual glaring back, to the verbal challenge "What are ya staring at?" These less severely sanctioned norms are called *folkways*.

There are other norms whose infractions carry more serious punishments. These norms are *mores*, and their violations are seen as more threatening and harmful to society, at least by some powerful segments of that society. Most crimes are violations of mores. Although most criminal laws (for example, those prohibiting homicide and theft) are mores, not all mores are laws. For a large part of our society, mores include the permanence of marriage, heterosexuality, and eventually having children. Divorce, homosexuality, and childlessness are not, however, crimes in Canada.

For many sociologists, crime is subsumed under the broader topic of deviance; deviant behaviour is defined as a violation of these folkways and mores, and generally involves, besides the violation of a norm, the possibility of punishment and the existence of a group that would want to punish the violation. Thus, sociologists are more interested in norm violations than in strictly legal definitions of crime. While there have been many attempts to summarize the sociological notion of crime, one of the best is still Gillin's (1945:9; cf. Heidensohn, 1990:3) classic statement that crime is

...an act that has been shown to be actually harmful to society, or that is *believed* to be socially harmful by a group of people that has the power to enforce its belief and that places such an act under the ban of positive penalties.

Gillin's definition includes the ideas that the harm involved can be a constructed (believed) harm and that power determines what will be defined as criminal — points to which we shall return throughout the volume.

THE LEGAL DEFINITION

Sutherland and Cressey (1978) in the tenth edition of their classic text asserted that the criminal law and thus the legal definition of crime is marked by four ideals: politicality, specificity, uniformity, and penal sanction. Politicality means that only governments, and in Canada this means the Federal Parliament, can make criminal laws; specificity, that the laws are quite precise in their wording, telling *specifically* and exactly what is forbidden (*proscribed*) or demanded (*prescribed*); uniformity, that the laws apply equally to all; and penal sanction, that violators are threatened with a penalty and punishment. *A crime is then any act or omission in violation of that criminal law.* [4]

Legally, then, a crime is a specific act forbidden to all Canadians by the Federal Parliament and punishable for all who perform that act. The Law Reform Commission of Canada discussed the legal definition of crime as well (1974:1-4), making the following additional points: (1) Not all acts against the law are crimes. *Torts*, or civil wrongs, for example, are not crimes. Criminal acts are proceeded against by *prosecution* and may result in *punishment*, while civil actions proceed by *suit* and may result in *compensation*. (2) Only the federal government can make a criminal law; the provinces cannot, according to the British North America Act. The provinces can create offences which, although treated like crimes, are technically not crimes. Examples of such legislation include driving and Sunday shopping rules. (3) Crimes are thought of as more serious than offences because (a) they are seen to involve greater harm to individuals, (b) they are more often a violation of fundamental rules, like *mores*, and (c) "they are wrongs that any person *as a person* could commit. Offences are more specialized...that we commit when playing certain special roles...." For example, individuals disobey speed limits as drivers; they commit murders or thefts as individuals (1974:3).[5]

Despite the distinctions between crimes and offences, the consequences to individuals caught for committing any of the many acts legislated against by the provincial and municipal governments and named "offences" may be similar to the consequences of committing a crime. For the individuals being charged, then, there may be only a technical difference between a federal *crime* and a provincial *offence*. Thus, for some purposes, the important component of a legal definition of a crime is that it is an act legislated against by any political body and deemed to be a criminal rather than civil (tort) matter by that body, and hence that criminal rather than civil proceedings may ensue.

In a still more technical and legal sense, for an act or an omission[6] to be considered a crime, several conditions are necessary. First, the act must have been legally forbidden before the act was undertaken, that is, the act or omission must be in violation of an *already existing law* that forbids or commands the act. This means that an act or omission, no matter how ugly, mean, or distasteful, is not a crime if no law exists against it. An *ex post facto* (after the fact) law thus cannot designate as criminal an act legal at the time it was committed. Actually, there are probably very few offensive acts not already covered by the Criminal Code, but the general ideal of *nullum crimen sine lege, nulla poena sine lege*, that is, no crime without law, no punishment without law, is still an important principle of Canadian jurisprudence. The main rationale behind the principle is that it would be unfair to punish persons who, when they acted, did so in good faith, thinking they were obeying the law.[7] One recent example concerns computers and computer software. The only law that could be applied to their misuse was theft of telecommunications (old Criminal Code 326), and it was only recently that the Criminal Code was amended to include 342.1, unauthorized use of computers. An implica-

tion of this principle is that laws must be quite specific and not vague, again applying the logic that the public should know exactly what it legally can and cannot do. Vaguely worded laws would make behaviour problematic, as people would not be sure if their activities would or would not result in penal sanction.

Second, there must be an *actus reus* or act. Merely thinking about or *planning* to violate the law is generally not a crime, with the exception of the crime of conspiracy (conspiracy to murder or falsely prosecute), Criminal Code section 465. In reality, there never were many conspiracy charges laid in Canada, even when the grounds were much broader than they are now. Thus, it is a fairly safe generalization that an *actus reus* is a requirement for a legal definition of a crime.

Mens rea[8] or criminal intent, is a third requirement for a crime. Intentions are not the same as motives (which are the reasons why individuals commit crimes), but instead involve determination and purpose — that the individuals *intend* the consequences of their acts. This means that they know what they are doing and thus mean to do what they are doing. Insane persons cannot commit crimes, since legally they are incapable of criminal intent. Accidents also are generally not counted as crimes, again for lack of intent.

Because they study criminal acts and not offenders, many criminologists find too strict the *mens rea* requirement for defining crime stated above. An alleged *actus reus* is sufficient for them to say a crime has taken place. Since most offenders are not apprehended, and thus *mens rea* or intent cannot be demonstrated, such criminologists choose to study all acts listed in police offence reports as being "founded" (see introduction to Part Two) and do not worry about *mens rea*.[9]

Finally, two additional requirements for the legal definition of a crime are that there should be a causal connection between the *actus reus* and any harm or outcome, and that the *mens rea* and *actus reus* must relate to the same act. These are general rules, ignored in certain circumstances, and sometimes a matter of dispute. For an excellent discussion of the technicalities of these and similar issues see Parker in this section of the book.

CHANGING LAWS CHANGE DEFINITIONS

Many people think of the law as being relatively static. Lawyers know that this is not so. The Criminal Code is frequently amended by Parliament. Minor changes occur often and are based on a "fine tuning" of legislation or on recent court interpretations. Changes with larger implications are less frequent and slower to occur. Two recent major changes, each with vast implications, include the introduction of the Canadian Charter of Rights and Freedoms as part of the Constitution Act of 1982 and the Young Offenders Act (1985), which replaced the Juvenile Delinquents Act (1970).

The philosophy and effects of the Young Offenders Act are well documented in the article by Bala that appears later in this section. For now, let us say that the changes to the old act and subsequent amendments have sometimes been controversial. Some feel that the philosophy of the old system, in which the court acted as a wise and judicious parent, was superior to the philosophy of the new act, which treats older children as more responsible for their acts. With the introduction of the YOA, youths basically gained the protection of due process (legal safeguards such as right to counsel) but lost some of the informal treatment previously routine under the old act. Some civil libertarians are especially concerned that the new system may lead to more frequent and longer custody for youths than occurred under the old act. At the other end of the spectrum, some feel that the new age definitions provided by the act (limited to ages 12 to 17 instead of the previous lower limit of age 7) allow younger children (up to age 11) to "get away with murder" (not to mention sexual assault, robbery, and arson). Children 11 or younger are now defined as incapable of having the *mens rea* necessary for crime. Perhaps the greatest public concern surrounds the maximum three-year sentence for those aged 12 to 17 who commit crimes. Cases like that of the 1989 Winnipeg boy who killed a woman, attempted to kill another, and engaged in break, enter, and theft can only increase that concern. Many feel both that three years is too small a price to pay and that society deserves more than three years' protection from this child. (We should note that the YOA does permit the transfer of youthful offenders to adult court and its penalties, but this is infrequently undertaken.). As this is being written, studies that attempt to establish the actual effects of the new act on the administration of juvenile justice in Canada are continuing (see Hudson et al., 1988). In reading Bala's article, the reader will find that one thing is certain — the changes have had vast implications for both offenders and the juvenile justice system.

The impact of the Charter of Rights and Freedoms on the adult system may be even greater than the effects of the Young Offenders Act on the juvenile system. Since the introduction of the Charter there have been numerous court cases testing the meaning of some of its sections. [10] Readers of the Charter will understand how these cases arose, as some of the sections of the Charter are vaguely worded and some even contradict other legislation. As a result, it has generally been left to the courts to decide their exact meanings and applicability. Of course, much of the Charter has nothing to do with criminal procedure or criminal law — but the proportion that does has created numerous test cases. Most of these cases do not deal with the creation of law itself or what the law will be, our topic in this section, but with the administration of justice and criminal procedure, that is, how the law will be enforced. For example, rules of evidence, warrants, illegal searches, burden of proof, presumption of innocence, and the illegality of minimum sentences have each been the subject of at least one Charter-based court challenge. Such procedural issues do, however, affect the treatment of crime, as they affect police and court activities and thus indirectly the statistics on whether crimes have been committed or not. For example, each time a search is deemed illegal, a *legally defined* crime technically will not have been committed.

And there were some substantive changes to the criminal law arising out of the Charter as well, including the striking down of the abortion law. The Charter's protection of free speech led to challenges to the law that made it illegal to solicit for purposes of prostitution (the Supreme Court in 1990 decided the law was constitutional) and to nullification of parts of the promotion of racial-hatred sections of the Criminal code. In addition, on the basis of the

Charter, the courts have struck down, in the Vaillancourt decision, the section of the code dealing with constructive murder, the old law that if someone was killed even by accident during the commission of another crime, the intent for the original crime was transferred to the intent needed for first-degree murder.

The process of defining crime and the law as based on the Charter of Rights and Freedoms will be a continuing one. One judge has said that the Charter has become a "pension for lawyers." When a lawyer runs out of all other appeals, there is always the Charter. In 1985, only three years after the Charter had been in place, Magnet produced a seven-hundred-page book documenting Charter cases to that point in time. Since then there have been several books on the same topic. The Charter caseload has become so heavy and the issues so complex that some books concentrate only on *portions* of the act (e.g., Atrens, 1989, deals only with sections 7, legal rights, and 11, proceedings in criminal and penal matters).

One effect of the Charter on criminal proceedings has been to make Canadian procedure more closely resemble its U.S. counterpart. For instance, in *R. v. Therens* (1985), 59 N.R. 122 (S.C.C.) cited in Magnet (1985), the defendant was made to take a breathalyser test after a single-vehicle accident. The investigating police officer failed to tell the defendant of his right to "retain and instruct counsel" (section 10 of the Charter). The judge excluded the "certificate of analysis" from evidence in the trial, reasoning that the police officer had flagrantly violated a Charter right and that such action would "bring the administration of justice into disrepute" (section 24). We expect that these and similar decisions will result in fewer convictions and more dismissals.

Other cases with implications for crime and criminal justice that have been, or are now being, contested under the Charter, include obscenity (p. 942ff.), unreasonable search and seizure (p. 1184ff.), arrest and detention (p. 1236ff.), cruel and unusual punishment (p. 1349ff.), and exclusion of evidence (p. 1550ff.) (all from Magnet, 1985; also cf. Morton et al., 1989, and Atrens, 1989).

Thus, pornography, the right to counsel, random spot checks for impaired drivers (deemed legal by the Supreme Court in 1990), and breathalyser tests have each come under challenge by way of a Charter appeal (also see *Maclean's*, 1988). Such scrutiny is no guarantee of a better criminal justice system, just a different one with different powers heard from (see the next section). It does not even guarantee a consistent system. In an examination of Lord's Day legislation (*Supreme Court of Canada-Her Majesty the Queen and Big M Drug Mart Ltd.*, April 24, 1985) the Court struck down Sunday closing in Alberta because it favoured one religion but basically accepted the same closing in Ontario because of the need for a day of rest.

CONFLICT VERSUS CONSENSUS DEFINITIONS

Durkheim, one of the founders of sociology, argued that a crime is a violation of a widely held societal norm or value, an act that attacks the collective conscience of a society (1964:79). Everyone in that society is outraged by crime because disobeying the rules weakens and attacks the very basis of society. This definition of crime is based on the assumption that the criminal law arises out of consensus, out of commonly agreed upon norms and values. Thus, since all or most people would agree that murder, sexual assault, and theft are serious threats to individuals and to society, these acts are defined as crimes.

For conflict theorists, on the other hand, crimes are more often seen as acts that the ruling class has made illegal in order to protect its own interests. These theorists see the law as a tool, part of the superstructure of institutions created by the ruling class to serve itself. The law, instead of arising from consensus and providing justice for all, is in reality a weapon of oppression. Conflict theorists disagree on whether the capitalist class alone (Taylor, Walton, and Young, 1973) or in concert with other power groups (sometimes called *moral entrepreneurs*) controls the enactment of law (Turk, 1976b), but they agree that it is conflict and power which determine the law, and not consensus. [11]

This discussion is germane to the definition of crime, since consensus and conflict theorists would come to quite different definitions. Whereas Durkheim would define acts that violate the Criminal Code of Canada as crimes, conflict theorists would argue that the crimes in the Criminal Code are often not crimes at all, but instead are expressions of the will of the ruling class. The capitalists pay poor wages and then create a crime of theft for those who cannot live decently on those wages. The real crime, they say, is the poor wages. Look to the system for the crime and not to its victim, the thief.

For conflict theorists, some of the basic values or aspects of capitalism should be defined as crimes, for example, the idea of profit, the practice of speculation, the encouragement of over-consumption, and the denial of the workers' rights to decent food, shelter, dignity, and self-determination. Hence, from a conflict perspective, the "real" crimes have not been defined as such; they are not illegal, because their victims do not control the law and thus the definition of what constitutes a crime. Thus the concept of ruling-class crimes, legal acts that "should" be illegal, provides us with but another definition of crime.

For one final example of the social construction and relativity of definitions of crime, Fattah (n.d.) reminds us that terrorism is a crime only if it is unsuccessful in overthrowing the authorities. Should the terrorists win their battle, their acts may become the cherished symbols of a successful revolution, as in the Boston Tea Party and the storming of the Bastille. The 1989 turmoil in the Soviet bloc displays how today's dissidents are tomorrow's leaders, yesterday's leaders, tomorrow's criminals.

Through the 1970s and 1980s conflict criminologists exerted a good deal of influence on the study of crime. Many of these scholars were more interested in political ideology and political activism (Ratner, 1984, 1986; Taylor, 1983a, 1984; Brickey and Comack, 1986; Fleming, 1985) than in the classical criminology orientations driven by strict adherence to the scientific method. Their orientation stimulated a good deal of research and had an important influence on the definition of crime. For example, in her 1980 article Comack-Antony presented a chart that compares and contrasts the ways in which radical and liberal crimi-

nology define crime. The chart, slightly modified and reproduced on the opposite page, illustrates well how perspective affects definitions of crime.

By 1990 some Marxist criminologists had admitted that studying crime through an idealistic framework may not be very fruitful. "...(L)eft idealism: tended to romanticize the criminal; ignored the victim of intra-working-class crime by drawing attention to the crimes of the powerful; viewed all crime as a product of class conflict; tended to explain why the state criminalizes certain people rather than explaining why certain people become criminal; ruled out the possibility of progressive reform; and argued that in a socialist political order the need for a criminal justice system (along with the state itself) would disappear" (Lowman, 1989, citing Lea and Young, 1984).

Some have now oriented themselves to something they call "left realism." This approach retains the conflict orientation while it "...evinces a new interest in crime, the victims of crime and crime control" (Lowman, 1989:243). As for Marx's prediction about the withering away of either the state or the criminal justice system, recent events in eastern Europe would suggest problems with those expectations.

SOCIALLY DEFINED CRIME

Therefore we have several definitions of crime from which to choose: (1) acts that violate norms; (2) acts that violate legal norms; (3) acts that the participants define as violations of legal norms; (4) acts that violate legal norms after the acts have been redefined by the agents of the Canadian criminal justice system; (5) acts for which *mens rea* and *actus reus* have been demonstrated; and (6) acts that are the "real" crimes (conflict criminology). Each definition may be appropriate under different circumstances.

Different definitions may not be that important in themselves. The crucial point to remember is that different definitions will yield different theories about the causes and the treatment of crime and delinquency. [12] The specific definition used determines what is studied and sug-

Liberal Criminology	*Radical Criminology*
definition of crime:	
legalistic approach: crime as behaviour.	legalistic approach: crime as a definition of behaviour made by officials of the State.
leads to an examination of the characteristics and life experiences of the criminal actor; general acceptance of the State.	leads to an examination of political authority and questioning of the State.
emphasis on cultural variables as they relate to explanations of crime, e.g., how failure in school could lead to crime.	emphasis on structural variables as they relate to explanations of crime, e.g., how the whole economic system causes crime.
role of the criminologist:	
criminologist as "expert advisor" to "enlightened leaders."	commitment to Praxis, to the *application* by scientists of their results to improve society.
social research used to provide information for the smooth and efficient running of the State system.	social research used to determine the means by which desired change can be implemented and inequalities between individuals and groups diminished.
image of crime and the criminal:	
crime as a universal phenomenon due to the inadequacies of human beings; deterministic (controlled by heredity and environment) image of people.	crime as a universal phenomenon due to the conflictual nature of society; human behaviour seen as purposive, intentional, and goal-oriented.
prescriptions for change:	
adherence to the rehabilitative ideal; emphasis is on changing the nature of the individual offender.	stresses the political nature of crime; emphasis is on changing the structural components of society.
adjustment of the individual to the needs of the system.	adjustment of the system to the needs of individuals.

Source: Adapted from Comack-Antony, 1980: 246-47.

gests treatment (cf. Jeffrey, 1990). Just imagine the differences between a consensus theorist and a conflict theorist, for the most obvious example, with the former treating "bad individuals" and the latter restructuring a "corrupt" society. Thus, as readers of criminological research, you should pay close attention to the researchers' definitions of crime. Such scrutiny will help you to evaluate the adequacy of their conclusions.

Whichever definition is used, it is important to remember that crime is made by people. There is not a universal definition of criminal behaviour. Crime is defined in a given time and place by those who have the power to act on those definitions. Most criminologists are then interested in those behaviours that are defined as crime. In contemporary societies this will usually mean those behaviours that have been dealt with by some form of legislation (i.e., the legal definition). Criminologists also sometimes study the way in which certain behaviours come to be defined as crimes, while other behaviours do not. Most often, though, they are interested in the patterns of "maladaptive behaviours" and the "causes" of those behaviours. Later sections of this book address those issues.

THE READINGS

The readings that follow were selected to illustrate and expand on the varying definitions of crime and the powers behind them. The legal aspects of crime are featured in Parker's "The Structure of Criminal Law," which introduces students to the fundamentals of Canadian criminal law. Criminologists who use only strict legal definitions of crime will find Parker's discussion most useful.

Doob in "The Many Realities of Crime" briefly discusses law and morality and the differing judicial, legislative, and public conceptions of crime and then devotes most of his discussion to public perceptions of both crime and the criminal justice system. The difficulties with public perceptions of crime are well illustrated in this piece.

In "The Young Offenders Act: A Legal Framework" Bala discusses the philosophy and specifics of that legislation as well as some of the court decisions that have arisen since its inception. In reading this article, students will clearly see the changes in the treatment of juveniles by the criminal justice system, compared with their treatment under previous legislation. As an exercise, students should try to imagine which forces fought for these changes and which fought against. Could a conflict model apply in this instance?

Finally, Schweighofer's "The Canadian Temperance Movement: Contemporary Parallels" examines the activities of the moral entrepreneurs behind the alcohol temperance movement and then makes comparisons with today's war on drugs. Misinformation and miseducation are shown as lying behind both movements.

NOTES

1. Nettler (1984:2) argues that the public are often ignorant of the broad extent of the criminal law, that they have a narrower definition of crime than legally is the case. It is illegal, for example, to give out trading stamps in Canada (CC 427), and to transport someone to a common bawdy house (CC 211), but few Canadians would be aware of these crimes.

2. To be more accurate, we might say that the popular conception of crime is what people consider bad or immoral, mediated by their perceptions of what the law is.

3. The changes to the law also represented attempts to lighten the complainant's burden; for example, now no corroboration is needed and one does not have to report the crime immediately. These changes also sought to remedy the fact that the complainant often felt that she was on trial, with her past sexual behaviour too often an issue. Her sexuality, like the wealth of a robbery victim, thus has become less relevant in defining the crime. Difficulties with the law remain, however; for example, in precisely defining the crime, including the issue of what unconsented touching is sexual and what is not, and in a reluctance on the part of the police to pursue charges if previous sexual activity can imply consent. Moreover, an honest but mistaken belief in consent is still a defense (Hinch, 1988).

4. Tappan (1947), among others, argued that this legal definition of crime should be used exclusively in criminology. The classic criminologist Sellin (1938), on the other hand, argued that the criminal law is irrelevant to the definition of crime. He believed in universals as a goal of science and said that criminology should not respect political or time boundaries. The law, being political and temporal, is too relative and unstable. Therefore criminologists should study behaviour that violates *conduct norms*, those universal and constant standards such as murder, assault, and theft, whether or not those standards have been formally enacted into the criminal law.

5. On this point we are in some disagreement with the Law Reform Commission. One may commit murder in his/her role as murderer (i.e., hired killer). Further, some "offences" may be punished more severely than some "crimes."

6. Omission offences include, for example, section 50: "Every one commits an offence who (b) knowing that a person is about to commit treason does not, with all reasonable dispatch, inform a justice of the peace or other peace officer thereof or make other reasonable efforts to prevent that person from committing high treason or treason"; section 129: "Every one who (b) omits, without reasonable excuse, to assist a public officer or peace officer in the execution of

his duty in arresting a person or in preserving the peace, after having reasonable notice that he is required to do so"; and section 215: "Every one is under legal duty, (a) as a parent, foster parent, guardian or head of a family, to provide necessaries of life for a child under the age of sixteen years; (b) as a married person, to provide necessities of life to his spouse; and (c) to provide necessaries of life to a person under his charge if that person (i) is unable, by reason of detention, age, illness, insanity or other cause, to withdraw himself from that charge, and (ii) is unable to provide himself with necessaries of life."

7. Mistake of law, knowingly acting but not knowing that you are breaking a law, is not an acceptable defence in Canada nor in most countries. Still, the arbitrariness of an *ex post facto* law, which in effect creates an earlier mistake of law, is considered a basic error in jurisprudence. Individuals would not be able to act rationally, because they would never know the legal consequences of their acts, due to the potential of these acts later being declared illegal.

8. A more accurate translation of *mens rea* is "guilty mind." We choose, however, not to use that term, as it is often confused with the concept of guilt. In fact, one can have *mens rea* but feel no guilt at all. Political assassins often feel moral righteousness in their acts and yet *mens rea* may be present.

9. Thus, these researchers allow the police or victims to define crime, and again there is a lack of concern with *mens rea*. Lawyers, however, and criminologists who demand a truly legal definition of crime would argue that *mens rea* is crucial in defining criminals and crimes. If *mens rea* cannot be demonstrated through a court conviction, then it is always possible that legally no crime has taken place. An act that resembles a crime has been committed, but until *mens rea* is established, technically no crime has taken place.

10. In an early reaction to the Charter, Alberta had to introduce an Omnibus Bill to change forty-eight laws in order to be consistent with the Charter's provisions concerning age discrimination (Peterson, 1985).

11. Pluralists, for example, Pound (1943), stand in between the conflict and consensus positions. They envision a society composed of competing interests, as opposed to consensus, but they see the law as impartial and reconciling these interests, rather than serving them, as the conflict theorists argue.

12. The many problems inherent in defining crime, and the alternatives available, are also operative in defining delinquency. In this book, as in many criminology texts, juveniles and adults are discussed under the same cover.

Chapter 1

THE STRUCTURE OF CRIMINAL LAW*

Graham Parker

SOME FUNDAMENTAL RULES

THE PRINCIPLE OF LEGALITY

The principle of legality is a fundamental rule built into any democratic system of criminal justice. This self-evident principle can be described as "the rule of law" — fairness in the formulation of the definition of criminal offences, the defences, and the rules that govern the determination of guilt. The old authorities express it as *nullum crimen sine lege, nulla poena sine lege* — there can be no crime or punishment unless it is in accordance with law that is certain, unambiguous, and not retroactive.

VAGUENESS AND RETROACTIVITY

The most obvious requirement is that criminal law should be prospective and not retroactive; the potential offender is entitled to know beforehand, with some precision, the kinds of behaviour that would attract criminal penalties. Totalitarian regimes often breach this principle. For instance, a Nazi decree of June 28, 1935 provided:

Punishment shall be inflicted when an act is committed which the law may declare to be punishable or which may appear to be deserving of punishment according to the fundamental idea of a penal law and according to healthy popular feeling. In the event of no penal law applying directly to the act, such act shall be punished under the penal provision whose basic idea is most suited to it.

This law also suffers from another defect that offends against the principle of legality, that is, the law should not be vague. This fault is also seen in the 1934 Soviet Code:

A crime is any socially dangerous act or omission which threatens the foundations of the Soviet political structure. In cases where the Criminal Code makes no direct reference to particular forms of crime, punishment or other measures of social protection are applied in accordance with those Articles of the Criminal Code which deal with crimes most closely approximate in gravity and in kind, to the crimes actually committed.

A similar provision is found in the Nazi decree "for the protection of the people and the state," which makes it an offence for "whoever provokes or incites to an act contrary to public welfare...to be punished with a penitentiary sentence, or, under mitigating circumstances, with imprisonment of not less than three months." The terms "contrary to public welfare" and "mitigating circumstances" are inherently vague and should be avoided if we wish to adhere to fundamental fairness.

* Edited version of Graham Parker, *An Introduction to Criminal Law*, 3d ed. (Toronto: Methuen, 1987), chapters 4 and 5. © Nelson Canada, 1987, A Division of Thomson Canada. Edited material.

    Editor's note: illustrations (appearing in boxes) have been integrated with the text, and the original numbering of illustrations used by Parker has been maintained. In the illustrations, names beginning with D are the defendant and names beginning with V represent the victim. Statute numbers have been updated to reflect the 1990 Criminal Code.

The United Nations in 1948 suggested a remedy for these infringements of the principle of legality in article 11(2) of the Universal Declaration of Human Rights:

No one shall be held guilty of any penal offence on account of any act or omission which did not constitute a penal offence at the time when it was committed. Nor shall a heavier penalty be imposed than the one that was applicable at the time the penal offence was committed.

The Canadian Criminal Code also contains provisions that are very broad and will no doubt be interpreted retroactively to impugn the behaviour of those who are troublemakers, anti-establishment, or considered potentially dangerous. Of course, the worst example, the War Measures Act, is found outside the Code. In the recent past we have seen the broad and immoderate use a government in panic, for retribution or propaganda purposes, can make of this broad provision.

The Code purports to embody the rule of law:

6(1) Where an enactment creates an offence and authorizes a punishment to be imposed in respect thereof.

(a) a person shall be deemed not guilty of that offence until he is convicted...

(b) a person who is convicted of that offence is not liable to any punishment in respect thereof other than the punishment prescribed....

9...no person shall be convicted

(a) of an offence at common law....

(c) of an offence under an Act or an ordinance in force in any province, territory or place before that province, territory or place became a province of Canada.

Section 12 of the Code provides that no person can be punished more than once for the same offence. All these sections are meant to be expressions of the rule of law. On the other hand, it is impossible to describe human behaviour with anything like precision; frequently legislative drafters use words such as "reasonable" or "probable" or "likely to." Ambiguity and uncertainty are inevitable.

Unfortunately, other ambiguities seem to be more avoidable. We do not have to look to overtly totalitarian regimes for provisions that seem unnecessarily broad. The following are some examples from the Canadian Criminal Code:

Section 46. Every one commits high treason who... (2)(d) forms an intention to do anything that is high treason... and manifests that intention by an *overt* act. (4) Where it is treason to conspire with any person, the act of *conspiring* is an *overt* act of treason.

Section 64. Unlawful assembly
(2) Persons who are lawfully assembled may become an unlawful assembly if they conduct themselves *with a common purpose in a manner* that would have made the assembly unlawful if they had assembled in that manner for that purpose.

Section 177. Every one who, in the home of a child, participates in adultery or sexual immorality or indulges in habitual drunkenness or *any other form of vice*, and thereby *endangers the morals* of the child or renders the home an *unfit place* for the child to be in, is guilty of an indictable offence and is liable to imprisonment for two years.

Section 175c. Causing a disturbance
Every one who *loiters* in a *public place* and in any way obstructs persons who are there.

Section 180.
(2) Every one commits a *common nuisance* who does an unlawful act or fails to discharge a *legal duty* and thereby
(a) endangers the lives, safety, health, property or *comfort* of the public, or
(b) obstructs the public in the exercise or *enjoyment* of any *right* that is common to all the subjects of Her Majesty in Canada.

THE LAW MUST BE ACCESSIBLE AND KNOWABLE

The most Draconian systems have an Alice in Wonderland flavour about them; hapless citizens have no way of finding out the law until they have already infringed it. The Nazi laws certainly had that quality. Some military codes of discipline have a blanket section advocating punishment of any behaviour "contrary to the good order and discipline" of the armed services.

These problems are closely related to vagueness. Even in our presumably democratic society, there are occasions when the bureaucracy becomes so overburdened with procedures and regulations that it is impossible for the average citizen to have access to the law. Trained law librarians would be severely taxed if they tried to keep on top of the torrent of paper produced by government departments. The basic rule (found in s. 19 of the Code) is that ignorance of the law is no excuse on the basis that everyone is presumed to know the law. Some courts have held that if it is impossible for the average lay citizen to discover the law, then a reasonable mistake of law might provide a defence despite the ancient rule that "every man is presumed to know the law."

At one stage the British Columbia government drew up regulations that were not published outside the minutes of the legislature. These circumstances would provide an appropriate case for acquitting an accused who infringed the regulations because he or she had no opportunity of knowing the law (or even being presumed to know it). There are a few instances where s. 19 does not apply. The decisions in which an accused has been acquitted are rare. In *Jollimore*, the accused had been convicted of impaired driving, which carried an automatic revocation of licence. The magistrate did not make an order in court and the Registrar of Motor Vehicles revoked the licence and notified Jollimore by mail. The accused was stopped by a police officer before he reached home, where the notice of revocation was awaiting him. He was charged with driving while his licence was suspended, the trial magistrate acquitted and four of five appellate judges agreed. MacDonald J. said there was "nothing in the enactment to overcome the general presumption that some conscious intention to break the law is essential." The motor vehicle statute was amended to solve the *Jollimore* problem: the failure of the magistrate to tell the accused that his licence was revoked "shall not affect in any way the validity of the revocation."

COINCIDENCE OF ACTUS REUS AND MENS REA

Any legal definition of a crime consists of two elements — the *mens rea* or mental element and the *actus reus* or physical element. The two must exist and co-exist.

Illustration 1 gives the simplest and most obvious example of this principle. No matter how "evil" Donald's intention might have been toward Victor, the latter's death in an automobile crash was purely accidental. The law would say that Donald's evil intent was not operating at the time his car collided with the taxi in which Victor was riding. Even if Donald had left a party with an urgent intent to kill his enemy, the situation would be the same providing the collision was accidental.

If Donald had been driving while very drunk, the situation essentially would still be the same. Undoubtedly, he would be convicted of criminal negligence, dangerous driving, or driving while impaired. Then his *mens rea* would be different and it would not be directed specifically to the murder of Victor. Donald could be convicted just as easily of criminal negligence causing the death of the taxi driver.

The bizarre facts of *Droste* provide a good factual illustration of the above. The Crown alleged that D had planned to impregnate the inside of his car with gasoline, fake an accident, and hit his wife over the head with a weighted pipe. He used gasoline on the interior of his car, and then set off with his wife and two children. While driving at thirty-five miles per hour, the car struck the abutment of a bridge. The car burst into flames and the children (but not D's wife) died in the fire. D claimed it was an accident. His car was in a "terrible state of disrepair." There was uncontradicted evidence

---

ILLUSTRATION 1.

Donald and Victor have always been sworn enemies. On more than one occasion Donald has said he would like to see Victor dead. One night Donald's car collides with a taxi in which Victor is an occupant. Independent witnesses are able to show that the collision was purely accidental.
(a) Is D criminally responsible for V's death?
(b) What if D had left a party half an hour before the collision, vowing to kill V that very night?
(c) Would it make a difference if D were very drunk when he was driving his car?

that D was devoted to his children. The Ontario Court of Appeal granted a new trial because the trial judge did not make it clear to the jury that although D may have had the *mens rea* to kill Ms. D, he would not necessarily be convicted of first degree murder of the children because the *mens rea* for first degree murder included the ingredients of planning and deliberation, specifically in relation to the deaths of the children.

In Illustration 2, David is not guilty of the murder of Vince. Indeed, he would be acquitted on the grounds of self-defence or justifiable

---

ILLUSTRATION 2.

David and Vince hate each other and each has made death threats against the other. One night D's mother, who is very nervous about many recent burglaries in the neighbourhood, tells him there is a prowler downstairs. D takes his shotgun and creeps down the staircase. He sees a movement behind a curtain and hears the click of a firearm being cocked. D fires both barrels at the curtain. To his astonishment, D sees V's dead body drop from behind the curtain.

Is D guilty of any criminal offence in relation to V's death?

ILLUSTRATION 3.

Drew has been involved in a brawl outside a tavern. He picked up a rock intending to hit one of his adversaries. The rock misses its human target but break's a window in the tavern. Should Drew be charged and convicted for
(a) damaging the window; or
(b) some other offence; or
(c) acquitted entirely?

ILLUSTRATION 4.

Dick is arguing with Vikki. He takes off his belt intending to hit Vikki. He misses but the belt buckle hits and wounds Vanda who is a stranger.

What offence, if any, has D committed?

ILLUSTRATION 5.

Dan is parking his car on a city street. Constable Vickers is guiding him into the space. One of the rear wheels of D's car comes to rest on the constable's foot. At that moment, the car's engine stops but the evidence does not make it clear whether this was because the engine stalled or because D switched off the ignition. V pointed out to D that the wheel was on his foot. D made an offensive remark and told the constable he could wait. V made further requests and finally D moved the car. D was charged with assaulting a police officer in the execution of his duty.

Can you imagine why there was any question of D being found guilty? Would the problem be different if D were charged with obstruction of Constable Vickers in the execution of his duty?

homicide in the killing or the apprehension of a potential criminal found in a dwelling house (per s. 40 of the Code so long as he used only "as much force as is necessary").

Illustration 3 is the English case of *Pembilton*, where the accused was acquitted because his *mens rea* was directed to assault but the *actus reus* was damage to property. Yet *Latimer* (described in Illustration 4) resulted in a conviction because his *mens rea* was directed to assault and the *actus reus* was also an assault. The only difference between Dick's intent and the result was the identity of the person assaulted. This is called transferred intent.

Transfer of intent applies only if the same kind of crime is committed. Sometimes, however, it is difficult to determine what is meant by the "same kind" of offence.

Illustration 5 describes the case of *Fagan*. Why should there be any question of Dan's guilt? His lawyer argued that, when the car wheel came to rest on the constable's foot, Dan performed the *actus reus* of an offence of assault but at that time he had no *mens rea*. When he had the *mens rea*, that is, when he finally decided to leave the wheel on the foot, he was not committing any *actus reus*. The defence further argued that criminal liability would have been more feasible if Dan's foot had been squashing the policeman's foot because that would have required a continuing willed pressure. The court did not accept this ingenious argument, which suggested that there was no coincidence of *actus reus* and *mens rea*. The conviction was upheld on the basis that the *actus reus* was an ongoing one, and when Dan decided that he would not immediately accede to the policeman's request, he committed the *mens rea* as well, and at that point there was coincidence of the two elements.

Glanville Williams (1961) has suggested an alternative rule that makes more sense than the legal fiction of the on-going *actus reus* in *Fagan* (above) and *Ashwell* (below):

...where the *actus reus* includes an act causing an event, and a person does the act without the mental element specified for the offence, but comes to know that it has caused or may cause the event and that he may be able to prevent the occurrence or limit the continuation of the event, it is his duty to take reasonable steps in that regard, and if he fails to take such steps then: (a) if after acquiring such knowledge he knew that the event or its continuation was practically certain unless action were taken, he is deemed to have acted intentionally in causing it, and (b) if after acquiring such knowledge he was reckless as to the continuation of the event, he is deemed to have acted recklessly in causing it.

Illustration 6 describes the Canadian case of *Ladue*. D argued that he could not be convicted, because he had no *mens rea* under s. 182, in that he thought V was alive. One way to approach the problem is to say that his *actus reus* was that of the offence under s. 182, but that he had no *mens rea* and certainly not the intention of committing an offence under s. 182. The British Columbia Court of Appeal did not accept the submission and convicted D. The court added that if D's contention were accepted, that would mean he was committing rape and could not use a defence that was, in effect, an admission of another offence. In terms of pure theory, this viewpoint is questionable: no one can be guilty of raping a corpse.

THE NEED FOR AN ACT

The most obvious reason for the requirement of an act in the structure of a crime is that the law will not punish mere thoughts. The

---

ILLUSTRATION 6.

Delius visited Veronica's apartment where he found her on the couch in a state that D took to be sleep. He had sexual relations with V who, at the time, was in fact dead. D was charged under s. 182 of the Code, with offering an indignity to a human corpse. His defence was that he did not know V was dead. In his own defence, he tried to explain his behaviour by saying that the dead woman was a drug addict and was often found in a comatose state.
    Should he be convicted?

efforts to describe "an act" in criminal law terms have generated much heat but little light. An "act" can be one of commission or one of omission. A difficult situation in the definitional search is the case of mere status, e.g., ex-offender, alcoholic, person addicted to a narcotic, dangerous offender, habitual criminal, or vagrant. Similarly, is it an act for a person to fail to fulfil a legal duty? The answer is yes, but it will depend on the circumstances.

Philosophers and lawyers have debated the meaning of an act in the criminal law. Roscoe Pound (1943) has defined an act as "exertions of the will manifested in the external world." This definition will often include omissions. The Model Penal Code (which is not legislation but the distillation of the best thought on criminal law prepared by the American Law Institute) says that a person is not guilty of an offence "unless his liability is based on conduct that includes a voluntary act or the omission to perform an act of which he is physically capable" (s.2.01(1)). In answer to Pound's definition, the following are not classed as voluntary acts:

2.01(2)
(a) a reflex or convulsion
(b) a bodily movement during unconsciousness or sleep
(c) conduct during hypnosis or resulting from hypnotic suggestion
(d) a bodily movement that otherwise is not a product of the effort or determination of the actor, either conscious or habitual.

The provisions of the Model Penal Code (M.P.C.) also show that it is impossible to separate the mind from the body or the *mens rea* from the *actus reus*. Though many forests have been sacrificed to a discussion of the distinction, we shall not concern ourselves with it here.

The same section of the M.P.C. discusses "possession," a difficult concept in the law that illustrates the problem of differentiating the mental element from the physical element. The M.P.C. drafters defined "possession" as:

an act...if the possessor knowingly procured or received the thing possessed or was aware of his control thereof for a sufficient period to have been able to terminate his possession.

Illustrations 7 and 8 show problems of possession. D in Illustration 7 was acquitted while D in Illustration 8 was convicted.

Section 4(3) of the Canadian Code defines possession as existing when a person "has it in his personal possession or knowingly":

(i) has it in the actual possession or custody of another person, or
(ii) has it in any place, whether or not that place belongs to or is occupied by him, for the use or benefit of himself or of another person.

Perhaps it would be best to follow Glanville Williams's definition of *actus reus* as "the whole definition of the crime with the exception of the mental element."

THE ELEMENTS OF THE CRIMINAL LAW

In the following pages we shall be concentrating on the mental element of the criminal law, which must usually be found along with an act before an accused can be convicted. (There are important exceptions to this rule, which will be discussed under Illustration 27.) The mental element, or *mens rea*, can consist of

---

ILLUSTRATION 7.

A man was charged with possession of a narcotic drug. He claimed that he thought the substance in his possession was harmless and not a narcotic. He claimed that he had a quantity of sugar of milk (which had the same physical appearance as heroin) that he intended to pass off as heroin because he wanted to hoodwink his intended victim. He said he was very surprised when the analysis showed that the substance was in fact heroin. The prosecution argued that the trade in heroin was so dangerous to society that liability for possession should be absolute.

Should he be acquitted?

ILLUSTRATION 8.

Doreen arrived at Vancouver airport from Asia and was clearing her baggage through customs. The RCMP became suspicious of a scuba tank that seemed abnormally heavy. When D was approached by a man she took to be a customs official, she said, "Oh, oh, looks as if I am in for it now." The man was from the RCMP, and he discovered that the tank contained a large amount of hashish. On being questioned by the police officers, D replied that she did not know the scuba tank contained hashish, she did not know that it contained a drug, she suspected that the tank contained something illegal, and she refused to divulge the address to which she was supposed to deliver the tank. She was charged with importation of a narcotic contrary to the Narcotic Control Act.

(a) Would you convict her on the evidence given?
(b) Would your answer be different if the trial judge had allowed the prosecution to admit evidence that the hashish had a street value of many thousands of dollars?
(c) What if she thought the scuba tank contained:
  (i) pornography;
  (ii) counterfeit money;
  (iii) jewellery;
  (iv) heroin; or
  (v) amphetamines?

---

intention, recklessness, or possibly negligence. Before formulating any more rules, we must remember that the terms *"guilty mind," "intention,"* or *"recklessness"* are not to be taken as having the same meaning in the law as they have to the intelligent layperson, the psychiatrist, or the philosopher. The psychiatrists' most persistent criticism of the criminal law is that it is based on free will and a theological ethic, while the behavioural scientists maintain that human conduct is determined.

The concept of *mens rea* is based on the Judeo-Christian ethic that humans are willing agents who can control their actions and the thoughts that precede them. A corollary of this is that persons should be punished only for those actions that they have willed. This concept would be quite rational and reasonable if humans were simply mechanisms that could be either totally switched on or totally switched off. Even if *homo sapiens* could be taught — like a laboratory pigeon — that if they pushed the button marked *mens rea* (or "crime" or "blame") they would receive an electric shock (or punishment or no rewarding pellet of food) and that if they desisted they would gain a reward, we might have a simple, workable system. Unfortunately, it is not that simple; legal guilt is not as mechanistic and obvious as a litmus test because there are grades of guilty

intent and shades of blameworthiness that we adopt in all our relations with other human beings.

There is a further complication. The ethos of the criminal law is based on the Old Testament rather than the New. The spirit of *lex talionis* or the Mosaic Code of an eye for an eye or a tooth for a tooth is applied in our system. Of course, it is not applied literally, but we have always lived, and continue to live, in a system where we insist on taking revenge on wrongdoers. Society insists that the criminal suffer degradation or denunciation. At one stage, this consisted of outlawry; at other times the disapproval of the State was expressed by capital punishment and mutilation. Now the offender is exiled to a penal system. The essence of all forms of penal treatment is stigma. The instinctive fold memory, which is only inarticulately expressed, is that there is a difference between those who wilfully transgress codes of behaviour and those who do it accidentally or negligently. Justice Holmes once said that even a dog knows the difference between being kicked and being tripped over. This phenomenon has also been explained by behavioural scientists in a number of ways — the need for guilt to be expiated (which also has been a common stance in Christian theology), the need to punish those who have fallen below standards that we have not yet transgressed or the feeling among the guilty that they should be punished.

As a general statement of *mens rea*, we might adopt the definitions of two commentators. Hall (1982) describes the principle of *mens rea* as the "ultimate summation of the moral judgements expressed in the proscription of the voluntary (intentional or reckless) commission of numerous social harms" done by normal adult offenders. Brett (1963) sets down an "overriding principle of criminal law, derived from its roots in the community ethic, requiring the presence of moral blameworthiness in every case." Both Brett and Hall stress that the moral connotation relates to the rule that forbids condemnation by the criminal law of a morally innocent person.

INTENTION

A typical legal definition of "intention" is found in Turner who says that it "...denotes the state of mind of the man who not only foresees but also desires the possible consequences of his conduct." The test of "intention" should be a subjective one in that the law is interested in the state of mind of the accused themselves rather than in an inference that the court might make about their behaviour; that is, what the accused foresee rather than basing liability on some exterior, objective test such as what the reasonable person might have foreseen. As we shall see there are many exceptions to the subjective rule.

Mens rea, in the form of intention, is not limited to cases where the accused admit they intended to do the prohibited act. The criminal law does not automatically accept the accused's story that they did not intend or desire to do the act. On the other hand, it is only the rare occasion in which police actually observe the crime being committed and see the accused doing it and, even more rarely, receive an immediate confession from the accused. Human behaviour is nearly always more ambiguous than the above situations indicate. Intention is a concept that must often be inferred from the circumstances, but the inference should come from the evidential data produced at trial, not from a supposition of the trier or an implication unsupported by the facts.

MOTIVE

Motive, as a general rule, is irrelevant to *mens rea*. In this context motive means the rationale for the accused's actions. The distinction between motive and intention is stated succinctly by Hall (1982):

...when we ask questions about a person's motives, we are asking for data relevant to evaluation of his character or at least of the morality of a particular act. Given a motive, a relevant intention can be inferred. But the converse does not apply, i.e., one may be positive that certain conduct was intentional without knowing any motive for it.

A confusion has existed because *mens rea* was once equated with sinfulness or evil at a time when crime had more religious than legal ingredients.

ILLUSTRATION 26.

Dupuis, who was partly a public-spirited citizen, partly a busybody, was convinced that the mayor of his town was a corrupt man. He wanted to test his hypothesis and persuaded his friend Albert, a road-building contractor, to try to bribe the mayor in exchange for a lucrative contract.

The mayor may have been dishonest but he was not stupid. He smelled a rat and reported Albert's attempted bribe to the police. Albert told the police the whole story and D was charged with attempting to bribe a public official. In his defence, D argued that he was a public-spirited citizen who wanted to keep city hall honest. What would the verdict be if

(a) subsequent events showed that D's suspicions were well founded; or

(b) D were head of the fraud squad of the city police?

Good motive is as irrelevant as bad motive. In Illustration 26, D's suspicions about the corruption of the mayor are irrelevant, although the prosecution might decide to exercise administrative discretion and not proceed with the charge in such circumstances.

If D had been the head of the fraud squad, the situation would be a little more complicated (and would involve questions that are discussed more fully under procedure). In theory, the case of *Ormerod* pointed out that police officers who breached the law, even in the course of their perceived duty, could be prosecuted. If their behaviour amounted to entrapment (rather than their merely acting as *agents provocateurs*), the accused might have a defence against conviction. In practice, of course, the police officer who acts as a thief to catch a thief is seldom prosecuted. Therefore, in Illustration 26(b) the *de jure* answer is that motive is irrelevant but the *de facto* situation means that the motive of the police officer is all-important.

In Illustration 17 we would not convict D of killing V simply because she was going to benefit under V's will. If that possible bad motive were the only proof of D's intention, then we could not and should not convict, but of course, there is often other evidence of intention, and in such circumstances, motive will be very important as a matter of evidence, although not as a direct contribution of the definition of intention.

RECKLESSNESS

Recklessness has been redefined by the English Law Commission (1968):

A person is reckless if,
(a) Knowing that there is a risk that an event may result from his conduct or that a circumstance may exist, he takes that risk, and
(b) It is unreasonable for him to take it having regard to the degree and nature of the risk which he knows to be present.

The Commission commented:

It is accepted that whether or not actual foresight or actual appreciation of the risk was present is a matter which in some cases may be difficult to prove, but we are not proposing any departure from the general principle that the court of trial may draw appropriate inferences from what in fact happened in order to reach a conclusion upon these matters.

The Commission did not see the unreasonableness test as a departure from subjectivity. The Working Paper stated:

The test of unreasonableness comes to be applied only when it is known that there is a risk and in that case the question is: "Did he, the defendant, behave unreasonably in taking the risk of which he knew?" The question is the same whether it is asked of the results or the circumstances of conduct:

The Model Penal Code also formulated a definition of "recklessly":

A person acts recklessly with respect to a material element of an offence when he consciously disregards a substantial and unjustifiable risk that the material element exists or will result from his conduct. The risk must be of such a nature and degree that, considering the nature and purpose of the actor's conduct and the circumstances known to him, its disregard involves culpability of high degree. [Al-

---

ILLUSTRATION 17.

Davinia, who was an unemployed spinster, lived with her elderly aunt, Violet. She paid no board but, in return for free food and board, she acted as companion to her aunt. Her aunt became ill and was so weak that she could not prepare food for herself or give herself her medicines. D simply ignored her. After a week or so her aunt died from a combination of the original illness, malnutrition and lack of attention. D was charged with manslaughter. Would it make a difference if
(a) D were not related to V;
(b) D were paid by V to be a companion;
(c) D would benefit under V's will?

ternative: its disregard involves a gross deviation from proper standards of conduct.]

We must note that recklessness implies advertence of foresight. If there is no foresight, then a person has only been negligent — something less than reckless behaviour, and negligence is usually not a sufficient mental element for criminal liability. In Illustration 8(a), *Blondin*, the court convicted the accused. The court decided that Blondin probably knew the scuba tank contained something illegal. If D did not know specifically that it contained hashish, then D had wilfully closed her eyes to the fact that it might contain an illegal drug under the Narcotic Control Act. In other words, Blondin had been reckless, which is a form of *mens rea*. If the accused had thought the tank contained something different, such as counterfeit money or pornography, she would not have been convicted.

ABSOLUTE LIABILITY

In many instances the courts have decided that if the prosecution proves that the defendant has committed the proscribed act, he or she is automatically liable. There is no additional need to prove that the defendant had intention, or was reckless or even negligent in relation to the act. This has been variously described as an absolute prohibition, absolute liability, strict responsibility, public welfare, or statutory offences (although the term "strict liability" should be avoided because the subsequent discussion will show it leads to great confusion). Most of these offences, which have proliferated greatly in the twentieth century, are found outside the Criminal Code.

The reasons for the recent increase in this type of offence are easy to find. Cities and towns have become massive conurbations. Technology has produced the machinery of "progress" — factories, automobiles, highways, and consumer goods. There are laws, regulations, and by-laws affecting every facet of our lives — the speed limits on highways, the labelling and processing of food stuffs, parking, the size and composition of garbage cans, the registration of pets, the control of infectious diseases, zoning regulations, and the construction of buildings. The list is endless. The minute

regulation of our daily lives is often explained in terms of the complex society in which we live. The rise of the welfare state and the expansion of government bureaucracy have also been contributing factors.

The penalties are usually trivial fines. A conviction does not often result in a criminal record. These offences are not "really criminal" and are sometimes called public torts or ways of enforcing a civil right. Lawyers claim that it is wrong for the legislatures and courts to interpret these laws as absolute prohibitions, that it offends the principle of legality, that no one should be convicted of an offence without the constituent elements of *mens rea* and *actus reus*.

A sampling of such cases can be found in Illustration 27. The cases are chaotic; some have acquitted on the basis of lack of knowledge, while others have admitted no excuses. Readers of these cases would be wrong in thinking that they all resulted in acquittals — or convictions. There appears to be little rationality. The courts sometimes acquit because they appear to have compassion for the accused, who could not possibly have avoided commission of the offence. In other instances, the courts convict because they find some overarching social value requiring absolute liability despite the protestations of the accused that they could not have intended, foreseen, or adverted.

The highest tribunals in both Canada and England have tried to make order out of the contradictory decisions of the past. They have not succeeded but they have, at least, provided some guidelines.

In *R. v. Pierce Fisheries Ltd.* (1970) the accused corporation had been charged under the Lobster Fisheries Regulations with having possession of "any lobster of a length less than that specified." In a catch of more than fifty thousand pounds of lobsters, an inspector found twenty-six undersized lobsters. The defendant company argued that no authorized officer or employee of Pierce Fisheries Ltd. had any knowledge that the undersized lobsters were on the company's premises. The president of the company had instructed his employees not to buy undersized lobsters. Consequently, the accused contended that there should be an acquittal because there was no *mens rea*. The magistrate who tried the case and the Nova

ILLUSTRATION 27.

Sometimes the law decides that some forms of social behaviour are so trivial (or so socially significant) that *mens rea* and procedural safeguards are not appropriate. The law does not require any proof (or perhaps not full proof by the Crown beyond a reasonable doubt) that the accused intended to do the act. The trivial cases may concern regulation of everyday problems such as traffic, liquor, pure foods, pollution, health or safety. These are public torts and not really criminal. The penalties will usually be fines or short terms of imprisonment. The idea of creating these quasi-criminal offences is based on expediency and deterrence.

There are a few serious offences that attract liability without full proof of intent; these include some narcotics offences and possession of many items that are potentially dangerous or very difficult for the prosecution to prove under ordinary evidential rules. These offences include possession of recently stolen goods, burglars' tools, counterfeiting equipment, or explosives. *(Editor's note: Several of these provisions are being challenged under the Charter of Rights.)* Should the following cases come within the definition of absolute liability offences?

(a) Drug control legislation provides that everyone who traffics in a narcotic drug or what is held out to be a narcotic drug shall be guilty of an offence and subject to severe punishment. D claims that he had been persuaded, against his better judgement, to sell heroin to a seventeen-year-old girl who wanted to find out what it was like. To protect her from becoming hooked, he substituted a mixture of milk powder and aspirin for the heroin which was originally in the capsule.

(b) Dobie and Dorion were driving on a city street at 2:20 a.m. when they were stopped by a police cruiser. A search by the police produced a crowbar, four screwdrivers, three credit cards, two flashlights, three pairs of gloves and two pairs of nylon stockings. They were charged under s. 309(1) of the Code which makes it an offence for anyone who "without lawful excuse, the proof of which lies upon him, has in his possession any instrument suitable for house-breaking...under circumstances that give rise to a reasonable inference that the instrument has been used or is or was intended to be used for housebreaking...."

(d) Dorey owned a tavern. There was a local law that no on-duty policeman could be served with liquor in a public bar. Policemen wore a checkered band on their left sleeves when they were on duty. Constable Abbott was on the beat on a very hot day. He felt thirsty. He removed his on-duty band and entered D's bar where he bought a drink. One of A's superiors noticed him in the bar and D was charged with an offence under the local law. D claims that he thought it was lawful to serve A as he had no band on his sleeve.

(e) On another occasion Dorey was charged with serving liquor to a man who was drunk. D claimed that he did not know the man was drunk — he seemed to be speaking clearly and was able to sit on his stool.

Scotia Appeal Court both thought the defendant should be acquitted. A majority of the Supreme Court of Canada decided otherwise.

The starting point for a discussion of the applicability of *mens rea* to "public welfare" offences is that in the criminal law there is a presumption that *mens rea* is "an essential ingredient in every offence; but that presumption is liable to be displaced either by the words of the statute creating the offence or by the subject matter with which it deals, and both must be considered." (The above is a famous statement from *Sherras v. DeRutzen*, on which Illustration 27(d) is based.)

Public welfare offences are not found in the Criminal Code but in provincial and other federal legislation and by-laws. Therefore, the common law defences available for Code crimes described in s. 8(3) may not apply. There are some indications that the defences may be available, but the burden of proof on the accused may be more onerous.

If the offences (found in this non-Code legislation) contain words or phrases similar to those extracted from the Code (and listed earlier), such as wilfully, knowingly, intentionally, with intent or without reasonable cause, then the wording of the statute will usually persuade the court that this statutory offence was not meant to impose absolute liability and to exclude *mens rea*. This test places unfounded reliance on the accuracy and planning of the legislative draftsman, but such words are useful rules of thumb.

The subject matter of the statute is also important. A statutory offence often will not be taken to include the ingredient of *mens rea* in the following circumstances.

1. Where the act is not criminal in any real sense but is prohibited under a penalty in the public interest. Instances of this class have arisen on legislation concerning such matters as food, drugs, liquor, licensing, the operation of motor vehicles.
2. Where the act is in the nature of a public nuisance.
3. Were the proceeding is criminal in form, but it is really a summary mode of enforcing a civil right.

In the Supreme Court of Canada decision in *Pierce Fisheries*, Ritchie J., for the majority, decided that it was an offence of absolute prohibition because the Lobster Fishery Regulations were "obviously intended for the purpose of protecting lobster beds from depletion and thus conserving the source of supply for an important fishing industry which is of general public interest." Perhaps it was only a coincidence that Ritchie J. was the Maritime provinces' representative on the Supreme Court of Canada but he was an appropriate spokesman for the social policy that absolute liability was necessary to protect the Atlantic fisheries.

The Court decided the question as a matter of social policy. The majority also relied, in part, on the wording of the regulations because, while another section contained the phrase "without lawful excuse," the provision relating to undersized lobsters contained no indication that the mental element of the defendant should be considered.

Another important consideration in these cases is the type of penalty that can be imposed by the court. If a jail term is a possible punishment, then mens rea should certainly be presumed to apply. If the punishment is a small fine that is meant to deter potential offenders from interfering with the smooth running of society, the mental attitude of the accused is usually considered irrelevant. Parking offences are an excellent example.

A middle ground, where the courts disagree, are those offences where the accused is not in danger of being imprisoned but is in danger of having his or her livelihood affected by conviction — a truck driver whose driving licence may be cancelled or a restaurateur who may lose his or her liquor licence. The courts have also considered the question of administrative convenience. If the granting of acquittals because of legal excuses would result in wholesale flouting of the law or if defended cases would clog the machinery of justice, then the courts might decide, as a matter of expediency, that no excuse would be allowed. This is based on the theory that if the law could not otherwise be satisfactorily enforced, then there will be absolute prohibition. Furthermore, the adherents argue that *mens rea* would be too difficult to prove.

THE DEFENCES

At least on a theoretical level, the accused has a right to remain silent. The prosecution must present sufficient facts relating to the charge against the accused to persuade the trier of fact (whether it is a judge or jury) that the accused should be convicted. If the prosecution evidence is ephemeral or unconvincing, the defence might invite the judge to decide there is "no case to answer" after the Crown has presented its evidence (and the defence has cross-examined the prosecution witnesses). This is an unusual procedure because prosecutors do not often waste their time bringing flimsy cases before the courts.

If the prosecution has a good case, it will be necessary for the accused to answer that case. Sometimes this will consist of a refutation of the prosecution case by means of cross-examination of the Crown witnesses, whose versions of the facts may be shaken so a reasonable doubt is raised. Witnesses for the defence may provide an alternative version of the facts leading to an acquittal.

Many acquittals are decided on the facts of the case. We are not concerned with these types of cases. We are most interested in those cases where the accused gives evidence or the defence lawyer puts forward a factual and legal argument that negates *mens rea*. This is the function of the "defence" of mistake of fact, which we will discuss presently. In addition, the law has developed a series of rules for circumstances where the accused clearly has carried out the physical act of the crime and was acting voluntarily, but where those acts are subject to certain excuses or justifications that will lead to acquittal. In addition, there are other circumstances, where the law, if it accepts the accused's explanation, will mitigate the grade of the offence (and punishment).

Mistake is not a true "defence" to a charge of crime. In most instances where a criminal charge is laid, the accused admits that he or she did the act and also admits that he or she consciously performed the act but claims that the behaviour was justified or should be excused. She says, "Yes, I did kill the victim but I acted in self-defence and, therefore, should be acquitted." Or he admits that he did have sexual intercourse with the victim but it was not sexual assault because he thought, in his drunken stupor, that she was consenting. Or the defence claims that the accused should not be convicted of an offence because she was legally insane at the time the alleged crime was committed.

The defences, which either provide full exoneration or partial mitigation, are value judgements. They decide that the accused lacked free will and should not be held criminally responsible. The granting of a defence recognizes in the accused's behaviour a value, such as self-defence or necessity, which society decides is worthy of recognition. The defence may be based on the idea that a person committing an allegedly criminal act in those particular circumstances is not deserving of punishment or should only be punished lightly. Or the law may be saying that a person performing such an act in those circumstances — for example, when suffering from mental disease — cannot be deterred and, therefore, punishment would be ineffectual or inhumane.

Some defences are very old. Self-defence, for instance, has been a legal defence for centuries and recognizes a natural response by human beings when attacked or when their home is invaded. Some aspects of the partial defence of provocation are similarly ancient. Other defences, such as necessity, duress, and superior orders, are also of old vintage but are rarely applied.

MISTAKE AND IGNORANCE

Mistake is not a true defence in the sense that the law has invented an excuse for the peculiar circumstances in which the accused find themselves: that they intended to do the act and willed the behaviour but claim that they should be excused.

When the accused claim mistake they are saying that they had no *mens rea* because they were acting under a misapprehension about the surrounding circumstances. In legal shorthand, the accused, with a conventional defence, are saying "*Yes*, I did it *but* I was acting under a misapprehension...."

As a general rule, a mistake of fact will lead to an acquittal, while ignorance of law will not be an excuse (see s. 19 of the Code). The basic rule is that when the accused have made an honest mistake of fact based on reasonable evidential grounds, the law will treat the situation as if the mistaken facts were actually true.

IGNORANCE OF LAW

The rationale for disallowing ignorance of law as a defence is that everyone is presumed to know the law, and it would make for an intolerable situation if an accused person could evade criminal liability by showing (or at least proclaiming) that he did not know that the act committed was contrary to the law. If a person is found with a blood-stained dagger in her hand and, at her feet, the corpse of a person to whom she is known to owe a large gambling debt, she can hardly claim that she should not be convicted because she did not know murder was a criminal offence in that jurisdiction.

But is ignorance of law always to be treated in this way? What if a merchant seaman returns to his home port and is found in possession of a substance (such as a drug) that was perfectly legal when he left but, during his absence, has become a criminal offence with a minimum punishment of three months' imprisonment? Should he be able to raise a defence of ignorance of law? One of the fundamental tenets of a democratic criminal justice system (under the general rubric of the principle of legality) is that the criminal law should not be retroactive and the accused should have prior notice of the provisions of the criminal law if he is to be presumed to have knowledge of it. The citizen might think it would be unfair to convict our sailor when he had no way of knowing about the change in the law, particularly when there is a mandatory jail term attached to it. Some courts have acquitted accused persons in such circumstances. Would that average citizen be prepared to acquit if the punishment were a mere fine? Or would the citizen think it makes no difference because, in both instances, the principle of legality had been breached? This question was recently (1980) addressed by the Supreme Court of the Northwest Territories in *Catholique*. The accused had been convicted of unlawful possession of liquor under regulations that had never been published in the government *Gazette*. The judge treated the regulations as a nullity.

MISTAKE OF FACT

We have already examined the fundamental principles of mistake of fact when we discussed *mens rea*. The defence of mistake of fact is best illustrated by the important case of *Beaver*, which is described in Illustration 7. The Supreme Court of Canada decided that if Beaver had an honest belief that the substance found in his possession was a harmless substance rather than heroin, as analysis proved, Beaver's belief that the substance was innocent was a good defence so long as it was an honest belief, and the honest quality of his belief was to be decided on a reasonable evidentially basis.

The courts have also taken a less lenient view when the accused claimed mistake of fact but was doing something else illegal (or perhaps immoral). *Ladue* (described in Illustration 6) resulted in a conviction because the court was not impressed by the accused's excuse that he made a mistake in thinking that the woman was alive. The court said that the accused could not use that mistake as a defence because the mistaken circumstances would amount to a crime in itself; the accused would then be committing the crime of rape. This is wrong in law because a corpse is not a human being, male or female, and therefore it could not be rape. If Ladue

were to be convicted of anything, it would be attempted rape because one can be convicted of attempting the factually impossible.

The courts have still not given a definitive answer to the scope of mistake of fact. There are three possibilities:

1. Must the accused have been completely innocent of all wrongdoing if the facts were as they mistakenly imagined them to be? Even this question is not completely unambiguous because by "innocent" we could mean devoid of any legal responsibility or lacking any moral fault. Even in *Beaver*, the accused admitted that he was planning to hoodwink or defraud the person who thought he was buying illicit drugs.
2. Should "innocent" have a narrower meaning, signifying that the accused is not guilty of the charge on the indictment or information? If the prosecution has made an error and charged the accused with possession of drug A rather than drug B, or charged the accused with possession of a drug under the Narcotic Control Act while the accused claims that he mistakenly and honestly believed he had possession of a drug prohibited or controlled by the less heinous Food and Drug Act, should we acquit the accused in either case and say that he is innocent *as charged*? The prosecution also made a mistake and should not succeed.
3. Finally, should we subscribe to a rule that if the charge relates to offence A, but the accused says that she thought she was committing the less serious offence, B, we should convict her of the lesser offence?

NECESSITY

Necessity in its purest form is not a common defence. Self-defence (as we shall see) is a special version of necessity and is more frequently found in criminal cases. The defence of necessity is based on the external forces of nature imposing themselves on the accused. In recent years we have had a few cases that could have evoked the defence of necessity if criminal charges had been laid. (No charges were laid because the necessitous circumstances were certainly obvious and the actors' harrowing experiences were no doubt considered sufficient suffering.) In both instances survivors of a plane crash had eaten the flesh of persons killed in the crash, which technically is an offence under s.182 of the Code. One of these cases occurred in the Northwest Territories and the other in the Andes.

DURESS, COERCION, OR COMPULSION

These terms are interchangeable, although the Code uses the last in s.17, which grants a defence but excludes its use in treason, murder, piracy, attempted murder, assisting in aggravated sexual assaults, forcible abduction, robbery, causing bodily harm, or arson (among others).

The compulsion imposed on the accused — threats of death or serious injury — is the same at common law and under the provisions of the Code. There must be no chance of escape, the threat must be immediate, and the fear must be reasonable.

DURESS AND SUPERIOR ORDERS

The harm done by the accused as a result of the alleged coercion must usually not exceed the physical danger that the accused was facing. Duress is never a defence to murder. The courts have always taken the attitude that if D were placed in the position that C said he would kill D if D did not kill V, then D has no excuse for the murder of V. The defence of superior orders in warfare is different because the soldier is obliged to obey the lawful orders of a superior. This, of course, begs the question of what is a lawful order and what is permissible behaviour in wartime according to the Geneva Convention or some other international agreement. These problems arose at the Nuremberg trials, the Eichmann trial, in the film *Breaker Morant*, and in the cases of Lieutenant Calley and Captain Medina. (See Illustration 36.)

Robert Jackson was chief U.S. prosecutor at the Nuremberg trials before he became a justice of the U.S. Supreme Court. He said at the time of those trials:

There is doubtless a sphere in which the defence of obedience to superior orders should prevail. If a

---

ILLUSTRATION 36.

(a) Dietrich, a soldier working in a Nazi concentration camp, was ordered by his superior — a non-commissioned officer — to deliver prisoners to Doctor Luger. After the war, L was charged before a war crimes tribunal because he carried out experiments on prisoners. Can Dietrich also be convicted of a crime against humanity? Would it make a difference if D had received his order from a very senior officer?

(b) Dorant is an officer commanding a small group of soldiers fighting a guerrilla war. The conventions of international law decree that the prisoners of war must be kept in custody until the end of the war and cannot be shot. A group of enemy terrorists carry out a raid, torturing and killing some of the soldiers' wives. In a fit of rage and revenge, Dorant's superior officer, Major Spencer, orders him to pursue the terrorists and "show them no mercy." Dorant surprises the terrorists in their beds and instead of taking any prisoners, he lines them up, and a firing squad shoots them.

(c) In another war, there is much guerrilla warfare. Soldiers have discovered that seemingly peaceable women and children have been often used to make booby traps and to throw hand grenades at unsuspecting soldiers. Lieutenant Dewar is ordered to go into a particular village (thought to be very sympathetic to the enemy and a place where many soldiers have been killed in ambush by the ordinary citizens) and told to carry out reprisals. He does so with his troops, killing many women and children.

conscripted or enlisted soldier is put on a firing squad he should not be held responsible for the validity of the sentence he carries out. But the case may be greatly altered when one has discretion because of rank or the latitude of his orders. And of course, the defence of superior orders cannot apply in the case of voluntary participation in a criminal or conspiratorial organization, such as the Gestapo or the S.S. An accused should be allowed to show the facts about superior orders. The Tribunal can then be allowed to determine whether they constitute a defence or merely extenuating circumstances, or perhaps carry no weight at all....

But none of these men before you acted in minor parts. Each of them was entrusted with broad discretion and exercised great power. Their responsibility is correspondingly great and may not be shifted to that fictional being, the state.

SELF-DEFENCE

This defence is a special application of the defence of necessity, although the forces of necessity are not usually human agencies. This is one of the oldest defences. Many of the early cases are of little relevance today. Many of the common law rules had been established when the usual weapons were swords, rather than firearms, which can kill from a distance. Therefore, many of these cases seem more appropriate to tales of the Count of Monte Cristo when they talk of "going to the wall" and retreating as far as practicable. If someone is threatening you with an automatic weapon, retreating to the wall or up the staircase is not likely to stop a bullet which can travel a great distance, while in sword-fights, one was safe so long as outside the range of the blade. The retreat rule is important in a symbolic sense; one should not retaliate with deadly force until it is absolutely necessary. These rules are a little academic because often the only witness to the killing (who is still able to give evidence) will be the killer.

Strictly speaking, the phrase "self-defence" is a little narrow because it only applies to defence of oneself. Approximately the same rules apply to apprehension of a dangerous criminal, suppression of a deadly fight, and defence of one's loved ones or dwelling house. Section 40 describes the justified behaviour of one in lawful possession of a dwelling house who can use reasonable force to prevent a forc-ible entry that is without lawful authority. Similarly, s. 41 allows a trespasser to be repelled with reasonable force if the trespasser is seeking forcible entry.

PROVOCATION

Most cases of self-defence are not clear-cut. Only in the minority of cases is the accused faced with a murderous attack by an axe-wielding homicidal maniac, by an ugly mob storming his or her peaceful abode, or by an armed attacker contemplating sexual assault, robbery, or arson. More frequently, the homicide arises from a drunken brawl where both parties have used some violence and it is impossible to say who was the initial aggressor or who was defending whom against what.

"A WRONGFUL ACT OR INSULT...OF SUCH A NATURE..."

The violent retaliation or response to the provocation must be proportionate to the act or insult. A homicide will not be reduced to manslaughter if the accused responded to a slap on the face by killing the provoker with a deadly weapon. Particularly sympathetic cases can be found that are exceptions: a one-legged man had his crutch kicked from under him and he killed his tormentor with a knife and was convicted only of manslaughter. In recent years, there have been several cases of abused women taking rather extreme retaliation against the abusers. Many have been convicted, at most, of manslaughter. *(Editor's note: In a 1990 case a woman was acquitted and the battered-wife defence became a reality.)*

"...TO DEPRIVE AN ORDINARY PERSON..."

Provocation does not exist for the benefit of the super-sensitive or those with extremely short (or unusual) tempers. An "ordinary person" is the average person with normal responses to stress and taunts. The common law used to refer to the "reasonable" person and some cases indicated that the "reasonable" person was an Anglo-Saxon with no physical abnormalities.

"...ON THE SUDDEN...BEFORE TIME FOR PASSION TO COOL"

The accused must act on the spur of the moment while he or she is actually provoked. Legal provocation does not arise as a mitigation if the accused is insulted or receives a blow and rushes halfway across town to fetch a weapon with which to kill the provoker. The accused cannot brood over the insult or blow for days and then seek revenge, calling it a manslaughter on sudden provocation.

Chapter 2

THE MANY REALITIES OF CRIME*

Anthony N. Doob

When some indefinite number of blind men find themselves confronting an elephant, they might, as the parable goes, describe the elephant in quite different ways, depending on what part of the elephant they happened to run into. However, the apparent conflicts in the manner in which the elephant is "seen" could easily be resolved: they could examine different parts and realize for themselves that the various parts of the elephant vary along a number of different dimensions. But more likely, if they were, indeed, wise, they would realize that the descriptions were not mutually exclusive. The elephant could well have all of the characteristics ascribed to it. The differences would then be readily explainable without having to examine the preconceptions, personal interests, or ideologies of the blind men. In a matter of minutes, the apparent conflict could be resolved and the blind men could go about deciding what to do about the great creature that was standing in their garden.

Three people — blind or not — describing crime or the operation of the criminal justice system, however, could not, probably, resolve

their differences quite so easily. There would appear to be a large number of ways of describing crime and the criminal justice system and there is little agreement on how these different views might be resolved. Indeed, even when one looks at a particular case being processed by the system, there are likely to be irresolvable differences that cannot be ignored.

The problem gets worse when we move to the question of describing the kind of criminal justice system we would like to have. If there is not, as I am suggesting, consensus in our criminal justice system on what crime looks like or what the criminal justice system does, it is hardly surprising that there is next to no agreement on the direction in which we should be moving in changing that system.

In this essay, I will be addressing some of the implications of this lack of consensus on the "reform" of the criminal justice system. Less optimistically, I should really, of course, be talking about "change" in criminal justice. Whether change will achieve reform is an empirical question that can only be determined some time after the change has been imple-

* Edited version of Anthony N. Doob, "The Many Realities of Crime," in A. N. Doob and E. L. Greenspan (eds.), *Perspectives in Criminal Law: Essays in Honour of John Ll. J. Edwards* (Toronto: Canada Law Book Inc., 1985), 61-67, 79-80. Reproduced with the permission of the author and of Canada Law Book Inc., 240 Edward Street, Aurora, Ontario L4G 3S9.

   Most of the data reported in this essay derive from two reports written for the Department of Justice, Canada: A. N. Doob and J. V. Roberts, *Crime, Some Views of the Canadian Public, 1982*, and A. N. Doob and J. V. Roberts, *An Analysis of the Public's View of Sentencing, 1983*. I would like to thank the Department of Justice, Canada, for its direct support of this research and the Ministry of the Solicitor General, Canada, for its indirect support of the research and the preparation of this essay by its direct support of the Centre of Criminology through its Contributions Program.

mented. As has been said in other contexts, it is hard to know where we are going if we do not know where we are.

WHAT IS CRIME?

The first problem we run into in examining the disparate views of crime and the criminal justice system is that we cannot even agree on what crime should be. One sees this, most obviously, in the margins of various definitions — for example, on whether it should be a crime to go to sleep, drunk, in the front seat of one's own parked car.[1] Though it is an oversimplification to say this, it would appear that the standard rhetoric of our courts is that their job is to determine whether something *is or is not* a crime, not whether something *should or should not be* a crime. Judges would lead us to believe that they would prefer to leave the difficult questions of what "should be" a crime to Parliament. It is an open question whether such a distinction is a real one.

Canadian trial judges appear to feel quite strongly that on the margins the public itself should not be encouraged to define the law. In a survey carried out in 1977 for the Law Reform Commission of Canada (1977:28), 94 per cent of Canadian judges having the jurisdiction to preside over jury trials indicated that they opposed having jurors instructed that "It is difficult to write laws that are just for all conceivable circumstances. Therefore, you are entitled to follow your own conscience instead of strictly applying the law if it is necessary to do so to reach a just result" (Doob, 1979a: 138). A majority (78 per cent) of the judges did, however, feel that "the jury is a good way of infusing community values into a trial" and slightly more than half (58 per cent) felt that it was a positive feature of the jury that it is "able to bend the facts in coming to a verdict in a manner that a judge could not" (Doob, 1979a: 135-36). Apparently, it is all right, our judges feel, for members of the public to modify the law to fit the needs of justice, but they, the judges, would prefer not to have the responsibility of telling jurors that they have this right. The Canadian public, however, according to a Gallup poll carried out in 1977, thought that the

instruction to bend the law in keeping with overriding principles of justice should be given, with 58 per cent thinking that such an instruction definitely should be given and an additional 18 per cent thinking it probably should be given (Doob, 1979b:1-26).

But the inclusion of "equity" considerations into a trial is only one issue in defining the breadth of criminal law. One can move from an operational level ("should this act be criminal") to a more conceptual level ("what kinds of acts should be considered to be criminal") and find that there is not much clarity there, either. The Law Reform Commission of Canada said, in 1976, that "Criminal law...primarily has to do with values." This would appear to be a normative rather than a prescriptive statement. But whose values are expressed in the criminal law? If kneeling at a church service is highly valued by some members of a church, but a change in church policy makes it inappropriate, can we determine, by looking at the values of "humanity, freedom and justice" whether this should be a criminal offence? I doubt it; indeed the court would appear to have decided the issue simply by closely examining the relevant law.[2]

It would be nice to think that by arriving at a simple and straightforward principle — even a principle that most could agree on — that we could solve the problem of what our criminal justice system should deal with. In that same 1976 report to Parliament, the Law Reform Commission of Canada said that the criminal law "has to stick to really wrongful acts. It must not overextend itself and make crimes out of things that most people reckon not really wrong or, if wrong, merely trivial. Only those acts thought seriously wrong by our society should count as crimes" (p. 28). They continue by stating that "Wrongfulness is a necessary, not a sufficient condition of criminality." In addition, it should cause serious harm to others and be best dealt with through the mechanism of criminal law. To return to the example of kneeling at a church service, the difficulty, obviously, arises from knowing in whose eyes one is to evaluate this act.

It seems reasonably safe to assume that those who decided to try to continue an old tradition of kneeling when receiving communion would have felt that they were not causing serious harm and that conflicts with the church over proper procedure would not best be dealt with in the provincial courts (criminal division). Even when we turn to the "tests of criminality" that the Law Reform Commission proposes, we find that it is difficult to imagine that there would automatically be consensus on the issues at hand. The Law Reform Commission of Canada (1977:33-34) recommends:

To determine whether any act should be a real crime within the Criminal Code we should inquire:
— does the act seriously harm other people?
— does it in some other way so seriously contravene our fundamental values as to be harmful to society?
— are we confident that the enforcement measures necessary for using criminal law against the act will not themselves seriously contravene our fundamental values?
— given that we can answer "yes" to the above questions, are we satisfied that criminal law can make a significant contribution in dealing with the problem?
Only if all four questions can be answered affirmatively should an act be prohibited as a criminal offence within the Criminal Code.

The Government of Canada in 1982 came out with a somewhat different formulation of the proper scope of the criminal law. It stated that "the criminal law should be employed to deal only with that conduct for which other means of social control are inadequate or inappropriate, and in a manner which interferes with individual rights and freedoms only to the extent necessary for the attainment of its purpose."[3] "The purpose of the criminal law is to contribute to the maintenance of a just, peaceful and safe society through the establishment of a system of prohibitions, sanctions and procedures to deal fairly and appropriately with culpable conduct that causes or threatens serious harm to individuals or society."[4]

The difference between the two formulations is important because of the nature of the "test" that is implied. The first three parts of the Law Reform Commission's test are, in a sense, moral ones and imply, in a way, that there is a high level of homogeneity of values in our society. The final part of the definition is obviously empirical: can the criminal law really do anything with respect to the issue in question? The Law Reform Commission at the time that it was formulating that report talked a lot about the role of the public in shaping the process of law reform. However, with a few notable exceptions like those involving their study of the jury, they have not systematically gone out to find out what the public thinks about crime or the criminal justice system. Had they looked systematically at the public's views, they might have been less optimistic about the usefulness of their "tests."

The Government of Canada's test for inclusion of an offence in the criminal law is essentially an empirical one: if some activity seems to disrupt a "just, peaceful, or safe society" and if "other forms of social control" seem inadequate to control it, then the behaviour involved should be criminalized. It would appear to be based on more pragmatic issues. Kneeling while receiving communion might, under the government's 1982 formulation, have failed to meet the test of criminality, but might have succeeded under the Law Reform Commission's depending on how one views the power of the church.

The remarkable thing about discussions of issues such as these is that it is easy to ignore the way in which the public see crime and the criminal justice system. Some might suggest that governments and individual politicians ignore the public at their peril. The alternate view is that politicians do not have to know what members of the public would want if they were informed about an issue; all they have to pay attention to is what the public *think* they want on the basis of whatever information is available to them. The distinction between giving the public what they think they want and giving them what will accomplish what they want is as important in criminal justice as in many other areas. A doctor who prescribes a sweet tasting pill to the patient who says he "knows" that his ailment can be cured with drugs is likely to be popular for a short time. When the ailment does not disappear, however, his popularity might drop. The doctor who prescribes a less pleasant but more effective cure and who explains the need for it to the patient may not only be a better doctor but also may, in the long run, win the popularity poll.

HOW IS CRIME MEASURED?

The first problem that arises in trying to understand how the public view crime and the criminal justice system is that there is not any real consensus among professionals about how one should really "count" crime. This is an important problem — not so much because the different methods come out with different estimates, but rather that the different methods (and their different resulting estimates) have, imbedded in them, different implicit theories of what the problem is. Much has been written about "crime statistics" and the various ways in which they are collected. There is little need, therefore, for me to repeat here what is covered in every introductory criminology textbook. Much discussion can be summarized by a simple statement: crime statistics reflect, to an extent that is hard to overestimate, the manner in which they are collected.

If, for example, one considers "official" police statistics as an indication of the "crime problem" one has to first understand that these numbers are a result of organizational decisions. These decisions — for example, not to include all missing merchandise from a retail store as a large number of "thefts" that will never be cleared, but to include only thefts (shoplifting) where there is an apprehended accused person — are probably sensible decisions when one is considering what the police department needs to know. However, if one really wanted to know how many people walked into department stores and walked out with goods that they had not paid for, these statistics would be almost useless. This particular example shows, also, the difficulty in interpreting crime trends: a trend (or lack of a trend) in shoplifting statistics might reflect only a change in the policy of retailers in the funds they are willing to spend trying to apprehend shoplifters. This point is an obvious one and a trivial one. However, it points out the obvious and non-trivial point that statistics such as these are of use for some purposes (e.g., in giving us some measure of the activity of police officers in filling out forms and charging offenders) but they may tell us little about our own society.

Recently the Government of Canada has embarked on what appears to be a rather large and expensive "victimization" survey to try to understand not only the "extent" of crime, but also something of its impact. Again, results like these are helpful in understanding crime from the perspective of those in the population that is sampled. Perhaps one might be so bold as to suggest that this is the most important perspective. However, one does have to worry about a number of important methodological issues. For example, whole classes of offences are not "countable" in such surveys. If someone is trying to defraud the telephone company by charging calls to a third number, such frauds are unlikely to be perceived as such by the customer (who might simply pay the bill or deduct the "wrong" charge from the bill) and might not even be seen as crime by the telephone company. Other examples could obviously be given. The point, however, is that once again the numbers created by such systems have meaning, but by no means can they really be thought of as perfectly accurate indicators of "crime."

WHERE DO WE GET INFORMATION ABOUT CRIME?

How then is the public ever to find out about crime or how can anyone ever be informed about it? Unfortunately, we all seem to be informed to an extent greater than is deserved, by information about individual cases rather than summary "statistical information." People hear about a case or read about a case in the newspaper or hear about a case on the radio or television and they generalize from it. Even knowing that the case may be unusual (and hence should not be given much weight in our overall understanding of the nature of the problem) does not seem to help us very much in getting an overall view of crime.

But let us look at this question: what would members of the public think crime looked like if all they had were newspaper accounts of crime? We looked at this in the City of Toronto. We chose three editions of each of Toronto's three daily newspapers for each week in a four-week period beginning December 26, 1983. Any article describing any criminal or other federal offence (or events that were likely to be construed as involving an offence) was noted. To nobody's surprise, crime (as reported in the newspapers) was quite different from the view of crime that one might get if, for example, one were to spend a few days in our courts. Not surprisingly, most crimes that were reported were serious ones. The results are shown in Table 1.

This, then, is the view that members of the public would get if they thought that the crime reported in the newspapers was representative of overall crime in their city. But we all know that the newspapers and other media cover the unusual or the important news. Hence, one might expect that members of the public would be able to weigh, in their minds, what the real frequency of a crime was, or at least whether a particular crime is increasing in frequency, by looking at crime reporting. People may do this, but if they do, they are almost certainly going to mislead themselves. A number of well-documented studies of the media coverage of crime (Fishman, 1978) have shown that news organizations themselves are capable of "creating" apparent, but not real, "crime waves." Hence, the evidence is that people are not likely to get a very useful or accurate overview of crime if they rely on the news media for their crime information.

WHAT DOES THE PUBLIC THINK CRIME "LOOKS LIKE"?

I have already pointed out that there does not, and probably cannot, exist any perfect measure of "crime" in our society. For most

TABLE 1
CRIMES REFERRED TO IN TORONTO NEWSPAPERS

Offence	Canada		Elsewhere		Total	
	N	%	N	%	N	%
Murder	73	20.1%	30	23.8%	103	21.0%
Attempt/Counselling murder	19	5.2%	4	3.2%	23	4.7%
Criminal negligence causing death	6	1.6%	0		6	1.2%
Various non-sexual assaults	16	4.4%	3	2.4%	19	3.9%
Sexual assaults	14	3.9%	7	5.6%	21	4.3%
Kidnapping	7	1.9%	11	8.7%	18	3.7%
Robbery (incl. attempts, etc.)	52	14.3%	7	5.6%	59	12.0%
Other offences involving violence	6	1.6%	12	9.5%	18	3.7%
Total violence	193	53.0%	74	58.8%	267	54.5%
Theft (including conspiracy, etc.)	16	4.4%	8	6.3%	24	4.9%
Break, enter, and theft	22	6.0%	11	8.7%	33	6.7%
Fraud (including attempts)	23	6.3%	3	2.4%	26	5.3%
Mischief, arson, vandalism	8	2.2%	3	2.4%	11	2.3%
Other property/economic offences	1	0.3%	1	0.8%	2	0.4%
Total economic/property	70	19.2%	26	20.6%	96	19.6%
Prostitution/pornography/nudity	17	4.7%	2	1.6%	19	3.9%
Perjury/fabricating evidence, etc.	7	1.9%	3	2.4%	10	2.0%
Contempt of court/obstruct justice	31	8.5%	2	1.6%	33	6.7%
Drugs	10	2.7%	14	11.1%	24	4.9%
Impaired driving	10	2.7%	1	0.8%	11	2.3%
Promoting hatred	7	1.9%	0		7	1.4%
Immigration	5	1.4%	0		5	1.0%
Various other	14	3.9%	4	3.2%	18	3.7%
Total various	101	27.8%	26	20.6%	127	25.9%
TOTAL	364	100%	126	100%	490	100%

people, however, official (usually police) statistics about crime are crime. Hence, it is instructive to see what image people have about crime and to compare this image to the "official" view of it. In two national surveys carried out by the Gallup organization in 1982 and 1983, people were asked the question "In your opinion, out of every one hundred crimes committed in Canada, what per cent involve violence — for example, where the victim was beaten up, raped, robbed at gun point, and so on?" In terms of official statistics and all that we know systematically about crime, the best guess would be that less than 10 per cent of crime involves violence. As can be seen in Table 2, this is not the view held by members of the Canadian public: to a very great extent, crime, for the Canadian public, *is* violence.

Remarkably, when asked "How does the violent crime problem in Canada compare to the violent crime problem in the United States?" — a question that I would have thought would have brought out our pride at being considerably less violent than those to the south — overestimates were still quite evident. Respondents were given five alternatives: Much less (one-fifth as great as in the U.S.); Somewhat less (about half as great as in the U.S.; About the same as in the U.S.; Somewhat greater (twice as great as in the U.S.); and Much greater (five times greater than in the U.S.). As shown in Table 3, a substantial number of people overestimate the comparative problem.

A final way in which the public's view of

TABLE 3

HOW DOES VIOLENT CRIME IN CANADA COMPARE TO THE PROBLEM IN THE U.S.?

Correct estimate (much less):	28%
Small overestimate (somewhat less):	39%
Large overestimate (same or greater):	29%
Do not know/not stated	4%

crime can be shown to have little to do with official views comes from a question concerning estimates of murder statistics following the abolition of capital punishment. In 1982, people were asked "As you know, five years ago Parliament abolished the death penalty for murder. Since that time, do you think that the number of murders has increased, decreased, or remained about the same?" The government was fortunate in the timing of the abolition of capital punishment in 1976: the mid-1970s appears, in Canadian statistics, to be the high point on a number of indices of violence in society, including homicides or murder. The general trend (looking at numbers, or rates, for victims or incidents, for total homicide or for murder only) is that violence, using these indices, has, if anything, decreased. This, however, is not what a majority of the public think. As shown in Table 4, a majority of the public appear to believe that murders have increased since the abolition of capital punishment.

It is easy to imagine why the public would have these views. Often when a particularly brutal murder takes place or a policeman or prison guard is killed, there are calls for the

TABLE 2

"IN YOUR OPINION, OF EVERY 100 CRIMES COMMITTED IN CANADA, WHAT PERCENTAGE INVOLVE VIOLENCE — FOR EXAMPLE, WHERE THE VICTIM WAS BEATEN UP, RAPED, ROBBED AT GUN POINT, AND SO ON?"

	1983	1982
Accurate (0 – 9%)	3.1%	3.8%
Small overestimate (10 – 29%)	14.7%	15.1%
Large overestimate (30 – 100%)	73.8%	73.9%
Do not know/not stated	8.4%	7.2%
TOTAL	**100%**	**100%**

TABLE 4

HAS MURDER INCREASED, DECREASED, OR STAYED THE SAME SINCE CAPTIAL PUNISHMENT WAS ABOLISHED?

Correct (stayed same or decreased):	30%
Overestimate of problem (increased):	67%
Do not know/not stated:	3%

return of capital punishment. These often come from people in the criminal justice system such as police spokesmen. For a member of the public without sophistication the inference (probably intended) in such matters is that if there were capital punishment, the offence would not have occurred.

HOW DOES THE PUBLIC VIEW THE CRIMINAL JUSTICE SYSTEM?

The public does not hold a very optimistic view of the criminal justice system's ability to deal with violence. When asked what percentage of those released on parole commit violent crimes within three months of their release, once again a large portion of the Canadian population overestimated the problem. Interestingly enough, it is difficult to get from official statistics a good estimate of the problem since the only reasonable data deal with those released from federal penitentiaries (presumably generally the most serious offenders convicted of the more serious offences) and include both those released on parole and those otherwise released (having been refused parole or having never applied for it). Using this method of calculating the "correct" answer it seems that about 13 per cent commit a violent offence within three years of their release. As shown in Table 5, however, a substantial portion of the population overestimates this figure.

Given these views of crime, it is not surprising that a substantial portion of Canadians indicate that they are concerned about crime. A

recent poll (University of Montreal, 1981) in three provinces showed that over 80 per cent of respondents were at least somewhat concerned about crime. Most, of course, were concerned in particular about violent crime. This would appear to translate into actual behaviour in that about a quarter of the respondents "often" or "very often" avoid going out at night because they are afraid about crime.

Overall, Canadians seem to be reasonably content with their criminal justice system, with about two-thirds indicating that it has more positive than negative aspects to it. However, almost three-quarters of the respondents in the same survey felt that "there should be some changes made" in the criminal justice system. Various surveys have indicated the kinds of changes that the public would like to make: one of the most consistently polled and one of the most controversial is the view that the sentences of the court are too short. A recent Gallup poll, for example, showed that almost 80 per cent of Canadian respondents thought that the sentences handed down by the court are too lenient.

CONCLUSION

It appears from our research that people vastly overestimate the likelihood that a first-time offender (property or violent crime) will be reconvicted. In terms of people's preferences for the way in which first offenders should be dealt with (or people's opposition to various kinds of programs that return such people to the community), it is clear that it would be worthwhile to keep in mind that the "reality" that people are thinking about is quite different from the "reality" of what we know actually is occurring.

Similarly, the criminal justice system's favourite whipping boy — parole — may owe some of its image to the belief noted earlier: people think that parolees are more likely to be involved in violence than, in fact, they are. These illustrations could go on and on. The point though is a simple one: those responsible for change in various aspects of the criminal justice system are faced with a number of difficult choices. They can decide what is politically

---

TABLE 5

WHAT PERCENTAGE OF THOSE RELEASED ON PAROLE COMMIT VIOLENT CRIMES WITHIN THREE YEARS OF THEIR RELEASE?

Underestimate of problem (0 – 9%):	4.1%
Accurate estimate: (10 – 19%):	7.0%
Small overestimate of problem (20 – 39%):	18.9%
Large overestimate of problem (40 – 100%):	62.0%
Do not know/not stated:	8.0%

possible (or politically attractive, if that is their major motivation) on the basis of the simple answers that the public give when they are asked simple questions. Or they can decide that part of their responsibility is to educate the public about the nature of the questions that should be asked and what the best educated guess might be as to the answer. There is every indication that the Canadian public are willing to consider the complexities of the issues related to policy decisions in the criminal justice system. On the other hand, if our political leaders and our news reporters pretend that the questions and the answers are both simple, then the public can be fooled into accepting these simple answers. To some extent, then, the future of our criminal law depends on which of these strategies predominates.

Only time will tell whether we will be influenced unduly by one blind man who may not even be touching an elephant.

NOTES

1. See, e.g., *R. v. Toews* (1983), 4 C.C.C. (3d) 450 (B.C.C.A.), leave to appeal to S.C.C. granted C.C.C. loc. cit., in which courts have differed on whether it is or is not a crime.
2. *R. v. Hafey et al.* (1983), 4 C.C.C. (3d) 344 (N.S.S.C. App. Div.), leave to appeal to S.C.C. granted 48 N.R. 400n.
3. *The Criminal Law in Canadian Society*, pp. 52-53.
4. Ibid., p. 52.

Chapter 3

THE YOUNG OFFENDERS ACT: A LEGAL FRAMEWORK*

Nicholas N. Bala

HISTORY

Since the beginning of legal history, there have been special rules for dealing with young persons who violate the law. Under English common law, the special *doli incapax* (Latin for incapacity to do wrong) defence developed. A child under the age of 7 years was deemed incapable of committing a criminal act. For children between 7 and 13 years, there was a presumption of incapacity, but this could be rebutted if there was evidence to establish that the child had sufficient intelligence and experience to "know the nature and consequences of the conduct and to appreciate that it was wrong" (Criminal Code, 1970, s.13). While the *doli incapax* defence afforded certain protections to children, those children who were convicted faced the same penalties as adult offenders, including hanging and incarceration in such places as the old Kingston Penitentiary.

In the latter part of the nineteenth century, social movements that sought to promote better treatment of children developed in Britain, the United States and Canada. These movements led to such reforms as the establishment of child welfare agencies and the creation of a juvenile justice system, which had a distinct philosophy and provided facilities separate from the adult system. The reformers of this time considered their paramount objective to be saving destitute and wayward children from a life of crime and destitution. Thus they did not draw a clear distinction between neglected and criminal children. W.L. Scott, one of the principal drafters of Canada's early delinquency legislation, stated that:

there should be no hard and fast distinction between neglected and delinquent children, but...all should be...dealt with with a view to serving the best interests of the child. (Archambault, 1983:2)

The efforts of these early reformers culminated with the enactment of the Juvenile Delinquents Act (JDA) in 1908. This federal legislation provided that children were to be dealt with by a court and corrections system separate from the adult system. The JDA clearly had a child welfare, or *parens patriae* philosophy. The Latin term *parens patriae* literally means "father (or parent) of the country," but it has come to mean a philosophy of state intervention based on an assessment of a child's best interests. This philosophy was reflected in section 38 of the JDA (1908):

* Edited version of Nicholas Bala, "The Young Offenders Act: A Legal Framework," in J. Hudson, J. Hornick, B. Burrows (eds.), *Justice and the Young Offender in Canada* (Toronto: Thompson Educational Publishing, 1988), 11-36. Reprinted with permission of Thompson Educational Publishing, Inc., and the author.

The author wishes to thank Deidre Rice (LL.M. candidate, Queen's University) for her helpful comments about a draft of this chapter.

...the care and custody and discipline of a juvenile delinquent shall approximate as nearly as may be that which should be given by his parents, and...as far as practicable every juvenile delinquent shall be treated, not as a criminal, but as a misguided and misdirected child...needing aid, encouragement, help and assistance.

The Juvenile Delinquents Act created a highly discretionary system, which gave enormous power to police, judges and probation officers, to do whatever they considered in a child's "best interests." There were no legislative guidelines governing judicial sentencing, and youths who were sent to training school (reformatory) were generally subject to indeterminate committals. Release from reformatory occurred when correctional officials felt that rehabilitation had been accomplished. While the system created by the JDA in 1908 marked an enormous improvement in the treatment of children and adolescents over earlier times, many serious, interrelated problems still existed, and by the 1960s juvenile justice in Canada was subject to criticism from a variety of different sources.

One major criticism of the JDA was that it created a system that tended to ignore the legal rights of children. This was true to such an extent that there were occasions when guilt seemed to be presumed so that "treatment" would not be delayed by "unnecessary formalities." In many parts of Canada, lawyers rarely, if ever, represented youths charged in Juvenile Court, and until relatively recently many of the judges in Juvenile Court lacked legal training. Thus, some critics charged that the juvenile justice system was unfair and unduly harsh with some youths. Other critics, however, pointed out that certain judges exercised their broad powers to promote their perceptions of the best interests of children in such a way that their dispositions were too lenient and did not adequately protect society.

The substantial discretion that the JDA gave to juvenile judges and probation officers was not the only reason for criticism. The Act also vested very significant control over the system in provincial administrators. As a consequence, there were enormous disparities across Canada in how juveniles were treated (Bala and Corrado, 1985). The maximum age of juvenile jurisdiction varied from province to province, ranging from the 16th to the 18th birthday, and the minimum age varied from 7 to 14 years; children under the minimum age in each province were dealt with exclusively in the child welfare system. There were also great disparities in respect of diversion from the formal juvenile justice system, access to legal representation and use of community-based sentencing options.

The 1965 release of a report on juvenile delinquency in Canada marked the beginning of a lengthy period of debate and gradual reform (Canada, Department of Justice, 1965). Some provinces, most notably Quebec, took steps to change their juvenile justice system by, for example, ensuring that young persons had access to lawyers and establishing a formal system of juvenile diversion. Other provinces lagged behind. On a federal level, discussion papers and draft legislation were released and commented upon, but no action was taken. The constitutional entrenchment of the Canadian Charter of Rights and Freedoms in 1982 gave a greater sense of urgency to federal reform efforts. Many of the provisions of the JDA appeared to ignore the legal rights guaranteed in the Charter and the provincial disparities invited challenge under section 15 of the Charter, a provision that guaranteed Equality Rights and was scheduled to come into force in April 1985. As a result, in 1982, with the support of all political parties, the Young Offenders Act received Parliamentary approval. Most of the YOA came into force April 2, 1984. Some parts of the legislation gave rise to controversy from the moment of their initial introduction in Parliament. Most notably, a number of provinces were dissatisfied with the establishment of a minimum age jurisdiction of 12 years, and a maximum age jurisdiction running to the 18th birthday. The proclamation of the uniform maximum age provisions was delayed until April 1, 1985, to allow all provinces sufficient time to adapt. It soon became apparent that there were a number of problems with the YOA and in 1986 some relatively minor amendments were enacted through the passage of Bill C-106. These did not alter the philosophy or basic provisions of the Act, but did facilitate implementation.

PRINCIPLES OF THE YOUNG OFFENDERS ACT

The YOA constitutes a clear departure from the JDA. There is a uniform national age jurisdiction of 12 through 17 years, as of the date of the offence, and the YOA is unmistakably criminal law, not child welfare legislation. The discretion of police, judges and correctional staff is clearly circumscribed by the YOA. The only justification for state intervention under the YOA is the violation of criminal legislation, and this must be established by due process of law. Society is entitled to protection from young offenders, and young offenders are to be held accountable for their acts. However, the YOA is not simply a "Kiddies' Criminal Code." It establishes a justice and corrections system separate and distinct from the adult system, and it recognizes that young persons have special needs as compared with adults, require special legal protection, and are not to be held as fully accountable as adults for their violations of the criminal law.

In section 3 of the YOA, Parliament offers an express Declaration of Principle for those responsible for the implementation of the Act.

3. *Policy for Canada with respect to young offenders.*
(1) It is hereby recognized and declared that
(a) while young persons should not in all instances be held accountable in the same manner or suffer the same consequences for their behaviour as adults, young persons who commit offences should nonetheless bear responsibility for their contraventions;
(b) society must, although it has the responsibility to take reasonable measures to prevent criminal conduct by young persons, be afforded the necessary protection from illegal behaviour;
(c) young persons who commit offences require supervision, discipline and control, but, because of their state of dependency and level of development and maturity, they also have special needs and require guidance and assistance;
(d) where it is not inconsistent with the protection of society, taking no measures or taking measures other than judicial proceedings under this Act should be considered for dealing with young persons who have committed offences;
(e) young persons have rights and freedoms in their own right, including those stated in the Canadian Charter of Rights and Freedoms or in the Canadian Bill of Rights, and in particular a right to be heard in the course of, and to participate in, the processes that lead to decisions that affect them, and young persons should have special guarantees of their rights and freedoms;
(f) in the application of this Act, the rights and freedoms of young persons include a right to the least possible interference with freedom that is consistent with the protection of society, having regard to the needs of young persons and the interests of their families;
(g) young persons have the right, in every instance where they have rights or freedoms that may be affected by this Act, to be informed as to what those rights and freedoms are; and
(h) parents have responsibility for the care and supervision of their children, and, for that reason, young persons should be removed from parental supervision either partly or entirely only when measures that provide for continuing parental supervision are inappropriate.

Some commentators have suggested that the principles articulated in section 3 are inconsistent and hence offer no real guidance for the implementation of the YOA. One youth court judge commented that section 3 reflects, if not "...inconsistency, [then] at least ambivalence about [what] approaches should be taken with young offenders..." (Thomson, 1983:27). It is apparent that there is a level of societal ambivalence in Canada about the appropriate response to young offenders. On the one hand, there is a feeling that adolescents who violate the criminal law need help to enable them to grow into productive, law-abiding citizens; this view is frequently reflected in media stories about inadequate facilities for treating young offenders. On the other hand, there is widespread public concern about the need to control youthful criminality and protect society. This view is reflected in media stories and editorials commenting on the inadequacy of the three-year maximum disposition that can be applied to young offenders, a particular public concern in regard to those youths who commit very serious, violent offences.

While it is not inaccurate to suggest that the Declaration of Principle reflects a certain societal ambivalence about young offenders, it is also important to appreciate that it represents an honest attempt to achieve an appropriate balance for dealing with a very complex social problem. The YOA does not have a single, simple underlying philosophy; there is no single, simple philosophy that can deal with all situations in which young persons violate the criminal law. When contrasted with the child welfare oriented philosophy of the JDA, the YOA emphasizes due process, the protection of society, and limited discretion. In comparison to the adult Criminal Code, however, the YOA emphasizes special needs and the limited accountability of young persons. There is a fundamental tension in the YOA between such competing ideals as due process and treatment; in some situations the Act gives precedence to due process, while in others treatment is emphasized at the expense of due process. The underlying philosophical inconsistencies and tensions in the YOA reflect the very complex nature of youthful criminality. There is no single, simple philosophy and no single type of program that will "solve" the "problem." Judges and the other professionals who work with young persons who violate the criminal law require a complex and balanced set of principles like those found in the YOA.

The balance of this chapter will be devoted to a consideration of the substantive provisions of the Young Offenders Act, with a discussion of how they reflect the principles found in section 3 of the Act and of how the courts have interpreted these principles in different contexts.

ARREST AND POLICE QUESTIONING

In addition to those rights guaranteed to all under the Charter of Rights, the YOA affords special rights and protections to young persons who are arrested. Some of these provisions are premised on the notion that many young persons lack the maturity and sophistication fully to appreciate their situation, and hence require special legal rights; other provisions are intended to involve parents in the process, both to protect the rights of their children and to recognize their supportive role.

The Charter of Rights provides:

s.8 Everyone has the right to be secure against unreasonable search or seizure.

s.9 Everyone has the right not to be arbitrarily detained or imprisoned.

s.10 Everyone has the right on arrest or detention.
(a) to be informed promptly of the reason therefor;
(b) to retain and instruct counsel without delay and to be informed of that right; and
(c) to have the validity of the detention determined...and to be released if it is not lawful.

The rights that are guaranteed to all under the Charter may be of special significance to young persons, as they are particularly prone to police supervision and even harassment in certain situations. In *R. v. Ina Christina V.* (1985:7211) a police officer observed a 15-year-old girl chatting quietly on a street corner in a place known by the officer to have an "...almost magnetic appeal for children who have run from home, some of whom have become the so-called `street kids' and acts as a focal point for many persons involved in prostitution and drug trafficking." The officer concluded she was either "loitering" (not a criminal offence) "or possibly a runaway," and purported to arrest her under provincial child welfare legislation. A struggle ensued and the girl was charged with assaulting the police officer. In acquitting the girl of this charge, the judge observed:

On the basis of the evidence presented, there is more than sufficient to find that Christina V.'s rights were infringed under ss...8 and 9 of the Charter and denied under para.10(b) of the Charter. In regard to the latter, although she was advised of her right to retain and instruct counsel without delay, there is no evidence that she was provided with the opportunity and means to do so. In advance of that, she was deprived of her liberty, the security of her person was invaded, her property was unjustly seized and searched and she was arbitrarily detained and imprisoned. These gross violations of her fundamental rights were totally out of proportion with the situation and prescribed nowhere by law. Even if the law had provided for such interference, it would be unreasonable to find that such was demonstrably justified in a free and democratic society....

The phenomenon of the runaway child is, in the first instance, a social problem. Left unaddressed, it too often escalates into a legal issue involving either or both child welfare authorities and law enforcement officers. The magnitude of the problem as it relates to downtown Toronto...requires an urgent response. Undoubtedly, as a result of pressure from concerned parents, politicians and business people in the area, the Metropolitan Toronto Police Department has felt obliged to provide that response. Unfortunately, the standard law enforcement approach to the problem is woefully inadequate as well as improper.

As was exhibited in this case, good faith and a sense of duty on the part of the police falls far short of adequately addressing the situation. The runaway child who has been reported missing but has not committed any criminal offence, *may* indeed be a child at risk. That is the issue that must be addressed first and it can only be accomplished in a competent and caring fashion by trained child care workers. (*R. v. Ina Christina V.*, 1985:7212)

In addition to the protections afforded under the Charter of Rights, special provisions found in section 56 of the YOA are intended to ensure that there is no improper questioning of young persons by police and other persons in authority:

s. 56(2) *When statements are admissible.* — No oral or written statement given by a young person to a peace officer or other person who is, in law, a person in authority is admissible against the young person unless

(*a*) the statement was voluntary;

(*b*) the person to whom the statement was given has, before the statement was made, clearly explained to the young person, in language appropriate to his age and understanding, that
  (i) the young person is under no obligation to give a statement,
  (ii) any statement given by him may be used as evidence in proceedings against him,
  (iii) the young person has the right to consult another person in accordance with paragraph (c), and
  (iv) any statement made by the young person is required to be made in the presence of the person consulted, unless the young person desires otherwise;

(*c*) the young person has, before the statement was made, been given a reasonable opportunity to consult with counsel or a parent, or in the absence of a parent, an adult relative, or in the absence of a parent and an adult relative, any other appropriate adult chosen by the young person; and

(*d*) where the young person consults any person pursuant to paragraph (c), the young person has been given a reasonable opportunity to make the statement in the presence of that person.

Section 56 is based on the recognition that young persons may lack the sophistication and maturity to fully appreciate the legal consequences of making a statement, and so require special protection when being questioned by police. It is also premised on the notion that some youths are easily intimidated by adult authority figures, and may make statements that they believe those authority figures expect to hear, even if the statements are false. It is hoped that consultation with a parent or lawyer will preclude the making of such false statements.

An interesting and difficult issue that has arisen in some cases is the extent to which individuals such as schoolteachers, principals or social workers may be "agents of the state" and hence should be expected to comply with the requirements of the Charter of Rights and section 56 of the YOA. In *R. v. H.* (1985) a 13-year-old boy was charged with theft and the prosecutor sought to have the court hear statements made by the youth to his teacher and the school principal. Prior to the statements being made, the teacher promised that if the money was returned, nothing further would happen. Not surprisingly, neither the teacher nor the principal complied with the Charter or section 56 of the YOA. The court ruled the statements inadmissible because of the violation of the YOA and section 10 of the Charter of Rights. *R. v. H.* does not require school personnel to afford young persons the right to counsel in all situations, but it does indicate that if this right is not afforded a youth prior to questioning, statements that are made may later be ruled inadmissible in youth court proceedings.

A somewhat different approach was taken in *R. v. J.M.G.* (1986), where a 14-year-old boy was charged with possession of a small amount of marijuana that had been discovered by his school principal after a search of the youth. The Ontario Court of Appeal emphasized that the search was carried out in the context of the principal's normal duties of maintaining discipline in the school, and hence did not constitute a violation of the Charter of Rights. The Court recognized that while the relationship between student and principal was not like that of policeman and citizen, "there may come a time when such [significant legal] consequences are inevitable and the principal becomes an agent of the police in detecting crime" (*R. v. J.M.G.*, 1986:712). In such a situation a school principal or teacher might be expected to strictly comply with the warning requirements of the Charter. *R. v. H.* and *R. v. J.M.G.* illustrate that the courts will closely scrutinize each situation to determine the extent to which a principal or other person should be treated as an agent of the state. It may also be significant that *R. v. J.M.G.* involved the seizure of physical evidence, which was clearly indicative of the fact that the crime in question had been committed, while *R. v. H.* only involved a statement and the YOA has special provisions in regard to statements.

Paragraph 3(1)(h) of the Declaration of Principle recognizes the role of parents in the lives of their children, and sections 9 and 56 ensure that parents have notice of arrest, detention and youth court proceedings. These provisions are premised on the notion that parents will normally provide emotional support and ensure that a youth's legal rights are protected. It should be emphasized that under section 56(2) it is the youth who has the right to decide whether or not a parent will be present during police questioning. Some youths may be unwilling to have parental involvement, and there may be cases where such involvement is clearly not appropriate. Parents will normally not be considered "persons in authority," and statements made to them by their children will usually be admissible, despite the absence of any form of caution (*R. v. A.B.*, 1986; YOA, 1982, s. 56(6)).

ALTERNATIVE MEASURES

Paragraph 3(1)(d) of the Declaration of Principle recognizes the value of "taking measures other than judicial proceedings" under the YOA. Section 4 of the YOA creates a legislative framework for "alternative measures," that is to say, for dealing with young persons outside the formal youth court process.

Alternative measures are a form of diversion from the court process and are typically used for first-time offenders charged with relatively minor offences. An alternative measures program allows a youth to be dealt with in a relatively expeditious, informal fashion and enables a youth to avoid a formal record of conviction. It is felt that some youths may be unnecessarily harmed by being "labelled" as "young offenders" through the formal court process, and that they may benefit from relatively informal treatment. Use of alternative measures is also consistent with the principle of "least possible interference," which is articulated in section 3(1)(f) of the YOA. Further, alternative measures programs may increase the scope for involvement of parents, victims and the community. Such programs may also be less expensive for society to operate than the formal youth court system.

In most provinces, responsibility for alternative measures is given to a community agency with a paid staff or volunteers, though in some provinces, government social workers or juvenile probation staff are responsible (Rabinovitch, 1986). Case referrals must initially be made by the police or Crown Attorney, who must be satisfied that alternative measures would be "appropriate, having regard to the needs of the young person and the interests of society," and that sufficient evidence exists to take the case to court. The program administrator then meets with the young person and proposes some form of alternative measures that might involve, for example, an apology, restitution, some form of volunteer work or a charitable donation. The young person is not obliged to participate, and always has the option of going to youth court for a judicially imposed disposition. Youths must "fully and freely consent" to participating and must "accept responsibility" for the offence alleged to have been committed; if the young person denies responsibility, the matter must go to court for a judicial finding of guilt or innocence. The young person must be advised of the right to consultation with a lawyer prior to participation.

If a young person agrees to participate and successfully completes the alternative measures agreed to, the charges must be dropped. Whether or not there is successful completion, no statement made by a youth, in the process of consideration of whether alternative measurers should be imposed, may be used in later court proceedings.

While there is some controversy over the efficacy of alternative measures as opposed to court in terms of reducing future offences (Moyer, 1980), until April 1988, every province except Ontario had implemented section 4 of the YOA. It is generally felt that alternative measures represent a socially useful experiment for dealing with first-time offenders in a humane, socially inexpensive fashion. The failure of Ontario to implement section 4 of the YOA has been successfully challenged in the Ontario Court of Appeal, as a violation of the Equality Rights guaranteed by section 15 of the Charter of Rights. In *R. v. Sheldon S.* (1988) it was held that the absence of such programs in Ontario constituted a "denial of equal benefit and protection of the law" on the basis of place of residence, and hence was in violation of section 15 of the Charter. This decision is under appeal to the Supreme Court of Canada and it remains to be seen whether the Charter can be invoked to force a provincial government to provide services and programs in accordance with the YOA. *Sheldon S.* may be a significant precedent for ensuring all youths access to a minimum level of services, regardless of their province of residence.

YOUTH COURT PROCEEDINGS

Proceedings under the YOA are conducted in a specially designated "youth court." In a number of provinces, the Family Court, which is responsible for such matters as child protection and adoption, has been designated as the youth court. In other jurisdictions, the Provincial Court, which deals with most adult criminal charges, has been designated as the youth court, although the proceedings must be held at a separate time from those involving adults.

Ontario and Nova Scotia have adopted a two-tier youth court model. As was the practice under the Juvenile Delinquents Act, 12- to 15-year-olds are dealt with in Family Court, while 16- and 17-year-olds are dealt with in Provincial Court, albeit with adult court judges who are nominally sitting as youth court judges. Critics have argued that Ontario and Nova Scotia have simply acted in an expedient fashion and have failed to implement the spirit of the YOA by maintaining the court jurisdiction in effect under the JDA (Bala, 1987; Stuart, 1987). However, the courts have held that the two-tier implementation model is permitted under the YOA and does not violate the Charter of Rights (*R v. R.C.*, 1987).

In section 52, the YOA stipulates that proceedings in youth court are to be similar to those governing "summary conviction offences" in adult court. This means that the proceedings are less complex and more expeditious than those applicable to the more serious adult "indictable offences." More specifically, this means that there are no preliminary inquiries, and all trials are conducted by a judge alone; there are no jury trials in youth court. It is felt that it is particularly important for young persons to have the more expeditious resolution of their cases available through summary procedures. The courts have held that the failure to afford young persons an opportunity for trial by jury does not violate the provisions of the Charter of Rights that guarantee equality and the right to a jury trial to persons facing imprisonment of five years or more. In *R. v. Robbie L.* (1986) the Ontario Court of Appeal emphasized that the maximum penalty under the YOA is three years, as opposed to the life sentence an adult may face for certain serious offences. Justice Morden wrote:

...the *Young Offenders Act* is intended to provide a comprehensive system for dealing with young persons who are alleged to be in conflict with the law which is separate and distinct from the adult criminal justice system. While the new system is more like the adult system than was that under the *Juvenile Delinquents Act* it nonetheless is a different system. As far as the aftermath of a finding of guilt is concerned, the general thrust of the *Young Offenders Act* is to provide less severe consequences than those relating to an adult offender...the establishment of the legal regime...for dealing with young persons, which is separate and distinct from the adult criminal justice system, is of sufficient importance to warrant the overriding of the equality right alleged to be infringed in this proceeding...(*R. v. Robbie L.*, 1986: 219, 225)

While a young person being tried in youth court is denied the opportunity to a preliminary inquiry and a jury, a youth is afforded all of the procedural protections that are given to an adult who faces a summary charge. There is a constitutionally based presumption of innocence (Canadian Charter of Rights and Freedoms, 1982, s. 11(d) with the onus upon the prosecution to prove its case. If a "not guilty" plea is entered, the Crown will call witnesses to establish its case and each witness will be subject to cross-examination. The youth is entitled to call witnesses and to testify, subject to the Crown's right of cross-examination, but there is no obligation upon the accused to adduce any evidence or testify. After all the witnesses are called, there may be submissions (or arguments) and the judge then renders a verdict. If the judge is satisfied. beyond a reasonable doubt, that the offence charged has occurred, a conviction is entered, and the case proceeds to disposition under the YOA. Otherwise, an acquittal is entered and this ends the YOA proceedings, though in appropriate cases the youth might still be dealt with under provincial child welfare or mental health legislation.

Most cases under the YOA do not in fact result in trials, but rather result in guilty pleas. Frequently the youth recognizes that an offence has occurred and wishes to plead guilty. If a guilty plea is entered, the Crown Attorney will read a summary of the evidence against the youth. Section 19 of the YOA has a special provision requiring a judge in youth court to be satisfied that the facts read by the Crown support the charge. If they do not, the judge must enter a plea of not guilty and conduct a trial. This provision recognizes that a youth may not appreciate the significance of a guilty plea as fully as an adult.

DISPOSITION AND DISPOSITION REVIEW

Young persons convicted of offences under the YOA receive a "disposition," or "sentence," pursuant to section 20 of the Act. Available dispositions consist of the following:

- an absolute discharge;
- a fine of up to $1,000;
- an order for restitution or compensation;
- an order for up to 240 hours of community service;
- an order for up to two years probation;
- an order for treatment for up to three years;
- an order for custody for up to three years.

Since the enactment of the YOA, appellate courts in different Canadian provinces have gradually articulated a dispositional philosophy for young offenders. In *R. v. Richard I.* (1985:523) the Ontario Court of Appeal acknowledged that in comparison to sentencing adults "...the task of arriving at the right disposition may be considerably more difficult and complex given the special needs of young persons and the kind of guidance and assistance they may require." In *R. v. Joseph F.* (1986:304), Justice Morden of the Ontario Court of Appeal wrote:

While undoubtedly the protection of society is a central principle of the Act...it is one that has to be reconciled with other considerations, such as the needs of young persons and, in any event, it is not a principle which must inevitably be reflected in a severe disposition. In many cases, unless the degree of seriousness of the offence and the circumstances in which it was committed militate otherwise, it is best given effect to by a disposition which gives emphasis to the factors of individual deterrence and rehabilitation. We do not agree that it puts the matter correctly to say the whole purpose of the Act is to give a degree of paramountcy to the protection of society with the implication that this is to overbear the needs and interests of the young person and must result in a severe disposition.

One controversial issue is the extent to which courts making dispositions under the YOA should take into account the principle of general deterrence. In *R. v. G.K.* (1985) the Alberta Court of Appeal declined to impose a custodial disposition on a youth without a prior record who was convicted of armed robbery, emphasizing that a psychiatric report indicated that there was no likelihood of recurrence of delinquent acts. Justice Stevenson wrote:

We...reject the suggestion that the young offender's sentence should be modelled on the sentence that would be imposed on an adult offender. If a custodial sentence is warranted then it ought not to be lengthier than that which would be imposed on an adult....In any event, deterrence to others does not, in my view, have any place in the sentencing of young offenders. It is not one of the principles enumerated...in s.3 of the Act which declares the policy for young offenders in Canada. (R v. G.K., 1985:560)

However, most other appellate courts have held that general deterrence may play a role in the sentencing of young offenders. The Ontario Court of Appeal specifically rejected the approach of the Alberta Court of Appeal in *R. v. G.K.*:

The principles under s.3 of the *Young Offenders Act* do not sweep away the principle of general deterrence. The principles under that section enshrine the principle of the protection of society and this subsumes general and specific deterrence. It is perhaps sufficient to say that...the principles of general deterrence must be considered but it has diminished importance in determining the appropriate disposition in the case of a youthful offender. (R. v. Frank O., 1986:377)

Another controversial issue is the extent to which courts should consider the promotion of the welfare of a youth as a basis for imposing a custodial sentence. In *R.R. v. R.* (1986) the Nova Scotia Court of Appeal upheld a sentence of five months' open custody imposed on a 14-year-old youth without a prior record who was convicted of the theft of a skateboard. The Court felt the youth "desperately requires strict controls and constant supervision" (R.R. v. R., 1986:3461-34). The commission of the offence was considered a justification for imposing needed care, even though the sentence was grossly disproportionate to the offence and far in excess of what an adult would have received for the same offence.

A more common approach, however, has been to reject the use of the YOA simply as a route for providing treatment. In *R. v. Michael B.* (1987) the Ontario Court of Appeal overturned an order for five months' open custody imposed upon a youth who committed a relatively minor assault and had no prior record.

The trial judge had been concerned that the boy was suicidal and neither his family nor the mental health facility he had been staying in wanted to accept him. Justice Brooke concluded that incarceration under the YOA "was not a sentence that was responsive to the offence, but in reality was what seemed at the time a sensible way of dealing with a youth who had a personality problem and needed a place to go" (R. v. Michael B., 1987:574). The Court of Appeal suggested that involuntary mental commitment was the appropriate route to follow; in fact this had occurred by the time the case came before that Court.

As a result of the YOA's distinctive dispositional philosophy and reflecting the fact that many youths involved in the criminal justice system have not committed serious offences, the vast majority of convicted young offenders receive dispositions that keep them in their communities. Section 20(1)(9) of the YOA allows the imposition of an absolute discharge if the court considers "it to be in the best interests of the young person and not contrary to the public interest." This disposition is usually reserved for minor first offenders and results in no real sanction being imposed, other than the fact of conviction. Restitution, community service and fines allow the court to impose a real penalty on the youth, without unduly restricting freedom. In appropriate cases, victims may be compensated by restitution.

The most frequently imposed disposition under the YOA is probation. The nature of a probation order depends on the circumstances and various conditions may be imposed. These might include that a youth maintain a curfew, attend school, or reside with parents. Probation may also entail regular reporting to a probation officer, and might even be used to require a youth to live in a foster home or with a suitable adult person (R. v. W.G., 1985).

The most serious disposition that can be ordered under section 20 of the YOA is placement in a custodial facility. For most offences the maximum custodial disposition is two years, but for offences for which an adult may receive life imprisonment, the maximum is three years. The YOA requires a judge placing a youth in custody to specify whether the sentence will be served in "open custody" or "secure custody."

A very disturbing trend immediately following the enactment of the YOA was a significant increase in the use of custodial placements for young persons who violated the criminal law (Leschied and Jaffe, 1987; Wardell, 1987). This trend can in part be attributed to the attitudes of many youth court judges who initially emphasized the protection of society and the youth's responsibility over recognition of special needs and limited accountability. It also seems that in those provinces where the age jurisdiction was raised, older youths who had been appearing in adult court as "first-time offenders" (their juvenile records being ignored), were appearing in youth court with long records of prior offences. Further, it seems that some youth court judges were making extensive use of open custody as a "middle option" for youths who had not committed serious offences but who "needed some help." Prior to the enactment of the YOA, many of these youths had been helped through the child welfare system.

It remains to be seen whether this trend toward increased use of custody will continue. There is some evidence that there may be a decline in the use of custody. In most provinces, the appellate courts have rendered decisions that reduce the length of custodial dispositions for young offenders, and emphasize limited accountability and recognition of special needs. As originally enacted, the YOA placed certain restrictions on the use of custody, requiring a predisposition report before any custodial disposition was made, and restricting the use of secure custody to cases where a more serious offence occurred or where there was a record of prior offences. In amending the YOA in 1986, Parliament also provided that a youth court should not place a young offender in open or secure custody unless this was considered "necessary for the protection of society....having regard to the seriousness of the offence and...the needs and circumstances of the young person" (Section 24(1)). Under the original legislation, this consideration only applied to secure custody. It is to be hoped that these signals from the appellate courts and Parliament may be having the effect of curbing the excessive use of custodial placements by the youth courts.

CONCLUSION

The Juvenile Delinquents Act came into force close to the start of the twentieth century, and by the 1980s major reforms were inevitable. The Young Offenders Act created a relatively uniform, national scheme for dealing with adolescents who violate the criminal law. While these youths are not afforded a child welfare approach, used for children under 12 whose behaviour may be a threat to others, nor are they subject to the full rigours of the adult criminal justice system.

The YOA has clearly achieved certain objectives, most notably protecting the legal rights of young persons, and provides recognition of the right of society to appropriate protection. It seems unlikely for the foreseeable future that Parliament will engage in a major revision of the YOA or change its fundamental principles. However, there remain many issues for the courts, provincial administrators, and the federal Parliament to address before we will have achieved a system of youth justice truly worthy of the close of the twentieth century. Our search for a youth justice system that fairly balances the needs and rights of young persons while adequately protecting society must be an ongoing one.

Chapter 4

THE CANADIAN TEMPERANCE MOVEMENT: CONTEMPORARY PARALLELS*

Anton R. F. Schweighofer

In the years preceding the prohibition of alcohol in Canada, liquor was vilified in increasingly vehement tones. After prohibition was instituted, the lies, violence and infringement of rights that accompanied alcohol prohibition led Canadians to reject it. The modern rhetoric condemning heroin, cocaine and other illicit drugs is similar to that which preceded and accompanied the prohibition of alcohol. These parallels will be explored in five sections entitled: Misinformation, Miseducation, The Unnecessary Ideal of Abstinence, War Mentality and Dangers to the Individual. The similarity of modern drug control policy and the prohibition policy, which was discovered to be inefficacious and counterproductive over sixty years ago (Brecher, 1972:265-66; Hallowell, 1972; Smart and Ogborne, 1986), may prompt a rethinking of the legitimacy of contemporary drug policy.

The Canadian temperance movement, one of the strongest lobby groups ever to have existed in Canada (Hallowell, 1972:11), was part of a larger movement of social reform that began in the nineteenth century. In addition to alcohol reform, groups throughout Europe and North America concerned themselves with wage rates, hours of labour, child labour, workmen's compensation, old age pensions, tariff reform, the single tax, direct legislation and women's suffrage (Allen, 1981:10; Thompson, 1972:287).

The first Canadian temperance society was founded in Montreal in 1828. The early societies emphasized moderation rather than abstinence and initially focused their attention on the excessive consumption of whisky, rum and brandy. Later, beer and wine were added to the list (Guillet, 1933:145). By 1835 the first of the Total Abstinence Societies began to form. These early temperance advocates were earnest and determined and their zeal was exemplified by their slogan "war to the death with the Demon of Intemperance" (Chiniquy, 1847:26).

Temperance groups were typically composed of well-educated members of the middle class (Hallowell, 1972; Smart and Ogborne, 1986). Although their actions can be seen as part of the turn-of-the-century progressive reform movement (Timberlake, 1963), they can also be seen as an expression of class conflict — an attempt to control drunkenness of "objectionable" members of society, including immigrants and the rising working class (Cloyd, 1982; Gusfield, 1963; McCandless, 1984; Vogt, 1984). Although beyond the purview of this

* Edited version of Anton F. Schweighofer, "The Canadian Temperance Movement: Contemporary Parallels," *Canadian Journal of Law and Society* (University of Calgary Press) 3(1988):175-93.) Reprinted with permission of the author and the *Canadian Journal of Law and Society*.

The author would like to thank Bruce Alexander, Michael Coles, and Brian Burtch of Simon Fraser University and an anonymous reviewer for their helpful comments and criticisms.

article — since it has already been well examined — it is interesting to note that the origins of Canadian drug legislation are also apparently based on class conflict and prejudice (Boyd, 1984; Comack, 1985; Mitchell, 1986; Small, 1978; Solomon and Green, 1988). Further, it has been asserted that contemporary drug prohibition continues to be supported by special interest groups, including doctors (Berridge and Edwards, 1981; Szasz, 1975) and law enforcement officials (Cloyd, 1982), in the effort to maintain and extend professional interests and power.

MISINFORMATION

The consumption of alcohol by Canada's early settlers did sometimes exacerbate the difficulties of pioneer life (Guillet, 1933; Smart and Ogborne, 1986: ch.1) and there was undoubted wisdom in the call for temperate use of alcohol. Temperance, however, soon came to mean total prohibition rather than moderation. The rhetoric that accompanied this shift was dramatic; alcohol was blamed for most if not all the ills of society. It was believed that:

Most of the robbers will tell you that liquor alone is the cause of the thefts they have committed, and that without the boldness which liquor gives, they would have been incapable of committing the crimes of which they are guilty. Penetrate into those dark and damp prisons, and if you encounter a monster who has imbued his hands in the blood of his father, and who in a few days, will expiate his crime by an ignominious death, ask him how he could have taken upon himself to commit such a willful murder, and he will answer you that it would never have happened to him, if he had not been addicted to drinking; that it was under the hellish influence of strong drinks he became a murderer. (Chiniquy, 1847:107)

Intemperance leads to crime, to insanity, and to pauperism. One-half of the crime annually committed, two-thirds of the insanity, three-fourths of the pauperism, are ascribable to intemperance. (Select Committee, 1849:86)

Such pronouncements were significant since they were often couched in the language of science and as such served a vital role in legitimizing the temperance cause. An increasing body of literature states, however, that such pronouncements have little basis in fact since crime, poverty, depression and other such problems tend to precede rather than follow addiction (Alexander and Dibb, 1975; Braucht, Brakarsh, Follingstad, and Berry, 1973; Browne and Finkelhor, 1986; Chein et al., 1964; Harlow, Newcomb, and Bentler, 1986; Helzer, Robins, and Davis, 1975/1976; Wurmser, 1978; Yeary, 1982).

Politicians now use remarkably similar hyperbole when discussing currently illegal drugs. Recently, Prime Minister Mulroney likened illicit drug use to an epidemic that threatens "our economic as well as social fabric" (Cruickshank, 1986: A1), in spite of evidence which shows that a Canadian drug epidemic does not exist. Even the use of cocaine, the most faddish illicit drug of the last few years, has grown far less and with far fewer harmful consequences than the media reports indicate (Erickson, Adlaf, Murray, and Smart, 1987:52; Maclennan, 1986).

It appears that recent Royal Canadian Mounted Police estimates of how much money Canadians spend on illicit drugs have also been excessive. For instance, RCMP figures for 1985 were inflated by approximately eight billion dollars because of an erroneous assumption that most of the drugs coming into Canada are consumed here. Much is actually re-exported (Vancouver *Province*, 3 September 1987). Although conviction rates are a crude measure of drug use the Bureau of Dangerous Drugs reports that during 1984 drug convictions in Canada fell 13 percent. In line with these data, experts in the field of addiction deny the presence of an epidemic (Poirier, 1986:A1).

Further hyperbole is also often evident in Canada's popular press. *Maclean's* magazine devoted its September 29, 1986 cover story to what it called "A crusade...to end the spread of killer drugs in Canada." "Killer drugs" refers to illicit drugs such as cocaine and heroin, but its use is unjustified. Of course, illicit drugs can cause death if taken in excess or in an especially hazardous manner, but so can hundreds of drugs that are not prohibited. It is not the case that illicit drugs inexorably cause death or even harm.

An exhaustive 1956 report on narcotics addiction discovered that not "even one scientific study on the proved harmful effects of [heroin] addiction" could be found. Earlier investigators had apparently assumed that the ill effects were so obvious as not to need scientific verification or they, too, *had accepted without question the traditional beliefs on the harmful effects of narcotics*" (Stevenson, Lingley, Trasov, and Stansfield, 1956:510 [emphasis added]). More recently, Brecher (1972:22) found that the most serious consequences of being a heroin addict or user resulted from "the risks of arrest and imprisonment, infectious disease and impoverishment — all traceable to the narcotics laws, to vigorous enforcement of those laws, and to the resulting excessive black-market prices for narcotics," rather than the drug itself. Similarly, an ethnographic study of cocaine users (Waldorf, Murphy, Reinarman, and Joyce, 1977) found that even among regular users there were few negative side effects (physical or social) and little evidence to indicate paranoid or violent reactions. Grinspoon and Bakalar (1976) and Erickson et al. (1987) have also reported that toxic or psychotic reactions were rare among cocaine users that they studied.

Of course, there are potential dangers associated with drug use and these should be expounded factually and clearly. However, to leave the impression that illicit drugs are "killers" is as misleading as many of the prohibitionists' descriptions of "demon rum."

The presentation of sensationalized and often misleading drug information by the mass media has been common for over a century (Silver and Aldrich, 1979). The effects are probably extensive since the media are an influential and trusted source of drug information (Erickson et al., 1987; Fejer, Smart, Whitehead, and Laforest, 1971; Sheppard, 1980; Smart and Fejer, 1972). Since the great majority of Canadians do not have direct experience with illicit drugs, it is safe to assume that most Canadians uncritically accept the often lurid images and descriptions that the media offer. An actual example of how these images can sustain the status quo was afforded when Canada's Minister of National Health and Welfare stated, in effect, that an epidemic of public concern about

illicit drugs is the matter of greatest importance and the lack of evidence for an actual epidemic of drug abuse is secondary.

The media (particularly news), due to their very nature, tend toward drama and action rather than time-consuming analysis (Bennett, 1983). The presentation of diverse viewpoints is also hampered by the tendency of the news media to rely heavily on government sources and mainstream perspectives (Bennett, 1983). In the area of illicit drugs this often results in the impression that there are no serious alternatives to "mainstream" thought (Bennett, 1983; Zinberg and Robertson, 1972: ch.2). This is not the case, however, and despite the difficulties of instigating opinion contrary to government policy (Ginsberg, 1986), recent changes in drug laws suggest that such movement is possible. For example, while marijuana is still illegal in Canada, thirteen American states have decriminalized its use. Significantly, decriminalization has been followed by negligible, if any, increases in marijuana use. Although many factors played a role, these changes were largely instigated by grassroots movements after mainstream images of marijuana had been dispelled (Josephson, 1981; Maloff, 1981; Roffman, 1977, 1980; Saveland and Bray, 1981).

The nature of drug information conveyed by the media, both today and during the temperance movement, plays an important and significant role. Drug information has the capacity to reinforce and sustain popular prejudices or it can stimulate new perspectives and thereby opinion that acknowledges, or at least explores, the potential value of new drug policies. The very nature of the mass media, however, militates against the second of those two alternatives and hence the critical appraisal of media pronouncements is a necessity.

MISEDUCATION

One activity of turn-of-the-century Canadian temperance advocates was "educating" the public, especially youth, about liquor. That "education," however, often consisted of half-truths and blatant inaccuracies. Temperance advocates often suggested that even one drink could produce a drunkard (Smart and Ogborne, 1986: 31). It was also asserted that alcohol could burn one's throat or cause spontaneous combustion (Bakalar and Grinspoon, 1984:83). These claims are distortions of the truth. The toxic effects of alcohol are actually negligible when it is used in moderation. It is only when alcohol is taken in sufficiently large doses with other drugs, or over an extended period of time that it becomes dangerous (Weil and Rosen, 1983).

Although we no longer provide alcohol education which relies on temperance misrepresentations, the lesson seems to have been forgotten by those who consider it legitimate to use comparable distortions when speaking of the feared drugs of our day. For example, Reginald Smart, (1983:69), a leading Canadian drug authority, has expressed such an opinion. Regarding amphetamines, Smart has written:

Most of the harmful effects of speed would not limit the lives of users in any significant way. Nonetheless, misleading as the phrase "speed kills" seems to be, it may have had a very positive effect in discouraging young people from trying amphetamines in any form.

Indeed, in the early 1970s Smart and Fejer (1974) even suggested that scare tactics may be a viable method of drug education.

Our current education policies are similar in other ways to temperance education. The "drug facts" that are given to today's youth often originate from those who espouse a complete abstinence view (Bakalar and Grinspoon, 1984:101; Chng ,1981) and who, in the hope of "doing good," provide one-sided information or misinformation (Fors, 1980; Sheppard, Goodstadt, and Chan, 1981; Sheppard, Goodstadt, and Williamson, 1985). Such practices often undermine drug educators' efforts. Chng argues that drug education, because of its emphasis on abstinence, has been "insidiously sabotaged" (Chng, 1981:13). Legal drugs are not subject to the strict abstinence ethos that is applied to illicit drugs and the existence of a clear double standard destroys the credibility of drug education.

The tendency of drug education courses to discuss "only the bad effects of using drugs" (Sheppard, Goodstadt, and Williamson, 1985:3) also discredits drug education programs when students learn that they have not been told the whole story. A classic example, the stepping-stone hypothesis of the 1960s, erroneously stated that marijuana use leads to heroin use (Le Dain, 1971:85; Weil and Rosen, 1983:120). Youths who realize the falsity of that and similar mistruths tended thereafter to disregard other drug information of real value (Brecher, 1972).

Not all drug education programs fall into the above categories. Nonetheless, many do. It is not surprising, therefore, that drug education programs have been found to be largely ineffective and in some cases even counterproductive (Goodstadt, 1980; Moskowitz, Malvin, Schaeffer, and Schaps, 1984; Schaps, DiBartolo, Moskowitz, Palley, and Churgin, 1981). Today, as in the early 1900s, the only route to sensible decisions and policies would appear to be through complete, accurate and unexaggerated information.

THE UNNECESSARY IDEAL OF ABSTINENCE

Advocates who campaigned for complete prohibition of alcohol attempted to strengthen their platform by arguing that moderate use was impossible as it inevitably led to debauchery (Levine, 1978:144; Smart and Ogborne, 1986:31). Although not true, this was a compelling statement. It is impossible to justify a drug whose use inevitably produces addiction. The contemporary media, and some academics, have advanced this same argument with regard to the most feared drugs of our day — heroin and cocaine (Cohen, 1985; Erickson, Adlaf, Murray, and Smart, 1987:28-31; Gold, 1984; Knox, 1984:23; McCormack, 1984:F3).

A study by Siegel (1984) found that social-recreational users of cocaine can maintain a low to moderate pattern of use without becoming dependent or addicted. These users apparently develop strategies that result in limited, or what Zinberg (1984) would term controlled, drug use. In a thorough and telling review of research from animal studies, clinical samples, population surveys and community studies, Erickson and Alexander also concluded that the addictive liability of cocaine has been overstated. In fact, of the total number of people that try cocaine, they estimate that the great majority (90-95 percent) do not become dependent and that most who do later regain control of their cocaine use.

The reality of moderate and controlled heroin and cocaine use is easily overlooked. Heroin and cocaine users who gain attention through media reports or word of mouth are typically those who have been unable to use these drugs in a moderate manner (e.g., John Belushi). Since such occurrences are more visible and more sensational than non-problematic drug use, people tend to remember these events more easily and vividly (Tversky and Kahneman, 1974). The public perception of illicit drug use is therefore skewed by the emphasis placed on those who are unable to use heroin and cocaine in moderation. Statistically, however, immoderate users are in the minority (Zinberg, 1984:250-53; Erickson et al., 1987:52).

The myth of inescapable addiction and degradation that has for so long lent support to extreme prohibition measures can be laid to rest.

WAR MENTALITY

Prior to World War I, despite their long and persistent efforts, temperance supporters had been unable to implement plans for the national prohibition of alcohol. But war, with its simultaneous concerns for patriotism and efficiency (Thompson, 1972) proved a boon for the temperance cause. Temperance advocates were able to muster new and powerful arguments in favour of a "dry" Canada and to tap the emotional fervour of wartime (Hallowell, 1972:60).

Temperance proponents, due to their years of experience, had become skilful publicists (Hallowell, 1972:19) and those skills were put into use with great effect during World War I. Temperance rhetoric increasingly used warlike metaphors that emotionally aroused one's sense of patriotic duty. For instance, it was stated that, just as Canadians should "despise the army of the Kaiser for dropping bombs on defenseless people, and shooting down women and children," they should also despise

the liquor traffic since it had "waged war on women and children all down the centuries" (McClung, 1915:163). A Reverend Hughson of Winnipeg counselled Westerners to "use ballots for bullets and shoot straight and strong in order that the demon of drink might be driven from the haunts of men" (*Manitoba Free Press*, 6 March 1916, p. 4). Even after the war it was declared that prohibition was a fight against "an enemy more mighty, more merciless, more beastly, more fiend-like, more diabolical than the Teuton" (*The Globe and Mail*, 29 Sept. 1919, p.8).

Likewise, current descriptions of anti-drug efforts continue to use war metaphors and to identify drugs with political enemies. The former Canadian Ambassador to the United Nations, Stephen Lewis, recently used the term "narco-terrorism" to link drug trafficking and international terrorism (*Vancouver Sun*, 9 Dec. 1985). The Americans have gone beyond metaphors. Rather than "ballots for bullets," real bullets and soldiers are used in authentic wars on the production and distribution of narcotics, cocaine and other illicit drugs. The recent involvement of American military troops in Bolivia illustrates this fact (McDonald, 1986:20). Although Canadians have not been involved in acts of such magnitude, it appears that they are also engaged in an escalating program that could lead drug enforcement policies to the excesses of a war that had originally served as only a metaphor (Ward, 1988).

The emphasis placed on patriotism was an important plank in the prohibition platform. The contention that liquor was the antithesis of patriotism was clearly embodied in such statements as: "anyone who will vote in favor of liquor might as well enlist under the Kaiser as far as patriotism goes" (Thompson, 1972:294).

The call to patriotism was especially potent since it enabled the temperance movement to enlist in its ranks those who otherwise would not have supported it, especially recent immigrants eager to prove their loyalty (Thompson, 1972:294). Furthermore, linking patriotism and support for prohibition served as a strong weapon to intimidate and denounce those who might speak against prohibition.

Groups such as the Liberty League, opponents of prohibition, attempted to defend themselves by stating: "We are not booze-fighters, nor are we bought by the liquor interests; we are just British subjects asking to live our lives under the laws of God and the reasonable laws of man" (*The Globe and Mail*, 30 July 1919, p.8).

Today, those who hold "liberal" drug views, those who suggest less restrictive measures for dealing with drug problems or those who suggest the "drug problem" has been exaggerated continually face the threat of being labelled soft on drugs, soft-headed, or even that their views may deserve legal censure (Bakalar and Grinspoon, 1984:111; Graham, 1987). If a person suggests that certain aspects of drug policies are incorrect s/he may even be suspected of being a "druggie" attempting to advance his or her own self-interests. Students in my own university debate whether the professor who lectures on drug issues is himself involved with marijuana or some other illicit drug. In contrast, other professors, who lecture on topics such as terrorism or fascism, do not risk the suspicion of harbouring motives other than curiosity and the quest for knowledge and explanations.

The temperance supporters' ability to "destroy most of their opponents' arguments by mere charges of selfishness or of collaboration with the liquor interest" (Hallowell, 1972:28-29) is a tactic that endures. It would appear that prohibitionists of the past and present use similar means to quiet and discredit those who should suggest alternative methods and ideas for dealing with drug issues.

DANGERS TO THE INDIVIDUAL

Another practice that grew from alcohol prohibition is the abrogation of normal individual rights. In turn-of-the-century Canada there was a strong belief in the sanctity of individual rights and the British ethos of "fair play." The enforcement of prohibition called these into serious question. For instance, the use of police "spies" and civilian "stool pigeons" was among the "arbitrary measures needed to keep the law" (*Victoria Times*, 9 March 1921, p.18). In the effort to enforce prohibition, youths as

young as eighteen and police officers were ordered to drink in order to detect and apprehend those who defied the prohibition edicts (*The Daily Colonist*, 28 April 1921, 20 October 1922).

Such cases as that involving Reverend Spracklin of Ontario received much publicity and served to highlight the loss of individual rights during prohibition. Spracklin, a practicing minister in Sandwich, Ontario was appointed a liquor licence inspector by the Attorney General of Ontario. He organized a squad of men who, in their roles as keepers of the law, carried clubs, guns and blank search warrants. On one occasion they boarded a yacht, pistols aloft, and proceeded to "carelessly [i.e., destructively] search the boat for liquor" (Gervais, 1980:122-23). Their search proved futile and Spracklin and his men left behind a group of frightened ladies rather than a gang of malicious rumrunners. Reverend Spracklin's most infamous adventure, however, involved Beverly "Babe" Trumble, the owner of a roadhouse. Contrary to the temperance laws of Ontario, Trumble continued to sell liquor, much to the chagrin of " The Fighting Parson." This situation came to a violent climax on November 8, 1920:

Spracklin, desperately wanting to question Trumble, broke a window of the hotel and climbed in. He raced through the main dining room, into the main hall and through to the bar in search of Trumble, but couldn't find him. He retraced his steps this time meandering through the pantry and kitchen of the roadhouse, then into Trumble's private dining room where he met him face to face.

It was then that Spracklin shot [and killed] Trumble claiming the hotel owner had flashed a gun (Gervais, 1980: 124-25).

Spracklin's subsequent trial and acquittal were the subject of intense media and public interest. The intensity was exemplified by an article in the *Christian Guardian*. Ironically, in view of the newspaper's name, it stated that the legitimacy of Spracklin's actions should not be obscured by "merely sentimental feelings stirred up by the thought of the taking of human life" (Hallowell, 1972:121). Ultimately, however, such extreme acts did lead the majority of Canadians to question and finally reject the "strong-arm" tactics necessitated by prohibition.

Nonetheless, the threat to individual rights has been recreated in modern drug laws. Today's police have "broader powers in even a minor drug case than they have in an investigation for murder, arson or some other criminal offence" (Solomon, Hammond, and Langdon, 1986:24). Furthermore, the actions of undercover officers continue to arouse scornful comment. A British Columbia judge recently commented that the undercover techniques employed by the RCMP were "scandalous" and "offensive in the extreme." The judge was referring to the most recent of a series of cases in which the RCMP used entrapment to obtain a drug trafficking arrest. In this case it was found that the RCMP had actually helped a drug informant escape criminal charges placed against him by other police departments. This occurred because the informant had been helping the RCMP entrap a man who, in the words of the judge, "was not ... a person who trafficked in drugs" (Needham, 1986:A12). It was also concluded that the RCMP had employed "a disturbing degree of persistence" in their effort to procure the trafficking arrest. In a similar case (*Amato v. The Queen*, 1982), the accused had been harassed for three months and threatened with violence before he finally agreed to acquire and deliver cocaine to a police informer. The threat of violence came from an RCMP constable (Boyd, 1983).

In another incident, a Surrey, British Columbia couple, who had been mistakenly identified by police as possessing illicit drugs, were subjected to the rigours of police drug search. The husband described the event as follows:

[a] man grabbed me with both hands around the neck... and started to squeeze. Another grabbed my hair and yanked out a handful of it... I think I swore at them, and the fellow who had been choking me said, "watch it buddy, or it will get tougher. You haven't seen anything yet." (Robinson, 1977)

The police apparently considered these tactics necessary since they had earlier seen a known heroin pusher brush against the husband outside a downtown Vancouver café, completing what appeared to be a drug transfer.

Although no drugs were found, the wife commented on that possibility: "Suppose the drug pusher had succeeded in putting a packet of heroin in [her husband's] pocket. The drug squad would have found it. How could we have proved our innocence?" (Robinson, 1977).

In some cases, proving one's innocence is the least worry of a police suspect. In a 1980 case, it was found that a British Columbia RCMP officer had apprehended a male heroin addict by the throat, holding him, in the words of the officer, "as hard as I could"; such a procedure being both a "common occurrence" and "standard operating procedure" when conducting a mouth search for drugs. The suspect in this case, however, choked on a package of heroin in his mouth and died. At the coroner's hearing the coroner stated, "It's a war between certain elements of society and law enforcement... Draconian measures...[are] obviously a must" (Trebach, 1987:299). The coroner's jury declared the death accidental.

CONCLUSION

The end of World War I spelled the demise of national alcohol prohibition in Canada. Arguments that had once been persuasive lost their force as the rallying cries of wartime efficiency and patriotism faded. The violence which accompanied the enforcement of prohibition could no longer be defended as a necessary corollary to the struggle to overcome the Kaiser. Coincidentally, the inefficacy of prohibition gradually became clear to increasing numbers of Canadians. The people of Canada acknowledged liquor policy should be changed and that more effective and moderate policies were available and could be achieved. Eventually, all the provinces which had instituted prohibition repealed it. In its stead grew a workable system that, although not perfect, proved serviceable for Canadians as a whole.

Hindsight shows that the arguments and "education" espoused by prohibition advocates were often distorted and sometimes patently false. These statements, even when made by those who had the community's best interests in mind, resulted in policies that ultimately proved counterproductive.

Alcohol is, however, a widely used drug and it was therefore possible for most people eventually to see through the exaggerations which supported prohibition. Exaggerations of the dangers of heroin, cocaine and other illicit drugs are much harder to expose since the majority of the public have only media sensationalism to provide knowledge of today's illicit drugs.

Although alcohol prohibition fell by the wayside, the rhetoric and mentality of alcohol prohibition live on. This is shown by the degree to which temperance-type slogans and tactics still inspire public belief and support. Few people question the slogans or tactics of the modern "drug war." Suggestions for change from the present course are usually accepted only if the suggested change is in the direction of ever greater controls and enforcement (Hadaway and Beyerstein, 1987).

Both alcohol and contemporary drug prohibition were, and are, responses to a desire to lessen the detrimental impact of drug use and addiction. In the clarity of hindsight, the futility of alcohol prohibition is unmistakable. However, that lesson has not been used to analyze the foundations of present drug policies. Doing so would expose excesses long ago recognized as repugnant to Canadians and counterproductive policies based on misinformation and exaggeration.

PART II

Measurement of Crime and Delinquency

As you read the title to this section and realize that a fair portion of this book is devoted to measurement issues regarding crime and delinquency, you must wonder why. After all, if you want to find out how much crime occurs in Canada, read your local newspaper. Between two and four times a year newspapers report the crime scoreboard. They tell us which cities are the murder and rape "capitals" of Canada. Inevitably, they tell us that the volume of crime has again increased (with few notable exceptions) and that the rate of crime is climbing. If we can learn all of that from a newspaper, why, indeed, should we spend so much time in a criminology book on the measurement of crime?

In Canada crime statistics are used for a variety of purposes. They are used in decisions involving funding of police and related agencies. At times they are used in the deployment of police. And from an academic point of view, they are used both to generate and to attempt to confirm explanations of criminal activity. "Crime statistics help establish the basic social facts of crime. For example, how does the crime rate vary by age, sex, race and income level of offenders and/or victims?" (O'Brien, 1985).

Since crime statistics serve such important purposes, it is critical that we know exactly what they represent. The criminal statistics that you read in the newspaper are not necessarily good indicators of what is happening in society. Most of the rest of this section is devoted to explaining how criminal statistics are generated.

CRIME FUNNEL

Crime statistics in Canada can be represented as a funnel, with the number of crimes decreasing as one moves through that funnel. Figure 1 illustrates that not all actual crime is detected, not all detected crime is reported, not all reported crime is recorded, not all recorded crime results in arrests, not everyone arrested is brought to trial, not everyone tried is convicted, and not everyone convicted is sentenced.

At the top of the funnel is the *actual crime rate*, the total number of crimes committed by all individuals in any given place and period of time, for example, in Canada during 1991. The total number of crimes is unknown but is at least theoretically knowable. However, we do not have a mechanism for knowing about all of the crimes and recording them. As things currently stand, we have only an approximation of *actual crime*.

Early criminologists, for example, Quetelet (1842), recognized that the "actual" crime rate was unknown. They assumed, however, that the *official crime rates* calculated from data gathered by the criminal justice system were good substitutes and reflected reasonably well the actual crime rate. Thus, they assumed that the direction (either up or down), the magnitude (either large or small), and the speed (either slow or quick) of changes observed in the official statistics were similar to the direction, magnitude, and speed of changes in the actual crime rate. The more criminologists learned about reporting and official recording of crime,

Figure 1

Theoretical Funnel of Crime

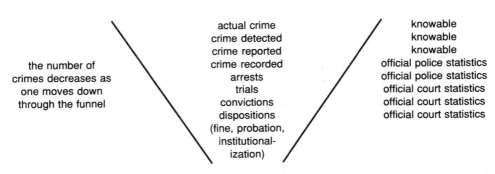

the number of
crimes decreases as
one moves down
through the funnel

actual crime
crime detected
crime reported
crime recorded
arrests
trials
convictions
dispositions
(fine, probation,
institutional-
ization)

knowable
knowable
knowable
official police statistics
official police statistics
official court statistics
official court statistics
official court statistics

the less they accepted these assumptions. For instance, criminologists learned that recorded crime statistics respond to forces in society that have little to do with the actual crime rate. Sometimes, political pressure to "clean up" an area or a type of crime results in an increase in police resources deployed, which in turn causes an increase in the crime rate as more police are able to arrest more offenders. The actual crime rate has not changed; only enforcement of the law has changed.

All three elements at the top of the funnel — actual crime, crime detected, and crime reported — are concepts for which only incomplete data exist. Later in the chapter we shall discuss the attempts to estimate those concepts using victimization and self-report data. For now, our discussion of crime statistics begins with the official police data on crime, crime recorded. (See the Appendix for an example of actual Canadian police statistics).

POLICE DATA ON CRIME

The police first become aware of crime either through their own observations or through public reports. In an early U.S. study, Black and Reiss (1967) estimated that 84% of crimes reported to police are citizen discovered, while only 14% are police discovered. Citizens do not report all crimes of which they are aware. The

Canadian Urban Victimization Survey (1984, *Bulletin 2*) found that 58% of victims in their seven-city survey did not report victimization incidents to the police. The police, in turn, have some discretion as to what types of crimes they will "discover," and these decisions also will affect criminal statistics (Ericson, 1981). Grosman (1975), for example, in his study of a Canadian prairie police department pointed out that the chiefs of police determine certain crime rates by the allocation of personnel to such areas as traffic, morality, and drugs. As indicated earlier, any increase in the number of police assigned, other things being equal, will increase the official crime rates for those crimes, at least initially, since there will be more police to undertake discovery of those crimes. The chiefs may look to the courts and the sentences handed out in order to make these deployment decisions. If for some crimes there are few convictions, they will not designate personnel to those crimes, thus "decreasing" the number of crimes.

Police discretion continues on the beat (Ericson, 1981; Sewell, 1985). Officers consider a variety of factors before deciding whether or not to intervene in criminal incidents. Most importantly, police officers consider how serious the crime is, but they also may consider the likelihood of successful prosecution, and even whether or not they are nearing the end of the shift (Wilson, 1968). All police officers have the option of continuing or not continuing the criminal justice process. Such discretion may not be officially sanctioned, but it occurs many times, every day, across the country (Ericson, 1981). These decisions have important effects on crime statistics.

Communications officers are the first to exercise discretion in responding to crime and thus to affect crime statistics (Silverman, 1977). If there are many calls coming in at once, such officers decide which sound the most serious, thus which will get attention and ultimately which will be recorded in official statistics. Major crimes are probably responded to and recorded, but minor crimes are especially vulnerable to such discretion. Sometimes, however, even for major crimes, there is some unofficial discretion. One frequent example is the crime of assault, especially if a drunk person calls in to complain about another drunk person's physical abuse and the communications officer, faced with several calls, fails to dispatch a car to the scene (Burris and Jaffe, 1983; Silverman, 1980). The case of wife battering provides an opposite example. As the social sensitivity to that event has changed, discretion has decreased and arrest rates have risen (Sherman and Cohen, 1989).

The police on the beat also exercise discretion in citizen-initiated crime reports. Wishes of the complainant for leniency and the seriousness of the offence are examples of factors that determine whether the crime is recorded. A citizen who wishes not to be involved in court proceedings may not wish to prosecute. While this is not, in fact, the victim's choice when the criminal law has been violated, the wishes of victims are most important, for without their testimony there can be no conviction. Hence, while the police could proceed with the offence on their own, they may be hesitant to do so without the cooperation of a primary witness.

More important for users of criminal statistics, this process of police discretion does not operate uniformly for all victims, for all types of crime, or for all population areas. Thus one cannot always estimate the distortions and inaccuracies such decisions have on official crime rates. In a 1980 study Silverman explored the effects of differential reporting of crime. His major finding was that the two Western Canadian cities he studied recorded minor crimes differently. In Calgary, minor crimes often did not get into the official statistics, while in Edmonton they did. Hence the actual amount of crime in the two cities was more similar than the official statistics indicated.

In an attempt to develop a system to enhance the quality of Uniform Crime Reporting (UCR) data the Canadian Centre for Justice Statistics (1990) undertook a study of procedures used in Calgary and Edmonton to generate crime statistics. (The two cities historically have very different crime rates even though they are demographically similar [Silverman, 1977[). In 1988 Edmonton's crime rate for criminal code offences was 69% higher than Calgary's. The study was an attempt to try to determine whether Edmonton's higher crime rate was real or was a result of reporting and recording differences (as suggested by Silverman, 1980).

In the CCJS study it was hypothesized that part of the differences in crime rates in the two cities could be attributed to differences in the structure, organization, and operation of the information systems in the two police departments. This hypothesis was confirmed in a number of ways. First, in each city there were a number of crimes that disappeared from the system of record keeping after the stage of the initial telephone call (from the public) about a crime. But the missing rate was twice as high in Calgary (9.9%) as it was in Edmonton (5.5%). The second part of the study traced the link between records in the communications area and in the records section. Calgary lost close to 11% of its cases as they moved from one section to the other, while Edmonton lost only 1%. That is, the information is lost before an offence report is even written. When the results of these two studies are combined, Calgary loses close to 20% of its cases, while Edmonton loses 6%. A third study examined the loss of specific offences. The conclusion is that there is a good deal of variability in the reporting of specific offences in the two cities, but that Calgary loses far more in the system than does Edmonton.

One final source of differences in the two crime rates is the population base. Crime rates are based on city populations. In 1988, about

15,300 people lived in the Calgary suburbs (2.3% of the city population) while in Edmonton there were 128,600 suburbanites (22% of the city population). If crime rates are based on metropolitan rates (inclusion of the suburban population and crime), Edmonton's crime rate is reduced by about 8.2%, while there is a negligible reduction of Calgary's rate.

In concluding the study, the researchers calculated the amount of difference in the crime rates that is due to data loss in the systems used in the two cities. The conclusion is that one-half the difference between the two cities is a result of loss of data in Calgary and the omission of the Edmonton suburbs when calculating these rates. However, even when these sources of difference are considered, Edmonton still has a criminal code crime rate 32% higher than Calgary's. The difference may be a real difference in crime rate of may be the result of other factors.

No doubt Calgary and Edmonton are not unique in the differences observed. There is good reason to believe that the kinds of differences observed between these two cities also occur in many other places across the country. It would thus seem that inter-city and interregional comparisons (which are constantly made in the national and local press) are risky (see also Hackler and Paranjape, 1983). On the other hand, the trends generated in any one city may be a reliable estimate of police activity for that city. Further, annual city statistics are likely a reasonable indicator of trends within that city.

As for victims, Black (1970) found that those who are not respectful to the police are less likely to have their complaints recorded than are the most courteous victims, and the police pay slightly greater attention to complaints from white-collar than from blue-collar victims. Murder, arson, robberies, and other serious crimes probably do not suffer from these biases and are probably recorded as reported, but assaults and most less-serious crimes may be less diligently recorded. Finally, as for location, police in smaller communities, because they are more likely to know the offenders, may be more likely to overlook or treat extra-legally some offences that police in large urban areas treat routinely as cases for the courts. A good

example of this variation in discretion is public drunkenness. In a small community, the police may know the offenders and thus let them dry out in a cell or take them home, whereas in urban areas the same offenders may be arrested (Neilson, 1979).

After police discretion has reduced the total number of crimes recorded, those that remain are sent for compilation to the Canadian Centre for Justice Statistics, Statistics Canada. The numbers forwarded to that body by the police are probably fairly close to those entered by local police into their own records. The exact methods used by the police for reporting those totals of officially recorded offences to Statistics Canada are discussed below. One should note here, however, that even some of the crimes initially recorded and forwarded by the police can later be discounted. In 1988, 4.5% of criminal code violations recorded were later listed by the police as *unfounded*, which means the police believe that those crimes did not happen or were not attempted (Statistics Canada, 1989). It is important to know how these decisions are made, as they may also affect actual crime data.

This discussion of how information on crimes is lost is not meant to be complete but instead is intended to give the reader an idea of some of the ways in which information about crime is omitted from the official records. The point to be remembered is that some of the crimes that the police are, or could be, aware of are not recorded in the official documents. Crime recorded will thus be a smaller figure than crime reported. This decreases the official crime rates, since the Statistics Canada data include only the smaller number.

At each stage in the criminal justice process subsequent to the police stage some crime statistics are generated. As the "crime funnel" shows, there are fewer people counted as the criminal justice process continues from police intervention to arrest, to court and final disposition of the case (see Boydell, 1985). Not all of this information is collected systematically and certainly not all of it is available to the public. For instance, in Canada, aggregate court statistics have not been available for many years. In this section, therefore, we are concerned mainly with police statistics, for they are most often used as the measure of crime in society.

As the noted criminologist Thorsten Sellin (1932) pointed out, they are closest to the commission of the criminal act.

GENERATING OFFICIAL STATISTICS: CANADIAN UNIFORM CRIME REPORTING, 1961-1988

The first step leading to a crime statistic usually occurs when citizens report a crime to the police or when the police observe a crime taking place. Every time a police officer investigates a crime a report is supposed to be written. These reports become a part of the official record. In the pre-1988 system, police departments entered their data on standardized forms that summarized their monthly crime data. Each police department's summaries were forwarded to Statistics Canada for compilation. Since 1982 this task has been handled by the Canadian Centre for Justice Statistics, which is part of Statistics Canada, and which produces *Canadian Crime Statistics* — books that display the crime data (see the Appendix for an example).

Police record crimes according to a set of rules that are contained in a Uniform Crime Reporting Manual. Statistics Canada and the Canadian Association of Chiefs of Police are responsible for the rules for recording crime in Canada, and those rules remained fairly constant (with only minor changes) between 1962 and 1988. Changes to the system planned in 1986 are currently being instituted and are discussed later in this chapter.

Canadian Crime Statistics presents information about crimes reported, persons charged, offences cleared, and crime rates for the country as a whole and for regions, provinces, and urban areas (as well as some other data). The report covers over 99% of the 607 municipal communities that have their own police forces in Canada, as well as those areas covered by RCMP and provincial police (Statistics Canada, 1989:20). The annual volume also offers a discussion of the rules used to report crime and some of the limitations of the data generated. Some of the rules that were used to generate the data resulted in interpretation problems, however, and these are discussed below.

OFFICIAL STATISTICS, 1961-88: SOME PROBLEMS

First, attempted offences were counted in the same category as completed offences. The only exception of this rule was attempted murder, which was counted separately from completed murder. For some purposes it would have been beneficial if attempted and completed acts had been counted separately. Certainly, the courts and the Criminal Code view them separately, and usually cut the maximum punishment for an attempt to one-half that for a completed act.

Second, the definition of what constitutes an offence varied with the type of crime. In offences against the person, one offence was counted per victim, while in the case of a crime against property one offence was counted for every "distinct or separate operation." A distinct operation is one that involves the "same time, location and circumstances." The difficulties that resulted from this distinction were numerous. For instance, if an offender entered a room and physically assaulted three persons, three crimes were committed. If, on the other hand, an offender entered a room and stole the belongings of three people at the same time, then, according to the official statistics, one crime occurred.

If there was a rationale for this inconsistency in the method of counting personal and property offences, Statistics Canada did not provide it. Within the category of property offences there were other problems of enumeration. Below are definitions used by Statistics Canada in describing the methods of counting robbery, break and enter, and theft.

Robbery — Count one offence for each distinct operation carried out or attempted: e.g., if three persons in a store are held up and the store is robbed, score a single offence of robbery. If four persons rob one, or one person robs four at the same time and location, only one robbery is scored.

Breaking and Entering — When a building contains several independently occupied residences such as apartments, suites, hotel rooms, or offices, each one entered would be scored. When a building has one occupant, for example, a warehouse, store, shop, etc., and is broken into, score only one offence. Score one offence for any number of box cars broken into when grouped in one location. Grouped in one location means the same spur or siding.

Theft — Property stolen from a number of persons located in one place constitutes one offence for scoring purposes. (Statistics Canada, 1986:7-2, 7-3)

The inconsistency that occurred is evident when robbery is compared with the other two offences. If four people lived in four different apartments in the same building and each had property stolen from his/her apartment, then four offences were counted in the official statistics. However, if four people happened to be gathered in the lobby of that apartment building and were robbed of their possessions, then only one offence was counted in the official statistics. If four boxcars on the same spur were broken into, one offence was counted; if two boxcars were on one spur and two boxcars were on an adjacent spur and they were broken into, two offences were counted.

Third, the instructions from Statistics Canada concerning multiple offences directed that "where several offences occur in one incident, score the more serious offence" (1986). Two problems arose from this method of counting. The first involved the process through which the most serious offence was determined.

Seriousness of the offences is determined by the maximum penalty allowed by law, or the offence that is considered the most serious by the police when the penalties are the same; or the offence which appears first in the offence classification. (Statistics Canada, 1977:11)

It is possible that this particular method of determining seriousness may not reflect the feelings of the community concerning the seriousness of the offences (see Akman and Normandeau, 1967; Sellin and Wolfgang, 1963; Shelley, 1980).

A further problem that resulted from this method of counting involved loss of information. In a hypothetical case a hitch-hiker flags down a car on the highway. The car, which contains a man and a woman, stops on the shoulder of the highway. The hitch-hiker goes up to the car, shoots and kills the man, sexually assaults the woman, takes the man's wallet with $300 in it, and drives off in the car, leaving the woman on the ground. In the official statistics, that multiple crime probably would have

been counted as one homicide and one sexual assault. Information was lost concerning the robbery, the auto theft, and a weapon's offence. (Note to students: While the statistics did not record those crimes, this loss would have had little effect on the prosecution of the case. The offender, if caught, would likely have been prosecuted for murder, sexual assault, robbery, assault, a weapon's offence, and auto theft).

Finally, the issue of "crimes cleared" continues to result in problems. Clearing a crime is essentially a housekeeping measure used by police. Crimes are cleared or "closed" either by apprehending a suspect and laying the charge (cleared by charge) or by some other means (cleared otherwise). The first category is relatively clear, but the "otherwise" category incorporates a wide variety of occurrences including, for instance, the case of a known offender who has diplomatic immunity and hence cannot be arrested, and the case of an offender who kills someone and then herself or himself and hence cannot be arrested. Both of the examples would be "cleared otherwise." The problem is that the category does not seem to be used in a consistent manner. In the 1977 Silverman study, it was shown that "cleared otherwise" rates were very different in Calgary and Edmonton, even though there was no apparent reason for the deference. Calgary and Edmonton are not alone in this varying interpretation of these categories. For instance, in some Canadian police departments when a known burglar is arrested, police may ask about other offences the person has committed. Often the burglar cannot remember the specifics of the cases in which he or she has been involved, but the police will use the apprehension of the burglar to clear "otherwise" a great many active cases even though they are not certain that the particular burglar was involved in those specific break and enter offences. As long as this is the case, the cleared categories are not very useful for comparative purposes.

CRIME RATES

Any increase or decrease in the absolute number of crimes recorded should be examined to see if they are due to an increase or a decrease in population. For this reason, crime rates, either crude, age specific, or sex specific are calculated. Crude crime rates based on official statistics take total population size into account and are calculated as follows:

$$\frac{\text{Number of Crimes Recorded by Police in a Particular Year}}{\text{Estimated Population for the Year}} \times 100,000 = \text{Crude Crime Rate}$$

Thus, while the number of crimes recorded by the police in a particular year may be a useful statistic, even with its inaccuracies, the crime rate for that year is even more useful because it takes into account population size. For example, in 1988 there were 2,392,419 violations of the Canadian Criminal Code recorded by Statistics Canada. The estimated population for that year was 25,911,800. The crude crime rate in Canada for Criminal Code violation in 1988 was therefore 9,233 per 100,000 population (Statistics Canada, 1989).

$$\frac{2,392,419}{25,911,800} \times 100,000 = 9,233 \text{ per } 100,000$$

Most criminologists would argue, however, that age-specific crime rates for each crime are more desirable than the crude rate (see, for example, Lee, 1984, and Maxim, 1985) because the crude crime rate may be affected by changes in the age compositions of Canada. For example, people between the ages of 14 and 30 commit most of the officially recorded crimes in Canada. Hence, if there are proportionately more people in that age group in particular years compared to previous years, perhaps due to the maturing of a "baby boom," then the overall crime rate may increase while the age-specific rates would remain unchanged for those years. Thus, rates that take into account shifts in age composition, perhaps due to increasing or decreasing birth rates, are desirable to avoid these misinterpretations.

Using conviction rates, fairly far down the

crime funnel, Hartnagel (1978) tested these notions by comparing crude and age/sex-specific rates across provinces. With the exception of the first-ranked Northwest Territories/Yukon, for which the crude rate is inflated due to the greater population of young males, there is only a negligible difference in rank orders and variations in rates of convictions across provinces using either type of data. The rates for British Columbia and Alberta are relatively high on both measures, while those for Newfoundland and Prince Edward Island are relatively low. Thus, for conviction rates at least, and for a one-year comparison, there appears little advantage in standardizing for age and sex distributions (see also Lee, 1984). However, for time comparisons, for example, a baby boom coming of age, such standardization is advisable.

It should be noted that the formula illustrated above can be used to generate other types of crime rates. For instance, by using the number of "victim incidents reported" (discussed later in this chapter) instead of "crimes reported to the police," victimization rates are computed.

OTHER ISSUES

Before making time comparisons one should also know that the techniques for collecting police crime statistics were improved and modified in 1962. Hence comparisons between police statistics pre- and post-1962 must be made with extra caution. For those interested in long-term trends of crime, any time series involving 1962 also presents problems of comparability.

Finally, an additional issue is that the system fails to collect some valuable information. Although the police collect information about crimes reported, persons charged, offences cleared, and crime rates for the country as a whole and for regions, provinces, and urban areas, no information is collected about the nature of the victims or offenders involved (except in the case of homicide).

In any event, however, crime statistics collected and published by Statistics Canada are the only statistics collected on a national and an annual basis in the country. Thus, for many purposes, they must be used by default. When used, however, their deficiencies must be kept in mind. If used with caution they can provide a useful social indicator of crime as defined by the law and by police activity in Canada. Moreover, the vast changes made to the data collection techniques after 1988 should improve Canadian crime statistics a great deal.

GENERATING OFFICIAL STATISTICS: CANADIAN UNIFORM CRIME REPORTING AFTER 1988 [1]

The statistics generated and published by Statistics Canada between 1962 and 1988 are based on police reports that summarize crime in police districts on a monthly basis. The information generated by the police and used by Statistics Canada is therefore aggregated statistics. Statistics from grouped data, however, are less useful for analytic purposes than information based on characteristics of individual crimes.

Recognizing these problems, the law enforcement program of the Canadian Centre for Justice Statistics, with the involvement of the Police Information and Statistics Committee of the Canadian Association of Chiefs of Police, undertook the task of developing a revised uniform crime reporting survey that would more fully satisfy the information needs of the criminal justice community.

The new system is designed to overcome some of the faults evident in the old uniform crime reporting system. Among other things, it is meant to generate more information for analysis. After being discussed at many levels of the criminal justice community, the new system was ready for testing in March of 1986. By 1988 the first police departments were actually using the system, and it is expected that 85% of eligible departments will be using the system by 1992. Hence, in the period between 1988 and 1922, two methods of reporting and recording crime occur simultaneously. The framers of the new system are, of course, aware of this inconsistency and have been careful to ensure that while the new system is an improvement on the old one, it is also compatible in the sense that comparisons between data collected using the two systems are possible.

The new system is *incident-based* rather than *summary*. That is, the unit of analysis is the crime incident rather than an aggregate of monthly crime data. Because data are available on an individual-by-individual basis, it is easier to analyze trends and to test theoretical propositions.

Because the new system is based on existing computer technology, the "respondent burden" remains manageable. (Respondent burden refers to the amount of work that the police expend in collecting these data.) The Canadian Centre for Justice Statistics captures police information about crime directly from the police computer. This requires that all systems are compatible to the extent that interface programs can be used to capture the same data from each participating police department. It also requires that all participating police departments utilize computer technology to record and store information about crime. While this may seem obvious, it should be pointed out that not all police departments in Canada have on-line computer systems, let alone systems that will mesh with the needs of the Canadian Centre for Justice Statistics. The Canadian Centre for Justice Statistics is providing the means by which police departments can join the system. They offer technical advice and access to the appropriate computer programs.

While the system itself its innovative and will be very useful for both the police community and academics, its utility is enhanced by the addition of data elements for analysis and by attention to some of the problems mentioned earlier. The following elements have been added to the uniform crime reporting content:

1. Information on victims: age, sex, victim/accused relationship, level of injury, type of weapon causing injury, drug and/or alcohol use.
2. Information on the accused: age, sex, type of charges laid or recommended, drug and/or alcohol use.
3. Information on the circumstances of the incident: type of violation (or crime), target of violation, types of property stolen, dollar value of property affected, dollar value of drugs

confiscated, type of weapon present, date, time, and type of location of the incident.

It is clear that these types of data will be useful to local law enforcement agencies for purposes of management, operational evaluation, program development and evaluation, and crime analysis. Also, the additional data are critical for theory testing by the academic community.

The new system yields other improvements over the old system as well. There is no longer any issue concerning different methods of counting crimes against the person and crimes against property (although appropriate differences in the specific information collected occur). Crime rates should be more easily calculated. Data on age and sex of victims and offenders (where available) make easier the estimations of age- and sex-specific rates.

Problems involving a multiple-offence rule (that is, count the most serious crime when more than one crime occurs in the same incident) have not been completely cleared up, but there is additional information on the lesser offences in a multiple incident. Initial feasibility tests indicate that multiple offences constitute a rather small proportion of crime and probably do not affect overall crime rates very dramatically.

The new system does not, in itself, address problems directly related to inter-city or inter-regional comparisons. The uniformity of the data elements generated by the new system will likely reduce between-jurisdiction problems but certainly not eliminate them completely. Differing styles of policing in different cities will still contribute to consistent differences between cities. Further, the new system does not affect levels of reporting by citizens. As a result, the new system will not get us much closer to the universe of crime than does the current system.

Nonetheless, the new system increases the quality of data being utilized in Canada. It is likely that Canada will be the first country to have this system fully in place and by the mid-1990s should have one of the best police data-collection systems in the world.

OTHER SOURCES OF DATA ON CRIME

Given the problems of police data, some criminologists have suggested that we go back up the crime funnel from recorded crime to reported crime. That is, data should be collected by criminologists at the police level itself, perhaps by sitting in police stations or police cars, or by walking beats and recording all the crime of which they become aware. This, of course, is a very large scale, clumsy operation, and virtually impossible at least at a national level.

Two alternative ways of measuring crime have been explored by criminologists in some detail. One method involves asking people what crimes they have been victims of (victimization studies), while the other involves asking individuals what crimes they have committed (hidden delinquency or self-report crime studies). We shall begin with the latter, since it was developed chronologically first by criminologists.

SELF-REPORT STUDIES

A dissatisfaction with official measures of crime led criminologists to look for other ways to determine the actual amount of crime in society. In self-report studies, individuals are asked about their own law-violating behaviour. While initial studies using the self-report technique were done in the 1930s and 1940s in the United States, they became very popular in the 1950s and 1960s, beginning with a study conducted by Short and Nye (1958).

In hidden delinquency/crime research, respondents are asked if they have committed specific delinquencies or crimes in a given time period. Think of yourself; have you done any of the following acts? Have you ever taken something from a store without paying for it? Have you ever driven a vehicle while even mildly intoxicated? Have you ever used marijuana or other illegal drugs? Have you ever struck someone in anger? Have you ever damaged public property? Have you ever taken anything from anyone by force? Have you ever taken office supplies for personal use? Have you ever taken goods into Canada without declaring them?

If you answered any of these questions positively, you probably violated a criminal law. Hundreds of similar questions could be used to demonstrate that at some time in your life you probably committed several acts that are punishable by law. And probably you committed a crime serious enough to be punishable by a jail or reformatory term. If the police did not become aware of your action, your behaviour is part of hidden delinquency or the "dark number" of crime.

Thus, to examine the extent of actual crime or delinquency in Canada, a sample of Canadians would be asked to respond to a list of crimes by indicating whether or not they had committed any of the crimes in question during a given time period. Crime descriptions are usually put into general language so that respondents are able to identify the act even if they do not know the legal terminology. The respondents are then asked for the frequency of commission of each event. Information on apprehension by police is also requested. With such data, comparisons can then be made between the amount of crime actually committed and the amount that the police record in official statistics. Studies using self-report methods generally conclude that most people have committed some crimes and delinquencies, some of them serious, of which the police are unaware. Most crime and delinquency does not result in police apprehension and punishment. Again, police statistics generally underestimate the amount of crime in society.

The early American studies using the self-report technique had a not-so-hidden agenda. They were attempting to show that there was no relationship between the social class of the offender and delinquent behaviour. In fact, the early studies (e.g., Short and Nye, 1958) found no relationship between the social class of the offender and delinquency, while the official statistics showed a negative relationship, with lower-class individuals committing more delinquency than middle- and upper-class individuals. Hence, the early studies concluded that a great deal of crime is unrecorded and that police may over-report lower-class delinquency. Later studies, however, disputed these findings (e.g., Elliott and Ageton, 1980; Braithwaite, 1981). While the controversy over the relationship between social class and delinquency continues today (Nettler, 1984), it would seem that lower-class youth are more highly represented in both police and self-report statistics, and commit more serious personal and property crime, more frequently, than middle- and working-class youth. [2]

But self-report studies have methodological problems (Nettler, 1984; O'Brien, 1985). For example, most of the statistics from self-report studies are not comparable to police-recorded statistics because of differing definitions of crimes, one legal and one unofficial (McClintock, 1970). Also, the time periods are not comparable, since police statistics are based on a year, while most self-report studies are based on six months to several years or longer. Thornberry (1967) criticized self-report delinquency studies on the basis of four criteria. First, the samples that have been used are often non-random. They deal primarily with juveniles, and as a result one cannot generalize with any confidence to either adult or non-sampled (usually non-school) juvenile populations (see also Braithwaite, 1981). Second, in selecting the questions for inclusion in questionnaires, most researchers systematically omit the most serious types of offences. Too many questions deal with non-dangerous, trivial delinquencies. Some of the later studies do take seriousness of delinquency or crime into account (e.g., Elliott and Ageton, 1980). Third, few of the studies use reliability tests to check the ability of the instrument to perform adequately in repeated studies. Last, and perhaps most important, any dishonesty on the part of respondents, any unwillingness to admit to committing crimes, biases the results of self-reports and makes them invalid. Only a few of the hidden delinquency studies tried to cope with the validity issue (Empey and Ericson, 1966; Hindelang et al., 1981). They came to inconsistent conclusions about the extent of dishonesty, either lying or selective recall, that was present in their respective studies. Coupled with these problems are problems of interviewer bias in administering questionnaires and eliciting responses (see Esbensen, 1982; Nettler, 1984). These problems are further complicated by issues of "telescoping" (bringing significant events forward in time) and memory decay, which seem to be common occurrences among subjects in self-report studies (Rojek, 1982; Schneider and Sumi, 1981), and the lack of national data. In the U.S. only a few national studies have been undertaken (e.g., Elliott and Huizinga, 1983) and none have been done in Canada.

Most hidden delinquency studies examine offenders rather than the offences they commit (O'Brien, 1985). The researchers are more interested in demonstrating that most individuals are offenders than in the variations in offences committed by different types of offenders. Thus, while researchers may argue that similar proportions of middle- and lower-class adolescents are delinquent, their statistics ignore qualitative differences in seriousness and/or quantitative differences in numbers of offences committed by the two groups. Lower-class individuals do engage in more frequent and more serious forms of delinquency.

On the other hand, for some kinds of criminal behaviour, self-report studies provide the only way of obtaining any information. For instance, researchers know that spouse assault is an underreported type of assault. In attempting to learn how much of that behaviour occurs in Alberta, Kennedy and Dutton (1989) used the self-report technique. They found that 12.8% of their urban sample and 8.3% of their rural sample reported such assaults. Despite the methodological flaws, the technique can provide valuable insights.

In sum, while hidden delinquency studies have added to our knowledge about the extent of delinquency and crime, methodological problems have handicapped their ultimate usefulness in measuring crime (Lab and Allen, 1984; Zimmerman and Broder, 1980; O'Brien, 1985; Nettler, 1984). Criminologists continue to seek better measures of the actual amount of crime in society. For many, a superior method of data collection is provided by victimization studies, described in the next section. Nonetheless, the self-report technique continues to be used, as it seems to be the only way to get at detailed offender information. And for purposes of exploring causes of delinquency it can serve a valuable function, as long as researchers are aware of and control for the methodological problems just noted.

VICTIMIZATION STUDIES

Victimization surveys ask respondents whether or not they were victims of crime in a given period of time, and may explore the circumstances of the crime and whether or not the individuals informed the police about the incident. These studies generally reveal that even when people know they have been victimized, a great amount of crime is not reported to the police, and, thus, crime detected is a much larger figure than either crime reported or crime recorded (the official data). The results of early victimization studies were first reported in 1967 (Biderman, et al., 1967; Ennis, 1967) in the United States. Since that time, a great deal of money has been poured into U.S. victimization studies and the level of sophistication has correspondingly improved. The U.S. National Crime Survey, the largest of its type in the world, collects data on 65,000 households every six months. This commitment to victimization studies no doubt reflects both the resources available in the United States and the seriousness of its crime problem.

Canada has taken advantage of the U.S. developments, and in early 1982 the Ministry of the Solicitor General of Canada, with the assistance of Statistics Canada, conducted a victimization survey in seven major cities — Greater Vancouver, Edmonton, Winnipeg, Toronto, Montreal, Halifax-Dartmouth, and St. John's. The survey collected information about reported and unreported crime during 1981, the risk of victimization, the impact of crime, public perceptions of crime and the criminal justice system, and victims' perceptions of their experiences (Solicitor General, 1983). In 1985, a follow-up victimization survey was conducted in Edmonton by the Solicitor General of Canada.

The 1982 study found that "for the year 1981, there were more than 700,000 personal victimizations of people over 16 (sexual assault, robbery, assault, and theft of personal property) and almost 900,000 household victimizations (break and enter, motor vehicle theft, theft of household property and vandalism) in the seven cities surveyed...Fewer than 42% of these had been reported to the police" (Solicitor General, 1983, *Bulletin* 1). The point made earlier concerning the incompleteness of police statistics is well documented in these findings (even though these figures are not directly comparable to any set of police statistics that could be generated. See also Skogan, 1984).

Of all crimes, motor vehicle theft is the crime most likely to be reported (70%), while theft of personal property is least likely (29%). The most common reasons for not reporting crimes are that the crime was "too minor," that "the police could not do anything about it" or that reporting it was "too inconvenient" (Solicitor General, 1983, *Bulletin 1*). The 1982 and 1985 studies generated ten reports and a modest amount of independent research (e.g., see Kennedy and Forde, 1990). A summary of findings from the 1982 and 1985 *Canadian Urban Victimization Surveys* follows:

1. About seventy incidents of personal theft per thousand population aged 16 and older occurred in the seven cities studied. More serious incidents occurred less frequently. (Solicitor General, 1983, *Bulletin 1*)

2. There is a strong relationship between engaging in activities outside the home and rates of assault, robbery, and theft of personal property, and a less dramatic, but still positive, relationship for rates of sexual assault. (Solicitor General, 1983, *Bulletin 1*)

3. The closer to home a violent crime occurred, the more likely it was to be reported. Violent crimes that occurred indoors were more likely to be reported than those which occurred outdoors. (Solicitor General, 1984, *Bulletin 2*)

4. Reporting rates increased with the extent of injury suffered by victims. (Solicitor General, 1984, *Bulletin 2*)

5. Reporting rates were not clearly related to either education level of the victim or to family income. (Solicitor General, 1984, *Bulletin 2*)

6. A profile of the average victim of crime suggests a "young unmarried male, living alone, probably looking for work or a student, and with an active life outside the home." This profile is not very different from a profile that might be drawn of the offender. (Solicitor General, 1983, *Bulletin 1*)

7. Over one-half of the incidents described to interviewers (58%) were never brought to the attention of the police. (Solicitor General, 1984, *Bulletin 2*)

8. Victims were more likely to report incidents that resulted in significant financial loss than those that resulted in pain, injury, and fear. (Solicitor General, 1983, *Bulletin 1*)

9. While women are about seven times more likely than men to be victims of sexual assault, they are also more likely than men to have their personal property stolen. (Solicitor General, 1983, *Bulletin 1*)

10. Violent crimes against females were more likely to be reported (46%) than violent crimes against males (34%). Reporting rates increased with the age of the victim, from 34% when victims were under 25 to 55% when victims were 40 or older. Violent offences against unmarried victims of both sexes were less likely to be reported than offences against married, separated, divorced, or widowed victims. (Solicitor General, 1984, *Bulletin 2*)

11. A higher proportion of assaults against women than against men occurred in the victims' residence (23% versus 5%) or in the vicinity of her home or in someone else's home (14% versus 9%). Women were more likely than men to be assaulted by relatives (12% versus 2%) or acquaintances (36% versus 25%). Women were the victims in 77% of the family-related assaults, 90% of assaults between spouses, 80% of assaults between ex-spouses, and 55% of assaults involving other relatives. (Solicitor General, 1985, *Bulletin 4*)

12. Women were more likely than men to be injured in assaults involving family members, especially is they were vic-

tims of "series assaults" (repetitions of the same kind of assault). (Solicitor General, 1985, *Bulletin 4*)

13. "Of the approximately 1,600,000 victimization incidents reported in the seven cities, fewer than 350,000 incidents (404,000 victims) could be classified as involving personal contact with the offender. Nevertheless, these resulted in 50,500 nights in hospital and 405,700 days lost due to some form of incapacitation." (Solicitor General, 1985, *Bulletin 5*)

14. While it is clear that there are emotional costs of crime, these are quite difficult to measure. (Solicitor General, 1985, *Bulletin 5*)

15. While elderly victims had a relatively lower chance of being injured, when they were injured, their probability of needing medical or dental treatment was higher than that of other age groups. (Solicitor General, 1985, *Bulletin 5*)

16. Elderly people, relative to others in urban centres in Canada, are rarely the victims of the types of crimes included in the victimization survey. (Solicitor General, 1985, *Bulletin 6*)

17. The consequences of victimization for elderly people are more severe than they are for younger people (both financial loss and physical harm). Elderly people are more fearful of crime than any other members in society. (Solicitor General, 1985, *Bulletin 6*)

18. Most crime was directed against property rather than people; serious and violent crime is relatively rare; many crimes could be prevented by employing simple target-hardening techniques (better locks, careful storage of small items, making houses look "lived in" during periods of absence, and so on). (Solicitor General, 1984, *Bulletin 3*)

19. About 8% of the households surveyed experienced a break and enter in the survey year. Of these, 14% experienced break and enter more than once, and 3%, three times or more.

About two-thirds of the break-and-enter incidents resulted in a loss to householders due to theft, damage, or both. (Solicitor General, 1986, *Bulletin 7*)

20. About 2% of the households surveyed experienced motor vehicle theft during 1981. (Solicitor General, 1986, *Bulletin 7*)

21. Almost one-half of the households interviewed experienced theft of household items, motor vehicle parts, bicycles, furniture, and so on. (Solicitor General, 1986, *Bulletin 7*)

22. Almost 8% of the households surveyed suffered damage to private property (vandalism) during the survey year. (Solicitor General, 1986, *Bulletin 7*)

Because the victimization survey was repeated in Edmonton in 1985, comparisons were possible between the 1982 and the 1985 periods. The early boom period in Alberta had ended by 1985 and unemployment had risen.

23. "A strong inverse relationship between age and rates of victimization was evident (in both 1982 and 1985). Those between the age of 16 and 24 experienced by far the highest rates of violent victimization." (Solicitor General, 1987, *Bulletin 8*)

24. Violent victimization rates were twice as high for residents of downtown Edmonton as for residents of the suburbs. (Solicitor General, 1987, *Bulletin 8*)

25. Multiple Victimization. The risk of at least one repeat victimization was considerably higher among victimized households than was the overall risk of victimization among all households. "For example, while 14% of all households experienced at least one incident of household theft, nearly 19% of all household theft victims experienced at least one other incident of household theft." (Solicitor General, 1988, *Bulletin 10*)

26. Many victims of personal crime were

also victims of at least one incident of a different type of crime during the twelve-month reference period. (Solicitor General, 1988, *Bulletin 10*)

Another, more recent, source on victimization in Canada is the Statistics Canada General Social Survey (Sacco and Johnson, 1990). In the 1988 survey a national sample of approximately ten thousand persons, 15 years of age or older, were interviewed by telephone, providing the most up-to-date information on victimization for Canada. In fact, because this survey involved the entire population (over age 15), it reflects victimization in Canada better than the 1982 survey, which involved only seven urban areas. Later in this part of this book Johnson and Sacco discuss selected findings from the survey.

Victimization surveys are not without their methodological flaws. Respondents may forget crimes or they may bring significant events (such as crimes) forward in time (telescoping) (Nettler, 1984; O'Brien, 1985; Skogan, 1986). In the latter case, the crime actually happened in a time period before the one in which researchers are interested, with the result that the data for the survey will be inflated and inappropriate for time-comparison purposes (Schneider and Sumi, 1981; Skogan, 1981). Further, the respondent's notion of being victimized may not correspond to a legal definition of crime. Worse, Levine (1976) argued that respondents may invent crime to please their employers, or respondents may simply not know that they have been victimized (Skogan, 1986). It is clear from some methodological investigations of victimization surveys that responses on these surveys may be quite inaccurate. In a 1977 study Schneider was unable to locate any record for about one-third of the crimes that her respondents indicated they had reported to the police. While researchers have pointed out that victimization data are not directly comparable to official statistics, there is not precise agreement on how one set of data corresponds to the other (Decker, 1983; Eck and Riccio, 1979; Skogan, 1981).

One other problem with victimization surveys is that they ask about a limited number of crimes. In fact, they leave out certain types of crimes completely. For rather obvious reasons murder is never one of the crimes on the list. More important in terms of data loss are decisions by the framers of the surveys to leave out consensual crimes (i.e., crimes in which the respondent was likely involved). By leaving out important crimes, those who develop these surveys operationally define victimization in a way that is likely different from other definitions of criminality.

While there are methodological flaws in victimization surveys, such surveys reveal that the majority of crimes committed in Canada are not known to the police. Further, they have specified the correlates of crime reporting, that is, they have told us who is and who is not likely to report a crime. They are by no means a perfect measure but they do help to fill in gaps in police statistics.

The ten bulletins of the *Canadian Urban Victimization Survey* provide a description of various specific aspects of urban victimization in Canada. They do not provide us with rural data or regional breakdowns, and the richness of the data has been tapped by few Canadian researchers. The data from the General Social Survey are just now being explored. Results from those data should further enhance our knowledge of victimization and the extent of crime.

SUMMARY

No perfect method of counting crime has yet been invented. The Uniform Crime Reports as utilized between 1961 and 1986 in Canada had some severe faults but were probably reliable as indicators of gross trends in Canadian crime statistics. The new system of uniform crime reporting offers a much richer data set and eliminates many of the problems inherent in the first CUCR.

Delinquency or self-report crime studies have methodological problems but when used with appropriate caution they may offer the only feasible way to get enough detail about offenders to test criminological theory. Nonetheless, as indicated several times in this chapter, caution must be the operative word.

Finally, victimization surveys seem to offer

more valid and reliable data than the other two methods in terms of volume of crime. However, here too caution must be used in interpreting these data, partially because the data are not directly comparable to police statistics.

In all social science, because of imperfect data, multiple measures are preferred for measuring any social phenomena. Hence, the student is advised to examine patterns generated by all sources of crime data and to do so with a critical eye.

* * * * * *

After reading about the problems with these sources of data, the student may well ask why it is so important to collect fully accurate crime data. The answer is quite simple. These data (particularly official statistics) are used to decide how much effort to put into any "fight against crime." For instance, they are often used to make policy decisions involving resources to be devoted to policing and crime prevention. Thus, incorrect data can mislead us into over- or under-reacting to a perceived crime threat. The latter may result in insufficient protection, while the former can mean wasted financial resources and unnecessary restrictions of civil liberties. Because of these policy implications, it is crucial that crime data be as accurate as possible. For social scientists, these data are used to test various hypotheses about crime (see Part Three). If the data are inaccurate, then we may draw erroneous conclusions about the causes of crime in Canada. While hypothesis testing does not lead directly to policy making, it often influences policy.

In concluding the introduction to Part Two, one final caution is in order. In Part One, we alerted you to the many definitions of crime. After reading this section you should be aware of several measures of crime. When you read reports about "crime" in this book and elsewhere, carefully examine both the definition and the measure of crime being used before you draw any conclusions.

THE READINGS

In "The Female Offender in Canada" Hatch and Faith provide an example of the uses to which "official data" can be put. They use Statistics Canada reports of crime commission to examine the frequency and types of crimes committed by females in the country. As they point out, this is an underexplored area of research in Canada. Students should think about the way in which these data were generated (the pre-1988 method) while reading the article.

O'Grady examines the meaning of violent-crime statistics in Newfoundland. He argues that statements about rising rates of violence are misleading when one does a thorough examination of the sources of data being used. He further argues that many forms of violence in society are not recorded in official statistics. In sum, he provides another view of the inadequacies of official statistics.

As indicated earlier, Sacco and Johnson examine the risk of victimization in Canada as estimated by the General Social Survey conducted by Statistics Canada. They are particularly concerned with the social and demographic correlates of victimization. Their findings are consistent with the earlier national victimization study done in Canada and with some U.S. studies. The article provides one of the most contemporary examples of victimization research.

The final article in this part, by Stoddart, shows how changes in a deviant community can result in increased reporting of crime. While the subject of a heroin-using community is inherently interesting, the revelation that subcultural lifestyle changes can result in more official crime reporting is of some import to those interested in the measurement of crime.

NOTES

1. The substance of this section was generated from materials provided by the Canadian Centre for Justice Statistics. These materials are not cited, as most are unpublished documents.

2. For examples of Canadian studies that have used the self-report technique see: LeBlanc, 1975; Tribble, 1975; Hagan, Gillis, and Chan, 1978; Gillis and Hagan, 1982.

Chapter 5

THE FEMALE OFFENDER IN CANADA: A STATISTICAL PROFILE*

Alison J. Hatch and Karlene Faith

The female offender has traditionally been ignored by criminologists with the rationalization that the relatively small numbers of women involved in crime do not warrant serious study. This omission has been rectified somewhat since the 1970s in the United States, where the controversy over whether women's liberation would produce more female crime served as impetus for a number of empirical, historical and theoretical studies (for example, Bowker, 1981; Chapman, 1980; Crites, 1976; Freedman, 1981; Klein and Kress, 1976; Leonard, 1982; Messerschmidt, 1986; Rafter, 1985; Steffensmeier, 1980). In the past decade, feminist scholars in the United Kingdom have likewise turned their attention to issues related to the female offender (for example, Carlen and Worall, 1980; Dobash, Dobash, and Gutteridge, 1986; Heidensohn, 1985; Morris, 1987; Smart, 1976). The same is now true of Canada, where the 1980s have seen the beginning of an analysis of national and provincial female crime trends. Just as the criminal justice system in Canada has been one of the last bastions of male occupational hegemony and even exclusivity, so did criminologists until recently continue to exclude discussion of the female from textbooks and scholarly work. The silence on the question of the female offender in Canada was first broken by the seminal work of Marie-Andrée Bertrand (1969), which anticipated the interest in the topic that was to develop in the U.S. Twenty years later, the Canadian Charter of Rights and Freedoms (1982) has stimulated an interest in the inequitable application of the criminal law to the behaviour of women (Boyle, Bertrand, Lacerte-Lamontagne, and Shamai, 1985). Feminist scholars have begun to analyse the unique position of Canadian women vis-à-vis the criminal justice system (Adelberg and Currie, 1987), and such discussion must proceed from an empirically based description of the Canadian female offender.

The focus of this paper will be women and girls who have been charged with criminal offences and officially processed through the Canadian criminal justice system. Statistics have been gathered from official sources and research surveys to offer a quantitative view of women in conflict with the law in Canada. It is intended that this descriptively straightforward presentation be useful to theoretical work, both in Canada and in cross-national comparisons.

SEX RATIO OF OFFENDERS IN CANADA

The difficulties associated with the official measurement of crime are well documented. In

---

*   Edited version of A. Hatch and K. Faith, "The Female Offender in Canada: A Statistical Profile," *Canadian Journal of Women and the Law*, 3(1989-1990): 432-56. Reprinted with permission of the authors and the *Canadian Journal of Women and the Law*.

the absence of an accurate indicator of the nature and extent of crime in Canada, information concerning the sex ratio of offenders is, likewise, unavailable. This absence explains, in part, why mainstream criminologists still ask the question: do women commit significantly fewer crimes than men or are they treated more leniently by decision-makers in the criminal justice system? (See Tjaden and Tjaden, 1981.) It is apparent that the latter view has been commonly held. Pollack (1950) first used the term "chivalry" to describe this situation. More recently, the Ouimet Committee (1969), for example, reported that the conviction rate for women rose steadily between 1901 and 1966, but the members assumed that women received preferential treatment at every decision-making juncture. Currently, there is not enough empirical evidence from Canada to support or refute this assumption.

Self-report surveys of delinquent and criminal behaviour have tended to add support to the chivalry hypothesis by indicating that the ratio of men to women is much closer than commonly thought, but methodological problems make this conclusion tenuous (Feyerherm, 1981). Another approximation of the relative role of men and women in crime can be obtained from victimization survey data, such as those collected in seven urban centres in 1982 (Solicitor General, *Bulletins No. 1, 2, 4*). Overall, the results conformed to those of previous American and British surveys. For example, it was found that a majority of incidents reported to the surveyors had not been reported to the police (58 percent). As part of the interview, sex of the offenders, for face-to-face crimes, was recorded. Five percent of robberies and assaults involved one or more female offenders, 91 percent one or more male offenders, and 4 percent some combination of the sexes (Johnson, 1986).

When examining incidents involving female offenders, relative to males, the following differences were noted:

females were the victims of female assailants in 78% of the cases while men victimized women in 35%;

the age distribution of offenders was similar for both sexes;

female assailants were more likely to be an acquaintance (50%) or relative (15%) of their victim than men (25% and five percent respectively);

weapons were used by 23% of female assailants and 34% of male assailants;

a higher proportion of the victims of females (64%) than the victims of males (48%) or victims of both sexes (59%) were injured in the incident;

an incident was most likely to be reported to the police if it involved males and females acting in a group (58%) than one or more male (35%) and one or more female (31%). If the attacker was a female acting alone, only 29% of incidents were reported; and,

respondents were more likely to describe the incident as a threat or attempt, rather than a completed crime, if the perpetrator was a man (49%) rather than a woman (32%). (Johnson, 1986)

Using victimization survey data as an indicator of the sex ratio of offenders raises interesting questions, such as the presumed hesitancy of a man to report being victimized by a woman, and the chance that similar acts committed by individuals of different sex may not both be interpreted as a "crime." Nevertheless, victimization data provide new insights into the role played by women relative to men in crime in Canada. Victimization data serve to support the picture provided by official statistics: women probably commit a small portion, about 10 percent, of all serious crime in Canada (Hagan, 1985b).

ARRESTS

From an examination of arrest statistics, it is apparent that the number of women against whom charges are laid is small, but increasing. Relative to men, the *number* of women charged is increasing more quickly but the *rate* is increasing more slowly (Johnson, 1986). This section will draw upon officially collected statistics of sex of adults arrested for selected offences.[1]

VIOLENT CRIME

Table 1 displays the number of adult women charged with crimes of violence. Overall, women constitute 11 percent of adults charged with such offences, although there is some variation among crime categories. Despite the title, the majority of incidents included under the category "violent crime" are relatively minor assaults and the statistics, as well as some research (Rosenblatt and Greenland, 1974), indicate that few women are charged with serious violent crimes. Women who commit homicide almost always do so within the domestic situation (Silverman and Kennedy, 1987a; Browne, 1987). Economic powerlessness, being the victims of chronic battering, and situational determinants may be key factors in many forms of violent acts committed by women (Hackler, 1988).

Abduction, the category in which women are most represented, rarely involves the frightening cases of strangers snatching children from the playground, despite media images to the contrary (Johnson, 1988). The majority of charges are laid against parents for abducting their own children, often when custody is in dispute or when sexual abuse is involved.

When examining charges laid over time, as in Figure 1, we find that between 1974 and 1982, the number of charges laid against individuals of both sexes evidenced a slow, steady increase, with a sharper rise beginning in 1983. From this figure, it is immediately apparent that women are arrested much less often for violent crime than are men. While 8 percent of persons against whom charges were laid in 1974 were females, by 1987 women

TABLE 1

ADULTS CHARGED WITH VIOLENT CRIME IN CANADA BY SEX OF ACCUSED, 1987

	Reported Offences	Males Charged	Females Charged	Females as %
1st Degree Murder	313	242	30	11.0
2nd Degree Murder	275	214	43	16.7
Manslaughter	49	46	9	16.4
Infanticide	5	3	1	25.0
HOMICIDE — Total	**642**	**505**	**83**	**14.1**
ATTEMPTED MURDER	**916**	**619**	**90**	**12.7**
Agg. Sexual Assault	412	198	3	1.5
Sex. Assault/Weapon	936	427	12	2.7
Sexual Assault	21,021	6,669	87	1.3
SEXUAL ASSAULT— Total	**22,369**	**7,294**	**102**	**1.4**
OTHER SEXUAL OFFENCE	**2,639**	**812**	**57**	**6.1**
ASSAULT — Total	**169,325**	**63,203**	**7,669**	**10.8**
Robbery w. Firearm	5,960	1,604	68	4.1
Robbery w. Other Offensive Weapon	5,772	1,478	125	7.8
Other Robbery	10,791	2,528	312	11.0
ROBBERY — Total	**22,523**	**5,610**	**505**	**8.3**
Abduction under 14	321	54	18	25.0
Abduction under 16	50	10	1	9.1
Abd'n Contravening Custody Order	347	74	38	33.9
Abduction with no Custody Order	249	55	9	14.1
ABDUCTION — Total	**967**	**193**	**66**	**25.5**
TOTAL VIOLENT CRIME	**219,381**	**78,236**	**8,572**	**11.0**

SOURCE: Statistics Canada, *Canadian Crime Statistics*, 1987 (Ottawa: Canadian Centre for Justice Statistics, 1988).

constituted 11 percent of this group. The proportion of women charged with violent crimes has varied only slightly, with minor fluctuations, since 1965, when 8 percent of persons charged with crimes of violence were women (Adams, 1978:17).

Overall, there was an increase of 171 percent for women and 100 percent for men between 1974 and 1987 (see Table 3). This increase in the *number* of women charged with crimes of violence would, for the most part, appear to be the result of the growth in the general population. But are arrests for violence increasing more rapidly for women than men? As Holly Johnson (1986:6) notes: "Because of the lower base number of women offenders, percentage changes will consistently give the appearance of greater increases in the number of women charged relative to the number of men." Using *rates* per 100,000 population, thereby using a common denominator, no dramatic change has occurred for women, with the exception of assault: the rate was 23.7 in 1975 and 34 in 1982 (Johnson, 1986). The rates for men showed a steady increase during the same period, with the exception of charges for homicide, which fluctuated too greatly to discern a general trend. Holly Johnson (1986) concludes that, between 1975 and 1984, the increase in rate of charges per 100,000 women was smaller than the comparable increase for men.

PROPERTY CRIMES

Table 2 shows the relative proportion of females arrested for property crimes. Women constituted a small percentage of those accused of offences characterized by Darrell Steffensmeier (1981) as "masculine property crimes": breaking and entering, auto theft and possession of stolen property. Shoplifting is the property offence for which women are arrested most frequently, females constituting 44 percent of the persons charged with shoplifting goods valued under $1,000 and 30 percent for over $1,000. Fraud offences, including passing bad cheques and fraudulent use of credit cards, is the second highest area, with women consti-

FIGURE 1

ADULTS CHARGED WITH CRIMES OF VIOLENCE BY SEX CANADA, 1974 TO 1987

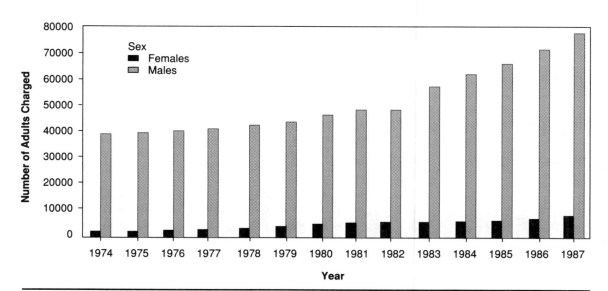

tuting 27 percent of the total number of adults charged.

Comparison of Figures 1 and 2 illustrates that females seem to play a greater role in property offences than in violent offences. In 1974, women constituted 22 percent of all persons charged with property crimes. In 1987, the figure was the same. But, the *number* of females charged almost doubled, with a 94 percent increase. The frequency with which charges were laid against men evidenced a less dramatic increase of 46 percent (see Table 3). Between 1975 and 1981, the *rate* with which charges were laid against both men and women rose quite significantly, except for auto theft.

PROSTITUTION

Technically, prostitution *per se* is not a crime in Canada. However, certain activities associated with prostitution, such as soliciting in a public place, operating a bawdy-house, procuring, and living on the avails of prostitution (e.g., pimping), are subject to criminal sanc-

tions (Criminal Code, R.S.C. 1985, c. C-46, ss. 210-13). Both prostitute and client are liable to arrest, but until recently prostitution was the only crime for which women were arrested more often than men (Table 3). Even though men are now slightly more likely to be arrested, we do not know if they hold that lead all the way through to the conviction stage. It seems plausible that arrest without prosecution may be used as a deterrent for the clients in some areas. A significant number of females arrested would fall under the jurisdiction of the youth court and, therefore, would not be reflected in these figures.

The number of arrests made for prostitution decreased dramatically during the 1970s. This has been attributed to various factors, a decrease in the actual incidence of prostitution not being one of them. It is commonly believed that several court decisions interpreting the soliciting law impaired the enforcement ability of the police. As a result of the perceived impotence of the legislation, the police reduced the frequency with which they invoked the criminal

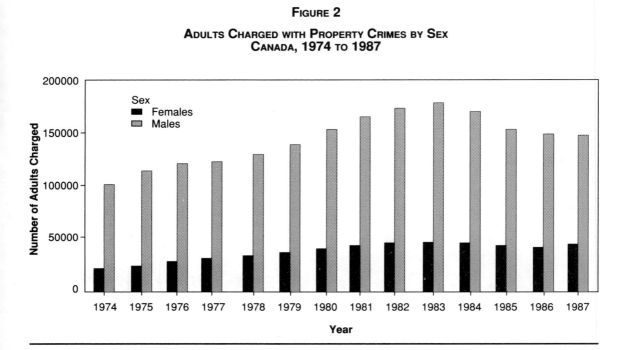

FIGURE 2

**ADULTS CHARGED WITH PROPERTY CRIMES BY SEX
CANADA, 1974 TO 1987**

TABLE 2

ADULTS CHARGED WITH PROPERTY CRIME IN CANADA BY SEX OF ACCUSED, 1987

	Total Offences	Males	Females	Females as %
B & E Business	99,733	13,619	448	3.2
B & E Residences	219,324	18,962	1,042	5.2
Other	45,087	4,449	161	3.5
BREAK & ENTER — Total	**364,144**	**37,030**	**1,651**	**6.0**
THEFT OF AUTO	**87,061**	**8,867**	**516**	**6.0**
Theft of Bicycle	1,481	34	3	8.1
Theft from Motor Vehicle	29,154	754	27	3.5
Shoplifting	2,278	301	127	29.7
Other	38,695	3,804	754	16.5
THEFTS OVER $1,000 — Total	**71,608**	**4,893**	**911**	**15.7**
Theft of Bicycle	117,693	1,000	64	6.0
Theft from Motor Vehicle	289,154	7,419	274	3.6
Shoplifting	103,652	31,188	24,333	43.8
Other	282,124	17,887	3,586	16.7
THEFTS UNDER $1,000 - Total	**792,623**	**57,494**	**28,257**	**33.0**
POSS'N STOLEN PROPERTY	**27,013**	**11,858**	**1,580**	**11.8**
Cheque Fraud	74,095	15,048	6,010	28.5
Credit Card Fr.	14,702	2,676	671	20.0
Other Frauds	37,345	9,467	3,216	25.4
FRAUD — Total	**126,142**	**27,191**	**9,897**	**26.7**
TOTAL PROPERTY CRIME	**1,468,591**	**147,333**	**42,812**	**22.5**

SOURCE: Statistics Canada, *Canadian Crime Statistics, 1987* (Ottawa: Canadian Centre for Justice Statistics, 1988).

law to deal with prostitution. Enforcement of various municipal by-laws and informal strategies such as harassing clients both proved unsuccessful.

Public concern over the issue eventually prompted the federal government to strike the Special Committee on Pornography and Prostitution. It was concluded that the law of the day was philosophically and pragmatically inadequate. The Committee also made the following observation:

Female street prostitutes are more likely to be arrested and convicted of prostitution-related crimes than any other category of person involved in the business. Pimps and customers are the least likely to be charged and convicted. Thus the enforcement pattern is uneven with respect to gender and occupation. It should be noted, however, that the low level of charges and convictions against pimps does not appear to be the result of biased law enforcement on the part of police forces, as much as a reflection of the difficulty of accumulating sufficient evidence on pimps' activities. (Special Committee on Pornography and Prostitution, 1985)

Rather than advocating more repressive criminal laws, they recommended decriminalizing prostitution engaged in by one or two adults (over 18) in their own residence, while prohibiting all other forms of prostitution, including any activities by juveniles. They also recommended tighter controls over those who would exploit prostitutes. These recommendations were ignored by the government when, soon after the Committee issued its report, the soliciting provisions were merely augmented and strengthened (Lowman, 1985).

NARCOTIC OFFENCES

The majority of drug-related charges laid in

TABLE 3

PERCENTAGE CHANGE OF ADULTS CHARGED WITH SELECTED OFFENCES BY SEX, 1974 TO 1987

	Males			Females		
	1974	1987	% Change	1974	1987	% Change
Homicide	417	505	21.1	73	83	13.7
Attempted Murder	357	619	73.4	40	90	125.0
Sexual Offences	3,763	8,106	115.4	25	159	536.0
Assault	29,644	63,203	113.2	2,700	7,669	184.0
Robbery	4,674	5,610	20.2	302	505	67.2
VIOLENT CRIME[1]	**38,885**	**78,043**	**100.7**	**3,140**	**8,506**	**171.0**
Break & Enter	25,978	37,030	42.5	923	1,651	78.9
Theft of Motor Veh.	11,091	8,867	−20.1	368	516	40.2
Theft	41,205	62,387	51.4	16,085	29,168	81.3
Poss'n Stolen Prop.	8,144	11,858	45.6	928	1,580	70.3
Fraud	14,641	27,191	85.7	3,811	9,897	159.7
PROPERTY CRIME	**101,059**	**147,333**	**45.8**	**22,115**	**42,812**	**93.6**
Bawdy-House	295	372	26.1	416	407	-2.2
Procuring	66	208	215.2	81	103	27.2
Other	269	4,760	1,669.5	1,885	4,428	134.9
PROSTITUTION	**630**	**5,340**	**747.6**	**2,382**	**4,938**	**107.3**
NARCOTICS	**48,822**	**34,344**	**−29.7**	**4,811**	**4,817**	**0.1**

SOURCE: Statistics Canada, *Crime and Traffic Enforcement Statistics, 1974* (Ottawa: Supply and Services Canada, 1975); and, Statistics Canada, *Canadian Crime Statistics, 1987* (Ottawa: Canadian Centre for Justice Statistics, 1988).
[1] Excludes abduction.

Canada are for possession of marijuana. Adult women comprised 10.6 percent of this group in 1987. Considering all types of drugs together, women constituted 12.8 percent of those charged with possession for personal use, 15.8 percent of those charged with trafficking, and 17.4 percent of those charged with importation. Although the cultivation of marijuana is not a very commonly used provision, 30 percent of those so charged in 1987 were women. Examining the changes in arrests over time, it is apparent that between 1974 and 1987 the number of charges laid against women for drug-related offences remained the same, while the number for men decreased substantially (see Table 3). For offences contrary to the Narcotic Control Act (i.e., opiates, cannabis and cocaine), the arrest rate has increased slightly. For women, the rate was 42.8 per 100,000 in 1981 as compared with 419.5 for men, showing increases of

27.4 percent and 30 percent, respectively, since 1974.

YOUNG OFFENDERS

The paternalistic philosophy of the Juvenile Delinquents Act[3] and the moral climate of the early twentieth century facilitated a system of juvenile justice that responded to girls in a manner quite distinct from the response to boys. Especially in the 1920s, with the eugenics and mental hygiene movements, emphasis was placed more upon the moral character of the delinquent than the nature or severity of the transgression.[4] In 1924, "sexual immorality or any similar form of vice" was added to the definition of delinquency, which already included incorrigibility and unmanageability in many provinces. Given the implications of sexual double standards, it is not surprising that girls were increasingly incarcerated for violations of contemporary moral standards or for living in what were regarded as unsuitable homes. Moreover, even the *possibility* of sexual behaviour was thought to be grounds for the preventive detention of girls and this quotation from the London, Ontario, Juvenile Court of 1925 was typical of the time. A girl was sent to the industrial school:

...to save her from being immoral through an extraordinary affection for a boy of her own age and she clung to this lad in spite of everything his or her parents could do, much to their annoyance and alarm, and finally when these children were caught drifting towards wrongdoing the girl was committed. (Warner and Bradshaw, 1925:8)

No mention is made of the fate of the boy.

Even in more recent decades, the reliance upon status offences as vehicles to involve non-criminal children in criminal proceedings sometimes resulted in harsher treatment of girls in the United States (Chesney-Lind, 1973, 1982) and Canada (Geller, 1987). More current Canadian research has demonstrated that, by the 1980s, neither boys nor girls were often brought to court for status offences, except perhaps in Ontario (Bala and Corrado, 1985). The overall proportion of girls in the juvenile justice system was, therefore, probably similar to that of adult females; but, contrary to the adult figures, a higher proportion of charges were laid against girls for violent crimes (16 percent) than for property offences (10.2 percent).[5] It is interesting to note that the same situation holds true now that the Young Offenders Act[6] is in effect. Overall, about 11 percent of charges for federal offences are laid against girls.[7] For fiscal year 1986/87, 10.6 percent of charges heard in youth courts for property offences were laid against girls. The comparable figure for violent offences was 15.4 percent. The question is raised whether girls have a greater propensity for aggression than women, or whether the criminal justice system is more aggressive in its response to female adolescent behaviours.

CONCLUSION

This chapter has provided an overview of the police statistics pertaining to women and girls who are arrested in Canada. We have seen that the number of female offenders processed through the criminal justice system is small, relative to men, and that the vast majority of charges laid against women are for property offences rather than for incidents which involve violence. The extent to which these data reflect the true incidence of crime by women is unknown but, with the sources of information available to us, these general statements seem valid.

Over recent decades, the rate of crime in Canada, as measured by police statistics, has been rising. But, are women playing a greater role in crime now than they ever have before? The arrest statistics indicate that this is not the case. Although the number of women arrested has evidenced a dramatic increase, the same is true of men. In Canada, at least, there is little support for the argument that the women's movement has caused either an increase in the proportion of crime which is committed by women or, more significantly, a less "chivalrous" response to women by decision-makers in the criminal justice system.

NOTES

1. Arrest statistics have been taken from the Statistics Canada publications from the years 1974 to 1987, originally titled *Crime and Traffic Enforcement Statistics* and more recently called *Canadian Crime Statistics*. As noted by Statistics Canada (1988:18), the category of "persons charged" is defined as follows: "The number of persons, not charges, is being counted... A person simultaneously charged with more than one type of offence is scored only once and against the most serious offence." It should be stated that these data are collected at that point in the process when the charges are laid. Hence, they may not reflect the charge for which the accused was ultimately convicted, which can differ from that originally

laid. Similarly, the pervasiveness of plea bargaining often results in police "overcharging."
This involves the laying of more charges, or of a
charge more serious than the evidence supports,
in order to accommodate the eventually negotiated reduction.

2. The rate per 100,000 population for women in
1981, and the increase evidenced since 1975, is
16.9 and 76.0 percent for breaking and entering,
234.1 and 45.1 percent for theft, 66.0 and 90.2
percent for fraud, and 5.4 and 35 percent for theft
of auto. For men, the highest rate in 1981 was for
theft (584.2), which represented a 44.2 percent
increase over the 1975 figure. Solicitor General, *A
Statistical Profile of Female Offenders in Canada*
(Ottawa: Statistics Division, Solicitor General
Canada, 1985).

3. R.S.C. 1970, C. J-3, now repealed.

4. Gordon, Hatch and Griffiths, forthcoming. For
an American discussion of moral character and
the juvenile court, see Emerson, 1969.

5. Statistics Canada, 1983. Figures for adults and
juveniles are collected separately, using different
units of count. It is not, therefore, possible to
compare the arrest figures directly. Quoting Statistics Canada: "Every *delinquency* for which
court action was terminated in the year specified
is counted. This is consequently a measure of
court activity and not of magnitude of delinquency. A juvenile may be reflected more than
once in tables having this basic unit of count
depending on the number of delinquencies with
which he/she was charged."

6. Young Offenders Act, S.C. 1980-81-82, c. 110, s. 4.
It eliminated status offences and requires the
commission of a criminal offence before court
proceedings can be commenced.

7. Canadian Centre for Justice Statistics, 1987a; Canadian Centre for Justice Statistics, 1987b; and
Canadian Centre for Justice Statistics, 1988. A
significant drawback of these data is the exclusion of the figures from Ontario.

Chapter 6

CRIME, VIOLENCE AND VICTIMIZATION: A NEWFOUNDLAND CASE*

Bill O'Grady

INTRODUCTION

In recent years Newfoundland has witnessed much popular concern about violent crime. Statements from a variety of social groups demonstrate a concern about the "growing crime problem" in general and about violent crimes such as armed robberies in particular. Accounts have come from business, groups, trade unionists, the clergy, the press, police, lawyers, judges and academics. Many groups and individuals have based their assumptions, by and large, on official statistics. However, assertions that Newfoundland is becoming more violent are not based on a coherent and thorough examination of official statistics. An increase in crime and violence is said to be typical of a population in turmoil or of a breakdown in traditional methods of social control. Rising levels of violence have been linked with economic crisis in general, and with rising unemployment in particular. Indeed, the unemployed, youthful, masked armed robber has become the symbol of danger and social malaise and has become the focus of many anxieties.

This paper starts by illustrating the clamour which was raised by a host of Newfoundland groups over rising levels of violent "retail crime." However, a critical examination of the "violent crime rate" and official statistics of other crimes of violence reveals no support for any significant shift in either the pattern or incidence of violent crime in Newfoundland. Changes in official statistics are best understood in relation to changed police practices and possibly greater citizen involvement and a greater willingness to see certain types of incidents as criminal offenses. Thus increased prison terms for armed robbery cannot be justified by the need for an increased general deterrent for this offense. After arguing that official statistics have been used to exaggerate public acts of violence associated with private property of relatively influential groups, this paper will demonstrate how official statistics either underestimate or else completely exclude harms perpetrated against less materially powerful victims: these being private acts of violence against women — particularly Native women — in the domestic context. To substantiate this claim, particular

* Edited version of B. O'Grady, "Crime, Violence and Victimization: A Newfoundland Case," *Canadian Criminology Forum* 10(1989): 1-16. Reprinted with permission of the author.

An earlier version of this paper was presented at the Annual Conference of the Atlantic Association of Sociologists and Anthropologists held at Saint Mary's University, March 10-13, 1988. The paper has benefited from the comments of the Forum editor and two anonymous reviewers. I am also grateful to Jim Overton, Julian Tanner, Elliott Leyton, and Nigel Rapport, who shared their ideas with me. Much of my research for the paper was generously funded by the Institute of Social and Economic Research, Memorial University of Newfoundland, and the Social Sciences and Humanities Research Council of Canada.

attention will be given to 'non-violent' crimes such as "drunk and disorderly in the home" and "weapon violations," as well as an analysis of homicide.

THE DATA

The statistical data in this paper come from three main sources. First, Statistics Canada's Uniform Crime Reports have been used to calculate provincial crime rates. These data, in combination with a second source, Annual Reports of the Royal Newfoundland Constabulary (RNC), will be employed to measure both "violent" and "non-violent" police reported crimes for the city of St. John's. Actual offender files obtained from the record office of the RNC for the period between 1955 and 1983 were a third data source. An investigation of these files will determine changes which have taken place in judicial dispositions for certain offenses over a twenty-eight year period in St. John's. Similar data, but on a provincial basis, are from RCMP "B" Division, St. John's. Statistics for Native people are also taken from police investigation files provided by the RCMP. Data on the media are drawn, in most cases, from the pages of the *St. John's Evening Telegram*, the only daily newspaper published in the province.

CONCERN ABOUT VIOLENT CRIME

In 1984 the *St. John's Evening Telegram* reported that statistics showed violent crime was on the increase in Newfoundland. In the report, the then Executive Director of the Canadian Centre for Justice Statistics told the Rotary Club of St. John's that, "For the country as a whole, it's a myth that violent crime rates are on the increase," but that detailed data showed the "violent crime rates are growing in Newfoundland. Between 1974 and 1983, the rate of violent crimes in Newfoundland rose by 39%" (*Evening Telegram*, 16 September, 1984).

In addition to the concern from experts whose job it is to compile and analyze "official statistics," other groups have been concerned about the "growing crime problem" as well. Indeed, some of the strongest concern about

increasing levels of violent crime in Newfoundland — particularly in St. John's — is coming from judges. For instance, a provincial court judge who passed an eleven year sentence on an unemployed 18 year old in a 1985 robbery trial, described this crime as "one of the most heinous crimes that society is aware of," and "one of the most frightening things that can happen to an individual" (*Evening Telegram*, 6 December, 1985). He also claimed that "there is great public concern about the incidence of this type of crime."

The police also share the view that violent crime has recently increased in St. John's, McGahan (1984) has noted that police officers in St. John's perceive an increase in the sophistication and frequency of criminal violence and that calls for services of the police more than tripled between 1979 and 1982. According to one of the police officers whom McGahan interviewed:

Ten years ago armed robbery was a big thing, a major crime. But now, it's getting to be an every day occurrence...there has been a large increase in the whole city in the last few years. (McGahan, 1984:193).

The impression that street crime is increasing in the province is also shared by the RNC Police Brotherhood who have been lobbying for some time now for the right to carry sidearms while on patrol as they do not wish to be "unprotected" against this new breed of criminal in the province. In 1984, over 70% of the RNC Association Members voted in favour of the RNC becoming an armed force.

The idea that armed robbery is increasing at an alarming rate has been fostered by the press and the electronic media.[1] Terms like "rash" have been used and considerable space in the news has been devoted to the issue of armed robbery in recent years. For instance, in the wake of a 1985 incident which took place in Gander, Newfoundland, when a convenience store clerk was killed during an armed robbery (in fact the first of this type of homicide to have taken place in Newfoundland) the *Evening Telegram* conducted a survey (who, how and where?) of employers and owners of convenience stores and gas bars on the subject of armed robbery and reported that "the consensus is that the courts are too soft on armed robbers," or, as one gas bar manager put it "...I'm really a believer in capital punishment for those who kill in these robberies. Being nice to these punks is not good" (*Evening Telegram*, 29 October, 1985).

A statement from a recent article entitled "A killer will kill you" printed in the *St. John's Metro Advertizer* both expressed and reinforced the sentiment that the danger of becoming a victim of a violent criminal act has very much increased in recent years in Newfoundland.

There's a killer on the loose right now... A stranger. You may pass him on the street and not know it. You may brush gently up against him in the supermarket while reaching for a fresh cut of steak... You never know... In the dark, hollow soul of the killer, you may form the perfect picture of a victim. You may die, screaming in tearful fear as life is torn from you... (*Metro*, 29 June, 1986)

As a response to these concerns the St. John's Board of Trade published a study in 1985 of what it called "A Case of Retail Crime in St. John's." This included shoplifting, break and enter, and robbery at retail locations. Using statistical information from the Royal Newfoundland Constabulary 1977-1983 Annual Reports, the study argued that "retail crime" (especially shoplifting) had reached "epidemic proportions" and that it must be controlled by a joint public and Government effort. According to the official statistics used in the study, between 1977 and 1983, shoplifting increased by 73%, break and enter increased by 97% and the robbery total rose by 26%. Although the increase in robbery was not as great as were increases in other retail crimes, the increase was considered "significant" because of the "seriousness and degree of violence involved" (St. John's Board of Trade, 1985:4). The study concluded with a call for more severe punishments for those convicted of retail crimes in St. John's. Heavier fines and tougher prison terms were seen to be the only measures which would act as a deterrent to the others. The study was presented to the Newfoundland Minister of Justice in an attempt to toughen sentences. Immediate action was called for to reduce the problem. Urgent action was seen to be necessary especially during the current economic climate, as "in times of recession, when crime

tends to rise, it makes it more difficult for recovery in the city's economy" (Ibid., 16) — this connection was only assumed, as no attempt was made to empirically associate increases in "retail crime" with increases in unemployment, etc. [2]

If the current economic situation gives cause for concern in general, workless youth seem to be the focus of particular fears. Youth is seen as a group which is particularly disaffected, estranged and demoralized. The fear is that they will become resentful and antagonistic and will resort to crime and violence; that excluded from society by being denied a useful role, they risk becoming hostile and dangerous. Discipline and careful control are seen to be necessary. Consider the following statement made in a rural community during the hearings of the recent Newfoundland Royal Commission on Employment and Unemployment:

I see the young people in our community getting very upset and possibly there could very well be a sudden rage of the people towards the Government, and maybe in our community, towards whatever groups of people they see as being in authority, which are seemingly not doing anything to help. It's like a time bomb which is very soon, I should think, ready to explode...The correlation between crime and unemployment is a reality. Many individuals find themselves in a rut. As long as the present unemployment situation continues, the crime rate will continue to rise due to the poverty cycle and the social and psychological effect that this cycle has upon the individual. (Clarke, 1986:1,2)

In recent years many people in Newfoundland have drawn attention to the very alarming consequences of lack of work. According to Overton (1988:18) who conducted a much more detailed account on this issue, there is in Newfoundland a strong "feeling that youth unemployment represents a great danger for society" and that it is "finding widespread expression at the present time...by those of all political persuasions...and in the statements of a variety of interest groups."

From this brief survey it is clear that there has been considerable anxiety about the level and character of violence in Newfoundland. Moreover, the feeling that youth unemployment represents a great danger for society is finding a large acceptance in Newfoundland society. Statistics have been used quite extensively to support calls for action, particularly from some powerful groups in the province. And there is some evidence that, as a response to the perceived increases in some types of violent crime, action has been taken by some members of the judiciary as incarceration rates have increased in Newfoundland in recent years. According to the *Annual Report of the Adult Corrections Division* of Newfoundland (1985:29):

The most disturbing aspect of the data is that the "offenses vs. the person" category now comprise 8% of the admissions when, in 1983-1984, the rate was only 4%. Since this change cannot be explained by a change in the method of data collection or a change in definitions, it is fairly obvious that the rate of admission for offenses...in which there was a confrontation between victim and offender did increase significantly.

The *Report* continues by stating that:

[There is] a slight shift towards longer prison terms being issued by the courts. For example, whereas in [fiscal year] 1983-1984, 52.5% of admissions were sentenced to terms less than one month, only 48.6% received such a sentence in 1984-1985. This could be a function of the increase in violent offenses...(Ibid.)

This trend towards longer sentences for violent offenses seems to have more than a one year history, at least for robbery, a crime which has attracted considerable attention in recent years. According to RNC police record files, prison sentences issued for robbery offenders have steadily increased. Between 1955 and 1983, the mean length of prison sentences issued by the courts increased from eighteen months for the 1955-1969 period to twenty-four months between 1970 and 1984. In fact, between 1980 and 1983 the mean was thirty-three months.[3]

Unfortunately there are no data available for determining the age and employment status of convicted robbers in Newfoundland. There are, however, good reasons to believe that many of these offenders are in fact young, unemployed males. In 1985, for example, most prison inmates in the province were single (60%), male (97%), under 30 years of age (67%) and had not completed high school (78%)

(Department of Justice, Newfoundland and Labrador, 1985). Also consider that 80% of those convicted of robbery in St. John's between 1980 and 1984 had had a previous criminal record, a background which would obviously make it extremely difficult for finding employment, particularly in a province where 30% of workers between the ages of 15-25 are unemployed.[4] Based on these statistics, then, it would not be unreasonable to predict that a high proportion of inmates incarcerated for robbery offenses are young, unemployed males.

However, when official crime statistics are critically examined there is weak evidence to support the assumption that these concerns and, indeed, the penal response to them, are reflective of a society which has suddenly become more violent. In other words, it would be too simplistic to account for these increases in custodial sentences for some crimes as simply the result of a process whereby:

[a]s unemployment increases, more individuals are tempted to break the law, and many of these have less reason to resist because — being unemployed or anticipating unavoidable future unemployment — they have fewer important economic or social bonds acting as brakes on their deviant motivations; consequently, the rate of criminal behaviour increases which, assuming a constant rate of crime reporting, arrest, and conviction, produces an automatic work load increase for the judiciary, and this results in more persons being sent to prison. (Box and Hale, 1982:20)

Let's begin with an examination of "armed robbery" statistics in Newfoundland as a first step of testing this conventional wisdom. According to the study of "retail crime" conducted by the St. John's Board of Trade referred to earlier, the robbery total had increased by 26% between 1978 and 1983. However, if the study had used other years, say 1978 and 1982, or 1979 and 1983, as comparison points, there would have been a decline in robberies. Along with this dubious use of statistics the figures used in the report were not standardized by population rates. This omission is serious as the jurisdiction of the RNC (whose annual reports were used as data for the study) was expanded by approximately 60,000 people, and now included the town of Mount Pearl (a suburb outside St. John's). If the report had compared rates, rather than incidents reported to the police, different results would have been obtained.

In addition to this oversight, another inaccuracy in the use of official statistics was made in the report when the statistical category of "robbery" was used to measure the incidence of robbery at retail locations. That is, the report used an aggregate total which included the sub-categories of: robbery with a firearm, robberies with other offensive weapons, and other robberies. Therefore, no attempt was made to differentiate between robberies which take place at retail locations (the type of robbery the report was most interested in examining), particularly involving the use of a firearm, with other types of robberies — all of which were contained together in the measure used in the report. If the Board of Trade had properly made these distinctions, they would have found that the majority of what are commonly referred to as "armed robberies" essentially comprise only a fraction of the total number of robberies which are reported to the police. For instance, between 1981 and 1985, approximately 50% of robberies which were reported to the police did not take place at retail locations, although the way they were included in the Board of Trades' measure would suggest they had. Furthermore, a critical examination of police files and criminal reports indicates that one-half of all robberies which took place in St. John's between 1981 and 1985 did not involve the use of a weapon. In fact, they were incidents which could be best described as "purse snatchings" or else "muggings." Therefore, the data used in the Board of Trade's study are simply misleading, as they do not reflect the incidence of armed robbery at retail locations in St. John's.

Looking at the "problem" of armed robbery on a provincial level, the incidence of robbery (all types) is relatively low in Newfoundland when it is compared with the Canadian average over time. In fact, between 1974 and 1984 the average incidence of all categories of robbery in Newfoundland which were reported to the police was 11 per 100,000 population, compared with the Canadian average over the same time period, which was 93 per 100,000

population. If an examination of "armed robbery" suggests that we must be skeptical of the uses to which official robbery statistics are put, we must be equally skeptical of how "violence" is officially measured and defined in general. For instance, what does it mean when Statistics Canada reports that violent crime, in general, has increased in Newfoundland by 39% between 1974 and 1983? Indeed, when this 39% increase is examined in some detail a problem arises suggesting that the "violent crime rate" is a very misleading statistic. Although the phrase has in fact been referred to a great deal — especially in the *Evening Telegram* — it is rarely defined, and its meaning is not described in any detail. What precisely does the violent crime rate measure? According to Statistics Canada, the crimes used to compute the violent crime rate are: homicide (including murder, manslaughter and infanticide), attempted murder, abductions, robberies and assaults (including sexual). Measured in this way, the types of crimes which comprise the violent crime rate would probably not be surprising to the lay person and, therefore, fall within the parameters of the convential images of interpersonal violence. What may be surprising, however, are the types of interpersonal violence which are most often reported to, and detected by police. This may be explained more clearly if, as illustration, the violent crime rate in Newfoundland is compared with the violent crime rate in Quebec for the year 1983. A province with a homicide rate three times greater than Newfoundland's and a robbery rate twelve times greater, nevertheless has a considerably lower violent crime rate.

These differences seem to be at variance with conventional wisdom, as the crimes of murder and armed robbery are likely the types of crimes people most often associate with violence. However, these puzzling differences in the two provinces' violent crime rates are essentially the result of variance in the two provinces' assault rates. In 1983, for example, Quebec had an assault rate of 288 per 100,000 population, while in the same year Newfoundland recorded an assault rate of 574 per 100,000 population — more than double the rate of Quebec. In this way, the proportion of assaults registered in the Newfoundland violent crime rate in 1983 was much greater than it was in Quebec. In Newfoundland, 88% of all violent crimes were assaults in 1983, while in Quebec the statistical category of assault was accountable for 60% of the number of violent crimes registered by police in that year — these differences have also generally remained constant in the past.

It is clear, then, that it is problematic indeed when we use the violent crime rate as an indicator of the "real" level of violence in Canadian society, that is, the forms of violence typically associated with the term violence — such as armed robbery. Consequently, we must be very careful in the way we interpret Statistics Canada's data which indicate that violent crime in Newfoundland increased by 39% between 1974 and 1983.

When this violent crime rate is examined on a yearly basis over the ten year period, we discovered that the greatest increase took place between 1981 and 1982. The violent crime rate in 1981 was 474 per 100,000 population, while in 1982 the rate had jumped to 580 per 100,000 population — an increase of 22%, by far the greatest annual increase over this ten year period. The question now to ask is: why did the assault rate increase so drastically in 1982? The explanation of this statistical increase is unlikely the result of Newfoundlanders suddenly becoming more violent over a one year period, but rather, the reason for this change lies in the way in which police began to deal with "family violence" (Figure 1: Rates/100,000 persons for all crimes of violence and assault in Newfoundland, 1975-1985). In 1982, police were encouraged by the Newfoundland Department of Justice to lay charges against assault suspects in

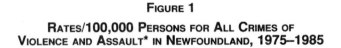

FIGURE 1

RATES/100,000 PERSONS FOR ALL CRIMES OF VIOLENCE AND ASSAULT* IN NEWFOUNDLAND, 1975–1985

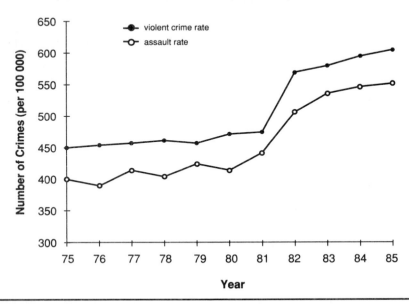

SOURCE: Compiled from Statistics Canada, *Canadian Crime and Traffic Statistics*, 1974-1986.

*   In order to be consistent, assault data for the years 1983-1985 were computed with the exclusion of sexual assaults. This is due to a change in legislation in 1983 in which the category of rape was replaced with sexual assault.

"domestic disturbances." In fact, in 1983 Manitoba experienced a similar increase in its violent crime rate which was also directly related to a recording reclassification of domestic disputes by police. In Figure 1 we see the very similar paths that both the assault and violent crime rates have taken, and both measures increased substantially in 1982. We can therefore explain the sudden increase recorded in the assault rate, as approximately 88% of violent crimes in Newfoundland are assaults. In fact, the assault rate increased from 422 per 100,000 population in 1981 to 530 per 100,000 population in 1982 — an increase of 25%. As with the violent crime rate, the assault rate failed to register any significant changes either prior to or following 1982.

The violent crime rate is therefore a problematic measure for determining the level and character of "violence." It is because the violent crime rate is so closely linked to the assault rate that the measure is almost meaningless in terms of understanding the nature of violent crime. Furthermore, these results indeed bring into question the established conventional wisdom I referred to earlier regarding high levels of unemployment causing more individuals to break the law, thus automatically producing a work load increase for the judiciary, which in turn results in more persons being sent to prison.

Another way of explaining increases in custodial sentences in Newfoundland for violent crimes is consistent with some recent work by Box and Hale (1982, 1985, 1986). There is preliminary evidence that, in Newfoundland, as Box and Hale argue to be the case in England and Wales, a correlation exists between economic crisis — particularly high levels of unemployment — and some members of the judiciary becoming increasingly anxious about the possible threat to social order posed by "problem populations," such as unemployed males. If people do embrace this assumption, and I have shown earlier that there is considerable evidence suggesting that many in Newfoundland do, then it is not surprising that judges may feel anxious at the present time and are more willing to accept stern measures being offered by powerful groups to deter and incapacitate. [5] Box and Hale's research has sup-

ported the idea that judges generally work with this set of assumptions about crime and that in the recent climate of growing unemployment this has been a strong influence on their sentencing behaviour. In England, prison incarceration rates have increased much faster than would be expected based on the number of crimes being committed in recent years. People are being sent to jail for longer periods in the late 1980s for offenses that would not have been treated as harshly a few years ago. There is some preliminary evidence that this is also happening in Newfoundland. More and longer prison sentences are being issued in Newfoundland despite the fact that, in statistical terms, violence is not increasing at an alarming rate. Thus, the reaction to the problem has taken on the characteristics of a moral panic (Cohen, 1973; Hall et al., 1978; Mungham, 1982; Tanner, Lowe and Krahn, 1984).

While there is no cause for complacency about robbery at retail locations — especially if you are a business person or retail clerk — there is always the problem of arriving at some "criteria of proportionality" by which a decision can be made as to whether or not a societal reaction to a given problem is reasonable or all out of proportion (Waddington, 1986:246). The number of armed robberies reported to police in Newfoundland are nevertheless small, and have not increased in recent years. Thus, there are no simple grounds for linking high levels of unemployment with violent crime in Newfoundland.

THE PRIVATE AND THE POWERLESS

This is not to say, however, that all concern about violent crime in Newfoundland may be explained in this way. In an attempt to debunk these popular and dangerous social constructions and images of crime and violence in Newfoundland, we do not want to fall into the trap of suggesting that all interpersonal violence is much exaggerated. To reject the assumption that violence can be measured in terms of the "violent crime rate" and at the same time turn our attention to a series of "nonviolent" police reported crimes in Newfoundland suggests that a considerable amount of violence is in fact taking place in Newfoundland, but is not being officially recorded as such because it does not seem to evoke a threat to dominant social values. However, when many police reported "non-violent" incidents are examined closely, very little distinguishes them from violent crimes such as sexual assault, other forms of bodily assault and in some cases attempted murder. By exploring the interactions between victim, offender and the state, and by defining who is at risk and how, as well as tracing the relationship between the victim and offender, we will show how violent crimes against women in Newfoundland are under-represented statistically in terms of criminal victimization. Doing so will reveal the overemphasis on public violence and the underestimation of private violence. Thus, an empirical examination of crimes typically categorized as "other provincial statutes" and "other offensive weapons," or, in other and more common terms, "drunk and disorderly in the home," "dangerous or careless use of a firearm," "pointing a firearm" and "carrying a weapon dangerous to the public peace" will demonstrate that the nature of violent crime in Newfoundland and the impact of victimization are being systematically misrepresented and underestimated, in effect ignoring risks faced by many women — particularly Native women. Let us begin by examining incidents which police label "drunk and disorderly in the home." It is very difficult to discern from the Uniform Crime Reports how many offenses are described in this way, as the offense, in Newfoundland, is subsumed under the category "other provincial statutes" — a category which includes crimes other than drunk and disorderly in the home. Based on conversations with police officers from the RNC, a drunk and disorderly in the home is typically a complaint made by a woman requesting that the police remove from her home a "trouble maker," usually the woman's husband or lover. Although drunk and disorderlies are not classified as violent crimes, evidence suggests that many of these incidents are indeed violent. While a police officer has never been killed in Newfoundland responding to a drunk and disorderly call, police officers nevertheless view these calls with caution. The following are

comments police have made regarding how they interpret drunk and disorderly calls in St. John's.

[D]runk and disorderly calls, you knock on the door, and stand back from it because you don't know what's going to come. We've had a number of close calls, doors blown off by shotguns. We've been lucky...they could say, "the old man is acting up", as the saying goes, "he's acting up," "he's drinking. He could have guns in the house... "Any guns in the house?" And she'll say "yes." Well right away we send an armed man because anything could happen. (McGahan, 1984:85-86)

This, along with discussions with counsellors working in battered women's shelters in St. John's, suggests that many women have been physically assaulted in situations police ultimately label as drunk and disorderlies. Unless the woman appears to be prepared to initially embark on legal action seldom are charges laid.[6] Thus, the level of police discretion is a very important factor in terms of defining what is violent crime in "domestic disputes."

According to conversations I had with a veteran RNC police officer, it was common police practice to not lay criminal charges in such incidents. Instead, police would usually usher the "trouble maker" away from the home in a police vehicle and then once a reasonable distance away from the home the "trouble maker" would be dropped off and made to make his own way back to the home. The intent of this strategy, according to police, was to allow the "trouble maker" sufficient time to sober up before returning home. Clearly, then, drunk and disorderlies are in many cases violent incidents, but due to police discretion they are not classified as such.

Let us now turn to the question of how many drunk and disorderly complaints police receive. Insofar as the RNC keep annual records on the number of complaints of drunk and disorderlies they receive from the public, it is possible to estimate the reported incidence of this "non-violent" crime. In 1985, for instance, the RNC reported in its annual report that there were, in total, 769 violations of "other provincial statutes" (RNC, 1985). And of this total, 461 were in fact drunk and disorderlies. In other words, roughly 60% of "other provincial statutes" in that year were drunk and disorderlies. Although this information is unavailable on a provincial basis, we may roughly estimate its occurrence in Newfoundland by using data from the RNC as a baseline. Assuming, for instance, that one-half of "other provincial statutes" across Newfoundland as a whole involve instances of "drunk and disorderly in the home," then it can be estimated that in 1985, for example, there were 1,800 of these reports made to the police. As such, the provincial rate for "drunk and disorderlies in the home" would approximate 250/100,000 population, a rate which is in fact almost one-half of Newfoundland's total assault rate in 1985! Considerable "violence" is taking place and is reported to the police in Newfoundland, but is not included in the province's violent crime rate. Like drunk and disorderlies, "offensive weapon violations" are not considered violent crimes. This general statistical category includes the sub-categories of: careless or dangerous use of a firearm, pointing a firearm or carrying a weapon dangerous to the public peace. However, an analysis of 78 randomly selected "other offensive weapon" files which were reported to the RCMP in Newfoundland between 1977 and 1983 reveals a great deal about the nature of those crimes. Twenty-eight percent of those police investigations involved a man threatening to kill his wife or lover with a firearm. In most cases the weapon involved was a hunting rifle or shotgun. The remaining files were essentially incidents involving other family members and relatives, neighbours or friends. Very few of these incidents involved strangers.[7] Although it was very difficult to determine the precise nature of what in fact took place during these "non-violent" crimes, based on information from the police files of incidents involving men and women living together, the motive held most often responsible for these types of confrontations was a "domestic dispute." And in most cases the offender, again, usually a man, was reported to have been drunk at the time of the incident.

In terms of the frequency of these official "non-violent crimes," they are, by and large, reported to police twice as often as incidents popularly defined as "armed robberies." In fact, the incident rate for offenses involving

"offensive weapon" violations in 1983, for instance, was more than double the robbery rate for that same year: 30/100,000 population versus 13/100,000 population.

Examining the "non-violent" crimes of "drunk and disorderly in the home" and "weapon violations" illustrates that many violent acts take place in Newfoundland and are reported to the police, but because of differences in legal, statistical, and police definitions and practices, they fail to be recognized as violent crimes despite the fact that a considerable degree of danger to human life, particularly for women, is present in many of these "non-violent" circumstances.

If offenses such as "drunk and disorderly in the home" and "weapon violations" provide reason to believe that a considerable level of violence, particularly against women, is underestimated in Newfoundland, a way of uncovering a more accurate measure of the extent of violence against women is to try and get at the rate of physical assault indirectly. It is generally accepted that the most accurate statistics concerning violent crime are homicide statistics; indeed "dead bodies are easier to count and harder to conceal than forms of violence that do not result in death, and with the exception of children and old people they may be taken as being tolerably accurate."[8] Based on data collected by reviewing over 100 homicide files in Newfoundland over a thirty year period, homicide in Newfoundland is typically committed by a man (88%) against a woman (50%) or another man (50%). In more precise terms, based on a total of 124 homicides in Newfoundland between 1953 and 1985 (representing roughly 80% of all homicides and attempted murders over that period) 109, or 88%, involved male offenders or suspects (we will use the term offender throughout the analysis) while women accounted for the other 12%. Most women homicide victims in Newfoundland have been killed by their husbands, lovers or ex-lovers, or by other members of the family. Indeed, this is so far 80% of women who have been murdered in Newfoundland during the past thirty years; a ratio which has, by and large, remained constant over time. One could reasonably expect that the ratio of men to women murdered would be reflected in the rate of men to women physically assaulted. Indeed, there are good arguments to suggest that in Newfoundland, as elsewhere, women are more vulnerable to physical assault (notably in the home) than men. Thus if women are as rarely assaulted as even the victimization survey statistics show by comparison to men (according to the *Canadian Urban Victimization Survey*, men in St. John's were victims of 70% of the total number of assaults which took place in St. John's in 1982, while women were victims of 30% of the total number of assaults), then we would expect many more men to be murdered than women. But this is not so. Women in Newfoundland overall suffer a murder rate only a little less than that for men. In other words, approximately one-half of all homicide victims in Newfoundland between 1953-1984 were women.

If violent crimes against women in Newfoundland are generally prone to underestimation, then there is good evidence suggesting that Native women in Newfoundland, specifically Inuit women living in Northern Labrador, are victims of violent crime a lot more often than official statistics (and victimization surveys) reveal. When homicide rates are compared between the island of Newfoundland and Labrador, we see striking differences. In 1981, Labrador, an area of Newfoundland with a population of approximately 32,000 people (with Native people accounting for approximately 5,000 of the total population for this region of the province), represented less than 6% of Newfoundland's total population. Yet Labrador accounted for 20% of the homicides and 10% of the attempted murders in the province between 1977 and 1984. And when these differences are examined more closely it becomes clear that a great deal of this carnage takes place between Native people living in Northern Labrador. In fact, between 1977 and 1984, nine homicides and three attempted murders took place in Labrador and, of this total, Native people were involved in seven of the homicides and one of the attempted murders. In other words, Natives, who comprise approximately 15% of the population of Labrador, accounted for 78% of the homicides and 33% of the attempted murders which were reported to police during that time. Looking at

these figures again in a different light, homicides and attempted murders which occurred between Natives accounted for 10% of the province of Newfoundland's homicides and attempted murders for this period — an alarming statistic if we consider that the Native population in Labrador accounts for less than 1% of the total population of Newfoundland. The homicide rate amongst Native people in Labrador, then, is 20 per 100,000 population while the average annual rate for the province in general over this period (which includes Native homicides) has never exceeded 1.8 per 100,000 population. When these incidents of Native homicides are examined in terms of gender, we find that the ratio between male and female offenders is very unequal; that is, for every nine male offenders there is one woman, whereas in terms of victims, women and men are roughly equally represented. These ratios, then, are quite similar for homicide incidents for Newfoundland in general. That is to say, the ratio between non-Native men killing non-Native women is, for all intents and purposes, identical to the ratio of Native men killing Native women — the difference between Natives and non-Natives differs only with respect to frequency.

The high levels of violent victimization for Native women are further revealed when police reported assaults are examined on a provincial basis. A random selection and analysis of RCMP assault files (N=85) revealed that roughly 20% of all incidents of assault reported to the RCMP in Newfoundland between 1977 and 1983 involved Natives residing in Labrador. And, of this 20%, 90% involved a male offender. Again these differences are very similar to assaults which were reported to the police involving non-Natives, as in 89% of assaults in this category there was a male offender.

In terms of established victim-offender relationship, 30% of assaults between Native people in Labrador were committed by men against their partners (includes married and common-law). Once again, these percentages more or less mirror victim-offender relationships of assaults which are reported to the police involving non-Native people in Newfoundland and Labrador.

Moreover, an analysis of 180 RCMP "family violence" files in Newfoundland for the years 1983 and 1984 (this total is not a sample, but rather the total number of these "family violence" files which were collected by the RCMP over this two year period) showed that 20% (or 37) of these files contained incidents involving Native people from Labrador. In all of these incidents men were labelled by police as offenders. In fact, in almost 90% of these reports Native men were reported to have assaulted their spouses. For non-Native men, 80% of these incidents took place where a man was, in most cases, charged for assaulting his wife. In fact, in 35 of these 37 incidents involving Natives, a Native man was charged either with assault or assault causing bodily harm.

Similarly (with differences between homicide for Natives and non-Natives in the province), on a per capita basis, Native men are charged with assaulting their spouses much more often than are non-Native men. Based on these statistics, then, Native women in Labrador are victimized by violent crime to a much higher degree than are non-Native women in Newfoundland. As well, there seems to be good evidence suggesting that many of these incidents of domestic violence are not coming to the attention of the police. For example, with regard to the "family violence" files, 54% of the Native women required hospitalization for the injuries they incurred. The percentage for non-Native women was 10%. Furthermore, in roughly 30% of these incidents, the police were notified of the incident by a hospital official. For non-Natives, however, hospitals informed police in 6% of total incidents. The most prevalent method for police being informed of non-Native incidents of "family violence" was from victims. This was the case in 77% of incidents.

No doubt, then, incidents of "family violence" involving Native women which come to the attention of the police are serious. For instance, in only 2% of the total number of reports of family violence involving Native people were there charges of "threats," as opposed to 8% for non-Natives. Perhaps the fact that in 24% of these incidents a charge of assault causing bodily harm was issued could also point to the fact that only the most serious assaults involving Natives come to the attention of the police.

Of course there are many factors which come into play suggesting that many assaults which happen to Native women don't come to the attention of the police. Unfortunately it is beyond the scope of this paper to investigate this process in detail. But what I wish to stress is one factor specifically related to Native people which may, in part, account for these reporting tendencies, that is, incarceration levels for Native people. In Newfoundland, Native offenders are seven times more likely to be incarcerated than non-Natives (Department of Justice, Newfoundland and Labrador, 1985:85). Native women may therefore refrain from reporting their spouses' violent acts to the police more so than non-Natives perhaps because they don't want their husbands jailed; they simply want only that the violence be condemned and stopped. Indeed, 30% of Natives convicted of assault (many for beating their wives) in Newfoundland between 1977-1983 were incarcerated for a period of three months or more. The comparable figure for non-Natives was 7%.[9]

It is quite evident from this empirical research that violent crime is underestimated and overestimated, but not randomly. Crimes of violence which affect women, particularly Native women, are underestimated in official statistics and no doubt in victimization surveys as well. The more materially vulnerable a social group is the less likely official statistics will reflect the real situation people from these groups face.[10]

Underestimation, then, is a product of power. One only has to compare the social response to robbery at retail locations and unemployed youth with the response to domestic violence to understand what is dominantly considered to be serious violent crime in Newfoundland. While public violence, such as armed robbery, can be argued as being subject to overestimation and moral panic, the same cannot be said for violence against women. It continues to take place with relative impunity and the legal system indeed consigns the problem of domestic violence — drunk and disorderly in the home as well as many "weapon violations" — to a status of relative unimportance. In fact, the police in Newfoundland have indeed questioned the appropriateness of becoming involved in situations of domestic violence; they feel it is not their job to mediate "family disputes" (McGahan, 1984:86). Consequently, violence against women in the private domain is viewed by police as being extraneous to "real police work," such as armed robbery investigations. Despite the fact that the Newfoundland Department of Justice has recently put some pressure on the public to lay charges against assault suspects in "domestic disturbances" and that there has been substantial change in some police force practices, the police in Newfoundland, like police in many other parts of Canada, continue to regard domestic violence lightly unless it results in serious injury or death.

The police, however, are but one institution in Newfoundland society which marginalizes violence against women by defining what is and what isn't violent crime. In fact, some members of the press in Newfoundland have viewed violence against women as more or less a "rubbish" crime. For instance, the editor of the *Evening Telegram* (who on a number of occasions has written about the growing menace of "street crime") recently wrote an editorial arguing that statistics issued by organizers of a "Take Back the Night" march were "made-up" as he felt the "issue is not sexual assault" but rather "figures which distort reality" and that the important question was "who benefits from such distortion?" In fact, the claim was made that there was "something to be gained" by feminists "by making a serious problem appear even worse" (*Evening Telegram*, 4 October, 1986).

When these editorial comments are juxtaposed with others published at roughly the same time on armed robbery in St. John's which were referred to earlier, one gets a strong impression that the editor is very selective in terms of how criminal statistics "distort reality." The editorial called for stiffer sentences for offenders despite the fact that, based on official statistics, the rate of armed robbery in St. John's was substantially greater six years previously.

It is quite easy to see then, the tendency for the largest newspaper in Newfoundland, business groups, judges as well as the police, to

embrace, with vigour, violence when associated with private property, while at the same time either lightly regarding violence against women, or else, with no statistical evidence, simply alleging that the problem is exaggerated.

CONCLUSION

This paper has argued that images presented by those concerned about violence associated with private property in Newfoundland are powerful and upsetting. The perceived increases in the character and level of violent "retail crime" have been explained as being largely the result of high unemployment. However, rigorous analysis of police files and statistics has revealed that violent "retail crime," for instance, remains low in Newfoundland when it is compared to most other provinces in Canada. Moreover, there is no concrete evidence suggesting that these types of crimes are increasing and thus approaching what are thought to be "mainland standards." Crimes of violence, for example, are much more likely to take place in instances where men beat their wives or lovers. As well as being prone to "official" underestimation, domestic violence in Newfoundland remains unrelated to dominant conceptions of the moral climate of Newfoundland society. Indeed, to understand the way in which crime and violence are officially defined, measured and produced, we must draw attention to the social relations out of which these practices arise. Thus, future research must consider the interplay between official statistics and the wider social, economic and political structures in society.

NOTES

1. The radio has been a popular medium where concern has been expressed about violence in Newfoundland. For example, Rapport's (1987:11-12) anthropological interpretation of conversations on violence in St. John's cites many comments from radio talk show callers on perceived increases in "violent and armed crimes" in St. John's.

2. A simple aggregate relationship such as this,

however, is unreliable for a large number of reasons. For example, Wright's (1981) review of research in this area suggests that there is considerable disagreement and uncertainly about the precise nature of the relationship between economic fluctuations and criminality. According to Wright, "Empirical research on the relationship has not found a consistent covariation" and "the proposition that if the economic situation declines then criminality will increase may not always be accurate nor extremely significant" (pp. 66-67). In a more recent review of this literature, Carr-Hill and Stern (1983:387) suggest that "It is possible that unemployment does cause crime, on the other hand in some respects it may reduce it, and it is quite wrong to pretend we know the answer."

3. This information was generated from police investigation files held in the records office of the Royal Newfoundland Constabulary. The figures were based on a quota sample of 65% of the robbery incidents which were cleared by charge in St. John's between 1955 and 1983.

4. These figures were calculated using information contained in Royal Newfoundland Constabulary criminal files.

5. For a paper that considers the pressure lobby groups have put on the authorities to stiffen penalties for "Retail Crimes," see Jim Overton and Bill O'Grady, "Popular Anxiety, Armed Robbery and Sentencing in Newfoundland." Unpublished paper, available from the author on request.

6. However, as I stated earlier, pressure has been put on the police in recent years to make criminal charges in these types of incidents.

7. Weapons violations involving strangers were, in most cases, events where police had been notified, and then responded to, situations where men had barricaded themselves in their homes with a weapon.

8. The method used here for uncovering a more accurate level of violence against women in Newfoundland is adopted from research from Kinsey and Young (1986:63).

9. In addition to this factor, services for battered women in Labrador have only recently been developed and most battered women living in isolated communities remain without emergency shelter. Moreover, Native people of Labrador, like Native peoples living in the Canadian North generally, are not "numerous or accessible enough to constitute an important political constituency or economic market. So for years they have either been largely ignored, marginalized or patronized" (Taylor, 1985:341). There is good reason to believe, then, that 'police/community relations' in these isolated communities are poor, so a lot of interpersonal violence is likely not being reported to police.

10. Victimization surveys are, according to Phipps (1986), "notoriously poor at uncovering unreported instances of violence to women, sexual assaults and rape." And, a good reason suggesting why this is so is that "Many such victims may be unprepared to report incidents of this nature to an interviewer; they may not feel that assaults of this sort fall within the survey's scope, or they may feel embarrassment or shame. Indeed, their assailant may be in the same room at the time of the interview" (Hough and Mayhew, 1983:21) as cited in Kinsey and Young, (1986). Also, for a good discussion of the concept "underestimation," see Kinsey and Young (Ibid).

Chapter 7

THE RISK OF CRIMINAL VICTIMIZATION: DATA FROM A NATIONAL STUDY*

Holly Johnson and Vincent F. Sacco

INTRODUCTION

The General Social Survey was initiated by Statistics Canada in order to reduce gaps in statistical information, particularly in relation to social and economic trends. The survey has two principal objectives: first, to gather data on trends in Canadian society over time, and second, to provide information on specific policy areas of interest. To meet these objectives, the GSS has been established as a continuing program with a single survey cycle each year.

The third cycle of the General Social Survey, which was carried out in January and February 1988, collected detailed information about personal risk of accidents and criminal victimization. Telephone interviews were conducted with 9,870 Canadians, 15 years of age and older. The sample covered the non-institutionalized population of the ten provinces.

The survey allowed for the investigation of the prevalence and the social and demographic distribution of eight specific types of victimization experiences that occurred during 1987: sexual assault, robbery, assault, break and enter, theft of motor vehicles and motor vehicle parts, theft of personal property, theft of household property and vandalism. Sexual assault, robbery and assault are classified as "violent victimization." These three offences and theft of personal property comprise the category

"personal victimization." The remaining types of victimization combine to form the aggregate category "household victimization." Non-victims were defined as those who did not report a victimization incident during the survey year.

Each time a victimization incident was reported by a respondent, interviewers were required to complete a "Crime Incident Report" in order to collect details about the incident. In all, 3,808 Crime Incident Reports were completed.

In addition to information concerning respondents' victimization experiences, the survey attempted to gather a variety of related data, for instance, attitudes toward the courts and the police, awareness of victim services and beliefs about personal risk of victimization. Sacco and Johnson (1990) provide a more detailed discussion of the methodology and the findings of the survey.

The present discussion focuses on the ways in which the likelihood of victimization varies across social and demographic categories. The rates described below are expressions of the estimated number of incidents per 1,000 persons (in the case of personal victimizations) or per 1,000 households (in the case of household crimes). In both cases, the rates are interpreted as indicators of victimization risk for the populations (persons and households) from which the samples were drawn.

* Adapted for this volume from Vincent F. Sacco and Holly Johnson, *Patterns of Criminal Victimization in Canada* (Ottawa: Ministry of Supply and Services Canada, 1990), chapters 1 and 2.

GENERAL RISK OF VICTIMIZATION

An estimated 4.8 million Canadians, 15 years of age and over, were victimized by 5.4 million criminal incidents in 1987. Over one-half of these incidents involved crimes committed against persons (54%). Approximately one-third (31%) were violent victimizations — sexual assaults, robberies, and assaults, and a further 22% involved the theft of personal property. Forty percent of the incidents involved crimes against households — break and enter, motor vehicle theft, theft of household property and vandalism. Approximately 7% of the incidents could not be classified with a high degree of certainty.

The rate of personal victimization was 143 incidents per 1,000 Canadians over the age of 15. The rate of assault was highest of all for personal offences (68 per 1,000), followed by theft of personal property (59 per 1,000) and robbery (13 per 1,000). There were too few incidents of sexual assault reported by respondents to allow the production of statistically reliable estimates.

The rate of household victimizations was 216 incidents per 1,000 households. The rate of vandalism was highest among household offences at 63 per 1,000 households, followed by break and enter (54 per 1,000), theft of a motor vehicle or motor vehicle parts (51 per 1,000) and theft of household property (48 per 1,000).

There is significant regional variation in patterns of victimization risk. Residents of Quebec face the lowest risk of personal crime (60 per 1,000) and residents of British Columbia face the highest (252 per 1,000). The data describe a general increase in personal victimization risk from eastern to western regions of the country, although Quebec does suggest a departure from this pattern. A generally similar pattern is demonstrated in the case of household crime: the overall rate for British Columbia is almost two and one-half times greater than the rate for the Atlantic region. A more detailed analysis indicates that households in the western regions of the country are at greatest risk of all types of household crimes covered by the GSS.

PERSONAL VICTIMIZATION

SOCIAL AND DEMOGRAPHIC CORRELATES

Table 1 describes the relationships among risk of personal victimization and several social and demographic variables. As the table indicates, rates are higher for males (148 per 1,000) than for females (138 per 1,000). In general, men face greater risks of criminal violence (90 incidents per 1,000) than do women (77 incidents per 1,000), whereas women experience marginally higher rates of theft of personal property (61 compared to 58 per 1,000).

Rates of personal victimization also vary markedly by age. Young Canadians (those between the ages of 15 and 24) experience personal victimization at rates nearly twice as high as those in the 25 to 44 age group and seven times that of those 45 to 64 years of age. A rate for the elderly (that is, those 65 years of age and over) cannot be estimated reliably. Differences between the youngest group of adults and those aged 45 to 64 are greater in the case of violent offences than in the case of theft of personal property; young adults are about eight times as likely as middle-aged Canadians to be victims of violence and about six times as likely to be victims of personal theft.

Data from the General Social Survey also allow an assessment of the relationship between personal victimization risk and socio-economic status. The survey found that personal victimization rates are higher for Canadians living in households with incomes of $60,000 or more (158 per 1,000), followed by households earning less than $40,000. Canadians who reside in households earning between $40,000 and $60,000 reported the lowest rates of personal victimization at 121 incidents per 1,000 population.

Data relating to the relationship between the risk of personal victimization and a second indicator of socio-economic status, education, are also presented in Table 1. It will be noted that Canadians with some postsecondary education reported the highest rate of victimization

TABLE 1
PERSONAL VICTIMIZATION RATES BY SELECTED POPULATION CHARACTERISTICS (PER 1,000)

	Total Personal	Theft	Violence
Total	143	59	83
Gender			
Male	148	58	90
Female	138	61	77
Age			
15 - 24	311	123	188
25 - 44	158	65	92
45 - 64	46	22	23
65+	-	-	-
Income			
Less than 15,000	142	46	96
15,000 - 29,999	149	55	94
30,000 - 39,999	146	61	85
40,000 - 59,999	121	56	65
60,000+	158	78	80
Education			
Some Secondary or Less	138	55	83
Sec. Grad., Trade School Dip., etc.	117	46	71
Some Postsecondary	174	74	99
Postsec. Degree or Diploma	153	64	88
Marital Status			
Married or Common Law	88	44	45
Single	274	107	168
Widow or Widower	-	-	-
Separated/Divorced	274	66	208
Residence			
Urban	158	70	88
Rural	114	46	68
Main Activity			
Working at Job or Business	145	62	83
Looking for Work	156	-	-
Student	360	151	210
Keeping House	81	28	53
Retired	-	-	-
Evenings Out (per month)			
Less than 10	55	26	29
10 - 19	88	46	42
20 - 29	153	63	89
30 or More	284	105	179
Alcohol Consumption			
Non-Drinker	90	42	48
Occasional	141	56	85
Total Current	164	67	97
< 1 Drink/Week	156	58	98
1 - 6 Drinks/Week	154	69	85
7 - 13 Drinks/Week	175	88	87
14+ Drinks/Week	294	-	220

— rate cannot be estimated reliably.

(174 per 1,000), followed by those with a degree or diploma (153). Those with some secondary school or less have a rate below the national average (138) while those who completed secondary school, but have no postsecondary training, have the lowest rate (117). This pattern holds true for both personal theft and violent victimization.

The relationship between education and victimization risk can be explained in part with reference to the relationship between education and age. Younger people are better educated and, as previously shown, younger Canadians have a higher than average risk of victimization.

When the relationship between education and personal victimization is examined separately for males and females, the data indicate that for females, risk of victimization increases with education while the pattern for males more closely resembles the national pattern. The greatest differences between male and female levels of risk are found at the highest and lowest levels of educational achievement. Among those with some secondary school or less, males have a rate of personal victimization of 161 per 1,000 compared to a rate for females of 117. However, females with a postsecondary degree or diploma have a rate of 171 compared to a rate of 133 for males at the same educational level.

With respect to marital status, the GSS data indicate that rates of personal victimization for those who are single or separated/divorced are twice the national average and three times higher than the rates for those who are married. As with education, this relationship probably reflects the fact that younger people are more likely to be single. In addition, marital status appears to have stronger effects upon the risk of violent victimization than upon the risk of personal theft. When the effects of marital status on victimization risk are examined within categories of gender, the data suggest that for males, rates are considerably higher for those who are classified as single (292), while in the case of females, those separated or divorced report the highest rates (329).

Table 1 also indicates that urban dwellers experienced rates of personal victimization (158 per 1,000) almost 40% higher than residents of

rural areas (114 per 1,000), and that urban dwellers are at greater risk of both theft of personal property and criminal violence.

LIFESTYLE

Table 1 describes the relationship between risk of personal victimization and three indicators of respondents' lifestyle. The first such indictor is self-reported "main activity" during the survey years. According to the data, students reported a rate of victimization two and one-half times the national average (360 per 1,000). Those whose main activity is described as "keeping house" had the lowest rate (81 per 1,000). Canadians employed outside the home reported average rates, while those looking for work had rates slightly above average.

A second lifestyle variable, the total number of times per month that respondents reported involvement in evening activities outside the home, also has important implications for victimization risk. As Table 1 shows, the risk of personal victimization climbs steadily as the number of reported evening activities increases. The greatest risks are faced by those who engage in 30 or more activities per month with an associated rate of 284 incidents per 1,000 population. This represents a rate over five times greater than that associated with the lowest activity level. This pattern holds true for males and females, although the rate of increase is marginally greater for females. The greatest risks are faced by those who are under 25 years of age and who engage in 30 or more activities per month. For this subgroup of Canadians, the rate of personal victimization is 403 incidents per 1,000 population.

The relationship between victimization risk and a final lifestyle measure, patterns of alcohol consumption, is also illustrated in Table 1. These data indicate that risk of victimization increases with the amount of alcohol consumed. Non-drinkers, for instance, have the lowest rate of violent victimization (48 per 1,000) while those who consume 14 or more drinks per week have a rate four and one-half times higher.

These patterns hold even when the relationship between alcohol consumption and victimization risk is analyzed separately within age groups. Thus, within each group (for which estimates can be made) the lowest rates are associated with the status of non-drinker and the highest rates are associated with the consumption of 14 or more drinks per week. Those between the ages of 15 and 24 who are in the highest consumption category have a personal victimization rate of 648 per 1,000 population compared to a rate of 56 per 1,000 for non-drinkers aged 45 to 64.

THE RISK OF HOUSEHOLD VICTIMIZATION

As with personal victimization, the risk of household victimization is not randomly distributed. As Table 2 makes clear,

several characteristics put certain households at greater risk of victimization than others.

Table 2 indicates that household income is linked to household victimization rates in such a way that these rates are lower for households with incomes of less than $15,000 and higher for households in the $40,000 or over income categories. This pattern holds for all types of household victimization with the exception of theft of household property.

It will also be noted that, as with personal crime, urban rates are higher than rural rates. Overall, households located in urban areas experience victimization rates (252 per 1,000 households) over 70% higher than rural households (146 per 1,000).

The risk of household victimization is also

TABLE 2

HOUSEHOLD VICTIMIZATION RATES BY SELECTED HOUSEHOLD CHARACTERISTICS (PER 1,000)

	Total Household	Theft Break and Enter	Motor Vehicle Offences	Household Property	Vandalism
Total	216	54	51	48	63
Income					
< 15,000	163	55	-	36	38
15,000 - 29,999	221	58	52	52	59
30,000 - 39,999	258	59	60	75	64
40,000 - 59,999	296	64	80	49	102
60,000+	277	63	-	-	101
Residence					
Urban	252	64	59	54	76
Rural	146	32	36	35	42
Household Size					
1 Person	159	48	42	28	41
2 Persons	208	63	47	44	54
3 Persons	263	61	57	57	88
4 Persons	249	44	64	61	80
5 or More Persons	246	-	-	73	76
Ownership					
Owned	207	52	45	44	66
Rented	231	57	60	55	59
Dwelling Type					
Single Detached	203	51	45	46	61
Semi-Detached, Rowhouse, Duplex	284	78	46	71	89
Low/High Rise	206	50	66	40	51

— rate cannot be estimated reliably.

affected by household size as measured by the number of household residents. Rates of motor vehicle offences and theft of household property increase directly with the size of the household. Rates of vandalism increase between one and three occupants and decline for larger households to above-average rates. Rates of break and enter are lower for the largest and smallest households and above average for those of moderate size.

Owning one's home puts occupants at somewhat lower risk of most forms of household victimization. For households owned, the overall victimization rate is 207 per 1,000 while for rental accommodations, the rate is 231 per 1,000. This pattern is consistent for break and enter, motor vehicle offences and theft of household property. In the case of vandalism, however, higher rates are associated with home ownership.

Type of dwelling also has an effect on risk of household victimization. Single-family dwellers reported moderate rates of all household offences. Residents of double houses, rowhouses and duplexes reported the highest rates of break and enter, theft of household property and vandalism. Occupants of apartment buildings reported below-average rates of all household offences except theft of motor vehicles and motor vehicle parts.

Finally, patterns of evening activity outside the home exert substantial influence not only upon personal victimization risk but also upon the risk of household victimization. Overall rates of household victimization climb steadily as the number of evening activities reported by respondents increases. The highest rates are experienced by those who report involvement in 30 or more activities per month (319 per 1,000 households), which represents a level of risk two and one-half times that associated with the lowest activity level (125 per 1,000).

DISCUSSION

The General Social Survey reveals social and demographic patterns of victimization risk that are consistent with the findings of previous research (Hindelang et al., 19878; Solicitor General of Canada, 1983, 1987). Canadians who are young, male, single, separated/divorced and who are students experienced the highest rates of personal victimization. Frequent involvement in evening activities outside the home and regular alcohol consumption also increased substantially the likelihood of personal victimization. In terms of regional variation, patterns of victimization followed an east-west trend with Quebec suggesting a departure from this pattern in the case of personal offences. The findings relating to the nonrandom nature of household victimization are also consistent with earlier studies (Statistics Canada, 1988). Rates of household victimization are linked to household income, household size, home ownership, dwelling type, level of occupancy and urbanism.

While there is considerable evidence to support conclusions about the empirical significance of the correlates revealed in this analysis, there exists somewhat greater uncertainty about the theoretical meaning of these relationships. With respect to personal crime, several writers have argued that the concepts of "lifestyle" and "routine activities" provide the key linkages between the social and demographic characteristics of victims and the nature and frequency of their victimization experiences. The essential logic of this position is that the role obligations and institutional constraints embodied in major social status dimensions such as age, gender, marital status and income affect patterns of customary behaviour and thus the degree of exposure to persons and situations that threaten criminal harm (Collins et al., 1987; Gottfredson and Hindelang, 1981; Hindelang et al., 1978). The higher victimization rates experienced by males, those who are single, divorced or separated, young adults, and those who are students may reflect differences in exposure to risk which the lifestyles of these groups typically entail.

Indeed, findings relating to the more direct measures of lifestyle employed in the GSS — that the risk of personal victimization increases as levels of evening activity outside the home and alcohol consumption increase — are consistent with this position. Yet, this analysis, like several others, finds that lifestyle/exposure measures are insufficient to account for all the variation in victimization risk across socio-demographic groups (Miethe et al., 1987; Solicitor General of Canada, 1987). Variation in victimization risk across gender or age groups persists even when, for instance, the effects of the differential involvement in evening activities outside the home are controlled. This suggests the possibility that such measures may be inadequate as indicators of differential exposure to victimization risk (Sampson, 1987).

Quite clearly, the concept of exposure may provide only a partial explanation of the relationships between characteristics of victims and victimization risk. These characteristics may also be indicative of the proximity of potential targets to potential offenders (Cohen, Kluegel, and Land, 1981). The fact that doubles, duplexes and rowhouses tend to be located in high density urban areas and thus proximate to high risk offender populations may help to explain the high rates of victimization that are characteristic of such residences (Solicitor General of Canada, 1986).

Variations in victimization rates across categories of persons and households may also be related to differences in their suitability as targets for potential victimization (Cohen, Kluegel, and Land, 1981; Reppetto, 1974). Target suitability may explain the relatively high rate of theft of personal property for residents of households with high annual incomes. Similarly, higher income households are more likely to have valuable property which increases their vulnerability to household theft (Solicitor General of Canada, 1986). They are also more likely to own motor vehicles which places them at higher risk of motor vehicle theft and vandalism (seven in ten vandalism incidents revealed by the GSS involved damage to motor vehicles).

Finally, social and demographic correlates of victimization risk may be indicative of variable effectiveness in preventing criminal victimizations (Cohen and Felson, 1979). For example, rates of break and enter are lowest for very small and larger households; as number of occupants increases so does household activity and regularity of occupancy, factors which have been shown to be important in reducing the risk of break and enter (Cohen and Felson, 1979; Solicitor General of Canada, 1986; Statistics Canada, 1988). Thieves prefer empty houses. The finding that rates of household crime increase as evening activities outside the home increase also may suggest that decreasing levels of guardianship amplify risk of victimization.

In a related manner, the lower rates of household victimization of owned as opposed to rented accommodations may be indicative of a greater ability and willingness on the part of owners to exercise guardianship over household property. Similarly, the restricted access into and limited escape from apartment buildings may reduce the risk of break and enter, theft of household property and vandalism (Solicitor General of Canada, 1986). However, limited surveillance over motor vehicles may leave these residences somewhat more vulnerable to motor vehicle offences.

Present knowledge does not permit an accurate assessment of the way in which, or the extent to which, many of the socio-demographic variables discussed here incorporate or combine elements of exposure, proximity, target suitability or guardianship. For instance, with respect to household crime, wealthier households may provide more suitable targets (which increase victimization risk) but may be subject to greater guardianship or crime prevention efforts (which decrease victimization risk). Quite clearly, a high priority of future research must be to elaborate the relationship between such risk factors and the frequency and nature of victimization experiences.

Chapter 8

IT'S EASIER FOR THE BULLS NOW: OFFICIAL STATISTICS AND SOCIAL CHANGE IN A CANADIAN HEROIN-USING COMMUNITY*

Kenneth Stoddart

INTRODUCTION

At one time, sociological concern with official rates of criminal behaviour was primarily of a practical sort. Guided by a conception of such data as potentially revealing of the features of the activities they recorded — the perpetrators of crimes, the distribution of crimes over time, space, and a host of other variables — sociologists found it most interesting to address such data under remedial auspices, with an eye to the enhancement of their revelatory utility. For sociologists concerned, official data were received as possessing little interest in and of themselves: they were interesting only as a means to study the activities they presumably indexed. Clearly, a prominent entailment of the practical stance is retreat from official data as phenomena worthy of study in their own right.

All this has changed, however. In the twenty-seven years since Kitsuse and Cicourel (1963) suggested that official statistics be understood as indices of organizational processes rather than potential indices of "actual" community law-breaking, sociological interest has focused on the production of such rates. Indeed, Kitsuse and Cicourel's reformulation has kindled a long-term proliferation of studies of police routines, practices, customs, discretion, and other enforcement-related matters (see Bittner, 1967; Black, 1970, 1971; Black and Reiss, 1970; Chambliss and Nagasawa, 1969; Piliavin and Briar, 1965; Smith and Visher, 1981; Stoddart, 1983).

Crucial as these studies are to an understanding of the meaning of official statistics, though, students of rate-producing processes have tended to ignore a matter of equally crucial significance. I am referring to the activities of participants in criminal and deviant "communities." While knowledge of what law enforcers do is undoubtedly important in coming to terms with official statistics, such knowledge represents only one side of the coin, albeit the one most frequently addressed.

Drawing on a corpus of data that was produced by (1) intimate observation of a heroin-using community over a six-month period, (2) a series of observational follow-ups in that community more than a decade later, and (3) an informal program of unstructured interviews

* Edited version of K. Stoddart, "It's Easier for the Bulls Now: Official Statistics and Social Change in a Canadian Heroin-Using Community," *Journal of Drug Issues* 1991. Reprinted with permission of the author and reprinted with permission, © *Journal of Drug Issues*, 1991.

Financial support for the research reported herein was provided by the Social and Epidemiological Research Division of the Non-Medical Use of Drugs Directorate (Irving Rootman, Chief). The author is solely responsible for the interpretations presented.

with both free-ranging and temporarily institutionalized participants in the community, this report turns the coin over and examines its other face, that is, what law violators do. Their activities, after all, provide the conditions under which rates are producible in the first place (see Chambliss, 1973).

While a number of interesting issues attach to the activities engaged in by participants in a heroin-using community, the present report addresses only one: the apparent change in activities over time. That the character of activities in any community should change is hardly surprising. What is notable about the changes in this particular community, though, is that they were of a sort that tended to facilitate the enforcement of narcotics statutes, a matter of no small concern to students of official statistics.

The remainder of this paper is organized as follows. After a characterization of the data and my experiences with the community under study, a discussion of enforcement-facilitating changes is undertaken. It is suggested that successful enforcement is easier in the current version of the community than in an earlier one because participants (1) are increasingly apathetic vis-à-vis their own and their colleagues' fates and (2) fail to persistently practise certain time-honoured strategies intended to minimize the risk of detection, apprehension, and arrest. Taken together, these changes make it possible for those familiar with the history of the Western City heroin scene to say:

The street's fucked. It's easier for the bulls now.

THE DATA

I spent nearly half of 1967 doing observational research in a Vancouver cafe that since World War II had been a gathering place for heroin users and traffickers, prostitutes, thieves, and a host of others whose lifestyle would be considered deviant by conventional standards (Stoddart, 1968). During the time I spent in and around the setting I became familiar with many of its habitués and observed firsthand their daily round of life. I sat with heroin traffickers as they dispensed their product; listened to junkies tell of the strategies they

used to obtain methadone from the local treatment centre; found out which physicians would issue a barbiturate prescription in exchange for oral sex and which pharmacists would sell synthetic opiates out of the back door; watched sex trade workers hustle tricks; dealt with suburbanites who had come downtown looking for drugs, sex, stolen merchandise, or all three; witnessed the necessary brutality of narcotics law enforcement; and so on.

Even though I had grown up in the portion of Western City that had for years provided this scene with a healthy percentage of its participants — I recognized (but was not recognized by) many acquaintances from junior high school — my early experiences in the field were unbelievably disorienting and disturbing. After all, I had been away from the public housing project of my youth for almost seven years. I was leading a relatively middle-class life, complete with attendant sensibilities.

With time, however, I underwent the fieldworker's usual transformation from someone who found the setting very strange and threatening to one who was perceptually comfortable there. Its shifting cohort of participants no longer did or said anything that surprised or confused me. It was at this point, of course, that I left the field.

More than a decade later, I chanced to have as a next-door neighbour a long-term member of the Western City Narcotics Enforcement Unit. Like me, he had spent a good portion of 1967 — and of each of the years following — observing the daily goings-on in what I pseudonymously referred to as the Family Cafe. His interests, unlike mine, were far from research-oriented. When he asked me how I liked "hanging around with a bunch of dope-fiends," I told him that while there was no likelihood at all that I would go native in such a community, there were elements of it that I enjoyed and, to a degree, respected. He agreed that certain elements were admirable and documented this with a couple of stories from his own experience on "the street," both as a beat policeman and, later, as a member of the Narcotics Enforcement Unit. As an epilogue — and as a way of ending a conversation I felt he did not want to continue — he added, without elaboration: "But it's not like that anymore. The street is a very different place from what it used to be." I would not appreciate the meaning of his comment for many months to come.

Later the same year, I received a telephone call from a colleague in the federal health department. He asked if I could provide some descriptive material on the then-current version of the local heroin-using community. In particular, he was interested in material that might explain the ever-growing number of local arrests and successful prosecutions for heroin possession. Indeed, Western City had recorded a five-fold increase in such events in less than a decade, a figure that was often cited as evidence of an increase in the actual number of drug addicts residing in the region.

I re-entered the city's heroin-using community the following week. Though its locale had shifted — the Family Cafe was now a pornographic movie arcade — to uptown beer parlours and diners, I felt certain that its standing pattern of behaviour had remained constant. Armed as I was with the folkways, mores, and argot (Stoddart, 1974b) of this particular subculture and of drug-using subcultures in general (Stoddart 1974a, 1980, 1981), I had every confidence that I could navigate through it with ease, blending in as I had done before. I could not have been more wrong.

Early in the first evening of my return to the field it became obvious that much of what I had learned about the community through previous investigations was irrelevant to its current version. I will not describe in detail the fear I experienced. This, I felt, was probably because of a bravado that has eroded as much as my hairline. Amongst other things, what I found incongruous and disconcerting was that even unsocialized eyes could detect goings-on that were previously the property of those in the know.

It would be weeks before I returned to the street after that first re-visit. When I went back, I would be able to engage a dozen participants in what sociologists would call unstructured interviews — they were conversations, actually. But before I returned to the local heroin-using community, I interviewed more than thirty of its incarcerated and in-treatment participants. Fortunately, two colleagues from my correctional-service days had risen to

"boss" positions. Both were within months of retirement and were more than willing to grant me access without my going through the usual governmental channels. With their help, I came to learn the meaning of the off-hand remark made by my neighbour. Its unpacking follows.

NOBODY GIVES A FUCK ANYMORE: THE ASSERTED EROSION OF COMMUNITY SOLIDARITY

Informants who had, in their words, "been around junk for a long time" frequently indicated that their community had undergone a dramatic transition "...since the old days." For them, the most disturbing aspect of this change related to the moral character of persons involved in heroin use. Time and time again, longtime participants in the community complained about its transition from a grouping composed largely of solid people, namely, ones who adhered to the local version of the convict code, to one increasingly populated by fuck-ups, goofs, heatbags, burn and rip-off artists, punks, and so forth.

One of the consequences of this asserted change in the moral character of many participants was portrayed as apathy towards their own and their colleagues' fates. This section explores the potential influence of this "changed morality" on official statistical representations of Western City heroin use.

HANDLING SICKNESS

Participants in the community under study asserted the existence of a relationship between the experience of withdrawal-related symptoms and the risk of apprehension and arrest. Specifically, it is held that "being sick" dramatically increases the likelihood that those events will occur:

Researcher: When's the most likely time you're gonna take a pinch? When's the highest risk?

Informant: Oh, when you're....if you're sick, that's the time it's gonna happen. That's the time, for sure it is.

Indeed, "sickness" was frequently offered as the reason why a person was arrested.

Informants claimed that in an earlier version of the community, sickness was less problematic than it is now, as "there was always somebody who'd take care of you":

R: So what about getting sick, before now?
I: Well there was always somebody who'd take care of you. People cared then.
R: How would somebody take care of you?
I: Well they'd fix you or lend you the money to score. Or somebody who was puttin' out would give you a few caps on the cuff, y'know.

Most informants were quick to point out that the extension of support to colleagues in need of it was not necessarily altruistic. On the contrary, they formulated "caring" in practical terms. Foundational to this conception was the realization that at some point in the foreseeable future one would oneself be sick.

You know you're gonna be in the same spot at some point. So if you're known as somebody who's taken care of other guys, then you're gonna get the same kinda treatment. If you've been an asshole and said "fuck you" well you're gonna get it back.

One of the ways in which those familiar with the history of the local community contrasted its current version with an earlier one was through reference to an observable erosion of supportive relationships. Apparently, sickness caused by a temporary inability to obtain narcotics is now a matter about which one's colleagues are apathetic. A prominent consequence of this change is a potential increase in the pool of easily apprehended heroin users. As one informant put it:

Sick junkies get careless, and when you're careless you're as good as had.

HANDLING COLLEAGUES' ENCOUNTERS WITH POLICE

Another of the ways in which community members participated in the fate of their colleagues was by offering gross physical assistance during encounters with the police. As one informant put it, "people got involved." Even though technically another's unfortunate confrontation was nobody's business but his own,

a physical demonstration of concern was seen as the "natural," moral thing to do:

Well, when somebody got jumped you just naturally pile in. You'd feel guilty if you didn't. Everybody did...you'd get four or five guys doin' battle with the bulls. People got involved, y'know.

That this was the case was reported by variously located observers. Consider the following field-note, which displays the closely paraphrased remarks of a policeman with more than fifteen years' experience in narcotics enforcement:

In a conversation about a variety of things Fred told me that narcotics enforcement didn't seem to be as violent as it used to be. "It used to be," he said, "that when you went after one guy you had to take on all his friends as well. Now they don't all jump in like they used to."

Such assistance was apparently offered despite the fact that it was potentially consequential to the samaritans.

In line with the sentiment that "...nobody gives a fuck anymore," informants claim that community members can no longer expect such intervention from colleagues. Now, the possibility of assistance is considered remote:

You can't count on anybody these days. All these guys care about is themselves. They don't care shit about anybody else. Fat chance of anybody putting their ass on the line to help you.

A prominent consequence of this refusal to get involved in the fate of a colleague is a potential increase in the ratio of successful to unsuccessful enforcement attempts. Indeed, from the point of view of longtime participants in the community:

It's easier for the bulls now.

HANDLING ONE'S OWN ENCOUNTERS WITH POLICE

Somewhat paradoxically, observers familiar with an earlier version of the heroin-using community suggested that the notion "nobody gives a fuck anymore" applied not only to an increasing number of current participants' relationships with their colleagues but also to their relationship with themselves. One aspect of this was revealed time and time again in informants' characterizations of the physical appearance and condition of "people on the street." In one interview, for example, heroin users were described as "walkin' around like a bunch of...animals." For the informant who so characterized her colleagues, the situation was received as a new one:

I: It's no wonder the bulls hate junkies so much. Look at 'em. Just look at the people you see on the street. Fuck, they're dirty, sloppy, they don't care about the way they look. Walkin' around like a bunch of fuckin' animals, y'know.

R: Well, the image, the picture the public has of hypes is like that. Just caring about dope and nothing else.

I: Oh yeah I know. Square johns could go down and see that kinda thing too. People all dirty, not carin'. It didn't used to be like that though...Guys'd be sharp, take care of themselves.

The most notable — and, for the purposes of the present explication, relevant — document of that apathy, however, was portrayed in interviews as consisting in a new stance towards the violence potentially associated with narcotics enforcement. An informant suggests the character of that violence:

R: What do they typically do? How do they get the dope?

I: Oh they choke ya, jump up and down on your gut. Stick keys in your mouth. Or handcuffs, and turn 'em. Things like that. Anything to get the stuff outa ya, y'know. They've even killed people in the process.

A stance that longtime participants in the community claim no longer exists, understood, in large measure, that encounters with enforcement-related violence were "part of bein' a junkie." The following excerpt from an interview displays not only the old stance but also the collision between an outside and a local understanding of "taking a beating."

R: Well what about after...the time you got say your first beating. Didn't you figure "well Christ it's not worth it if this kinda thing's gonna happen." I mean broken teeth and things.

I: Oh no, that's part of it. That's part of bein' a junkie,

takin' a beatin'. It's part of it. You expect it's gonna happen and you don't want it to but you expect it. It's just part of your life if you're a junkie.

Informants claim that considerations of avoiding arrest by preventing police from obtaining their heroin properly exercise an overriding priority when choosing amongst alternate courses of action on the occasion of a violent encounter. Plainly, one "puts up a fight."

R: Well do you fight back, or what?

I: Do I fight back? Well of course. You kick and punch and do...and ... anything to keep them from you.

It is not the case that heroin users cannot assert the priority of other "considerations": indeed, they are free to elect amongst possible courses of action in ways suggestive of the priority of short-term well-being, such as the preservation of teeth. It is the case, however, that the subordination of considerations of arrest-avoidance to any others is received by informants as strange, somehow unbelievable. To wilfully permit the police to obtain the very evidence that could imprison you — just to avoid taking a beating — was formulated as something that "...nobody in their right mind" would do.

As suggested earlier, the stance towards arrest-avoidance that was once dominant in the community is now portrayed as having faded. As one informant put it:

...a lot of your kids seem to think different now, I guess. Like they don't put up the fight they used to.

Informants were not without theories regarding the apathy of many colleagues toward their own fate. Some accounted for it by reference to such objective factors as the declining quality of narcotics available on the street:

Well it used to be that if you went to jail...the junk was really good then, 15 to 20 percent, not like now. If you went to jail you got sick. Now the stuff's so shitty, there's not the drive, I guess. I guess it doesn't matter that much.

or the comparatively short sentences given out for possession of narcotics:

Guys are now getting what...thirty days, sixty days. You could count on six months at least, before. People're just getting short time...maybe they figure a shitkickin's not worth it, just for a month or so.

Others accounted for this observable change by referring to a change in the character of the heroin-using population:

These kids now have got no backbone, no strength. They're a much weaker bunch today than we used to be.

Some invoked the "degenerative" properties of substances used by newer participants prior to their involvement with heroin:

A lot of the younger people that are...a lot of the younger types started out dropping acid and the like. Some of them still do, believe it or not. Well that stuff's no good, as far as I'm concerned. It does things to you. Junk does too but I mean different things. You know. It does something to your mind, I'm sure. A lot of the younger ones just aren't like us at all. They've got no morals, they're fuckin' degenerates, some of them. It's that psychedelic shit.

And others claimed that apathy and change in general could be tied to lack of appropriate socialization:

I: The trouble with these young kids is they haven't been around, y'know.
R: No. How do you mean "around."
I: Well they haven't been...Well look at me for example. I've been involved in crime since...as long as I can remember. I'm not braggin' but I was doin' B & E's when I was thirteen, me and a bunch of other guys in the East End. I was in Oakalla at sixteen for god's sake. They wouldn't do that now. I didn't get into junk until I was twenty-three or twenty-four. By that time I was more or less established as a thief. Other guys I knew — the same thing, the same pattern.
R: I don't know...
I: Well the point is we'd all done time, we were all solid people. Now these kids that are on the street now. Seventeen, eighteen years old. They've come up from different ranks so to speak. They haven't got a clue about how to be decent.

Whatever the reason, the informants felt that fewer of their colleagues were resisting police efforts at enforcement with the vigour portrayed as characteristic of an earlier period in the history of the local community. Rather than

"do battle" with the police, it was held that users were more likely to "turn over the dope so they won't take a beating." One informant called this "doing up."

I: A lot of people now will do up to the bulls rather than take a beating.
R: How do you mean "do up"?
I: Well they'll just hand over the dope to the cops, or else just spit it out as soon as one of them grabs by the throat. Fuck, that was just unheard of before! It's better to have a few bruises or broken bones and still be on the street.

Quite obviously, participants' apathy towards their own legal fate has as a consequence a potential increase in the ratio of successful to unsuccessful investigations.

HANDLING BURNS

A burn can be described as an offence against the marketplace ideal that consumers should get what they believe they are paying for, that the seller's representation of the product should correspond in a reasonable way with the product-in-fact. In the heroin-using community the burn can take a variety of forms. For example, that title can be used to describe a situation wherein one pays for heroin but receives another substance or a short measure.

Reference to an increasing number of burns was amongst the ways in which participants in the community under study contrasted its current version with an earlier one. Consider the following excerpt from an interview.

R: I've been hearing a lot about burns...
I: That's 'cause there's a lot of 'em happening. Lots. You gotta be careful all the time, now.
R: More than before, say ten to twelve years ago or so?
I: Oh fuck yes. For sure. People didn't do that kinda thing then.

Burns occur in virtually every sphere of merchandising, but in legitimate spheres the consumer has legal recourse, and recent legislation has made *caveat venditor*, let the seller beware, a rule of the marketplace. The ideal is thus officially enforceable and, on occasion, officially enforced.

The informant whose remarks were just displayed indicated that while *caveat venditor* used to be operative in the heroin marketplace, it is increasingly less so. She understands the erosion of that principle as a further aspect of the description "...nobody gives a fuck anymore." It is suggested that burning a colleague is not as consequential as it was at an earlier period in the history of the local community.

Participants in the local heroin-using community indicated that they received burns as somewhat more than just fraudulent transactions. Indeed, for them a burn prompted frustration and with it the possibility that one would do "stupid things." Doing "stupid things," it was held, facilitated apprehension for the violation of narcotics law. Consider the following excerpt from an interview:

I: ...so I was really pissed off, y'know. There I was with no dope and my money's gone. So I got some more bread...
R: How did you get it?
I: Trick.
R: Oh, okay. So you got the money...
I: Yeah, then I scored off somebody else... By this time I was gettin' a bit edgy, y'know. I did a stupid thing, crazy. I dashed in to fix right in the john and of course the harness bulls nabbed me.

In general, colleagues' talk and activities provided informants with ample evidence to document the notion that "...nobody gives a fuck anymore." For informants, however, more than just the morality of community members had changed. The next section describes a further aspect of the transition.

PEOPLE AREN'T AS CAREFUL: ASSERTED CHANGES IN ADAPTIVE PRACTICE

In characterizing the differences between the earlier and current versions of the heroin-using community informants often indicated that

...people aren't as careful anymore. The way they do things they're just askin' to be pinched.

For them, the notion that "people aren't as careful" implied that the performance of certain drug-related activities had changed in ways that facilitate — perhaps invite — enforcement. This section examines user-asserted changes in two crucial activities: buying heroin and transporting it to the place where it will be administered.

SCORING

Participants in the community under study regarded police observation of scoring — purchasing heroin — as the initial event in a series of events that could lead to arrest for the possession of narcotics. In line with this belief, informants claimed that scoring should be done in such a way as to minimize police identification of it as scoring. Obscuring the reason for one's presence in a copping area was portrayed as a common way of accomplishing this. Typically, one embeds scoring in a round of "ordinary" activities, such as visiting friends or having coffee. Consider the following excerpt from an interview with a female heroin user who attributes her arrest to her failure to obscure the fact that she had purchased narcotics:

R: How do you mean it was your own fault?
I: Oh I was...I was too quick about it, y'know. I just went in and out, in and scored and came right out. It'd be obvious that I was just there to score. I shoulda sat down and hung around for awhile, y'know. Make it look like I was just bein' social, havin' a visit or something.
R: Is that what you'd done...is that what you'd normally do? Hang around and things.
I: Oh yeah, but for some reason I didn't. I don't know why.

Another way of preventing police observation of scoring is by keeping the dealer invisible. As one informant put it:

If the bulls don't know who's puttin' out they won't know who's scorin' will they?

This is often accomplished by having one person score for a number of colleagues, thereby reducing the amount of traffic to, say, a particular table or booth in a restaurant. Indeed, informants claimed that it is largely through traffic that dealing is inferred by police observers:

...so if they see people goin' back and forth, back and forth then they can say "Well I see so-and-so's puttin' out tonight."

Informants familiar with an earlier version of the community claimed that many participants in the current version could be characterized as "uncool" with regard to scoring. Whatever the underlying reason, however, it remains the case that, for longtime observers, scoring is considerably more detectable than it was at an earlier period in the history of the community. For them, this is a document of the fact that

...people aren't as careful anymore.

PACKING

For informants, the obscuring of scoring is in no way a guarantee that one has not been selected as a candidate for pursuit and investigation. Indeed, as one heroin user said of the police:

You can think you've got it made. You've been really cool and all of a sudden bang, there they are.

The next problem is transporting the heroin to the locale where it will be administered. Traditionally, participants in the local community have transported or "packed" heroin in their mouths. The heroin, made water-resistant in "score paper" (usually the foil from a cigarette package), a condom, or a balloon, can be swallowed should the police be encountered, and regurgitated intact at a more convenient time. In an earlier version of the heroin-using community this was received as the only sanctionable mode of packing. To do otherwise was understood as strange or foolish, the activity of someone not attuned to the reality of life-as-a-heroin-user. For example, an informant from that period answered the question:

Do you ever carry it anywhere else, like in your pocket or someplace?

in the following manner:

Oh fuck no. That's askin' for it if they jump ya. It'd be crazy to pack it anywhere else. Y'gotta be able to choke it down, unless you want to get pinched.

Current data, however, suggest that the practice of transporting heroin in the mouth is not as general as it was in a previous version of the community. The following excerpt from an interview reports a convicted trafficker's observation of a new diversity in packing styles:

R: So is it still pretty much the case that people pack in their mouth?
I: Some do, some don't. It used to be everybody did. You'd get score papers ready for them.
R: So there's people who aren't packing in their mouth?
I: Oh yeah. I think they're crazy but that's their business, y'know. If they get pinched that's their business.
R: So where do they carry it?
I: Oh in their pocket or their hand. Figure they can throw it away if they see the bulls.

For informants, transporting heroin in other than the traditional manner heightened the probability that police would be able to successfully obtain arrest-producing evidence. Thus,

...it's easier for the bulls now.

Early in the course of the research it was ascertained that, for the most part, heroin users did not regard arrest as the outcome of fate, chance, or bad luck. While some arrests were formulated as fortuitous it was understood that a clear majority could have been prevented had one only been more careful, less careless, or wiser. For longtime members of the community, the likelihood of arrest was minimized by following a set of time-honoured adaptive strategies. Recently, however, informants claim that numerous participants in the community are disregarding the strategies. In the words of informants, successful enforcement of narcotics violations has been facilitated because

...people aren't as careful anymore.

CONCLUDING REMARKS

The notion that official statistics have an unknowable relationship to the "actual" volume and morphology of criminal activity is, for most sociologists, no longer a matter of debate: that official statistics index something else is now well-established.

For the most part, the "something else" has been formulated as enforcement procedures. Indeed, over the past two decades many well-known and thoughtful studies have documented the role of official statistics in the construction of official portrayals of community law-breaking. Important as these studies are, however, they are neither definitive nor exhaustive of the "something else" such figures may index. While its parameters are unknown, the "something else" could include variations in criminal skill and technique, improvements in the technology of security, shifting community tolerances, and the like.

Drawing on a corpus of data produced by getting physically and perspectively "close" to participants in a heroin-using community, this report has examined a seldom-addressed element in the repertoire of possibilities that official statistics might reveal — the nature of the deviant community itself. In particular, focus has been upon the changes it is alleged to have undergone over time. As was shown, the erosion of community solidarity and the abandoning of certain adaptive practices have facilitated the enforcement of narcotics statutes. This, of course, should be a matter of significance for students of official statistics.

PART III

Theories of Crime and Delinquency

Before attempting to summarize and evaluate the many theories of crime and delinquency, it is necessary to indicate several of the problems involved in such a task. A first difficulty, as discussed in Parts One and Two, is that criminologists do not always agree on how concepts such as crime or delinquency should be defined. For obvious reasons, these disagreements prevent the establishment of any wide consensus regarding what it is that requires explanation.

For example, in Part One we introduced the consensus and conflict positions on the origins of criminal law. Briefly, consensus theorists argue that the criminal law arises out of agreed-upon norms, out of consensus (Carey, 1978; Hagan, 1985a). From this perspective, the law is viewed as an expression of the common will, and therefore needs no examination or scrutiny. It is those who break the law, rather than the law itself, that require study. Why did they break agreed-upon rules? What individual quirks or social conditions caused these norm violations? Consensus theories of crime therefore generally focus on the offenders (Hagan, 1985a).

On the other hand, conflict theorists see the law as reflecting the interests of the more powerful segments of society. Thus, from this viewpoint, it can be argued that the "causes" of crime are implicit in law and in the social interests behind the law. Conflict theorists argue, therefore, that explanations of crime should focus on the study of how laws are formed and how they are used to control the behaviour of the more powerless members of society.

Even if criminologists were to agree on a definition of crime, a second problem in explaining crime stems from the fact that criminal behaviour is so diverse that any one theory or explanation will almost certainly be inadequate. We need different explanations for the behaviour of a man who murders his wife than of a student who uses marijuana. Incest, embezzlement, mail fraud, and bank robbery, each a crime, may share little in common as to cause. Because of the diverse nature of criminal behaviours, some criminologists have argued that instead of seeking one theory for all crime there should be separate theories for different crimes (see Brady, 1983) or even several theories for each and every crime (see Scully and Marolla, 1985; Wittingham, 1981, for examples).

Only rarely, however, do criminologists attempt to integrate several theoretical positions or to synthesize the insights of the various disciplines — for instance, sociology, psychology, economics, and geography — that study crime (Pfohl, 1985). At present most of the explanations of crime are sociological, in that they attempt to locate the social causes of crime. This is because most criminologists are trained in sociology. Reflecting this bias, most of the theories presented in this text are also sociological. Before examining them, it may be instructive to present their predecessors, the earlier biological theories.

BIOLOGICAL THEORIES

One of the earliest criminological theorists was a nineteenth-century Italian physician named Lombroso (1876), who with his colleagues advocated biological theories of criminality (see Fink, 1938). Lombroso's work was based upon and followed closely Darwin's theory of evolution. Lambroso and his colleagues believed that many criminals are *atavists*, humans with animal-like traits who are lower on the evolutionary scale than non-criminals and thus more susceptible to crime. These individuals can be recognized by visible physical signs, such as excessive length of arms, or ears of unusual size. Unfortunately, these "born criminals," who account for about one-third of the entire criminal population, according to Lombroso, cannot be helped, as they are born that way and thus biologically determined. Other categories of Lombroso's typology include the *insane* (idiots, imbeciles, and hysterical women), the *criminaloid* (for whom situational factors play a part in precipitating crime), the *habitual criminal* (for whom crime is a way of life), and finally the *passionate criminal* (whose crime, such as murder, is committed in a fit of passion and is thus not likely to be repeated).

Lombroso's methodology was crude and his findings were later found to be incorrect. Problems with his physical measurements and his inadequate use of a control group of non-criminals for comparison purposes (he examined only criminals) proved to be Lombroso's downfall (Goring, 1913). Another weakness was that he ignored the problem of how criminal law is created, concentrating only on the motivations of the criminals. This oversight stemmed from his belief that there is a natural law, absolute and common to all societies. (We discussed this essentially consensus position and its shortcomings in Part One.) On the positive side Lombroso tried to be objective and deterministic, as opposed to the then popular free-will and self-determinist doctrine, and advocated the study of interrelated rather than single causes (Vold and Bernard, 1986). Perhaps Lombroso's two most significant contributions were: (1) his demand that the scientific method be applied to the study of crime, and (2)

the subsequent research his ideas stimulated.

However, biological theories are still being advanced and there is a biological chain stretching from Lombroso to the present day. In recent years, biological theories of crime have re-emerged as part of an interdisciplinary approach to explaining crime and deviance. One Canadian researcher has suggested, for instance, a direct link between neurological problems and criminal behaviour (Yeudall, 1977; see also Jackson, 1977). Yeudall argued that brain damage almost always afflicts the left side of the brain, the side that controls both moral and learning functions. Much of the damage is a result of nutritional deficiencies during pregnancy or severe illness (which may be class-related). Brain damage leads to learning problems, which lead to a chain of events that may result in conflict with the law.

A similar causal link is found in learning disability research (Carrier, 1986; Crealock, 1987; Dunivant, 1982). That research attempts to tie neurologically based learning disability (e.g., dyslexia, aphasia, hyperkinesis) to juvenile delinquency through a chain of events that includes learning problems, poor school performance, labelling by adults and peers, association with similar peers, dropping out of school, and, finally, increased susceptibility to delinquent behaviour (see, for examples, Murray, 1976; Ross, 1977; and Coons, 1982, for negative evidence). The causal chain suggested here is not inconsistent with most of the sociological theories discussed later in this chapter, nor is it inconsistent with sociological findings concerning the link between poor school performance and delinquency (Wolfgang et al., 1972; Hirschi, 1969). However, learning disability research emphasizes a different major cause — neurological malfunction. Unfortunately, this research is fraught with problems, not the least of which is the difficulty involved in measuring the independent variable (learning disabilities).

More generally, Wilson and Herrnstein (1985) have pointed out that if all influences on crime were cultural we would expect to find variance in the patterns of age and gender difference in crime commission. But instead we find a persistent relationship, in that young men from very different cultures are most likely to be involved in crime commission. These researchers have further argued that both intelligence and temperament are heritable and that either or both may be related to crime commission. The causal links between these factors are social (at times similar to the chain of events suggested by those studying learning disabilities). Wilson and Herrnstein maintained the existence of a causal chain that involves biological, psychological, and sociological factors. They interpreted the fact that identical twins have more similar rates of crime than fraternal twins as supportive of their position. Other writers, however, remain skeptical regarding the suggestion of a link between heredity and crime. In a review of the relevant research literature, Walters and White (1989) concluded that, although genetic factors are associated with various measures of crime or delinquency, research limitations prevent any simple interpretation of the data. They argued that one should not dismiss the genetic literature but that much better research is needed before criminologists can feel comfortable about the link between heredity and behaviours that are defined as criminal.

Most social scientists would probably agree that both biological and environmental factors play a role in antisocial behaviours. What they probably would not be able to agree on is the relative contribution of each to particular cases. One of the major problems with the research on biology and "maladaptive behaviours" is that virtually all studies use correlations to "prove" cause. That is, they find correlations between biochemical influences (particularly hormones) and maladaptive behaviour (Fishbein, 1990); and between psychophysiological variables (i.e., central nervous system disturbances) and psychopharmacological variables (i.e., drug use and personality) and maladaptive behaviours (Fishbein, 1990). Of course, social science cannot prove cause using correlation. After a rather exhaustive review of the literature in these areas Fishbein concluded:

How biological variables interact with social and psychological factors to produce human behaviour generally and antisocial behavior specifically is unknown...The bulk of biological studies...have examined only a few isolated variables and have generally failed to evaluate dynamic interrelationships among biological and socioenvironmental conditions. (1990:55)

Fishbein argued for more sophisticated models that interlink biological and environmental factors.

The conclusions of Fishbein (1990) and Walters and White (1989) are rather similar. That is, the research to date on biological factors and crime has not been adequate, and more sophisticated models and research are necessary. Unfortunately, the research that is needed to establish causal links between biology and crime may not be possible at this time. That is, the tools both for biological research and social research may not be complex enough to establish causal links with any certainty.

SOCIOLOGICAL THEORIES

Sociological explanations of crime causation have, as their basis, cultural or social determinism rather than biological determinism. In other words, they seek to understand how crime is made more likely by particular kinds of social arrangements, cultural environments, or patterns of interaction.

A review of the most influential sociological theories of crime and delinquency must be preceded by two caveats. First, any attempt to summarize several decades of sociological thought on the causes of crime requires the sacrifice of the subtleties of many of these arguments. The reader should be aware that more detailed reviews of the relevant theoretical and research literature are readily available (Downes and Rock, 1988; Pfohl, 1985; Nettler, 1984). Second, the classification scheme employed below is somewhat arbitrary, since many explanatory accounts reflect the influence of more than one theoretical tradition (Williams and McShane, 1988).

ECOLOGICAL THEORIES

Ecological theories attempt to understand the causes of crime in reference to environmental characteristics that make crime more or less likely. Such theories do not ask why some individuals tend to commit crimes but rather what social conditions make it likely that many people will (Blau and Blau, 1982). In general, ecological approaches are directed toward an understanding of why some communities (neighbourhoods or cities) have higher rates of crime than other communities.

The suggestion that an understanding of the structure of communities is important to an understanding of differences in levels of crime (Reiss, 1986) may be traced to the work of several sociologists who were affiliated with the University of Chicago in the first several decades of this century.

On the basis of his observations of the city of Chicago, Burgess (1923) suggested that modern cities exhibit a pattern of five concentric circles or zones, from the center out, with each area reflecting distinctive living arrangements. Zone one is the central downtown business core of the city, zone two the downtrodden slum area of transition waiting to be annexed to the business core, zone three the working-class homes, zone four the middle-class residential area, and zone five the commuter suburbs. Shaw and McKay (1942) then applied this concentric-zone model to the study of delinquency. They found that as one moves toward the city core and away from the suburbs one finds not only increasing rates of delinquency, but also increasing rates of crime, truancy, mental disorder, infant mortality, and tuberculosis.

Furthermore, Shaw and McKay found that these forms of social pathology were unrelated to changes in ethnic population or population composition. They argued that regardless of which ethnic group inhabits the transitional run-down area, the social pathology rates are high and they stay proportionately the same in zone-by-zone comparisons. This implies that factors associated with the zones, such as denial of economic opportunity, ethnic segregation, and physical deterioration, rather than the specific characteristics of the people living there, are associated with the relative incidence of social problems such as crime and delinquency.

For Shaw and McKay and others whose research followed the Chicago tradition, the concentration of crime in inner-city urban neighbourhoods is best explained with reference to the high levels of "social disorganization" that may be said to characterize such areas. Althought the term social disorganization has been defined and used in a number of different ways, it generally refers to the breakdown of the formal and informal mechanisms that are normally thought to regulate behaviour and thus to discourage juvenile as well as adult criminal conduct. Specifically, it may be argued that the greater degree of poverty, family dissolution, ethnic heterogeneity, and other associated conditions prevents the effective exercise of community control and in turn leads to higher delinquency rates.

The work of Shaw and McKay stimulated considerable debate among subsequent generations of sociologists. Much of this empirical research and theoretical thinking criticized their initial efforts. Some writers argued, for instance, that the charge that high-delinquency areas were socially disorganized reflected nothing more than the value biases of the Chicago sociologists and their unwillingness or inability to recognize that such areas were not disorganized but rather were organized differently from the middle-class communities with which they were more familiar (Mills, 1943; Whyte, 1955). A second problem identified by critics concerns the fact that although ecological theory can be used as a predictive model of gross rates of crime and delinquency in terms of their general location in a metropolis, it is not as useful in predicting *individual* crime and delinquency — that is, which individuals in the area will become criminal. Third, empirical attempts to replicate the findings of Shaw and McKay have frequently been unsuccessful (Lander, 1954). Finally, it may be argued that many of the ecological studies that employed official crime data have been unable to determine whether there are more or different *reactions* to crime in some areas, rather than more actual crime)see, for example, O'Brien, 1985; Hagan, Gillis, and Chan, 1978). More will be said about this in the section on labelling.

In recent years, ecological approaches to the study of crime and delinquency have undergone a resurgence of interest (Byrne and Sampson, 1986; Reiss and Tonry, 1986; Figlio et al., 1986). This resurgence has been spurred by the development of more powerful techniques for data analysis and by the availability of alternative data sources (such as victimization surveys, see Sampson 1986c; Laub, 1983). While this recent work finds its origins in the pioneering efforts of Shaw and McKay and other Chicago sociologists, it represents a more sophisticated approach to understanding the relationship between levels of crime and the dynamics of community life.

For example, Sampson (1986a) investigated how variations in rates of urban crime are related to city differences in levels of formal and informal social control. For research purposes, formal control was defined in terms of jail-incarceration risk and police aggressiveness, while family structure was employed as a measure of informal control. Such an analytical framework suggests continuity with the view of Chicago sociologists of crime as the product of poorly regulated communities. Using data from 171 American cities with a population greater than 100,000 in 1980, Sampson found that as levels of both types of control decrease, rates of crime increase.

Sherman, Gartin, and Buerger (1989) argued that much ecological research has tended to restrict itself to the study of relatively large aggregates (cities or neighbourhoods) and in so doing has obscured important distinctions among places that constitute such aggregates. They stressed instead the study of "hot spots" of crime (street addresses and intersections), which allow finer distinctions to be made with respect to the manner in which crime is distributed across the urban landscape. Using data on more than 300,000 calls to police in the city of Minneapolis over a one-year period, Sherman and his colleagues found that relatively few hot spots produced most of the calls to police. Thus, 50% of the calls involved only 3% of the 115,000 addresses and intersections. Such findings raise important questions about the importance that researchers have traditionally attached to larger ecological units.

Stark (1987) has attempted to synthesize several decades of ecological research in order to develop a theory of "deviant places." In essence, the theory argues that:

(1) high crime-rate areas are characterized by several distinct physical and social characteristics, including poverty, density, and a transient population

(2) residents may react to such conditions in ways that promote "moral cynicism," increased criminal opportunities, increased motivation to deviate, and diminished social control

(3) these reactions not only increase the amount of crime directly but also do so indirectly by attracting deviant people to the area, by driving out those who are least deviant, and by further reducing social control.

Stark's theory, which is stated in the form of thirty interrelated propositions, is likely to generate considerable research interest in the future.

Generally, applications of ecological theory to the study of crime and delinquency in Canada have been few and relatively recent (see, for instance, Jarvis and Messinger, 1975; Hagan, Gillis, and Chan, 1978; Engstad, 1980; Gabor and Gotteil, 1984). One possible reason for the lack involves the inapplicability of American models of urban process to the study of Canadian cities (Goldberg and Mercer, 1986; Guest, 1969; Sacco, 1985).

STRAIN THEORIES

Strain theories locate the causes of criminal conduct in the attempts that people make to solve problems that society presents to them. Merton's (1938) theory of *anomie* is probably the version of strain theory that has gained the most attention. Material success is the main goal of North American society, according to Merton, and almost everyone is expected to try to be successful. The capitalist economy in which we live, however, is based on inequalities and thus not everyone is able to obtain that material success. (Changing or lowering one's goals or aspirations is not recognized as a desirable option. Merton calls individuals who lower their goals "ritualists," and those who "drop out" "retreatists" — neither of which concerns us here.) Hence, persons lacking legitimate means to success may feel pressured to use illegitimate means to achieve the goals society says they should be achieving. Merton uses the term *anomie* to describe this discrepancy between the goals of a society and access to the legitimate means to obtain them. The more anomie that exists in a society, the greater the pressure toward crime.

Merton added that lower-class individuals are more often denied legitimate means; thus most feel the pressure of anomie and more frequently become criminal offenders, or "innovators," in Merton's terminology. Such an image of the class distribution of crime is consistent with images provided by official statistics (Pfohl, 1985).

Critics of Merton have pointed, however, to the great amount of upper-class or white-collar crime, which anomie theory is less successful in explaining. They argue that many people with access to legitimate means are also criminal, while most lower-class individuals with curtailed access to legitimate means do not engage in serious criminal activity but instead lower their goals, becoming "ritualists." Many writers, such as Tittle (1983), question the relationship between social class and crime; others, like Agnew (1984b), argue that *low*, not high, aspirations may be related to deviance.

The theory also does not provide us with guidance regarding why individuals differ in their choice of deviant adaptations. In other words, why do some people lower their aspirations and use legitimate means, while others refuse to lower their aspirations and thus adopt illegitimate means (Cloward and Ohlin, 1960; Jackson, 1984)? Moreover, the utility of the theory may be limited to the explanation of "instrumental crimes" that involve some type of material goal; it may be less useful in explaining expressive-emotional crimes, for example, a murder in the heat of passion, or a barroom assault. Finally, like most traditional accounts of crime and deviance, Merton's anomie theory would seem to have relatively little to say about the occurrence of female crime or delinquency (Pfohl, 1985).

From the perspective of Canadian criminology, one may speculate whether Merton's anomie theory can be applied to the Canadian case without a review of what our major values are and how they compare with those of Americans. In fact, in one study, Rokeach (1974) suggested that Canadians are less materialistic, and if this is generally true, then Canadians may have fewer anomie pressures toward crime than U.S. citizens.

In an important reformulation of strain theory *Cohen* (1955) argued that many working-class male adolescents cannot achieve according to middle-class standards, and find it especially difficult to do well in the middle-class-dominated school system. These boys then tend to gravitate toward one another, and together attempt to develop new norms and standards by which they can succeed. Sensing failure and contempt, they create new criteria for success that are directly opposite to middle-class standards, but that are achievable (Cohen, 1955:65-66). These new norms take the form of a rejecting counter-culture, then antisocial behaviour, and, ultimately, gang delinquency. Essentially these boys are of the type Merton called innovators — individuals who lack conventional means to achieve common success goals.

Cloward and Ohlin (1960) developed a theory of delinquency and opportunity that suggested an important refinement of Merton's original argument. They argued that while the strain toward anomie may encourage criminality, it does not determine the types of criminal conduct in which anomic individuals become involved. This will depend upon the illegitimate opportunities available to them.

In substantive terms, Cloward and Ohlin focused upon the study of lower-class urban juvenile gangs and argued that these youth become delinquent because they experience "a marked discrepancy between culturally induced aspirations ... and the possibilities of achieving them by legitimate means" (1960:78). Because lower-class youth cannot achieve as easily as middle-class youth, they may become alienated from the dominant society. They then may externalize the blame for their failure onto that society and seek a group solution to their perceived problems. Delinquent acts occur after this alienation develops. Cloward and Ohlin see these acts as far more rational than Cohen does. In their opinion, the acts serve as solutions to the anomie problem faced by the youth. Such solutions are found in groups organized around specific delinquent activities, and in these groups ideologies and rules of behaviour take shape.

Concerning opportunity, Cloward and Ohlin hypothesized two opportunity structures for attaining society's success goals. One is legitimate; delinquents aspire to this but cannot realize it. The other opportunity structure is illegitimate; it is attractive, but not always available to delinquents. This structure offers illegal means for attaining success. Since there are differing opportunities to learn particular illegal means, there are three possible delinquent subcultures: the *criminal*, the *conflict*, and the *retreatist*.

The *criminal* gang flourishes where younger adults and youths of all ages mix, and where petty criminals freely interact with non-criminal individuals. Youths in this situation have the opportunity to learn criminal activity from others who are slightly older than themselves. They also have adult role models to emulate, for example, successful pimps or gamblers. The major activities of the criminal juvenile gang involve offences like theft and extortion.

In areas where youths do not mix with older people and/or there are no criminal adult role models, the type of delinquent group that develops is known as the *conflict* gang. These gangs develop in disorganized slums, and behaviour is centered on fighting and gang wars.

The third subculture is called the *retreatist* subculture (cf. Merton, 1957). Possessing neither the conventional nor the criminal means, the individuals attracted to this subculture are, in essence, double failures. Their activity revolves around some kind of illicit consumption, such as drug taking. There is often some theft involved as well, since theft may be necessary to maintain drug habits.

The major contribution of Cloward and Ohlin's theory to criminology has been to direct attention to the role played by illegitimate means in criminogenic processes. Although the theory has not been fully supported empirically (for example, see Agnew, 1984b), it is also worth noting that some aspects of the theory have proved useful in the examination of the neglected topic of female criminality (Adler, 1975). Steffensmeier (1983), for example, described how women are denied equal opportunity in crime.

As Downes and Rock (1988:111) noted, it is probably correct in the present period to characterize strain theory as "distinctly out of fashion." Its dominance as an explanation of crime was successfully challenged in the 1960s by a number of competing accounts including labelling, conflict, and control theories. Still, there continues to exist interest in the development and refinement of the strain argument. Blau and Blau (1982), for instance, utilized the basic premises of strain theory in their analysis of urban variations in rates of violent crime. They theorized and attempted to illustrate empirically that urban violence is markedly influenced by levels of income inequality, particularly when income inequality is reinforced by strong patterns of racial inequality.

Agnew (1985) offered a revised version of strain theory intended to correct many of the limitations of earlier formulations. While older versions of strain theory focused upon the blockage of goal-seeking behaviour, Agnew viewed strain as resulting from the blockage of pain-avoidance behaviour. Adolescents, he argued, are forced to remain in certain environments such as the family or the school, and if these environments are a source of pain or hardship for the adolescent, there is little that he or she legally can do to escape. This blockage is likely to be a source of frustration and may lead to illegal escape (running away from home) or anger-based delinquency (violence or vandalism). An empirical test of the theory using data collected from a national sample of American youth lends considerable support to the argument.

Mitchell (1984) also attempted to reformulate strain theory so as to increase its usefulness. His revision of the argument rests upon a distinction between "anomic" and "alienated" individuals. The former, identified by Merton and others, are most suitably described as people who feel less than competent to perform the roles that society expects them to perform. Alienated persons, on the other hand, are those who feel that their abilities exceed their role expectations. Whereas the former type of disjunction as a source of deviance has been recognized since the publication of Merton's original argument, Mitchell suggested that less attention has been paid to the latter type of imbalance, which may also be a source of strain and thus of deviance. For example, assembly-line workers who do not feel challenged by the nature of the work may commit acts of sabotage by purposefully misusing equipment or damaging products. The value of Mitchell's analysis is that it suggests how the logic of strain theory may be applied both to an understanding of many non-traditional forms of crime and deviance and to an understanding of nonconformity in the middle and upper classes.

CULTURAL THEORIES

Cultural theories argue that people become criminals because their socialization experiences expose them to beliefs, values, and norms that permit or encourage nonconformist conduct. These sources of crime are thus seen to reside in the cultural environments that individuals inhabit rather than in the individuals themselves.

Edwin Sutherland provided criminology with perhaps the most influential version of cultural theory. His theory of *differential association* maintains that one learns criminality in the same manner that one learns any other behaviour. For Sutherland, society could be characterized as being in a state of "differential social organization" such that there exist groups that carry and transmit conventional conformist values and groups that carry and transmit criminal values. As individuals associate with one of these groups rather than the other, they will come to see the world through the cultural lenses that that group provides. Thus, people become criminal because they learn to be criminal through association with others who transmit cultural values and beliefs supportive of criminality. For Sutherland, then, one learns but be criminal in essentially the same manner that one learns any other occupational, recreational, or cultural activity. This position may not sound radical in the 1990s, but, when initially formulated, Sutherland's theory had to compete with the previous biological theories, which argued that criminality is not learned but innate. Sutherland's theory gained wide popularity and the differential association hypothesis was expanded and refined, as several editions of his book *Principles of Criminology* were published (Sutherland, 1939; Sutherland and Cressey, 1978).

On the whole, differential association theory is today less prominent than before, despite attempts to broaden (Glaser, 1956) and reformulate (Burgess and Akers, 1966; Akers, 1985) the central argument. Because of the difficulty of testing the theory and its omission of the "causes" of the transmitted culture of crime, it is used either in conjunction with other theories or as a general orientation, rather than as a specific explanation of crime.

Differential association theory in many respects resembles Thorsten Sellin's (1938) theory of culture conflict. For Sellin, crime in complex heterogeneous societies results from the clash between the traditional cultures of ethnic groups and the culture of the dominant society, which is codified in law. For example, because Canada is a multi-ethnic society, there are groups of people in our society with allegiance to two sets of cultural values — the culture of the "larger Canadian society" and the culture of a specific ethnic group. Sellin argued that culture conflict involves those situations in which ethnic norms conflict with the norms embodied in legal codes. Thus, some immigrants to Canada may bring with them the belief that it is appropriate to use physical violence in the defence of personal honour. The law, and the wider society from which the law might be seen to derive, may define the violent defence of personal honour as criminal assault.

It might be argued that since Canada is frequently claimed to be more of an "ethnic mosaic" than a "melting pot" it is therefore a society in which cultural groups are more likely to maintain their separate identities and in which the potential for culture conflict is greater (Martin and White, 1988). However, it can also be argued that the fundamental norms of this society are not markedly dissimilar from the norms of the cultures from which we draw the bulk of our immigrants. Moreover, since most crime in Canada is committed by people born in Canada, culture conflict cannot be used as a major explanation of criminal activity.

Sellin's theory of culture conflict became

very popular in a historic period during which much of the crime in North America was attributed to rapid and large-scale immigration. The argument has also been applied to other societies that have experienced rapid immigration (Rahav, 1981). Although the value of the culture conflict model has been disputed by some empirical researchers, it may still have some limited utility. For instance, Ribordy (1980) discussed how the culture conflict experienced by Italian immigrants in Montreal is related to levels of criminal offending.

Wolfgang and Ferracuti (1967) applied the logic of cultural theory to an understanding of the specific problem of criminal violence. Their theory is more focused than many theories of crime or delinquency, since it concerns itself with only one type of behaviour. At the same time, however, it is more general, since it is intended to have applicability beyond the North American context. In fact, the data in support of their "subculture of violence" argument are drawn from many nations and many historical periods.

Their thesis suggests that there are subgroups of individuals within any society in which the use of violence is valued and encouraged:

The development of favourable attitudes toward, and the use of, violence in this subculture involves learned behavior in the process of differential learning, association, or identification. The use of violence in a subculture is not necessarily viewed as illicit conduct, and the users, therefore, do not have to deal with feelings of guilt about their aggression. (Wolfgang and Ferracuti, 1967:314)

Thus violence is a learned value, which is acquired in the same manner as are other values. If individuals are raised in a violence-approving subculture and learn to positively regard violence as either an appropriate means to an end or as an end in itself, then it is likely that they will behave violently when the situation is conducive to their doing so.

The subculture-of-violence theory may prove useful in explaining at least some urban violent crime in Canada. However, empirical tests of the thesis have, thus far, been discouraging. While some researchers continue to argue that geographic differences in levels of violence lend support to the subculture argument (Rosenfeld, 1986), others maintain that these differences are better explained by reference to socioeconomic rather than cultural factors (Blau and Blau, 1982; Loftin and Hill, 1974; Parker, 1989).

As a final example of cultural theory, Claude Fischer (1975, 1976) has attempted to wed ecological and subcultural accounts in order to explain why cities generally have higher rates of crime than less urban places. With respect to crime, or any type of cultural activity, he argued that the sheer size of cities allows for the development of a "critical mass" of individuals that permits and sustains distinctive lifestyles. Thus, the concentration of people in one place who share an interest, talent, or preference allows for the development of subcultural worlds that are frequently organized around unconventional values. In towns or villages, on the other hand, the absolute number of deviant or criminal individuals will be smaller, and when crime does occur in such settings, it is less likely to take a subcultural form. Because big cities facilitate subcultural growth and diversity, urbanism is inevitably associated with crime and other forms of deviance:

Large population size provides a "critical mass" of criminals and customers for crime in the same way it provides a critical mass of customers for other services. The aggregation of population promotes "markets" of clients — people interested in purchasing drugs or the services of prostitutes, for example; and it provides a sufficient concentration of potential victims — for example, affluent persons and their property. Size also provides a critical mass of criminals sufficient to generate organization, supportive services (such as fences, "bought" policemen and a criminal underground) and full-time specialization. (Fischer 1976:93)

While Fischer (1976) marshalled considerable evidence in support of his subcultural theory of urbanism, a comprehensive test of the hypothesis by Tittle (1989) produced mixed findings.

In general terms, the utility of cultural and subcultural theories for Canadian criminologists resides in the fact that they can be applied to any setting in which a group of people have norms and values that are different from the majority norms and values. As mentioned above, this is descriptive of the Canadian case as well as of other large, heterogeneous societies.

On the other hand, however, such theories are judged by many to be deficient in several respects. Nettler (1984) and Hagan (1984) suggested that their reasoning is circular. Such theories explain illegal or delinquent behaviour by arguing that the individuals so engaged possess values that are supportive of such activities. Thus, in a sense, they merely describe what we already know and do not tell us which conditions are conducive to holding the values that are favourable to illegal or delinquent conduct. Also, the proportion of criminality or delinquency accounted for by cultural rather than by individual factors is not known. It is possible that much of what has been labelled "subcultural" crime is in fact "situational" crime, in that it occurs in response to opportunities available in particular areas at particular times, or that it results from pressures placed on individuals in groups, even when they do not share a common culture (Matza, 1964).

SOCIAL CONTROL THEORY

Social control theories proceed from the assumption that people will refrain from engaging in criminal or delinquent conduct only to the extent that they are pressured to do so. Rather than emphasize the factors that motivate nonconformity, they attempt to account for the factors that discourage or control it. When such factors are weak or non-existent, rule-breaking behaviour will be an inevitable result. Whereas other theories assume conformity and attempt to explain deviance, control theories argue that it is safer to assume that people will deviate and that it is therefore necessary to explain why so many conform.

Control theorists maintain that if individuals are to conform to normative expectations, they must be taught the lessons of conformity. From a sociological point of view, the training of individuals to conform is known as *socialization*. The essence of socialization involves reward and punishment. While psychological principles indicate that reward techniques are more effective than punishment techniques in producing desired outcomes, most of those involved in the socialization of children (parents and teachers) combine punishment and reward. Society expects from such efforts a group of individuals who share a core of common values and who possess the skills necessary to interact with one another with only minimal conflict. The interactive techniques of etiquette, politeness, and good citizenship are all examples of these trained behaviours.

Not everyone, however, responds to the training in the same way. Some respond quickly, some slowly; and some trainers are more effective than others. Thus in the long run, some individuals are more likely than others to conform. Individuals who do not conform might be thought of as products of poor or inadequate socialization. In speaking of adult criminals we may indicate that "something went wrong with their childhood or upbringing." Perhaps their antisocial impulses were not punished enough or their pro-social activities not rewarded sufficiently. When we make such comments, we are tacitly accepting the tenets of control theory.

Research concerning social control and crime generally examines either how socialization leads to conformity or how punishment decreases nonconformity. Probably the greatest amount of research and theory involves this latter, negative, aspect of social control, that is, the potential of punishment for deterring criminal activities. Beccaria (1764) and Bentham (1843), early social control theorists, for example, saw people as hedonists or pleasure seekers, and argued that in order to deter crime the state must make the potential punishment and pain for crime greater than its potential pleasures and rewards. Rational individuals would then conform in order to avoid the pain and punishment that would follow criminal activity. More specifically, they argued, the more certain, the more severe, the more public, and the quicker the punishment, the less crime there would be.

Over the last several decades, considerable research attention has been directed toward the study of crime deterrence (Gibbs, 1975; Fattah, 1983; Zimring and Hawkins, 1973). While theoretical and methodological approaches to the problem do not allow this literature to be easily summarized, it appears that "(s)everity of punishment is probably less important in deterring crime than certainty of punishment" (Conklin, 1986:409). In addition, in a review of relevant experimental studies, Clark (1988) concluded that although the swiftness (or celerity) of punishment appears to be an important aspect of the deterrence process, its importance is diminished when other factors are taken into account.

As stated, a second variant of control theory is less concerned with punishment and emphasizes instead the "positive" role that socialization plays in the promotion of conformity. Thus, from this perspective, socialization is seen as the process that results in the establishment of strong social bonds between the individual and others in society who are carriers of conformist values. When such bonds are effective, they discourage delinquent or criminal conduct.

The best known version of this argument has been provided by Travis Hirschi (1969). According to Hirschi, when our connections to conformist others are meaningful, we are forced to take their opinions into account when we act. If, however, we are detached from those who hold values of conformity, we are free to do as we please — and frequently this may mean that we are free to behave in a criminal fashion. For Hirschi, the "bond to society" can be conceptualized as being made up of four distinct but related strands. The first element, *attachment*, refers to the degree to which individuals are sensitive to the expectations of others who represent the world of conformity. The second element, *commitment*, refers to investments of time and energy made to conventional lines of activity; the greater these investments the more likely they are to discourage criminal behaviour that might place them in jeopardy. *Involvement* refers to the extent to which time and energy are used up by non-criminal pursuits and thus made unavailable for the exploration of criminal opportunity. Finally, what Hirschi terms *belief* refers to perceptions that conformist values are deserving of respect. Hirschi's version of control theory suggests that, rather than threatening punishment, one should attempt to induce conformity by attaching individuals to society with positive bonds, that is, by making them want to conform.

A somewhat more complicated version of the control argument is found in the work of Matza (1964; Sykes and Matza, 1957), who suggested that the relationship between the bond to society and delinquent behaviour must be understood in situational terms (Liska, 1981). Matza maintained that in order to commit delinquent acts, youths must be able to rationalize their behaviour and thus be released from the moral constraints that would normally prohibit the performance of these acts. The rationalization process that allows youth to "drift" in and out of delinquency is known as *neutralization*. Through this process the law may be temporarily and sporadically deprived of moral constraint to the point where the offender is able to transgress it. Matza describes a "negation of events," a feeling on the part of the delinquents that the deviant acts are not really important, that people act that way all the time, or that adults are allowed to get away with similar acts and thus there is no reason why they should not also get away with them. For example, alcohol regulations may be considered irrational by juveniles, auto theft may be redefined as "joy-riding," and vandalism may come to be viewed as a harmless prank. Hence the juveniles question the moral validity of such rules, find them wanting, and feel free to violate them. By neutralizing the law, they create a situation in which they are free to choose whether to violate it.

Hagan (1984) criticized Matza's neutralization theory by arguing that it underestimates the pleasures of delinquency, and ignores the fact that delinquents engage in criminal activities because of the rewards they reap. Moreover, delinquents may not need to neutralize guilt, because they do not feel all that guilty. Remorse, if present at all, results from being caught, rather than from the harm of the act. As well, their neutralizations may be offered as justifications *after* the act and may not be the causes of the act itself. Still, the concept of neutralization continues to be viewed by many as offering a useful insight into the problems of crime and victimization (Ferraro and Johnson, 1983; Scully and Marolla, 1985).

The most recent and most sophisticated version of control theory has been formulated by Hagan, Simpson, and Gillis (Hagan et al., 1979, 1985, 1987, 1988). Their work offers an analysis of why male rather than female adolescents are more frequently involved in delinquent activity. In constructing a theoretical account of this pattern they attempted to integrate the logic of control theory with insights offered by Marxian and feminist criminologists.

Their theoretical approach, which Hagan and his colleagues term "power-control theory," maintains that gender differences in delinquency are rooted in historical changes that have assigned men and women to different social realms and have created differences in the kinds of social control to which each gender group is subjected. Specifically, as modern industrial economies developed, there emerged a sphere of consumption and a sphere of production. The former is best typified by the home environment (to which women were largely segregated), while the latter is best typified by the workplace (in which men have largely been dominant). The growth of the criminal justice system, which coincided with these economic changes, was largely concerned with the regulation of behaviour in the public sphere. As a result, criminal justice has had more to do with controlling the behaviour of men than the behaviour of women. By contrast, the household has come to be characterized by informal rather than formal control processes in which women are more actively involved than men. Hagan and his colleagues argued that these changes have stratified social control in such a way that men more than women have become both the "instruments" and "objects" of formal control, while women more than men have become the "instruments" and "objects" of informal control.

They also argued that the family, because it is the social agency primarily responsible for early socialization, provides the means by which these differences are maintained from one generation to the next. This implies that mothers more than fathers are assigned the responsibility for the control of children and that daughters more than sons are subjected to these control processes. The authors argued

(and attempted to illustrate empirically) that these differences are maintained through patterns of social control of offsprings' attitudes toward risk taking. The socialization of daughters may encourage passivity and in so doing may prepare females for "the cult of domesticity." The socialization of sons, however, frees males from many of the forms of control that might discourage risk taking and thus prepares them for activities associated with the production sphere. Since much delinquency may be understood as risk-taking activity, gender differences in delinquent conduct follow logically from these more general differences in socialization processes.

As several writers have noted, the body of evidence that has accumulated in support of the general logic of social control theory is quite impressive (Hagan, 1985b; Vold and Bernard, 1986). Still, some critics question the assumptions from which such arguments proceed. Thio (1988) for instance argued that the distinction that is frequently made in control theory between individual deviants and the world of "conformist others" is too simplistic to capture the cultural pluralism of complex societies. Others doubt the generalizability of control arguments, given that most of the supporting research has involved the study of adolescent populations only. Perhaps the most frequently voiced criticism of control theory, however, concerns the charge that it is inattentive to the possible ways in which the application of social control might increase — rather than reduce — the propensity to criminality. This is a theme that has been pursued in the context of societal reaction theories.

SOCIETAL REACTION THEORIES

Societal reaction theories attempt to understand crime or delinquency as outcomes that result from interactions involving offenders and agents of social control such as police or judges. Thus, crime is not seen as something that emerges full-blown from the motivations or values of the criminal but rather as rooted in the social exchange between those who are judged to be law-breakers and those who make those judgements. Societal reaction theories attempt to demonstrate that the behaviour of those who are supposedly involved in the control of crime may actually have consequences that produce the opposite effect.

Most of the research and theorizing on the role of societal reaction in generating crime has been organized in terms of a set of arguments known as the labelling perspective. This approach to the study of crime and control gained considerable popularity in the 1960s and 1970s and exerted considerable influence on an entire generation of sociologists.

In simple terms, labelling theorists argue that the response of control agents to a presumed law-breaker may create conditions that increase the probability of further (and perhaps more serious) rule breaking. Thus, the application of labels such as "criminal" or "delinquent" may create a self-fulfilling prophecy such that the individual who is so labelled comes to behave in ways that are consistent with the behavioural expectations that such labels embody. Labelling theorists encourage us to ask two important questions about the relationship between crime and the labelling process: (1) what factors determine who does and who does not end up being labelled?; (2) what consequences does the application of these labels have for the labelled individuals?

With respect to the first question, labelling theory suggests that criminality is more evenly distributed throughout the social system than police or other types of official statistics would lead us to believe. Thus, the over-representation of crime in the lower social classes or among ethnic minorities may be thought to reflect the uneven application of legal control rather than the greater tendency on the part of some groups in society to engage in criminal conduct. Several factors such as race or economic status may be thought to affect the likelihood that an individual will be arrested by the police or sentenced by the court. It has also been argued that offence characteristics (such as the visibility of the act or the relationship between the victim and the offender) as well as characteristics of the social control agencies themselves (the size of the agency, organizational priorities, resources available) may also affect the directional flow of social control activity. For example, Pfohl (1985:289) states:

imagine a police officer late at night on a darkened street. She has just received word that a burglar is nearby. She turns the corner and sees a figure in an alley. Will she apprehend the person? Will a formal deviant label be applied? Think of all the social contingencies which might affect the officer's actions: the person's gender, size, color, age, mode of dress, way of walking, manner of speech. Also of importance might be pressures from the department to make more arrests, the presence of witnesses, or the kind of neighborhood and whether the suspect is perceived as the type of person who would normally be found in such a place. The interaction of all these factors is important to an analysis of the formal labeling process. [From Pfohl, *Images of Deviance and Social Control*, (New York: McGraw-Hill, 1985). Reproduced with permission.]

Moreover, labelling theorists argue that societal reactions tend to be less punitive and less frequent in the case of upper-class crimes, such as price fixing or bribery, which cost us huge amounts of money (Snider, 1988a; Goff and Reasons, 1978; Pontell et al., 1982 for medical fraud), rather than in the case of under-class crimes, such as robbery and break and enter.

As stated, the second set of issues raised by labelling theorists concerns the effects of labelling processes. One of the first sociologists to focus attention on this problem was Tannenbaum (1938). He argued that if children are labelled as "bad" and then segregated from "good" children, they are more likely to continue their deviance than if they are simply ignored. A change in self-concept occurs *because* of the labelling, and this change gets worse with each subsequent labelling. These children come to think of themselves as bad and isolate themselves, or are isolated from, conforming others. Eventually they move closer to deviant groups that have antisocial values, they spend much of their time attacking the labellers, and ultimately they engage in deviance because they are cut off from legitimate alternatives. This cycle is repeated with each new "delinquent" act.

Lemert (1951) attempted to understand this process in a somewhat more systematic manner, introducing a distinction between what he called "primary" and "secondary" deviance. According to Lemert, primary deviance refers to those types of rule-breaking behaviour that are engaged in by many members of society, but do not attract the attention of control agents and have no serious implications for the self-concept of the rule-breaker. Although most of us have at one time or another broken the law (i.e., fighting, shoplifting, etc.), we do not see ourselves as criminal for having done so. Lemert would suggest that this is largely because our actions are transitory and episodic and, in most cases, do not attract the attention of social control agents. Lemert argued that there is an important difference between such acts of primary deviance and what he defined as secondary deviance. The latter term refers to the behaviour of the person who is immersed in a deviant role and whose self-concept is organized around a deviant lifestyle. For Lemert, the central task of the sociologist is to explain how the processes of societal reaction transform primary deviance into secondary deviance. In a similar manner, Becker (1963) maintained that an understanding of nonconformity requires an appreciation of the role of societal reaction in the development of *deviant careers*.

For Lemert, Becker, and many other labelling theorists, the societal reaction process is a complex one. If an individual on the basis of an isolated criminal act attracts the attention of control agents, this may have very important implications for the ways in which others see that individual and ultimately for how that individual sees himself or herself. The application of an emotionally laden label such as "criminal" or "delinquent" will influence the quality and quantity of subsequent interaction in which that individual is involved. The individual may be stigmatized (Goffman, 1963) and isolated from conformist others. As opportunities for association with conventional others become blocked, opportunities for association with criminal others may open up. When conventional people do interact with the stigmatized individual, they may do so largely in terms of the negative stereotypes (Simmons, 1969) that they have come to associate with people who bear these labels. These stereotypes may encourage the individual to adopt a self-image consistent with the expectations contained in these stereotypes. The overall effect of the societal reaction according to this logic is to increase the likelihood that sporadic acts of nonconformity will coalesce into stable patterns.

Analyses such as those provided by Tannenbaum, Lemert, Becker, and other labelling theorists have been useful in forging a reconceptualization of the relationship between crime and social control. However, in recent years, the influence of labelling theory has diminished considerably, in part due to the growth of a large body of critical literature which has questioned the validity of the perspective (Nettler, 1984; Sagarin, 1975; Wellford, 1975). The central arguments of labelling theory have not been consistently supported by the available empirical evidence. While some studies do verify these theoretical claims (Farrington, 1977; Jensen, 1972; Schwartz and Skolnick, 1962), many do not (Gove, 1975; Nettler, 1984; Sagarin, 1975). Moreover, much of the supportive evidence is impressionistic and anecdotal (Gibbons, 1979) and does not stand up well to methodological scrutiny (Nettler, 1984).

In the absence of a compelling empirical case, critics have concluded that, while labelling processes may play a role in the development of criminal careers, they are probably not as important as proponents of the perspective make them out to be (Nettler, 1984; Vold and Bernard, 1986) — especially in the case of serious, repetitive, criminal offending (Hagan, 1985a).

Finally, although societal reaction theorists have directed most of their attention to the study of labelling processes, control responses may increase crime in other ways as well. Gary Marx (1981), for instance, identified three such processes. The first, *escalation*, refers to those situations in which an event occurs because of an intervention by control agents. For example, if the police "over-react" to a peaceful protest, a riot could result. A second process, *non-enforcement*, involves the police allowing some types of crimes to occur in order that they may pursue what they believe to be larger control objectives. In such cases, the police may, for example, allow an underworld informer to pursue a life of crime as long as the individual agrees to supply the police with information that they deem useful. Finally, Marx notes, control authorities may engage in *covert facilitation*, which involves deceptive actions taken by authorities in order to promote criminal activity. We recognize covert facilitation in the behaviour of the "decoy" intended to attract the attention of potential muggers or in the actions of the undercover police officer who attempts to initiate a drug deal.

The general value of societal reaction approaches derives from the fact that they encourage us to recognize that it is useful to conceptualize the activities of control agents such as the police as something other than mere reactions to the behaviour of criminal offenders. While many critics appreciate the insights derived from such an approach, they argue that societal reaction theorists do not pursue the issues that they raise to their logical conclusions. In other words, while societal reaction theorists focus our attention upon the role of power and conflict in the creation of crime, they do not draw explicit linkages between the activities of control agents and the larger social structure. This question was taken up by conflict theorists who, while building upon the work of societal reaction writers, took the study of crime and social control in new directions.

CONFLICT THEORIES

The distinct types of theories that we label conflict theories construe social conflict as the most central dynamic to which theoretical explanations of crime and delinquency must be attentive. These theories reject the assumption that societies are based upon a shared consensus about important norms and values. Instead, they assume that the most noteworthy feature of any complex society is the presence of conflict between segments of that society that differ from each other in terms of the social power and other resources to which they have access. The important task for criminological theory, conflict theorists argue, is to understand processes of law making and law breaking in a manner that takes the conflict-oriented nature of society into account.

At the risk of over-simplification, it is possible to recognize two broad categories of conflict theory (Williams and McShane, 1988; also see Bernard, 1981; Gibbons, 1979; and Turk, 1986). Conservative conflict theorists tend to view social conflict as involving a wide variety of groups in society. They conceptualize conflicts as emerging in response to particular situations or particular events that bring into sharp relief their competition for social or economic advantage. In contrast, radical theories of social conflict, which derive primarily from the writings of Marx, conceptualize social conflict primarily in terms of a struggle between social classes in the context of the structured inequalities of capitalist societies.

George Vold (1958; Vold and Bernard, 1986) provided an early example of conservative conflict theory in criminology. Vold's argument begins with the assumption that people are fundamentally "group-involved" in that their lives are both a part of, and a product of, group belonging. Groups are formed because individuals have common interests and common needs that are best met through collective action. Moreover, Vold maintained, groups come into conflict with each other as "the interest and purposes they serve tend to overlap, encroach on one another and become competitive" (Vold and Bernard, 1986:272).

Vold suggested that law making is one arena in which the processes of group conflict are especially apparent. Groups with the power to do so will attempt to influence the content of law so that it reflects their interests and preferences. Those in society who promote the passage of a given law will likely abide by it, while those against whom the law is directed will be more likely to violate the law, since it defends interests and values that are in conflict with their own.

Seen in this way, criminal behaviour is the behaviour of a minority group, that is, a group in society that lacks the power to exert its will through the legal machinery of the state. Vold maintained, for instance, that much juvenile misbehaviour could be understood in precisely this way. The law (and the behaviour of police, judges, and others who enforce law) may be said to reflect the interests, values, and preferences of the adult world. Thus, juvenile crime and delinquency are very much reactions against the rules and regulations that the adult world attempts to impose upon the behaviour of youth. Juvenile crime, which is very often a group phenomenon, according to Vold, represents a minority response to the domination exerted by the more powerful adult majority.

As Vold's work makes clear, an important theme in conflict theory is "criminalization," the processes by which behaviour comes to be designated as criminal. Criminalization is not seen to emerge, conflict theorists argue, from the common will of the members of society but rather from the ability of more powerful members of society to impose their definition of behaviour upon those who are less powerful. Thus, Austin Turk (1976a) argued that it is useful to think of the law as a "weapon in social conflict." Turk rejected older consensus views of law as a reflection of the compromise between conflicting segments of society. Instead, he maintained, law should be viewed as a resource that more powerful groups may be able to secure in order to resolve conflicts in their favour. The law does not express a common morality but rather the morality of the group that is able to influence the content of the law.

Gusfield (1963) argued, for example, that the passage of prohibition laws in the United States involved a symbolic struggle in which the relative prestige of competing lifestyles was at stake. Abstinence from alcohol, Gusfield showed, was part of a complex of values associated with the traditional lifestyle of nineteenth century rural, middle-class, Protestant Americans. These values were threatened, however, by the large numbers of Catholic European immigrants who settled in large urban areas. The conflict over alcohol use, Gusfield held, was merely symbolic of the larger struggle over the relative prestige that should be awarded these competing styles of life. The process by which one set of informal group norms regarding the use of alcohol became enshrined in law is the process by which the state came to recognize, officially, the legitimacy of one of these lifestyles at the expense of the other. Thus, Gusfield concluded, the criminalization of alcohol use in the last century symbolized the victory of rural Protestant over urban Catholic values in the struggle for prestige and recognition.

A number of writers have attempted to demonstrate the value of conservative conflict approaches to an understanding of the development of Canadian laws (Cook, 1969; Green,

1979; Hagan, 1980). Some critics have questioned, however, whether the conflict between interest groups characterizes the emergence of all laws or merely those that are directed toward the regulation of "vices" such as drug or alcohol use (Hagan, 1984). Other critics have maintained that while the movement away from the study of crime and toward the study of criminalization was an important step, conservative conflict theorists offered only limited insight into these processes. In particular, Marxian criminologists maintain that the emphasis that conservative conflict theory places upon interest groups detracts attention away from the study of how social conflict is rooted in the structure of society.

These more radical theories of social conflict proceed from general Marxian assumptions about history and social change. These more general theories are not easily summarized. Pfohl (1985:347), however, characterized these assumptions as follows:

The Marxist image of deviance suggests that the social organization of material existence is a primary factor in determining the style and content of social control. Following Marx, this perspective asserts that the foremost task of any society is to secure the conditions of its own material survival. To do this society must have adequate physical or material resources, a sufficient population of workers, and a capable technology. All of these things are necessary for the survival of the human group. They are not, however, in themselves sufficient. Material resources, human population, and technological know-how must be socially organized if they are to provide for a stable economic environment. Economic production is a social art. It is structured by organized social relations. The way this structuring occurs is what Marx referred to as the "mode of production." Central as it is to the very survival of the social group, the mode of production is said to influence all other social relations, be they legal, religious, formal, or whatever. How the mode of production influences the relations of social control is central to the critical understanding of social deviance ... The Marxist interpretation of history stresses the impact of unequal economic resources on the entirety of social life.

Building upon these assumptions (and upon the insights provided by the writings of more conservative conflict theorists) Marxian criminologists have attempted to understand the relationship between crime and social control, and the structured inequalities of capitalist societies. Consistent with much Marxist scholarship, they have argued that capitalist forms of economic production contain within them the elements of a conflict between a capitalist class, which controls the mode of production, and a labouring class, which must sell its labour in order to survive.

During the 1970s many Marxist scholars argued that processes of criminalization could be understood as the means by which the capitalist ruling class attempts to control the labour class and thereby maintain its advantage (Chambliss, 1975; Hepburn, 1977; Michalowski and Bohlander, 1976; Quinney, 1974). Criminal law, as a social institution, was thus viewed as an instrument of class oppression. Behaviour that threatened the interests and privileges of the ruling class was seen as subject to criminalization. Moreover it was argued that while "capitalist crimes" such as price fixing, union busting, the pollution of the environment, or the endangerment of worker safety may result in greater harm than the garden-variety offences of robbery or assault, they are either ignored by the state or defined as less serious regulatory offences.

Proponents of more mainstream criminological approaches maintained that these attempts to develop a Marxian theory of crime were too simplistic and almost impossible to verify empirically (Nettler, 1984). Similar criticisms have also been articulated by a subsequent generation of Marxian scholars who have attempted to refine the approach and to offer a view of the relationship between capitalism and crime that is considerably more sophisticated.

Some writers have shifted the focus of the study of criminalization away from a notion of class rule and toward a notion of class conflict (Chambliss, 1979; Greenberg, 1981). Thus, law is not seen to result merely and inevitably from the absolute power of a unified ruling class. Instead, it is viewed as the product of a struggle between classes. From this perspective, law is seen to reflect the struggle, divisions, and compromises that characterize class relations in complex capitalist societies.

Another recent trend in Marxist criminology, "left realism," has faulted earlier approaches for their insensitivity to the kinds of crimes about which most members of society evidence the greatest concern (Lea and Young, 1984; Matthews and Young, 1986; MacLean, 1989). The left realists argue that while Marxist criminology must increase awareness of the crimes of capitalists, it must also attempt to understand the origins and consequences of street crimes, since such offences disproportionately victimize women, the poor, and others who are made vulnerable by capitalist economic relations.

The range of theoretical approaches that may be labelled Marxian is extremely broad, and as a result, it is difficult to describe the limitations that they share in common. Two points, however, require comment. First, as many critics have pointed out, Marxian theories have frequently evaded empirical test. This was especially true of the first wave of Marxian theory, which was frequently distrustful of traditional criminological methodology and thus resisted attempts at empirical verification. In general, however, the empirical evidence supportive of Marxian models of crime and social control is safely characterized as piecemeal and frequently inconsistent (Hagan, 1985a). Second, the value of a Marxian theory of crime ultimately rests upon the more general assumptions that such a theory makes about the nature of social organization and social change and such assumptions have not gone unchallenged (Parkin, 1979; Turk, 1986).

VICTIM-CENTERED THEORIES

As the above review makes quite evident, criminological theory has, for the most part, been focused on the study of offenders. Thus, in the study of, for instance, murder, robbery or theft, attention has been directed toward an understanding of the murderer, the robber, or the thief. How, these theories have asked, does social status, association with the carriers of deviant values, the deployment of social control, or the process of criminalization affect those who engage in such conduct? Such theories have generally not been concerned with the study of crime victims.

Recent years, however, have witnessed the emergence of a large body of criminological theory that is intended to place the victim rather than the offender at center stage. Whereas previous theories assume a steady supply of victims and attempt to explain the behaviour of offenders, these victim-centered theories are more likely to assume a steady supply of offenders and attempt to understand, instead, the behaviour of victims.

The growth of victim-centered theories may be traced to three important developments. The first is the emergence of the "crime victim" as a social and political issue in the 1970s and 1980s (Elias, 1986). The second development concerns a disenchantment on the part of many criminologists with the explanatory utility of the offender-based theories that have dominated criminology since its inception (Fattah, 1979). Finally, the emergence of victim-centered theories may be linked to the proliferation of victim surveys, which have yielded a wealth of information relating to the social characteristics of victims and victimization.

One important line of theoretical inquiry into victim processes emphasizes the *situational* nature of victim-offender interactions. Such explanations attempt to understand crime as a product of the exchange that occurs between the victim and the victimizer, rather than a product of offender motivation only. In an early empirical study Wolfgang (1958) discovered that in about one in four of the homicides that occurred in the city of Philadelphia between 1948 and 1952, the victim, rather than the offender, was the first party in the exchange to engage in some sort of aggressive action. Wolfgang conceptualized such murders as "victim-precipitated." He intended the term to describe such homicides in terms of the situational dynamic that led to the lethal outcome. Typical of the victim-precipitated homicide would be the situation in which:

The person who ended up the victim was the one who had started a barroom brawl. His friends tried to break up the fight, but he persisted. Finally, the tide turned, and the aggressor was knocked down; he hit his head on the floor and died from the injuries. (Karmen, 1984: 79)

Wofgang's general point was that in a rela-

tively large proportion of the homicides that he studied, the stereotypical image of an exchange between a completely innocent victim and a completely guilty offender was not applicable.

Although the concept of victim-precipitation has been very influential in forcing a rethinking of the situational determinants of criminal incidents, it has also been widely criticized. Much of this criticism has centered on the tendency toward victim blaming that is seen as implicit in any view of crime as precipitated by the crime victim (Clark and Lewis, 1977; Karmen, 1984; Fattah, 1979; Silverman, 1974). Thus, in recent years, attention has "moved beyond victim-precipitation, looking to the full round of interaction between the offender and the victim" (Luckenbill, 1984:31). In a study of seventy California homicides, Luckenbill (1977) analyzed murder as a "situated transaction." His analysis reveals that homicide is generally the result of a "character contest." Such contests take the form of a gamelike confrontation in which offender and victim each attempt to save face at the expense of the other. In a similar way, Felson and Steadman (1983) analyzed the ways in which the escalation of offender and victim aggression eventuates in criminal violence. While such analyses may be said to find their theoretical origins in the concept of victim-precipitation they provide important elaborations and in doing so provide a more balanced assessment of the role played by victim-offender exchanges in the generation of crime.

A somewhat different approach to the study of crime victims is provided by lifestyle-exposure theory. This theoretical position, originally formulated by Hindelang et al. (1978), tries to explain why some groups in society (males, the young, racial and economic minorities) face much higher risks of victimization than do other groups. For Hindelang and his colleagues, the principal link between the social and demographic characteristics of people and the victimization risks that they face is the concept of lifestyle. This concept is defined by the authors in terms of routine daily activities of both a vocational and leisure nature. Stated differently, lifestyles may be defined as the patterned ways in which people distribute their time and energies across a range of activities. We can recognize without much difficulty that a retired middle-class female typically has a different lifestyle than a young male working-class high school student. The retiree and the student would differ with respect to how they put in an average day, how they spend their leisure time, how often they go out in the evening, where they go when they do go out in the evening, and with whom they routinely associate. According to Hindelang et al., these lifestyles emerge out of the differential adaptations that people make to the institutional constraints that are placed upon them and the social roles that they are required to play.

Hindelang and his colleagues argued that some types of lifestyles are more likely than others to put people at risk of criminal victimization. For example, to the extent that the style of life regularly puts a person on the street or in bars late at night, or brings the person into regular contact with people who have the social and demographic characteristics of typical offenders, the risk of criminal victimization increases. Young members of minority groups, therefore, have a higher level of victimization than middle-class retirees because the lifestyle of the former group entails much more exposure to victimization risk than does the lifestyle of the latter group.

An allied approach to the study of victimization is known as "routine activity theory." As originally developed by Cohen and Felson (1979) routine activity theory attempts to explain variations in victimization rates independently of changes in the size of the offender population. They argued that in order for a direct-contact predatory victimization (such as assault, personal theft, or break and enter) to occur, three elements must come together in time and space. Thus, a *motivated offender* must come into contact with a *suitable target* in the absence of *capable guardianship* (that might otherwise prevent the occurrence of the victimization).

While most criminological theorists have emphasized the study of the factors that motivate offenders, Cohen and Felson wanted to concentrate on the other two factors as well as upon the changes in society that affect the rates at which offenders, targets, and the lack of guardianship converge. Beginning with these

assumptions, Cohen and Felson argued that since the end of the Second World War, several changes have occurred in North American society to increase the likelihood of victimization. In general, they argued, the world beyond the household, rather than the household, has increasingly become the locus of routine activities. People are, for instance, more likely to eat out at restaurants or to take longer vacations than in earlier periods. In a related way, many women who in previous times would have been homemakers are now in school or in the paid labour force. Moreover, the growth in the number of single-person households brought about by rising divorce rates and the tendency on the part of many people to marry at a later stage in the life cycle has accelerated the shift in routine activities away from the home.

According to Cohen and Felson, such changes have important implications for the levels of victimization. First, the dispersion of activities away from the home increases the probability that people will come into contact with strangers who might threaten them with criminal harm. Second, these changes mean that homes are occupied at a much lower rate than in previous decades and, as a result, households and their contents are subject to generally lower levels of guardianship. Finally, these changes have increased consumer demand for lightweight durable consumer goods (such as portable radios, television sets, computers, and VCRs) that are defined by offenders as desirable targets.

Overall, Cohen and Felson maintained, these broad social changes have increased the likelihood that motivated offenders and suitable targets will converge in time and space in the absence of capable guardians and, as a result, rates of direct contact victimization will be expected to climb. Importantly, however, their analysis implies that these changes will increase victimization levels even if the number of motivated offenders does not increase. Crime is not simply the product of an offender's intention but of the spatial and temporal combination of this intention with other elements.

It is apparent that lifestyle-exposure and routine activity theories share many common themes. In fact, some writers suggest that the differences between the approaches are more apparent than real (Garofalo, 1986; Maxfield, 1987b; Sampson, 1987) and that both positions should be viewed as aspects of a more general theory of victimization opportunity. To be sure, empirical tests of these theories blur whatever distinctions may exist and many researchers use the term lifestyle/exposure and routine activity interchangeably.

In any case, these approaches have generated a large body of empirical literature in recent years and analysts have attempted to apply the logic of these arguments to a broad range of victimization problems (Messner and Tardiff, 1985; Cohen and Cantor, 1980; Cohen, Cantor, and Kleugel, 1981; Sampson, 1987). Although victimization research in Canada has lagged behind that of other countries, researchers in this country have also begun in recent years to apply lifestyle and routine activity models to the study of crime. Corrado et al. (1980) and Kennedy and Forde (1990), for example, utilized data from the *Canadian Urban Victimization Survey* to investigate the relationship between lifestyle and victimization risk. Employing national homicide data, Kennedy and Silverman (this volume) have analyzed the problem of elderly homicide as it relates to age-graded differences in patterns of routine activities.

Victimization opportunity theories have significantly reoriented the study of direct contact predatory offences. In so doing, they have overcome some of the obstacles that have beset traditional offender-based explanations of such behaviour. Moreover, such accounts are well supported by the existing body of empirical evidence (Garofalo, 1986; Maxfield, 1987b). Critics suggest, however, that the utility of such theories ultimately will depend upon the ability of investigators to overcome the limitations of current formulations. For instance, victimization opportunity theories have, to date, utilized rather crude conceptual and operational definitions of "lifestyle" and "routine activities" (Miethe et al., 1987) and have failed to devote sufficient attention to the relationship between lifestyle activities and wider community settings (Sampson and Wooldredge, 1987; Kennedy and Forde, 1990; Jackson, 1984). Other critics have argued that there is a need to

shift attention away from the general relationship between routine activities and victimization and toward the study of such relationships in the context of specific domains such as the workplace (Lynch, 1987), the school (Garofalo et al., 1987), or the household (Maxfield, 1987a). It should also be re-emphasized that thus far the applicability of lifestyle and routine activity theories has been limited to the study of direct contact offences and thus has had little influence in the study of the victimless, corporate, or white-collar crimes in which criminologists are also interested.

THE READINGS

This section has provided an overview of the major theoretical perspectives that have occupied the attention of criminologists for the last several decades. How is the relative utility of these perspectives to be assessed? Most simply, we might ask about the degree to which a given theory appeals to "common sense" or about the extent to which it is consistent with strongly held ideological or cultural beliefs. Most criminologists, however, would not be content to rely upon common sense or ideology in attempting to judge the merits of a given theoretical explanation. Instead, they would argue that if theories are to be reliable and valid guides to understanding behaviour, they must be supported by research evidence. It is worth noting that when we employ the criterion of empirical validation, the theories that we have reviewed in this section do not fare equally well. The empirical predictions of labelling theorists, for instance, have been less consistently supported by research than have those of control theorists (Nettler, 1984).

All of the articles contained in this section demonstrate an awareness of the intricate relationship between theoretical explanation and empirical research. In the first selection, "A Power-Control Theory of Gender and Delinquency," Hagan details the criminological foundations of power-control theory and the types of empirical questions that the theory encourages researchers to ask. The discussion emphasizes how the long-standing sociological interest in class and crime may be combined with the emerging body of theory and research on crime and gender.

In "Critical Criminology in Canada: Past, Present and Future," Snider reviews important developments in Marxian criminology in this country. Her article discusses the major research issues that have engaged the interest of Marxian scholars and provides important commentary with respect to the theoretical assumptions upon which such scholarship rests.

In "Chinatown's Immigrant Gangs," Joe and Robinson examine the structure and processes of four gangs operating in the Vancouver area between 1975 and 1978. Their analysis, which utilizes data from a variety of sources, reaffirms the value of cultural models of delinquent conduct.

Kennedy and Silverman ("The Elderly Victim of Homicide") employ data on elderly victims of homicide in order to provide an empiri-

cal test of some of the predictions of lifestyle/ routine activity theory. Their finding, that the elderly are disproportionately victims of theft-based homicide, suggests a need to modify the routine activity approach.

In "Designing Crime," Tremblay provides an analysis of a "crime wave" that involved credit card bank frauds in Montreal and Toronto. His research reveals that the crime wave emerged, in large part, as a response on the part of experienced offenders to changes in the structure of illegitimate opportunity.

Finally, "Urban Crime in Canada" by Hartnagel and Lee offers a recent example of the social ecology approach to the study of crime. Their research, which examines the relationship between urban location and crime rates in a large sample of Canadian cities, reveals strong support for opportunity theories of victimization.

Chapter 9

A POWER-CONTROL THEORY OF GENDER AND DELINQUENCY*

John Hagan

In its most general form, power-control theory asserts that the class structure of the family plays a significant role in explaining the social distribution of delinquent behaviour through the social reproduction of gender relations. "Family class structure" and "the social reproduction of gender relations" are not commonly used concepts in sociological criminology, and so we begin with some definitions.

Family class structure consists of the configurations of power between spouses that derive from the positions these spouses occupy in their work inside and outside the home. Spouses often gain power in the family through their work outside the home. So the occupational advances of women in recent decades are of particular interest to our understanding of family class structure.

The social reproduction of gender relations refers to the activities, institutions, and relationships that are involved in the maintenance and renewal of gender roles, in the family and elsewhere. These activities include the parenting involved in caring for, protecting and socializing children for the roles they will occupy as adults. According to power-control theory, family class structure shapes the social reproduction of gender relations, and in turn the social distribution of delinquency.

POWER, PATRIARCHY AND DELINQUENCY

The concepts of power and control typically are treated as being respectively, macro and microstructural in content. The macro-micro distinction may or may not be one of simple aggregation, as for example when classes are thought of as all persons found in common social relations of production, or as in addition sharing views of these conditions that result in group-based actions organized and carried out in ways that go beyond any simple summation of individual preferences (see Coleman, 1986). In either event, conceptual and empirical considerations of power typically occur at higher levels of aggregation and abstraction than do discussions of control and they therefore are characteristically kept separate.

Considerations of power and control nonetheless have important features in common: for example, they are both relational in content. Power theories often focus on relations of domination in the workplace, while control theories frequently focus on relations of domination in the family. We do both here. Essential to the conceptualization and measurement in both areas of theory construction is the effort to capture a relational component of social struc-

* Edited version of J. Hagan, *Structural Criminology* (New Brunswick, N.J.: Rutgers University Press, 1989), 145-58. Copyright © 1989 by Rutgers, The State University. Reprinted with permission of Rutgers University Press.

ture. In power theories of the workplace, the relational structure may be that between owner and worker, or between supervisor and supervisee. In control theories of the family, the relational structure may be that between parent and child, or between parents themselves. In both cases, however, it is a sociological concern with relational and hierarchical structure that drives the conceptualization and measurement.

Power-control theory brings together these relational concerns in a multi-level framework. In doing so, this theory highlights another concern that the power and control traditions share. This common concern is with the conditions under which actors are free to deviate from social norms. Both the presence of power and the absence of control contribute to these conditions. A particular concern of power-control theory, for example, is to identify intersections of class and family relations that provide the greatest freedom for adolescent deviation. Power-control theory assumes that the concept of patriarchy is of fundamental importance in identifying such intersections.

Curtis (1986:171) persuasively argues that patriarchy should not be seen as a theoretical concept with a standard definition, but as a generalization about social relations that calls for sociological investigation and explication. This generalization involves the propensity of males to create hierarchical structures through which they dominate others. It is important to emphasize here that these others may be male as well as female. So the study of patriarchy includes within it the analysis of structures through which men exercise hierarchical domination over both males and females, for example, including children of both genders in the family. Curtis goes on to point out that patriarchy is extremely widespread, including structures of the state (such as police, courts, and correctional agencies) as well as the workplace and the family. But the source of patriarchy nonetheless is assumed to be the family. Millett (1970:33) calls the family patriarchy's "chief institution," suggesting that the family is the fundamental instrument and the foundation unit of patriarchal society, and that the family and its roles are prototypical.

We are now in a position to begin sketching the outlines of a power-control theory of delinquency. We begin with the three levels of the theory, as illustrated in figure 1. These include, in order of level of abstraction, *social-psychological processes* involving the adolescents whose behaviours we wish to explain, *social positions* consisting of the gender and delinquency roles in which these adolescent are located, and the class *structures* by which families are socially organized. Five kinds of links, described further below, bring together the social positions

---

FIGURE 1

A POWER-CONTROL THEORY OF GENDER AND DELINQUENCY

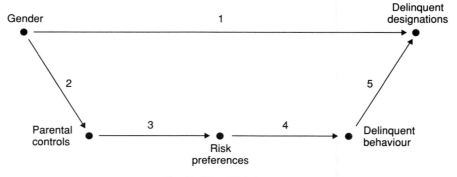

Family Class Relations

and social-psychological processes that are the core of power-control theory.

We begin with the connections between the social positions and social-psychological processes identified in figure 1. Link 1 is the correlation between gender and state-defined delinquency that criminologists long have observed. We need only note here that gender and delinquency both constitute ascribed positions that are socially designated and legally identified. Our interest is in establishing the family class structures and social psychological processes that account for these social positions being joined in the correlations so consistently recorded by criminologists. Note that the interest of power-control theory is in individuals only insofar as they are located as occupants of these positions, and not, therefore, in these individuals *per se*. By virtue of the premises noted above, the question power-control theory inevitably asks is: how and why are individuals located in male adolescent positions freer to deviate in ways defined by the state as delinquent than are individuals located in female adolescent positions?

The reference to state definition above indicates that the connection between officially defined delinquency and delinquent behaviour is not assumed. Nor is a consensus assumed about what is to be called delinquent behaviour. Indeed, it is assumed that police and court practices sometimes operate to inflate the gender-delinquency correlation. As we will discuss further below, the effect of this inflation is to reinforce a sexual stratification of family and work activities, with females ascripted disproportionately for the former, and males appropriated disproportionately for the latter. Nonetheless, a sufficient consistency is hypothesized between police processing and delinquent behaviour to make the above kind of question relevant in behavioural terms.

Note also that while the above question makes no value judgements as to the "goodness" or "badness" of delinquency, it does nonetheless imply that there is a pleasurable or enjoyable aspect of delinquency. Indeed, power-control theory assumes that delinquency can be fun, if not liberating, as well as rewarding in other ways. Bordua (1961) notes that theories of delinquency too often, at least

implicitly, assume that delinquency is a grim and somewhat desperate pursuit. In contrast, our assumption is that delinquency frequently is fun — and even more importantly, a kind of fun infrequently allowed to females. Said differently, delinquency may involve a spirit of liberation, the opportunity to take risks, and a chance to pursue publicly some of the pleasures that are symbolic of adult male status outside the family. One reason why delinquency is fun, then, is because it anticipates a range of activities, some criminal and some more conventional, that are more open to men than women. The interests of power-control theory are in how a sense of this sexually stratified world of licit and illicit adult pleasures, and restrictions of access to them, are communicated and reproduced across generations through gender relations.

Link 2 takes the first step in addressing such issues by explicating a connection between gender positions and the parental control of children. This link first calls attention to the proposition that parental controls are imposed selectively: that is, daughters are controlled more extensively than sons. Conceptually we represent this by noting that parents are characteristically the instruments of familial controls, while children are the objects; but most significantly, *daughters* are disproportionately the objects of this socially structured domination. So the instrument-object relationship established between parents and children is applied more selectively and extensively to daughters than sons. Beyond this, within patriarchal family structures mothers are particularly likely to be placed in the primary position of implementing this instrument-object relationship: that is, mothers more than fathers are assigned responsibility for perpetuating this instrument-object relationship.

Of course, control can be established through ties of affiliation as well as through subordination. Indeed, it might well be argued that a lot of affiliation and a little subordination is the most effective basis of social domination. Again, however, power-control theory predicts that ties of affiliation selectively and more extensively will be applied to daughters than sons. We will refer to these affiliative ties as relational controls, as contrasted with more instrumental kinds of controls involving supervision and surveillance. However, it is again the sexual asymmetry that is of greatest importance here, with power-control theory predicting that the larger burden of these controls is imposed on daughters rather than sons. Furthermore, it is mothers more than fathers that the patriarchal family holds responsible for the everyday imposition of these controls, again, on daughters more than sons.

Links 3, 4, and 5 in our theoretical framework lead us to a consideration of the consequences of this sexual stratification of social control. In link 3 the focus is on the risk preferences of adolescents. Risk-taking can be regarded as an expression of freedom, an expression that power-control theory predicts will be allowed selectively and more extensively to males than females. Delinquency can be regarded as an adolescent form of risk-taking (hence links 4 and 5) that we have argued can carry with it an element of pleasure, excitement, and therefore fun. The interest of power-control theory is in how a taste for such risk-taking is channelled along sexually stratified lines.

Link 3 in our theoretical framework predicts that gender differences in risk preferences will be observed and that they are mediated by the structures of parental control introduced above. That is, parents control their daughters more than their sons, and in so doing they diminish the preferences of daughters to take risks. The logical links in this theory therefore predict that daughters will be more risk-averse than sons, and that therefore daughters will be less delinquent in their behaviour than sons. In an important sense, then, what a power-control theory of delinquency is saying is that the higher likelihood of delinquency among boys than girls, and ultimately the higher likelihood of crime among men than women, is an expression of gender differences in risk preferences, which in turn are a product of the different patterns of parental control imposed on daughters compared to sons. In a still more ultimate sense, however, power-control theory goes beyond this to locate the source of such gender differences in a patriarchal connection between the family and the world of work outside it. We

turn next to an explication of this connection between work and family.

CLASS, STATE AND HOUSEHOLD

We have made recurring references to the role of the patriarchal family in reproducing the five links presented in figure 1 as the core of power-control theory. In this section we will argue that the patriarchal family is one distinct type of family class structure. Power-control theory predicts that the links identified in figure 1 are strongest within this family class relation, and therefore that this type of family structure plays a central role in accounting for a strong connection between gender and crime. Because patriarchal family structures historically have played such a prominent role in the development of industrial capitalist societies, the effects of this family structure may be seen throughout our society, even within families that seek to reduce or eliminate patriarchy. We live, in short, in a patriarchal society. Nonetheless, if power-control theory is correct, it should be possible to identify variations in the effects of patriarchy across family class structures. First, however, we consider the historical roots of the patriarchal family structure to which we attach so much importance, and the place of this family structure in the theory we propose.

Power-control theory focuses on the social organization of gender relations. it is concerned with the way in which gender relations are established, maintained, perpetuated, or in other words, reproduced. The social reproduction of gender relations occurs across generations, and so adolescence provides a crucial context in which to address such issues. Meanwhile, societies vary in the social organization and reproduction of their gender relations, and so it is highly significant that our development of power-control theory occurs within an industrial capitalist society. Indeed, the question we must initially confront is: what is it about the macrolevel development of industrial capitalist societies that accounts for the way in which they reproduce gender relations?

Weber (1947) answers this question by noting that an important juncture in the development of modern capitalism involved the separation of the workplace from the home. Two distinct spheres, which Weber regarded as crucial to the rationalization of an industrial capitalist economy, resulted from this separation: the first was populated by women and focused on domestic labour and consumption, and the second was populated by men and centered around labour power and direct production. Weber referred to these respectively as the consumption and production spheres.

The differentiation of the production and consumption spheres is significant for the social reproduction of gender relations. The reproduction of gender relations occurs in both spheres. The state (through police, courts, and correctional agencies) assumes responsibility for reproductive functions in the production sphere, while the family assumes responsibility for such functions in the consumption sphere. These reproductive functions are inversely related and sexually stratified.

The inverse relationship derives from the fact that as the reproductive activities of the family and kinship groups decline, the reproductive activities of state agencies increase. So, for example, we have elsewhere (Hagan et al., 1979) tested the thesis that as informal social controls of family and kinship groups decrease, contact with state agencies such as the police increases. This inverse relationship between state and family based systems of social control is discussed by Donald Black (1976) and Andrew Scull (1977), among recent sociologists interested in issues of social control. The important point here is that this differentiation of state and family reproductive functions, and the inverse relationship between them, also has its source in the separation of the workplace from the home that accompanied the emergence of Western capitalist societies. So the separation of the workplace from the home brought a change in production relations that in turn resulted in changes in reproductive relations, both of which had profound implications for gender relations. Among the most significant of the new gender relations was an intensification of the sexual stratification of reproductive functions.

The sexual stratification of reproductive functions in the production and consumption spheres inheres in the fact that while females disproportionately are the instruments and objects of the informal social control activities of the family, males disproportionately are the instruments and objects of formal social control agencies of the state, such as the police. The overall effect of the sexual stratification of these functions is to perpetuate a gender division in the production and consumption spheres, with females restricted to the home-based consumption sphere, and males appropriated to the production sphere; where, among other things, males are more liable to police contact.

The new family that emerged from the separation of work and home assumed responsibility for reproducing the gender division of the production and consumption spheres (Vogel, 1983). This family was patriarchal in form and created a "cult of domesticity" around women (Welter, 1966). Today, however, Coser (1985) notes that there is a declining division of the consumption and production spheres which is reflected in the increased participation of women in the labour force. Coser goes on to note that as women have joined the labour force, they have gained new power in the family, particularly in the upper classes. We consider a highly abridged version of a model of family class structure, noting that these structures vary between two extreme family class relations that form real-life counterparts of two ideal-type families.

The first of these ideal types is largely a residue from an earlier period in which the consumption and production spheres were more strictly divided by gender. To reflect this legacy, we will call this the patriarchal family. Of the family class relations we identify, the one that should most closely correspond to the ideal-type patriarchal family consists of a husband who is employed outside the home in a position with authority over others, and a wife who is not employed outside the home. Power-control theory predicts that patriarchal families will tend to reproduce daughters who focus their futures around domestic labour and consumption, as contrasted with sons who are prepared for participation in direct production. We say more about how this happens below. Here we simply repeat that Weber regarded this process of social reproduction, and implicitly the social reproduction of gender relations, as crucial to the rationalization of industrial capitalism.

At the other extreme is an ideal type we call the egalitarian family, in which the consumption and production spheres are undivided by gender. Of the family class relations we identify, the one that should most closely correspond to the ideal-type egalitarian family includes a mother and father who both are employed in positions with authority over others outside the home. Power-control theory predicts that egalitarian families tend to socially reproduce daughters who are prepared along with sons to join the production sphere. Such families are therefore a part of an overlapping of the consumption and production spheres, which a post-industrial society no longer so clearly keeps apart; such families are a part as well as a product of changing economic relations.

So the patriarchal family perpetuates a gender division in the consumption and production spheres, whereas the egalitarian family facilitates an overlapping of these spheres. The question is how this occurs. How does this happen and what are its consequences? Power-control theory answers these questions by joining a class analysis of the family with an analysis of the division of parental social control labour discussed above. The link is that parents socially reproduce their own power relationships through the control of their children. The key process involves the instrument-object relationship described under link 2 of figure 1 above, which is assumed to be at its extreme in the patriarchal family. Here fathers and especially mothers (i.e., as instruments of social control) are expected to control their daughters more than their sons (i.e., as objects of social control). In regard to mothers, we should emphasize that our point is not that they are, in any ultimate causal sense, more important than fathers in the control of daughters, but rather that mothers in patriarchal families are assigned a key instrumental role that involves them more in the day-to-day control of their children, especially their daughters. This imbalanced instrument-object relationship is a product of a division in domestic social control labour and it is a distinguishing feature of the control of daughters in patriarchal families. This instrument-object relationship is a key part of the way in which patriarchal families socially reproduce a gender division in the spheres of consumption and production.

Alternatively, a reduction of this relationship enables egalitarian families to reproduce an overlap of the production and consumption spheres. This does not mean that in these families fathers are as involved as mothers in the parental control of children; indeed, evidence mounts that this is not the case (e.g., Huber, 1976). What it does mean is that parents in egalitarian families will redistribute their control efforts so that daughters are subjected to controls more like those imposed on sons. In other words, in egalitarian families, as mothers gain power relative to husbands, daughters gain freedom relative to sons. In terms of the social reproduction of gender relations, the presence of the imbalanced instrument-object relationship helps perpetuate patriarchy, and its absence facilitates equality.

Our final task at this stage is to link this discussion of ideal-type families and the instrument-object relationship with predicted gender differences in common delinquent behaviour. This final intervening connection involves the attitudes toward risk-taking involved in the discussion of links 3 and 4 in figure 1. At one extreme, the patriarchal family and its acute instrument-object relationship between parents and daughters engenders a lower preference for risk-taking among daughters. Risk-taking is the antithesis of the passivity that distinguishes the "cult of domesticity." So, in patriarchal families, daughters are taught by their parents to be risk-averse. Alternatively, in egalitarian families, daughters and sons alike are encouraged to be more open to risk-taking. In part, this accommodation of risk is an anticipation of its role in the entrepreneurial and other activities associated with the production sphere, for which daughters and sons are similarly prepared in egalitarian families.

Control theories often regard delinquency as a form of risk-taking (Thrasher, 1927; Hirschi, 1969), sometimes as an unanticipated consequence of a rewarded willingness to take risks. The result is a correspondence in delinquent and entrepreneurial orientations that is reflected in Veblen's frequently quoted observation that "the ideal pecuniary man is like the ideal delinquent in his unscrupulous conversion of goods and persons to his own ends, and in a callous disregard of (i.e., freedom from) the feelings and wishes of others or the remoter effects of his actions" (1967:237). Power-control theory does not regard this parallel as simple irony, but as an unintended consequence of a patriarchal social structure that is valued for its capacity to foster entrepreneurial, risk-taking orientations. With this in mind, power-control theory predicts that patriarchal families will be characterized by large gender differences in common delinquent behaviour, while egalitarian families will be characterized by smaller gender differences in delinquency. In egalitarian families, daughters become more like sons in their involvement in such forms of risk-taking as delinquency.

Chapter 10

CRITICAL CRIMINOLOGY IN CANADA: PAST, PRESENT AND FUTURE*

Laureen Snider

INTRODUCTION

This article examines the development and growth of critical criminology in Canada. Critical criminology is an approach, not an area of study, based on certain premises about the nature of Canadian society. "Cui bono" (in whose interests) is a central question critical criminologists ask about law. They reject approaches which define crimes as antisocial acts committed by deficient individuals; which see punishment, therefore, as a necessary defence employed by a concerned society for the benefit of all. Critical criminologists want to know who benefits by a justice system which defines stealing a car as more serious than killing workers through exposure to dangerous chemicals; which criminalizes and imprisons almost exclusively the poor and the young, mainly for offences against property; whose imprisonment rates (the number of people locked up for each 100,000 in the population) are higher than every western country except the United States (even though Canadians remain convinced that the system is lenient, that most defendants "get off", and that most of those arrested have committed violent offences — all false) (Canada, 1982). There may indeed be consensus about the amount and nature of serious crime in this country; there may even be widespread agreement that more and heavier punishment is the proper response — but it is an engineered

not a spontaneous consensus. It is built on an ignorance about crime and criminality which is exceptionally, and not coincidentally, useful to the benefactors of the unequal status quo which characterizes Canadian society today.

Like every approach, critical criminology, sometimes called conflict, radical, or Marxist criminology, rests on a group of assumptions based in theory. It assumes, first, that crime and societal responses to it (that is, the laws passed and the police, parole, and prison systems devised) cannot be divorced from the larger socio-economic picture. Different societies have different definitions of crime, different rates of crime, and different responses to acts they define as crime. Thus the fact that Canada is a capitalist society with great inequalities in the distribution of income, the ownership of property, and the amount of power vested in each social class, gender, and ethnic group, is important in understanding the nature and shape of law and corrections.

This theoretical orientation, not surprisingly, has led to increased attention to the responses a society takes to crime, rather than to its individual causes. Critical criminologists, therefore, are more likely to study the police, parole, and prison systems than to ask why a 14-year-old Jamaican immigrant in Toronto breaks into an unoccupied apartment. If such an offence were studied, the explanation would be likely to employ the frameworks of eco-

---

*Written for this volume.

nomic deprivation and racism. On the other hand, consensus-based approaches, (which assume that members of a democratic society broadly agree that certain acts should be defined as crimes, and that laws should be passed to punish and deter people from engaging in them) would be more likely to look at the correlates of juvenile lawbreaking, focusing on the offender's peers, attitudes to education, success or failure in the school system, and identification with law-abiding role models such as teachers or scout leaders.

A second characteristic of critical criminology is its emphasis on how and why behaviours are defined as criminal. To answer this question, historical studies have become common, and we now know a great deal about the origins of criminal law as it developed in Britain and France (Ratner et al., 1987; McMullan, 1987; Tigar and Levy, 1977). Before the industrial revolution and the rise of liberal capitalism, criminal law was very different, and concepts of individual rights and due process ranged from rudimentary to non-existent. Critical criminologists see the justice system in use today, with its safeguards against the arbitrary use of power and its emphasis on universalistic rather than class-based justice, as the product of a struggle by the then-emerging capitalist class to wrest power from the land-based aristocracy. Criminal justice and law as we now know them represent the outcome of earlier class struggles over legality and legitimacy (Fine et al., 1979; Holloway and Picciotto, 1978; Ratner et al., 1987). As the modern state developed, and the middle and working classes grew more powerful, justice became less the direct tool of an upper class. Power, which had earlier shifted from the aristocracy to the business/ corporate elites, shifted again as the modern state and its myriad of middle-class employees took over. And as the power structure of the society changed, so did the behaviours which were seen as crimes, and so did enforcement practices and accountability.

Critical criminologists have also examined the reverse process — that is, why other acts, equally harmful to life and limb, escape criminalization. Acts which kill or maim employees, or destroy the life chances of the poor; assaults on women and children; profit-making behaviours which destroy the environment — all have resisted the stigma of criminal law with considerable success. Studies of corporate crime show that class-based power is still a major factor in law passage and enforcement (Snider, 1978, 1986; Goff and Reasons, 1978; Reasons et al., 1981). Studies arising out of the feminist movement document the extensive victimization of women and argue that both law and the criminal justice system have been dominated by male, patriarchal interests, with the result that crimes against women have been ignored or trivialized (Daly, 1987, 1989; Boyd and Sheehy, 1989).

Of course, critical criminologists have no monopoly on any of these issues and areas. People of every ideological stripe have studied police, women, prisons, the history of crime, and even corporate crime. It is the approach, the concepts used to explain the results, the tendency to make dominance and power key variables in the explanations, which distinguish the critical approach. I must also caution the reader that "critical criminologists" are not a group one can generalize about with any confidence. One cannot take any group of living scholars (and, given the newness of this approach in criminology, most of the authors we will discuss are still active in the field), and assign them forever to one theoretical approach. People change their minds about correct interpretations, or develop allegiances to new ways of thinking. Moreover, sociological knowledge, while certainly socially constructed, is not wholly defined by the subjective. People can set out to study something with the expectation that they will find one set of answers, and come up with results that force them to adopt different ones, answers which support an opposing theoretical perspective. What we find out, then, is not totally determined by the way we approach our subject matter, or the theoretical mind-set we have at the beginning of our inquiries. If this were so, there would be no sense in doing empirical work.

Because it is new, many of the major tasks of critical criminology remain ahead. This paper will initially examine parts of the Anglo-Canadian literature which have become the roots of critical criminology. Then, it will look at four areas or themes which have preoccupied critical criminology in the last decade. Discussion will focus on both the theoretical issues and the empirical studies which characterize each area, because it is impossible to rigidly separate the two in the critical literature. The close relationship between theory and empiricism is, in fact, one of the most important characteristics of this approach. Following this, future directions will be set out.

DEVELOPMENT AND BACKGROUND

Both sociology and criminology are disciplines which date back to the nineteenth century, but both experienced their greatest expansion during the post-World War II period. The number of sociologists in Canadian universities grew from 61 in 1960-61, to 917 in 1976-77 (Hiller, 1980). While some sociologists (along with psychologists, economists, and others) had been studying crime for some time, the establishment of four Centres of Criminology between 1960 and 1972 marked criminology's official coming of age in Canada (Arnold, 1984). Until very recently, however, criminology has been isolated from Canadian sociology, taking its inspiration primarily from the more conservative American discipline. In part, this is because mainstream sociological literature in Canada has been predominantly critical in nature, and Canadian criminology has not.

Critical criminology here developed, in part, as a reaction to this conservatism. In the fifty-odd years since criminology came of age in Canada, a variety of studies and texts, providing information on various parts of the criminal justice system and various types of crime, have been done. Scholars have used a variety of methodological perspectives as well, ranging from the most positivist and quantitative large-scale questionnaires to the most qualitative techniques, exemplified by participant observation. And they have employed, for the most part, labelling or consensus theoretical arguments to explain the findings (see, for example, Silverman and Teevan, 1975, 1980, 1986; Hagan, 1984; Connidis, 1982; Griffiths et al., 1980; McGrath, 1976; Kelly and Kelly, 1976;

Horgarth, 1971; Boydell et al., 1974). The problem with this literature, from a critical perspective, is not that the studies are poorly done or useless (they provide detailed and essential information), nor that they uncritically praise existing procedures, institutions, and officials (they do not). The problem is at the level of explanation, in that the explanations employed are for the most part divorced from structural and historical realities. That is, by inference or explicit statement, the problems in the population under analysis have been attributed to factors such as educational deficiencies or maladjustment, improper role models or socialization, too few legal opportunities to attain societal goals, or peer pressure (to name only a few which have been said to cause criminal behaviour). The role that the power structure — the corporate and political elites in Canada — plays in perpetuating the conditions which give rise to traditional crimes, and in maintaining the structures which so inadequately prepare the felon for release, is never examined.

Gradually, inspired at first not by the political economy tradition in Canadian sociology but by developments in Great Britain (an intellectual dependence typical of colonial societies), macro level explanations incorporating structural factors arising out of capitalism became more common and critical criminology began to take shape. However, criminologists were soon forced to recognize that the theoretical perspectives they were using, imported from the United Kingdom or Europe, had limited applicability here, being rooted in societies whose history and political economy were very different. Hence, critical criminologists began looking for approaches which explained and characterized their own society, discovered the political economy tradition, and began using these insights to study crime.

Political economy has been defined as "the study of power derived from or contingent on a system of property rights; the historical development of power relationships; and the cultural and social embodiments of them" (Marchak, 1985:684). The emphasis, therefore, is on property rights and the power they confer. This power may originate in the ownership or control of the mode of production (the economic power which standard Marxism used to see as the force which determined everything — culture, religion, education, crime, and so forth). But power derived from one's gender (male), ethnicity (white), or region (Ontario and Quebec versus the peripheries) may also be significant.

Originally, political economy in Canada was rooted in the staples theories of Harold Innis, who argued that the basic commodities a society depended upon for its subsistence and wealth led to the formation of distinctive societal patterns. Societies dependent on staples (lumber, fish, minerals, and so forth), such as Canada, would therefore exhibit different political, economic, and cultural patterns from those based on peasant labour (such as China) or those with a wage-earning industrialized proletariat (such as Britain). This was an early recognition that, while capitalistic systems operate according to certain universalistic rules — for example, all owners of industry have to maximize profit in order to survive — these rules are articulated differently, according to the particular features of the individual society. Thus, the culture and history of social relations in a given country, as well as its material basis, will condition the forms that the institutions of that society will take.

In addition to applying political economy, critical criminologists have focused upon the role and concept of "the state." The state refers to a set of political institutions, and the elites at the top who run them. It is usually defined to include major governing bodies (for example, the prime minister, his cabinet, and deputy ministers of key civil service portfolios, in provincial governments as well as the federal one), the military and police (the top officialdom), and the judiciary (especially the Supreme and higher county courts). State theories have tried to understand the relationship of these bodies to the forces of capital, specifically to the giant corporations and their chief executive officers. Simplistic theories in the past often assumed that capitalist governments automatically followed the dictates of the economic elite, eschewing policies antithetical to the rich. Thus, those acts which actually or potentially threatened the interests of the rich and powerful would be transformed by law into crimes, while the destructive, antisocial acts of the economic elite themselves, on the other hand, would be ignored or minimized. Credibility was lent to this formulation by studies which demonstrated that the officials who run the state (the cabinet, senior bureaucrats and judges) often have direct links with the capitalist class, through identical class backgrounds, schools, clubs, and a wide network of personal and professional connections (Miliband, 1969; Clement, 1975; 1979).

This formulation, known as instrumentalist theory, has been attacked for oversimplifying the relationship between capital and the state. It ignores the diversity of interests and needs within the capitalist class, in that a policy which benefits some interests of capital may hurt others, as the recent free trade debate illustrates. Moreover, if the main function of the state is to directly serve capital, how does one explain occasions on which the state acts against it, as in laws which impose a minimum wage on employers or require corporations to alter manufacturing processes to protect the ozone layer?

More complex views of the state, epitomized by the myriad theories usually referred to as structuralist, have developed to get around these problems (Poulantzas, 1973). In structuralist theories, the state is seen as having a qualified independence from capital, under certain circumstances, because some independence is necessary to protect the long-run interests of capital. The state must sometimes act, then, against the dominant class, or factions of it, in order to preserve the status quo, if this is threatened by serious dissent or unrest. But the independence is limited, because the state must in the final analysis provide capital with conditions under which it is free to generate and control the profit which comes from paying employees less than they are worth (that is, less than the income their labour generates for the employer).

Law plays a central role in persuading workers to accept the inherently exploitative bargains offered by capital. As explained by Antonio Gramsci (1971), the capitalist state is strongest if its citizens believe in the system under which they live. The state and capital, therefore, foster acceptance of a complex of beliefs and opinions which support the status quo, resulting in a social order known as hegemonic order. Securing hegemony — getting people to freely accept the terms of capitalism — is not easy, because capitalism is riven by contradictions and inequalities. There is, for example, the contradiction between the freedom to elect representatives and call them to account which characterizes the political sphere, and the dictatorship which prevails in the workplace, characteristic of the economic sphere; or the fact that, while all citizens are purportedly equal, and equally deserving as human beings, some are wealthy while others are, and remain, poor. Law makes this system more palatable, because it theoretically guarantees everyone the same rights and protections. Here, as nowhere else, then, everyone is equal.

To be specific, the state in capitalist societies is now seen as possessing a limited autonomy from capital, and as filling three important roles: accumulation, legitimation, and coercion (O'Connor, 1973). Accumulation refers to the state's responsibility to secure the political, social and economic conditions under which the capitalist class can profitably operate. This means that the major social institutions — the laws, working conditions, educational system, religious beliefs, and so forth — must reinforce capitalist values and serve capitalist needs. And since capitalism needs enthusiastic, willing employees, not incipient revolutionaries, the majority must accept their place, and the minority must be rendered ideologically and physically impotent. Thus, when key groups such as workers become dissatisfied, legitimation is threatened, and the state puts in place reforms which control the excesses of capital, in effect saving capitalism from itself. Unemployment insurance, health and safety regulations, old age pensions, mother's allowance, welfare, and workers' compensation provide examples of this. Should these mechanisms fail, coercion, exercised by police forces and armies, is the third state option. However, it is a two-edged sword which may jeopardize consent, because the population has been socialized to believe that the society runs on freely given consent. Therefore, it is wise for state authorities to ensure that populations against whom force is used are discredited and powerless. The aver-

age person who is labelled criminal (young, unemployed, often from a non-dominant ethnic group or a racial minority) is a perfect example of a safe target group for state coercion. And the mythical equality and universality of criminal law are used to demonstrate that the exercise of coercion is both deserved (the criminal broke the law) and responsible (the state's reactions are controlled by law).

FOUR MAJOR THEMES

With this background, we can now turn to four major themes which have preoccupied critical criminologists in the last decade. These are, first, the Canadian response to the crisis of capitalism; second, the role of ideology; third, the presence or absence of state autonomy in the operation of the criminal justice system; and fourth, critical feminist studies.

THE STATE AND THE CRISIS OF THE 1980s

Critical criminology has been concerned with linking the study of crime to broader socio-economic conditions, to figure out how responses to crime are related to the prevailing political and economic climate. It is generally accepted that the expansionary phase of capitalism is over. High rates of unemployment coupled with inflation and economic slowdown marked the 1970s and much of the 1980s. Profit margins have been falling, traditional markets are saturated, competition has heated up with the arrival of the Japanese, Koreans, and Taiwanese, and whole industries have become obsolete. The capitalist class, those who own and control the factories and corporations, have responded to this crisis in particular ways. New technology has been introduced, both to cut costs and to reduce the power of the working class. Corporations have "downsized" their working force, leaving thousands unemployed, turfed out in middle age. Minimum wage, part-time jobs in the service sector (at fast food restaurants, for example), the only area where employment opportunities have become plentiful, are pitifully inadequate substitutes. In addition, corporations try to get more surplus value out of the labour they retain, the aim being increased profitability. In the economic sphere this movement is often referred to as "austerity capitalism," and is justified in terms of corporate and national needs to stay competitive internationally. Whatever the rationale, the result is increased pressure on labour to accept less and give more, while corporate taxes are reduced and corporate privileges increased (Horton, 1981).

Politically, austerity capitalism is allied with the development of the exceptional state and the rise of the New Right. Exemplified by the regimes of Reagan in the United States and Thatcher in Britain, the state responds to the crisis of capital by passing laws to restrict the rights of labour, making it harder for unions to fight cutbacks, and by removing government regulations over business (repealing environmental statutes, or weakening laws governing health and safety in the workplace, for example). At the same time, the state reinforces its coercive strength to deal with the expected resistance, hiring more police, building more prisons, and passing more restrictive laws. In addition, attempts are made to strengthen right-wing ideologies and legitimate this agenda, through appeals to nationalism and religion (for example, "We have to make the country great again under God"), calls for a return to so-called "traditional values," as well as naked appeals to greed and self-interest. This is coupled with attacks on blacks, homosexuals, feminists, and any other group which can be used to symbolize decline, decay, and the loss of traditional white male authority (Comack, 1988; Horton, 1981). Crime in this scenario becomes an all-important symbol to divide the subordinate classes, providing them with a scapegoat (someone to hate, and to blame for their worsening economic plight), and diverting their attention away from developments in the workplace, allowing capital to get on with making ever more of them obsolete. [1]

Although this model describes the recent history of Britain and the United States very well, it has some deficiencies when applied to Canada. On the economic and political levels, it is true, monetarist policies are widely found, with state retrenchment and cutbacks to Medi-care, unemployment insurance, education, hospitals, welfare, and so forth. Recipients have been asked to pay a higher proportion of the costs of government services through user fees. Crown corporations are being privatized or, if this is not politically feasible, savaged like the CBC and Via Rail. Increased coercion is evident in labour relations (Panitch and Swartz, 1985). Expenditures on criminal justice have multiplied too, precisely as they did in Britain and the States. The criminal justice system has been tightened, typically through unpublicized rule changes; many of its functions have been decentralized; while overall control has been reinforced federally. Spending on crime control has increased at a rate greater than all other public sectors (Ericson, 1987; Taylor, 1983b). In a slow and steady fashion, then, Canada is increasing the power and scope of its coercive systems (Comack, 1987; McMullan, 1986; Ratner et al., 1987).

But all this has been done without an ideological crisis. Spending cuts in popular programs have been enacted without major ideological shifts in government philosophies — in fact, the prime minister has defended his economic policies by denying that they threaten the government's "sacred trust" to take care of vulnerable groups. The validity of this statement is not the issue; it is the fact that the prime minister is reverting to the rhetoric which characterized the post-war Canadian welfare state rather than appealing to "New Right" ideologies. A moral panic over crime, then, has not been created. Indeed, the visible policy changes made by the Conservatives in the 1980s, on drunk driving, victims' rights, prostitution and pornography, could hardly be seen as progressive, but they are not draconian shifts to the right (Hatt et al., 1989). Instead, the system has been tightened invisibly, by "brazen executive fiat" (Ratner and McMullan, 1983:40), rather than by Parliament.

The key question for critical criminologists, then, is this. Why has the federal state in Canada, experiencing the same economic crisis as other capitalistic democracies, played the law and order issue so differently from the United States and the United Kingdom? Some argue that this is a temporary phenomenon (Taylor, 1983b). Others assert that no moral panic is necessary to increase the level of social control, tighten up laws, and remove civil liberties, because Canadians do not resist such measures. Canada, the argument goes, is historically a conservative and bourgeois social order which never developed an allegiance to genuine social-democratic, anti-capitalist values. Politicians therefore have a free hand, as long as they deliver the material goods and status with which the population is obsessed (Taylor, 1987; Gaucher, 1987). Elizabeth Comack (1987), on the other hand, thinks that such an interpretation imposes the patterns and experiences of other countries onto Canada, rather than looking for explanations that fit this society. The controversy continues.

THE ROLE OF IDEOLOGY

Ideology is important in understanding crime and law because it is the key to consent, and securing consent to a social reality in which a small elite control a disproportionate share of money and power is a difficult and never-ending task. Ideology can be defined as: "elements of consciousness operating and originating in social practices which resonate throughout a society and which mirror and mediate its main societal relations and institutional forms" (Sumner, 1978:6). In other words, it is a set of beliefs people have about their social world and the way it works. It is not necessarily a factually incorrect view of the world, however, or one which reflects only the perspective of the ruling class (defined as those who own and control the means of production) (Hunt, 1985). Ideologies are part of people's lived experience in a given social order, influencing how they see the past and how they interpret new experiences. They both "act upon" people, and are acted upon by people; they are both cause and effect, subject and object.

This does not mean that individuals, classes, genders or ethnic groups construct their belief systems in a totally voluntary fashion. Some choice is involved, as people accept and reject different components according to their individual and collective experiences and personalities. To some degree, then, they do build their own idiosyncratic and unique views of the world. But within every social order are domi-

nant ideologies which form the belief systems that are taken for granted. These are "the conventional wisdoms ... which permeate institutions, allowing members to interact ... and perform according to the requisite social goals" (Marchak, 1981:2-3). Dominant ideologies are reinforced by societal traditions, that is, selective readings of the past which privilege certain historical accounts and deny others. As contradictions between dominant ideological accounts and people's lived realities occur, as people see that what they were taught and what they experience are two different things, counter-ideologies challenging the dominant versions begin to appear. If people cannot organize and share collective experiences, these tend to remain at the individual level. They do not become the basis of a social or political movement. If, however, people are able to organize and point out the inaccuracies of the dominant version of reality to others occupying similar positions in the social order, a counter-ideology can take root. For example, workers, women, and native peoples have organized and shared experiences through various "consciousness raising" devices, and forced modifications in dominant ideology.

Law is frequently the first tool those generating counter-ideologies or challenging accepted ones seek to use. Getting new laws passed or repealing old ones is important to any challenge to the status quo, both symbolically and practically. For example, replacing the old rape laws with sexual assault legislation signals official acceptance, on the symbolic level, of the validity of feminist arguments. This is an important ideological victory. Law reform is also sought to increase the power of one group at the expense of another — in the example above, the aim is to strengthen women and victims versus men and aggressors. The legal system can also be used to get existing laws declared "ultra vires," or to enshrine new rights.

However, law, especially criminal law, can get in the way of reform. The claims that law embodies the principles of universalism, due process and impartiality are crucial to the status quo; they transform and depoliticize struggles by turning them into battles over the rights of individuals, obscuring the fact that such grievances are not individual legal problems, but are disadvantages suffered by collectivities, be they classes, ethnic groups or genders (Hunt, 1985; Althusser, 1971; Pashukanis, 1978; Balbus, 1973, 1977). In fact, Mandel (1986c:86-89) argues that passing new laws is the easiest way for the state to pacify dissenters without making any substantive change. The courts will ultimately rule in favour of existing property relations, and a potentially revolutionary fight between classes can be transformed into a dispute about which side has a better legal case. Native peoples' land claims, for example, have become contests over the legality of treaties. Law makes both the unequal position natives occupied vis à vis whites when they signed the treaties, and the morality of one group displacing another by force equally irrelevant. Indeed, because courts ignore class-based power, the focus upon equal rights can actually increase the power of the privileged. In the area of corporate law, for example, equal rights mean that the car buyer and General Motors have the same opportunity to prove that a car is (or is not) defective even though they patently do *not* enjoy equal power, knowledge, or resources. Finally, law impedes reform by serving as a superb delaying strategy; cases can and do drag on for decades.

Looking at the literature which examines the relationship between the state, ideology, and law, we begin with Hastings and Saunders's study of the Law Reform Commission of Canada (1987:142-44). The Law Reform Commission was set up by the federal government in 1971 to modernize Canadian legal statutes. Canada's Criminal Code, enacted by Parliament in 1892, was based on a penal code originally developed for Britain, but rejected by the British Parliament as unduly punitive. Although many sections have been altered over the years, the original orientation survives largely intact. The Law Reform Commission, then, was charged with rethinking not only the substance of criminal law (removing obsolete laws), but also with reforming its philosophical base. Hastings and Saunders's analysis of the LRC shows, however, that attempts to significantly liberalize criminal law have been abandoned, because a major shift in the ideological climate occurred between the inception and the completion of the major recommendations.

The original mandate of the agency derived from the non-punitive, expansionary 1960s. However, shortly thereafter, the state had entered a neo-conservative, punitive phase, wherein progressive changes to criminal law were unwelcome. The LRC, then, abandoned its reformist strategy and adopted a position which was "ideologically compatible with current social arrangements" (Hastings and Saunders, 1987:129).

Studies of the media also illustrate the close relationship between crime and dominant ideology. Ericson et al. (1987) point out that accounts of deviance and control, whether fictionally as dramas or "factually" as news, dominate newspapers, television, and radio. And although the amount and nature of "crime news" vary both by and within each medium, changes in the level of coverage do not reflect increases or decreases in the actual number of crimes occurring, as measured by police statistics. This distortion of reality is not random; media coverage always overrepresents certain crimes (murder, sex, and serious crimes of violence), and underrepresents others (corporate crime, theft). The fact, therefore, that *The Toronto Star* suddenly features on the front page a rash of convenience store robberies or sexual assaults does not mean that these offences are occurring more often. Incidence may, in fact, have decreased. Media respond to their own internal and external pressures in deciding how, whether and where to place stories, and the "news judgment" exercised by individual editors is an essential part of this process.

From a theoretical perspective, media accounts of deviance and control are crucial to the maintenance of ideological hegemony. They tell us what kinds of activities are crimes (robbing a store is, but despoiling a water supply through industrial waste is not), and they spell out the range of causal factors deemed legitimate. In recent years this has meant that defects in the offender, such as poor education, laziness, permissive, absent or inconsistent parents all cause crime, but poverty and inequality do not. Media also discuss solutions, but once again focus on those which fit into dominant ideologies — longer jail terms are debated, but universal day care or a minimum wage high enough to support one's children is not. The media in general, then, focus attention on certain social problems and solutions and not others. Particular incidents, groups (such as women on welfare or the mentally ill), or habits (such as taking illegal recreational drugs) are periodically highlighted and become the "Problem of the Week" (Ericson et al., 1987:70). In all of these ways, then, crime news becomes a force which shapes people's view of the world in a way which serves the interests of powerful political and economic elites.

STATE AUTONOMY AND CRIMINAL JUSTICE

A third area examined by critical criminologists is the potential of criminal law to create meaningful, humane social change. Empirical studies of change in the institutions of criminal justice demonstrate that most reforms have backfired and ended up strengthening existing systems of social control rather than humanizing or transforming these systems. Such results force us to look specifically at the role criminal law and the criminal justice system play in supporting the status quo and preventing revolutionary change.

The critical criminologist does not pretend to be value neutral or "objective" about the changes he or she seeks. Critical criminologists tend to believe that the entire penal process should be drastically reduced in size and scope, with only the tiny minority of offenders who commit seriously violent acts remaining subject to official processing. Humane alternatives, such as restitution, re-socialization, and non-punitive community programmes, are generally preferred. In the long run, critical criminologists believe that changing the conditions which cause traditional crime (inequality, exploitation, misogyny, the attitudes of greed and competition fostered by capitalism) is the only real solution to the problem of antisocial behaviour. However, they are not sanguine about the possibilities of securing such changes, because the existing system is seen as serving very real benefits for both state and economic elites. Those at the bottom of the social order have the most to gain and the least to lose by committing criminal acts, since such behaviours jeopardize

a future which would only be spent in minimum wage jobs or unemployment anyway (excluding those few for whom upward mobility is a real possibility). Hence, they must be brought into line, and where socialization and education fail, criminal law and the coercion of the penal system will be brought into play. Criminal justice officials recognize this need to control surplus populations, and respond by concentrating enforcement efforts on the lower and working classes (Snider, 1988b; Reiman, 1982). Indeed, the vaunted "discretion" of criminal justice officials, from police to parole officers, is typically the ability to weed out those deemed to pose no threat to the existing relations of production — the middle-class youth or the white-collar offender, for example. And lawbreaking which is in defence of the status quo, such as police planting illegal bugs or using coercion against defendants to secure confessions, tends to be overlooked or treated with the greatest leniency (Mandel, 1987:156).

Despite this, critical criminologists continue to look for evidence that Canadian criminal law can be used to fight injustices and secure reform. In part, this is because the dominant theoretical position, namely structural Marxism, insists that law can be autonomous from the needs and interests of the capitalist class. Such autonomy is demonstrated, it is believed, by state actions which liberalize the criminal justice system, increase the power of defendants and prisoners, or take control away from judges, lawyers, and prison wardens. However, as we shall see, there is very little evidence that criminal law can be a liberating force.

Let us look first at the police. Have they been controlled by the state, forced to obey the laws they enforce, and respect the civil liberties of the population? Police forces in Canada have, over the last twenty years, continually expanded in power, size, budget, and coercive potential. There is no federal registry to monitor police arsenals, and forces in small towns and provincial cities have amassed an array of computerized systems and weapons which would be a match for the worst drug barons of Colombia. How appropriate such weapons are for facing down the amateur thief or irate husband that officers more typically encounter is less clear (Taylor, 1986). In fact, 80%-90% of police work in Canada is taken up with maintaining order and providing services, not with enforcing law or catching criminals (Ericson, 1981; Ericson and Baranek, 1982). Police blunders are frequent, but seldom threaten the widespread public approval police enjoy. Policing is not a very dangerous job in Canada — police are far more likely to shoot civilians than be shot by them. Police officers on the job killed a minimum of 125 civilians in Canada between 1970 and 1981, far outnumbering the number of police killed by citizens (Chappell and Graham, 1985:8-9); they shot unarmed black civilians in both Toronto and Montreal; they launched massive raids on non-criminal populations, as in the bath-house raids in Toronto; and were directly implicated in major miscarriages of justice involving native people in both Manitoba and Nova Scotia (Fleming, 1985; McMahon and Ericson, 1987; Shearing, 1981).

Despite this, their criminal acts have typically been viewed as exceptional and atypical lapses ("bad apples in a good barrel"), and the few dissenting or critical voices raised were silenced. Very few police officers have been punished for their offences, in part because the investigation and definition of complaints is done by allied police forces (or even senior officials in the same one), and the police subculture is notorious for its solidarity in the face of threats from outsiders. Moreover, there is little political support for such punishment. Newspapers and MPs who dare to criticize police wrongdoing have been subjected to intense criticism themselves, and have even lost elections over the issue (John Sewell's mayoralty defeat in Toronto in 1980, for example).

McMahon and Ericson (1987) studied a citizens' organization in Toronto (CIRPA), a group whose original aim was to reform the police and make them accountable to the public. They conclude, however, that the group was no match for the combined and virulent opposition of the police, allied state agencies, and the media. In summarizing the transition group members underwent, they say: "Within 20 months ... CIRPA had displaced its original goals from independent review, particularly of citizen complaints against the police, to accommodation with the official review procedures of the Public Complaints Commissioner's Office; from democratising the police commission to working within its parameters; from bringing allegations of police abuse ... to making standard recommendations regarding policing policies and management; from collaborating with a broad base of citizens groups to representing a very narrow constituency ..." (McMahon and Ericson, 1987:63). Challenging or reforming the police has been found to be a difficult task, because they are a national symbol and remain "legitimacy incarnate" (1987:65 - 66). After a lengthy search for evidence of police autonomy from the forces of capital, Ratner et al. conclude in a similar fashion: "in theory and deed they [police forces] reinforce state power and class dominance" (1987:109).

Studies of the prison system reinforce skepticism about the potential of criminal law to gain independence from the interests of capital. While descriptive studies of prison life abound in the traditional literature, many extolling the giant strides which have been made in reforming prisons, critical criminologists ask about the impact such changes have had on prisoners. It is generally accepted that prisons today rely less on physical violence than ever before. The disappearance in the twentieth century of whippings and the rule of silence, and the diminished use of solitary confinement or bread and water diets to punish inmates, all indicate that punishment of the body, while still employed, is no longer the foremost weapon in the arsenal. However, if physical control has lessened, mental control has increased. Sophisticated mechanisms of surveillance, drugs which break down mental reserves, operant and aversive conditioning programs, and even individual and group therapy (to the limited extent therapy is available in penitentiaries) all aim at the psyche of the prisoner. Overall, then, critical criminology does not interpret the historical record as a transition from blackness and cruelty to humanitarianism. It sees, instead, a transition from an ineffective, expensive, and crude mode of control to a technologically modern, efficient one. This new prison system, as far as we can tell, is no more effective in turning prisoners' lives around than the older models, and may be less humane.

The latest development to be touted as an example of enlightened penal attitudes has been the bestowal of legal rights upon federal prisoners through court decisions arising from challenges under the Charter of Rights. The position formerly taken by Canadian courts was that prisoners had no rights because, once incarcerated, all power over them rests with prison authorities. Wardens, and therefore guards, held the power of life and death over inmates, restricted only by the regulations of the Correctional Service of Canada (which allowed them to take any action they deemed necessary to preserve the "peace and good order" of the institution). Recent court decisions, however, challenged this authority. For example, disciplinary tribunals inside prisons formerly had unlimited power. They sentenced inmates to lengthy stays in solitary confinement or took away good time they had earned (thus extending the inmate's prison term) for a variety of offences on no more evidence than rumours overheard in the exercise yard or the uncorroborated word of a guard. Such internal courts have now been told to redraft their evidentiary rules and procedures and allow inmates limited rights of defence. Inmates' communication channels with the outside have been broadened, and the stringent censorship of the past has been relaxed.

However, critical criminologists conclude that such changes are not as far-reaching or humane as they might at first appear. Securing limited legal rights for prisoners is not an unalloyed blessing, and may represent nothing more than a concession by the state to maintain the legitimacy of the legal system. Even if the state is committed to protecting powerless populations from arbitrary and capricious authority, can limited legal rights really change the balance of power inside prisons? The closed nature of the prison system means that change cannot be monitored from the outside, so groups which fought for rights are not present to oversee their crucial translation into day-to-day operating procedures. The translation process is controlled by prison employees who probably oppose any changes which give more power to prisoners. And yet they decide, in the context of their interactions with prisoners, exactly what each new directive from the war-

den means. Legal rights for prisoners challenge not at all the structural relationship between the prisoner and the state which is the root cause of exploitation and mistreatment (Mandel, 1986c:88).

Studies show that, in general, prisons have resisted attempts to impose change from the outside. Sometimes rules reflecting the newly secured right are written into the regulations, but not enforced; sometimes even this, the minimal procedural level of conformity, is never accomplished (Jackson, 1983, 1986; Mandel, 1986a, 1986b, 1986c; see also Ekland-Olson and Martin, 1988). The main effect on Canadian federal prisons to date has been to force prison officials not to change their goals or philosophies but to set up new bureaucratic procedures (to accomplish the same repressive ends) (Mandel, 1987; Ratner et al., 1987:112-14). The paucity of external support for prisoners' right is an important factor in understanding the fragility of reform efforts. Prisoners, as a despised out-group, lack powerful supporters. Legal rights were not demanded by a ground swell of Canadians outraged at their treatment. Few people outside the legal and penal communities know the conditions under which prisoners live; and prevailing sentiments are punitive rather than humane. Making prison life more bearable for inmates was never a realistic goal to seek through legal reform alone, and it certainly has not been realized.

CRITICAL FEMINIST STUDIES

A final area critical criminologists have discovered, quite recently, has been the relationship of women to crime and law. Feminist work in criminology began by questioning the claims that law operated in an objective fashion, independent of class or gender. Feminists maintain that what we accept as "knowledge" has been constructed by (privileged) men and reflects their interests and values. The different position women occupy in the social structure, symbolized by their unique role in the reproduction and rearing of children, necessarily creates different interests, needs, and a different view of the world. The fact that some women have "bought" dominant male ideology does not invalidate this, any more than the acceptance by workers of the ideology of capital means they have the same interests as General Motors.

Feminists have argued, then, that the criminal justice system is patriarchal in the extreme, from the (male) lawyers and politicians who formulate and pass the laws to the police, to the attorneys and judges who enforce them, to the corrections system which deals with the convicted. This inspired studies of female victimization, epitomized by wife battering and rape, and it soon became apparent that women's suffering was not treated seriously. Assaulting another individual has always been an offence outlawed by the Criminal Code. However, feminist studies found that assault, when committed by men against their spouses or children, was largely ignored. Police were reluctant to press charges; prosecutors encouraged women to drop them if they were laid; justices of the peace were loathe to accept the validity of a woman's uncorroborated account; and judges trivialized the few offences which made it to court by refusing to convict or handing out very light penalties (Macleod, 1980; Dutton, 1984; Patterson, 1979; Dobash and Dobash, 1975). Such realities demonstrate the reality of patriarchal attitudes which specify that men have a right if not a duty to exercise authority over women and children, and that force is justified in this endeavour.

The study of rape provides another example of critical feminist initiatives. In Canada, as in most western countries, rape until 1983 was defined as "sexual intercourse by a male with a female who is not his wife without her consent, or with consent if it is extorted by threats or fear of bodily harm, is obtained by personating her husband or by false representations of the nature and quality of the act" (Macdonald, 1982b:3). This meant that a husband who forced his wife to have sex could not be charged with rape, and that coercive sexual acts which did not involve vaginal penetration were not defined as rape. Moreover, unlike ordinary assault cases where it is assumed that the victim did not consent, the burden of proof worked the opposite way in rape cases, with the result that the woman had to prove she did not consent. Since providing non-consent is difficult,

conviction was therefore unlikely unless there were serious physical injuries.

The legislation had other problems as well. First, the doctrine of recent complaint specified that, if a woman did not report the offence at the earliest possible juncture, the judge was entitled to tell a jury to "draw conclusions adverse to the complainant" (Macdonald, 1982a:6). In other words, if the rape victim did not tell police she was raped as soon as she was released, despite the fact that she may have told her mother or best friend, the law presumed she was lying. Secondly, the victim's testimony alone was insufficient to obtain a rape conviction; it had to be corroborated, either by a witness or by evidence of coercion such as injuries. Thirdly, the victim's previous sexual activity could be introduced as evidence by the defence; and women who showed signs of independence from men, women who were neither virgins living in their parents' home nor good wives living with husbands, found their credibility attacked. Not surprisingly, successful rape convictions were rare (Clark and Lewis, 1977:56). The conclusion reached by feminist criminologists was that rape laws plainly embodied patriarchal interests: women were viewed in law as the property of men whose value to them was lowered by rape; women were spiteful and unreliable creatures prone to false accusation; their word could not be trusted; and if they were independent or unchaste, not living in ways sanctioned by the patriarchal order, their victimization was of no concern (Brownmiller, 1975; Clark and Lewis, 1977; Medea and Thompson, 1974; Snider, 1985).

Critical feminist criminology has examined many other areas, including laws which govern the family, prostitution, pornography, and the plight of female criminals. Where laws have been revised, it is now possible to scrutinize the effectiveness of legal reform over, in some cases, ten years or more. Sadly but predictably, legal reform has run up against many of the same structural problems discussed elsewhere, and studies are reporting that the twin forces of capitalism and patriarchy have blunted its ameliorating potential (Snider, 1990; Faith, 1989; Boyd and Sheehy, 1989).

CONCLUSION

This paper has summarized the issues critical criminologists examine and the perspectives they employ. Themes such as power, class, exploitation and repression represent consistent undercurrents in every area of study, and law reform does not seem to have altered this pattern in any significant way. The percentage of the population at risk of criminal records is continually increasing, as new laws are constantly passed (without eliminating old ones), and punishments become ever heavier. The fear of being (or appearing) lenient, rather than the desire to be humane, dominates the political agenda. The damage caused by traditional crime (assault, break and enter, robbery, and so forth) is exaggerated, while the more widespread financial losses, personal injury, and deaths caused by crimes against health and safety laws in the workplace, crimes against the environment, and corporate crime of all sorts, are minimized or ignored. The challenge for critical criminologists is to determine what kinds of social action and struggle have the potential to be effective in a capitalist democracy. Taking the actions necessary to change oppressive conditions, however, is the most significant and far-reaching challenge.

NOTES

1. See Hall et al. (1978) for the classic analysis of the British government's use of the offence of "mugging" to both signal and justify its shift towards increased repression and decreased benefits for the working class

Chapter 11

CHINATOWN'S IMMIGRANT GANGS*

Delbert Joe and Norman Robinson

Over the past decade and a half Chinatowns in the major urban centers of North America have ceased to be islands of law and order and have instead become places in which crime is increasingly prevalent. The rise in crime is largely the work of gangs of immigrant Chinese youth who view themselves as a new young warrior class. The trouble began in the mid-1960s, when both Canada and the United States adopted less restrictive immigration laws, under which substantial numbers of poorly educated and disaffected Hong Kong youth began to enter Canada and the United States (Rice, 1977:61). A number of these youths formed gangs which have created a wave of crime and fear in the Chinatowns of San Francisco, Vancouver, New York, Los Angeles, and other cities.

PURPOSES OF THE STUDY

This study investigated the characteristics and processes of four Chinese youth gangs (Phantom Riders, Golden Skippers, Blue Angels, Golden Wheels) in the Chinatown region of Vancouver (B.C.) over a four-year period (1975-1979). Specifically, the study attempted to answer three main questions:

(1) What group characteristics do these Chinese youth gangs possess?

(2) What is the nature of the group processes operating in these gangs?

(3) To what extent can the sociocultural antecedents, functions, and characteristics of these Chinese youth gangs be explained in terms of current sociological theories of gang delinquency?

RESEARCH PROCEDURES

Data from five sources were collected and analyzed: (1) structured, in-depth interviews with a sample of members from each gang; a total of 13 members was interviewed by one of the researchers who speaks Cantonese; (2) structured interviews with individuals in the community who had contacts with the gangs (e.g., school personnel, youth workers, police); (3) school, police, and welfare records; (4) interviews with victims; and (5) on-site observation of gang activities.

FINDINGS

GROUP CHARACTERISTICS OF THE GANGS

Member Characteristics. The members in all four gangs were immigrants recently arrived from Hong Kong. All were males between the

* Reprinted from D. Joe and N. Robinson, "Chinatown's Immigrant Gangs," *Criminology* 18(1980): 337-45. Reprinted with permission of the authors and *Criminology*.

ages of 13 and 19. There were no Canadian-born Chinese in the gangs, nor were there any gang members who had come to Canada during their preteen years. Moreover, the gangs did not contain any youths who had attended English schools in Hong Kong.

All of the gang members interviewed reported past or present school problems, particularly with learning English. About half of the gang members were dropouts. Those who were still in school attended irregularly. Gang members revealed that most of them were having problems with their parents. They said that their parents objected to their style of dress, their preference for Western food, their poor school performance, and their use of leisure time. They also reported problems in developing contacts with people in their own age group. As immigrants, they attended special English classes, which led them to be perceived by other students as members of an "out-group."

Structural and dynamic characteristics. In terms of size, all four of the gangs had active core memberships of between 10 and 20 persons, with a larger fringe membership that participated in gang activities from time to time. Membership stability was relatively low, with a 25% turnover each year.

In terms of group uniformity, the gang members held very similar beliefs and attitudes. They felt discriminated against by the Canadian-born Chinese, the older China-born, and the larger Canadian society. On the other hand, the gang members expressed a strong desire to acquire stylish clothes, fancy cars, and other material symbols of success. They believed this could happen only if they learned English, obtained an education, and got a good job, but they felt blocked in this objective. Those gang members who were in school felt they were failures and objects of ridicule, and those who worked felt stuck in their menial jobs. As a consequence, the gang members felt that they had to stand together for mutual support.

Behavioral characteristics. School personnel reported a high incidence of "ah fai," a form of antisocial behavior practiced in schools. Imported from Hong Kong, "ah fai" behavior derives from movies (such as *The Blackboard Jungle*) to which Eastern influences (e.g., the martial arts, Oriental actors such as Bruce Lee) have been added.

Within the Chinatown community, the four gangs were involved in extortion, shoplifting, picking pockets, possession of illegal weapons, refusing to pay for goods and services, beating of Canadian-born Chinese, trafficking in soft drugs, and gang fighting. The Phantom Riders were the only youth gang that had any contact with the young-adult gangs operating in Vancouver's Chinatown. Members of the Riders would be recruited from time to time to assist a young-adult gang in its criminal activities.

During this study (1975-1979) the Blue Angels underwent considerable change. When first formed in 1971, the gang was very active in crime. In 1976 the gang came under the influence of a youth worker who involved them in a community program for the elderly in Chinatown. Soon after this, gang membership began to drop.

GROUP PROCESSES IN THE GANGS

Interstimulation. In terms of the basic form of face-to-face behavior in the gangs, the observational data showed a good deal of playing at the martial arts. This activity was important, not only for fighting purposes, but also to develop and strengthen the gang members' image of themselves as "young warriors."

Recruitment. Each of the four gangs emerged from some community-organized activity for immigrant youth. The Phantom Riders and the Golden Skippers emerged from school classes. The Blue Angels began at the local YMCA. The Golden Wheels began at a local church. A fresh supply of recruits for the gangs came from new immigrants who came to the organized activities.

Goal-setting. The data showed that the primary goals the gangs pursued were: (1) the acquisition of money and (2) manly image building. Money was needed for flashy clothes, cars, and so forth. The constant display of tough behavior was designed to show others that gang members were young warriors who commanded respect and fear.

Status management. Contrary to the findings

of some other gang studies (Thrasher, 1963:230; Cartwright, 1975:8), there appeared to be little struggle for status within each gang. There were, however, distinct status differences between the gangs, based on: (1) the degree of contact with young-adult gangs and (2) fighting ability. The Phantom Riders enjoyed the highest status. The Blue Angels also enjoyed high status but began to decline after 1976, when they became more involved in legitimate activities. The Golden Wheels increased in status from 1976 on, as it established greater contact with young-adult gangs.

ANALYZING THE GANGS IN TERMS OF CURRENT GANG THEORY

Sociocultural antecedents. Most studies of delinquency among immigrant youth have stressed bad economic conditions, conflict of cultural norms, and conflict between parents and children as important factors contributing to the development of delinquency (Empey, 1978; Gibbens and Ahrenfeldt, 1966). Two decades ago, however, Eisenstadt (1959) suggested that immigrant delinquency among youth can be better understood in terms of:

(1) the diminution of the immigrant family's ability to satisfy the needs and aspirations of its members, particularly adolescents
(2) the limitations of the social sphere and functions of the family, leading to the emergence of specific youth groups
(3) the extent to which the immigrant group establishes a positive identification with the new society and the extent to which this identification is not blocked by the "absorbing" environment

This study's data suggest that Eisenstadt's three points on the sociocultural antecedents of delinquency among immigrant children are particularly useful in explaining the origin and development of Chinese youth gangs. First, there is evidence that families in this recent wave of Chinese immigrants are not satisfying the needs of their members, particularly the adolescents. Fathers and mothers of gang members were found to be working long hours,

often at two or three jobs each. Youngsters were left on their own and there was little supervision or guidance (Tisshaw, 1976:3). The traditionally close Chinese family unit did not exist. Second, there was evidence to suggest a limitation in the traditional sphere and functions of the Chinese family. Social workers reported that the traditional Chinese extended kinship group did not exist among the families of the gang members. Rice (1977) and Sung (1967) have pointed out that recent immigrants from the pseudo-Western urban society of Hong Kong are dramatically different from pre-World War II immigrants, who came from the stable rural environment of China with their strong kinship ties. In this study, workers reported constant challenge of parental authority by gang members (Tisshaw, 1976:3). In earlier times, this rebellious behavior would have been dealt with by parents and relatives (Sung, 1967:179, De Vos and Abbott, 1966) or by self-appointed community courts (Sutherland and Cressey, 1955:74-81). The absence of kinship groups thus encourages the formation of adolescent peer groups which fill the social vacuum between the nuclear family and the community. But why do some peer groups become delinquent and others not?

A likely answer to this question emerges from an examination of Eisenstadt's third point — the immigrant's degree of positive identification with the host society and the extent to which this identification is blocked by the "absorbing" society. The Chinese people see education as the key to success, and parents will make almost any sacrifice to ensure that their children receive schooling. The parents of the gang members studied here expected their children to succeed in school. The difficulties the youth encountered in learning English made success unlikely. They saw around them the material and status evidence of what success in school could bring, particularly among Canadian-born Chinese, but success was denied them because of their inadequacy in English. As Cloward and Ohlin (1960) point out, delinquent groups develop when a society establishes success-goals for youth and at the same time provides youth with few legitimate opportunities to attain them. In the absence of legitimate opportunities for attaining the success-goals, delinquency becomes an alternative means of attaining them.

Gang characteristics. The data from this study tend to support the concept of the gang as a near group (Haskell and Yablonsky, 1974). The gangs had shifting memberships, distributed leadership, diffuse expectations and roles for members, limited group cohesion, and a variable life-span. Like the gangs studied by Miller (1975, 1977), the Chinese youth gangs were less concerned with "turf" than with money. As such, the gangs could be typologized as essentially criminally oriented (Cloward and Ohlin, 1960). Like the criminal gangs of Spergel (1964), the Chinese gangs had two principal suborientations: (1) racketeering and (2) theft. The Phantom Riders had contacts with the young-adult gangs, and thus, ample opportunity to learn and use the illegitimate means (racketeering) needed to achieve success-goals (money, manly status). The other three gangs had no contacts with adult gangs, and therefore theft became their way of attempting to achieve success-goals.

CONCLUSION

By late 1979, none of the four gangs existed as it had in 1975. The Blue Angels had dispersed and members largely entered the work force. The Golden Skippers still existed, but were not active. Many in both the Phantom Riders and the Golden Wheels had graduated to young-adult gangs.

The problem of Chinese youth gang formation is likely to continue if Canadian and American immigration policies remain as they are. Youth will be admitted who have only a limited chance to succeed in the host country.

Gang formation can be inhibited only if immigrant youth are able to

find and acquire new, permanent and recognized social roles and to participate in close personal relations with the old inhabitants. The existence of personal channels through which the immigrants can be introduced to new social settings is the prerequisite of absorption. In many cases, the existence of such channels mitigates the results of unfavorable family settings.... and the negative identification between the families and the community. (Eisenstadt,1959:208)

Chapter 12

THE ELDERLY VICTIM OF HOMICIDE: AN APPLICATION OF THE ROUTINE ACTIVITIES APPROACH*

Leslie W. Kennedy and Robert A. Silverman

INTRODUCTION

Accepted doctrine in criminology has been that the elderly experience low rates of victimization and high levels of fear of violent crime. While some questions have been raised about the latter (see Ferraro and LaGrange, 1988), their vulnerability does make them good targets. If a perpetrator knocks down an elderly woman and steals her purse, she is less likely to get up and give chase than a younger, more agile victim. At the same time, routine activities/lifestyle theory (Felson and Cohen, 1980; Hindelang, Gottfredson, and Garofalo, 1978) credits the elderly's low victimization rates to their self-protective tendency not to venture out alone, thereby decreasing their vulnerability. In other words, by their actions the elderly try to reduce the probability of victimization. Victimization in their homes will likely be by those who routinely occupy the same space — their family and/or close friends (Messner and Tardiff, 1985).

Some recent findings from American and Canadian studies of homicide contradict this predicted pattern. One Canadian study finds that the elderly are victimized at a rate proportional to their numbers in the population, but suffer violent death during the course of a theft-related crime at a rate greater than expected (Silverman and Kennedy, 1987b). Similarly, Copeland (1986), working with Dade County data, and Maxfield (1989), with the U.S. Supplementary Homicide Reports, find that the elderly are victims of felony related homicide more than expected.

Our study attempts to unravel some of the incongruity between routine activities theory and the empirical findings concerning elderly victims of homicide.

ROUTINE ACTIVITIES THEORY

In a study that anticipates the routine activities approach, Hindelang, Gottfredson, and Garofalo (1978) present a set of propositions about victimization based on lifestyle. "Lifestyle refers to routine daily activities, both vocational...and leisure" (p.241). They offer

* Edited version of L.W. Kennedy and R.A. Silverman, "The Elderly Victim of Homicide: An application of the Routine Activity Approach," *Sociological Quarterly* 31(1990): 305-17. Reprinted with permission of the authors and JAI Press Inc., Greenwich, Conn.

This research was supported by a Contributions Grant from the Solicitor General of Canada through the Centre for Criminological Research at the University of Alberta. Data were provided by the Canadian Centre for Justice Statistics, Statistics Canada. The authors would like to thank David Forde for his assistance in data analysis and John Gartrell and three anonymous *Sociological Quarterly* reviewers for comments on an earlier draft.

eight propositions that link lifestyle with victimization patterns and suggest that age, sex, marital status, family income, and race are all bound up with lifestyle and help predict victimization. First, the amounts of time spent in public places, especially at night, relate to victimization. Second, the probability of being in public places varies with lifestyle. Third, social contacts and interactions occur disproportionately among those who share lifestyles. Fourth, the chance of being a victim varies with the extent to which victims and offenders share demographic characteristics. Fifth, the proportion of time spent among non-family members varies as a function of lifestyle. Sixth, the probability of personal victimization (particularly theft) increases with the amount of time spent among non-family members. Seventh, variations in lifestyles are associated with persons' ability to isolate themselves from those with offender characteristics. Eighth, variations in lifestyle relate to the convenience, desirability, and vincibility of the person as a personal victimization target (Hindelang, Gottfredson, and Garofalo, 1978:251-64).

These propositions suggest ways that people will act and interact in various environments and some strategies they use to accommodate to the conditions in this milieu. Emphasis is placed on the relationship between offenders and victims and on the location of the offense.

Routine activities analysis became widely accepted in criminological work with the publication of Cohen and Felson's (1979) innovative study of social change and crime rate trends. They argue that much behavior is repetitive and predictable and that, at a minimum, each predatory crime requires an offender willing and able to do the crime, a target suitably accessible and vulnerable, and the absence of any target protector. When these elements converge in time and space, risk of victimization is high. Timing of the acts is based on what the offender thinks he (or she) knows about the target's activities.

Most research directly related to routine activities involves macro level analysis (Cohen and Felson, 1979; Felson and Cohen, 1980) that examines the effects of urban structure, including community size and density, on crime rates. Such research appears to reinforce the predictions of routine activities explaining overall patterns of urban criminality. Miethe, Stafford, and Long (1987), however, report strong support for routine activities hypotheses about property crime but not violent crime. Unlike the former, which may materially benefit the offender, the latter often involves interpersonal conflict or disagreement. These researchers suggest that the spontaneity of much violent crime defies the theory's assumption of rationally motivated criminals who are reasonably able to calculate the risks of their crimes. Equally important, enhanced potential of victimization through routine activities alone seems insufficient to explain criminal violence.

Using data from the *Canadian Urban Victimization Survey* (CUVS), Kennedy and Forde (1990) report findings related to property and personal crime that require adding into our explanation of victimization the degree of exposure experienced by following certain lifestyle patterns. They find that the most vulnerable to personal assaults are young, unmarried males who frequent bars, go to movies, go out to work, and spend time out of the house walking or driving around. It appears that this public lifestyle creates exposure to risk and, while violent crime may be spontaneous, its targets are more likely to be in places where conflict flares up. This evidence belies the claim by Miethe and associates (1987) that routine activities poorly predict these crimes.

ROUTINE ACTIVITIES AND ELDERLY VICTIMS OF HOMICIDE

The victimization literature consistently finds the elderly to be the least victimized age group in American and Canadian society (Centers for Disease Control, 1986; Eve, 1985; Goldsmith and Goldsmith, 1976; Hindelang, Gottfredson, and Garofalo, 1978; Yin, 1985; Solicitor General of Canada, 1985, *Bulletin 6*). It is argued that their lifestyle leads to isolation, contributing to a lower rate of victimization (Solicitor General of Canada, 1985a). While such rates remain relatively low, recent studies show a rising rate of homicide against this age group (Copeland, 1986; Wilbanks, 1981/82; Kunkle and Humphrey, 1982/83).

Dussich and Eichman's (1976) early attempt to delineate the effects of lifestyle on victimization of the elderly suggests that for vulnerability to attract an offender it must be obtrusive: offenders must be able to locate targets they consider prime for attack. For instance, an elderly person alone in an isolated area is "obtrusive and vulnerable." Generally, though, the lifestyle of most elderly is unobtrusive, lowering their degree of blatant vulnerability, which should inhibit their victimization.

Following from this research, Messner and Tardiff (1985) and Cohen and Felson (1979) suggest that because the elderly (and the young) spend more time in their homes and interact primarily with "family" members, they more often than others will be killed by family members in or near their homes. Hence, while their routine activities protect them from strangers and predatory crime, they do not thwart family (and perhaps friends) who would prey on their vulnerability. Messner and Tardiff's (1985) analysis of age-specific homicide distributions in New York City confirms that the elderly and the young are more likely to be killed at home than elsewhere. At the same time, they are as likely to be killed by a family member as by a stranger (p. 254).[1]

Other research on routines of the elderly does not support Dussich and Eichman's hypotheses or Messner and Tardiff's findings. Copeland (1986) reports from research done in Dade County, Florida, that homicide among the elderly is more common than expected (though still relatively low), accounting for approximately 5% of all murders in the county during the previous five years. Contrary to both conventional wisdom and previous findings, he finds that homicide of the elderly most commonly involves robbery or burglary. Further, over 60% of the homicide of the elderly in Dade County occurs in their home, most often by gunshot wound but also commonly by blunt force injury, sharp force injury, and asphyxia (p.261).

Maxfield, using selected metropolitan areas from the Supplementary Homicide Reports, concludes that the elderly are disproportionately victims of murder in connection with an instrumental felony (1989). Such felonies include theft-based homicides. Hence, Maxfield's findings are consistent with both Silverman and Kennedy (1987b) and Copeland (1986).

The vulnerability of the elderly when outside of the home with no protectors provides the minimum requirements for predatory crime, particularly theft. In the home, those people thought most likely to protect the elderly may in fact perpetrate violence. But, the predictions of routine activities theory seem unable to account for Copeland's (1986) finding that frequently a stranger perpetrates homicide against the elderly at home. This contrasts with murders for other age groups, in which victim and offender are most often family members or friends involved in arguments.

HYPOTHESES

We combine the empirical findings with the routine activities/lifestyle orientation to produce a set of testable hypotheses concerning the elderly homicide victim:

1. Previous research and the elderly's self-protective behavior indicate that the elderly's rate of victimization will be lower than other age groups'.
2. Lifestyle of the elderly suggests that their murder is most likely to occur in their own home.
3. Routine activities predicts that murder of the elderly most often will be by family member or friend, least often by stranger (although Copeland [1986] finds otherwise).
4. Routine activities suggests that murder of the elderly will most likely be in their homes by family members or friends and by means similar to those used to kill other individuals in the home. The most common means of homicide in Canada is shooting, followed by stabbing and beating; its most common setting in the case of intimate relationships is the victim's home (Silverman and Kennedy, 1987b). Hence, this pattern is expected

in homicide of the elderly.

5. Consistent with lifestyle/routine activity theory, the elderly are less likely than other age groups to experience crime-(theft-)based homicide, as they are less exposed to high target salience situations in which these crimes occur.

METHOD AND MEASUREMENT

Data for this study originate with the homicide project of the Canadian Centre for Justice Statistics, Statistic Canada. Canadian police departments supply the data by means of the Homicide Return. The data type, which consists of summaries of the Homicide Returns, includes detailed incident-based information on victims and offenders. Our study comprises all homicides[2] committed between 1961 and 1983.

In Canada, as in the U.S., homicides are "officially" tallied by a count of victims. Between 1961 and 1983 there were 9,642 homicide incidents involving 10,627 victims.[3] The unit of analysis in our study is the incident.[4] This presents some problems when dealing with multiple offender and multiple victim cases. Thus we examine only one offender and one victim from each incident. We use all incidents and the principal offender for analytic purposes. Victim/offender relationship is coded in terms of the closest relationship between the principal victim and any offender in an incident; this biases the data slightly towards intimate relationships. Victim/offender relationship is divided into four categories. The most intimate group is labelled *spouse/lover* and includes husbands, wives (legal and common-law), estranged lovers, and those identified as involved in a love triangle. It represents those relationships where there was likely "romantic involvement" and a good deal of intimate interaction. The second group consists of any *family members* (legal and common-law), such as parents, grandparents, nieces, nephews, uncles, aunts, and siblings. The third, more socially distant category of *other relationships* comprises victims and offenders involved in business relationships, friendships, casual acquaintance-

TABLE 1

LOCATION OF OFFENSE [a]

Place	Age				
	<18	18 – 25	26 – 45	46 – 64	≥65
Victim's Home	484	568	1563	967	485
	(52.0)	(33.5)	(45.7)	(56.5)	(72.4)
Suspect's Home	63	195	332	111	21
	(6.8)	(11.5)	(9.7)	(6.5)	(3.1)
Private Place	105	307	577	281	97
	(11.3)	(18.1)	(16.9)	(16.4)	(14.5)
Public Place	183	443	703	274	50
	(19.7)	(26.2)	(20.5)	(16.0)	(7.5)
Institution	2	31	53	13	3
	(0.2)	(1.8)	(1.6)	(0.7)	(0.4)
Other (i.e., car)	93	149	194	65	14
	(9.9)	(8.8)	(5.7)	(3.8)	(2.1)
Total N	930	1693	3422	1711	670
Row Percentages	(11.0)	(20.1)	(40.6)	(20.3)	(7.9)

NOTES: N = 8426.
 Unk = 779.
 [a] Column percentages in parentheses except as noted.

TABLE 2
VICTIM/OFFENDER RELATIONSHIP [a]

	Age				
Relationship	<18	18 – 25	26 – 45	46 – 64	≥65
Spouse/Lover	36	450	1218	441	74
	(3.9)	(28.3)	(40.0)	(28.0)	(12.5)
Other Family	507	176	311	259	114
	(55.0)	(11.1)	(10.2)	(16.5)	(19.3)
Other Relationship	174	636	993	494	139
	(18.9)	(40.0)	(32.6)	(31.4)	(23.5)
Stranger	204	329	520	379	264
	(22.1)	(20.6)	(17.1)	(24.1)	(44.7)
Total N	921	1591	3042	1573	591
Row Percentages	(12.0)	(20.6)	(39.4)	(20.4)	(7.7)

NOTES: N = 7718.
Unk = 1387.
[a] Column percentages in parentheses unless otherwise noted.

ships, and other non-kinship relationships. *Strangers* includes those who shared no known domestic or other relationship.

About 15% of the homicides in Canada are unsolved. These are distributed among the age (of victim) groups in proportions similar to the known cases and we suspect involve more distant victim-offender relationships. As we are mainly interested in characteristics of the victim and the crime, this category rarely has an impact on our analysis. Although it does have an effect in the case of victim-offender relationship and precipitating crime, because a small proportion of the cases are involved, their exclusion from one part of the analysis likely has no major effect on the results.

Age and gender are provided for both offenders and victims. The age categories for victims and offenders are (1) <18; (2) 18-25; (3) 26-45; (4) 46-64; (5) 65 and over (the elderly).

Means of offense are grouped into shooting, beating, stabbing, and a composite category including strangulation, suffocation, drowning, arson, and all other means.

For this study, location is grouped as victim's home, suspect's home, other private place, institution, public place, and other.

Precipitating crime is derived from a vari-

able that asks about motive. In the initial analysis, both theft and sex precipitated homicide are examined.

FINDINGS

Among all homicide victims in Canada, 1961-1983, the elderly suffer the lowest proportion (8%, N = 732) of homicide compared to other age groups (40% for those 26-45, 20% each for those 18-25 and 46-64, and 12% for those under 18). However, this is directly proportional to their numbers in the general population (8%, [Statistics Canada, 1984]). Unlike Wilbanks' (1981/82) data, Canadian national data reveal no upward trend in homicide against the elderly. Over these 23 years homicide of Canadians averages 2.02 per 100,000 compared to 1.62 per 100,000 elderly. The rate for the elderly ranges from a low of 1.06 per 100,00 elderly in 1962 to a high of 2.4 in 1976 and declines between 1977 and 1983.

Hypothesis 2 predicts that homicide of the elderly is most likely in their homes. That 72.4% of homicides of the elderly (vs. 33.5% of those of persons 18-25) occur in the victim's home supports this hypothesis (see Table 1). Most researchers suggest that younger individuals spend more time outside of the home and are therefore more likely to be victims in public places than the elderly who spend more time at home. Hence, according to lifestyle theory younger people will be homicide victims more often than other age groups.

Building on the lifestyle hypotheses and the notion that the elderly spend more time at home than in other places, Hypothesis 3 suggests that the elderly victim of homicide will more often suffer at the hands of someone known to him or her than at those of a stranger. While Table 2 confirms this (55% vs. 45% respectively), stranger offense is almost twice as high for the elderly as for those aged 46-64 and over twice as high compared with other ages. The elderly have apparently more to fear from strangers than do other age groups.

The fourth hypothesis deals with means of homicide. As their greater vulnerability to physical violence suggests, the elderly are more likely than any others to die as a result of beatings (see Table 3). Contrary to the hypothesis, stabbing is at a lower proportion in this group than in any other age group other than those under 18. The proportion of shooting is lowest for this group, and the ordered likeli-

hood of means is first beating, followed by shooting, then stabbing.

Hypothesis 5 predicts the elderly least likely of all age groups to fall to crime-based homicide, where a theft or robbery precipitates death. In fact, the elderly are more than twice as likely (41.1%) as others to be victims of theft-based homicide (see Table 4), supporting Copeland's (1986) findings in smaller, more local samples. Another 4% of all homicides with elderly victims involve sex related crime.

To summarize thus far, the elderly are victims of homicide most often as a result of blunt force in their own homes. Although the location is as expected, beating, rather than shooting or stabbing, is the most prevalent means of homicide commission against the elderly. Further, they are victims of theft-based murder more often than anticipated. Proportionately, they suffer this kind of homicide far more often than any other age group.

DISCUSSION

Editor's note: The original article included a more sophisticated multi-variate analysis. This dis-

TABLE 3

MEANS OF OFFENSE COMMISSION [a]

Means	Age				
	<18	18 – 25	26 – 45	46 – 64	≥65
Shooting	217	861	1744	646	151
	(21.8)	(46.3)	(47.8)	(35.7)	(21.8)
Beating	246	258	693	501	272
	(24.7)	(13.9)	(19.0)	(27.7)	(39.2)
Stabbing	150	500	831	416	138
	(15.1)	(26.9)	(22.8)	(23.0)	(19.9)
Other	381	242	377	244	133
	(38.3)	(13.0)	(10.3)	(13.5)	(19.2)
Total N	994	1861	3645	1807	694
Row Percentages	(11.0)	(20.6)	(40.5)	(20.1)	(7.7)

NOTES: N = 9001.
        Unk = 104.
        [a] Column percentages in parentheses unless otherwise noted.

TABLE 4

PRECIPITATING CRIME [a]

Crime	Age				
	<18	18 – 25	26 – 45	46 – 64	≥65
Theft	17	89	274	319	250
	(2.0)	(5.5)	(8.6)	(19.8)	(41.1)
Sex	152	81	71	32	25
	(18.0)	(5.0)	(2.2)	(2.0)	(4.1)
Other Crime	17	21	32	22	19
	(2.0)	(1.3)	(1.0)	(1.4)	(3.1)
Other	659	1431	2820	1235	315
	(78.0)	(88.2)	(88.2)	(76.8)	(51.7)
Total N	845	1622	3197	1608	609
Row Percentages	(10.1)	(20.6)	(40.5)	(20.4)	(7.7)

NOTES:　N = 7881.
　　　　Unk = 1224.
　　　　[a] Column percentages in parentheses unless otherwise noted.

cussion includes both analyses.

These findings, along with earlier research findings, are inconsistent with some of the predictions made by routine activities. But it is possible to mesh theories and findings into a new formulation that retains the logic of the situational orientation of routine activities/lifestyle.

Predictions that the elderly can become victims by isolating themselves at home are correct, as are those that suggest they will most often be killed by someone they know. However, inconsistent with our predictions, homicide of the elderly at home is often by a stranger intent on committing theft.

To explain the anomalies in our findings, we re-examine the conceptual bases for the hypotheses. Routine activities theory suggests that at a minimum, the conditions for predatory crime require a convergence in space and time of motivated offenders, suitable victims, and a lack of victim protectors. Using these criteria to predict elderly victimization, researchers have concluded that being outside of their home increases the target-likelihood for elderly persons as this exposes their vulnerability (frailty). Yin (1985) reports that the elderly are often victims of predatory street crimes. But their most usual routine activity is isolation in their homes, making them less vulnerable (accounting for the low general victimization rate). While we do not have direct measures of routine activities for victims of homicide, patterns in victimization surveys should apply. Data from the CUVS show that while 90% of the elderly report that someone is home for all or part of the day, only 63% of those under 65 do. The elderly report much more constrained evening activities than do younger persons.[5] In addition, measures of location and social relationship to offenders in homicide cases give some indirect clues about these routines.

Interpretations of routine activities have emphasized the activities of both offender and victim that generate the crime situation. For the elderly, the routine activity is to stay at home. In other words, the activity is inactivity — a state not generally considered by the routine activity theorists. The social isolation that virtually every researcher has thought lowers victimization rates is sometimes a liability. The activity of the burglar coupled with the inactivity and vulnerability of the elderly renders crime possible and, for some, perhaps irresistibly attractive. Reppetto's (1974) study of burglary shows that young burglars are more concerned with ease of dwelling entry than with the goods therein. Further, areas with low daytime occupancy rates are the most likely to be considered good targets.

From this altered perspective, routine activities theory might now consider that the elderly person is not the target of the crime, but the dwelling and its contents. Taking into account the work of Reppetto (1974), Miethe, Stafford, and Long (1987), Copeland (1986), Warr (1988), and Maxfield (1989), routine activities theory could predict that the elderly person, living quietly alone in an area with low daytime occupancy, is not detected by the burglar, or if so, is not a threat because of perceived vulnerability. In a confrontation, the elderly individual, if alone, may resist or not but is beaten. While a younger person might recover, the elderly victim dies.

Thus for the elderly, the safety of the home is offset by the vulnerability to attack during a crime and the difficulty in recovery from beating. Why are there such high levels of crime-based homicide against the elderly when compared with other age groups? Recent literature on the effects of injury on individual well-being provides clues. Findings on the impact of personal theft against the elderly support the idea that they are especially vulnerable to the consequences, which are sometimes fatal (Dussich and Reichman,1976; Eve, 1985; Hindelang, Gottfredson, and Garofalo, 1978; Kosberg, 1985; Skogan and Maxfield, 1981). The CUVS reports that while elderly are no more likely than younger victims to have suffered injuries as a result of victimization from any crime, the consequences of their injuries are typically more serious. "For example, elderly victims who were injured were twice as likely as younger victims to have required medical or dental attention" (Solicitor General of Canada, 1985, *Bulletin* 6:2). Medical statistics substantiate that the death rate from injury is higher among the elderly than younger people even though injury is the leading cause of death among the latter (Committee on Trauma Research, 1985:19).

In his discussion of rape and burglary, Warr (1988) suggests that one type of rape results from chance encounter. That is, a burglar inadvertently encounters a vulnerable woman and rapes her. This scenario is very similar to that suggested above for elderly victims of homicide. While Warr argues that this type probably does not account for a large proportion of all residential rape, it is likely (according to our findings) that death is the unanticipated outcome of some home burglaries of the unaccompanied elderly.[6] Following Warr, we can suggest that the elderly whose dwelling's characteristics attract burglars are probably at higher risk of death through theft-based homicide than are those in less targetable dwellings.

CONCLUSION

Our explanation of elderly homicide fits a slightly modified version of routine activities theory. The lifestyle of elderly individuals who live alone makes some vulnerable to theft and injuries that may prove fatal. Their isolation, coupled with the offender's motivation to burglarize (or with the burglar's simple choice of target) creates a potential homicide situation.

This re-formulation does not undermine the activity-based portion of the lifestyle/routine activity theory most often used in recent research. That conception can explain homicide against the elderly by a friend or family member. The value of the re-formulation is that it explains the inconsistent research findings cited earlier. It can take account of both inactivity and activity as precipitators of crime.

NOTES

1. Messner and Tardiff analyze the young and the old in their sample together, making it difficult to assess the effects of routine activities separately for each.
2. We exclude infanticide and manslaughter from the data set as these crimes have been recorded only since 1974. Excluding these crimes from the analysis does not alter the results.
3. Canada's population is about one-tenth that of the U.S. and its homicide rate about one-fourth.
4. The exclusion of manslaughter and infanticide from the analysis lowers the number of cases observed in the tables.

5. These data were extrapolated from the *Canadian Urban Victimization Survey Data Tape* (Solicitor General of Canada, 1981).

6. As Warr (1988) points out, the problem of measuring motive hinders verification of this. Few data sets have direct or indirect measures of that psychological contingency, if indeed any can be developed.

Chapter 13

DESIGNING CRIME*

Pierre Tremblay

Criminal opportunity analysis specifies the set of conditions that explains why a given crime occurs as it does, when it does and where it does. This kind of inquiry owes much to Cloward and Ohlin's (1960) insight that access to illegitimate means is an important pre-condition that structures crime participation. This paper will focus on a recent wave of credit card bank frauds — the "cheque guarantee scheme" — and will describe in some detail how this fraud presupposes functional tie-ins or links between different criminal practices, and furthermore requires access to one or more specific illicit markets. We will also try to understand the decision-making process underlying the geographical dynamics and life expectancy of what we consider here as a group event. As Clarke and Cornish (1985) have pointed out, criminal opportunity analysis has been rather neglected, the dominant research perspective in criminology being to explain why people involve themselves in crime. On the other hand, what research there is on criminal opportunity structures has concentrated mostly on modelling residential burglary or shoplifting target selection processes. What we will deal with in this article is a criminal practice whose targets are less physical and to which access is more restricted and structured.

DATA COLLECTION

Crime analysis can rely either on aggregate data (victimisation surveys, police statistics, samples of offender's self-reports) or individual data (police files, offender's life history, newspaper stories, interviews with related victims or bystanders). Whereas "arm-chair" crime analysis usually operates at an aggregate level, "investigative" crime analysis concentrates on a given crime occurrence or a given set of one or more known offenders and victims (Adler and Adler, 1983; Brady, 1983). In this paper we offer a case-study of the dynamics of a specific group event (a particular crime wave). The data collection strategy was designed as follows:

1. Interviewing offenders about their actual participation in specific crimes has obvious shortcomings. Besides, life histories and life styles of any particular offender may also have no direct bearing on the situational dynamics of crime occurrence itself. Finally, offenders as

* Edited version of Pierre Tremblay, "Designing Crime: The Short Life Expectancy and the Workings of a Recent Wave of Credit Card Bank Frauds," *British Journal of Criminology*, 26(1988): 234-53. Reprinted by permission of Oxford University Press.

A preliminary version of this paper was presented at the 1985 Annual Meeting of the American Society of Criminology, San Diego, California. In facilitation of this study, I am grateful to the members of the Economic Crime Unit of the Quebec Police Force, especially André St.-Pierre, Jacques Cloutier, and Gary Budge. I also wish to thank Bernard Poirier and Jim Mathews.

individuals are not necessarily able to provide information that one needs to uncover the specific collective social and economic configuration underlying a crime opportunity structure. In this research, we did not rely extensively on offenders as informants. We limited ourselves to a three hour interview with a "checkman" who had been actively involved in the cheque guarantee fraud.

2. The most important data set has been provided by the banks who had been defrauded in this scheme. It just so happened that, in this particular instance, banks were quite willing to provide police investigators with all the necessary data: loss reports by victims whose credit card or cheques had been stolen; and a number of boxes containing all the fraudulent cheques, cards and opened accounts related to the cheque guarantee fraud. They were also willing to provide to the author access to relevant internal security and administrative memos, as well as aggregate estimates of the stolen credit card market. Much of this information was not really needed by the police investigation routine, but was actively sought out for research purposes. In fact, the investigation process has a logic of its own (Ericson, 1981) and evolved independently of the crime analysis itself. In this paper we do not dwell on detective work.

3. The research site was a specialized investigative unit in "economic crimes." These units are relatively better equipped for crime analysis (as we see it) than patrol-oriented police stations or all-purpose investigation teams. When given access to such a research site, crime students should preferably be assigned to current rather than past investigations. First, much of the information gathered during an investigation is "talked about" but never gets written down because it is not necessary or useful for prosecution purposes. Secondly, assistance in obtaining information of no direct relevance to detective work (which is offender rather than crime oriented) is also easier to obtain during an on-going investigation. The main problem in "past files" is that one cannot assess the extent to which the set of data exhibited has been shaped by the organizational contingencies that structure routine police investigations (Ericson, 1981). Although working in a police unit has the advantage of giving access to other sources of data, the information specifically generated by the police investigation of the cheque guarantee fraud must also be used. Written confessions from a number of suspects, hand-writing analysis of cheques cashed fraudulently, transcripts of wire-tapping (and on-the-scene "mug shots" provided by the banks) have been relied upon mainly to estimate roughly how many different offenders participated in the crime wave and their individual offending rate. Past investigations and other current investigations conducted on the research site, as well as the rap-sheets of known offenders who got involved in the cheque guarantee scheme, were also analysed in order to assess how this particular fraud related to other kinds of cheque and credit card frauds.

The reliance of "investigative" crime analysis on incomplete and biased secondary data can be readily acknowledged. We have tried to overcome the deficiencies partly by making use of multiple sets of data, and by relying mainly on a set of victimisation incidents that was fortunately complete (no crime "dark" figure in this case). Furthermore, police files (as well as the transcripts of an interview with an offender in the process of being charged and convicted) were not used as precise descriptive accounts of what "really" went on, but as provisional evidence of some previously developed argument or hypothesis. It may also be pointed out that group offending is a less than well researched topic (Reiss, 1980), and that passing cheques and cards has not been systematically analysed since Lemert's (1967), work on naive cheque forgers, so that an exploratory inquiry into the matter is not totally unjustified. Finally, text-book enumerations of data weaknesses are to be assessed in relationship to the stated interest of any given piece of research. The paper's main purpose has been to understand the workings of a specific crime so as to be capable of engaging oneself, intellectually of course, in this crime with some reasonable confidence of making it work in a worthwhile fashion for a sufficient period of time.

THE OCCURRENCE OF A CRIME WAVE EVENT

Banks usually greet requests for cheque cashing from non-customers with much reluctance, precautions and suspicions. In February 1978 one of the five chartered Canadian banks decided that this could indeed be a market opportunity for the first bank to abandon this traditional defensive stance and adopt, instead, a more "co-operative strategy," namely the cheque guarantee programme. This strategy was quite successful (other banks had to follow) and developed in three stages. In phase one (1978-1980), the cheque guarantee programme operated so that account customers could cash their personal encoded cheques for a certain amount on an advance basis, once a day, at any other of the domestic branches of the bank. The only thing they had to do was to present their credit card to the teller, the credit card guaranteeing, in fact, the transaction. Phase two started in January 1980. Account customers could cash not only their personal encoded cheques but any cheques they wished. Phase three started in December 1980. Not only did the daily withdrawal limit go up from $200 to $500, but most importantly, the programme extended to all credit card holders, whether customers or not of the bank from which they were to draw their cheques. This was still another market opportunity for attracting non-customers. And it was precisely at that time that the wave of credit card bank fraud started (as shown in figure 1).

To "ride" a (stolen) credit card in this scheme

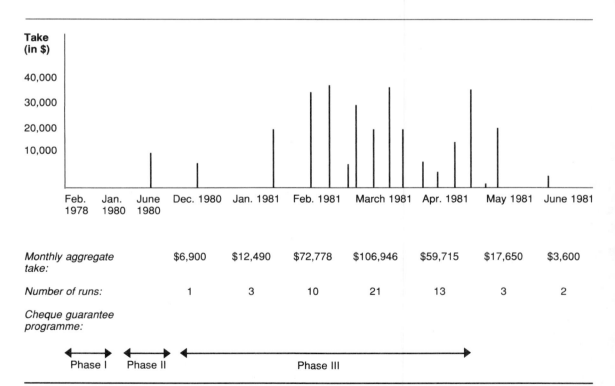

FIGURE 1
THE CHEQUE GUARANTEE FRAUD WAVE

	Feb. 1978	Jan. 1980	June 1980	Dec. 1980	Jan. 1981	Feb. 1981	March 1981	Apr. 1981	May 1981	June 1981
Monthly aggregate take:				$6,900	$12,490	$72,778	$106,946	$59,715	$17,650	$3,600
Number of runs:				1	3	10	21	13	3	2

Cheque guarantee programme:

Phase I   Phase II   Phase III

meant cashing cheques in a maximum number of different banks' branches in the shortest time possible. The number of banks visited per run is approximately 15 to 20. The total number of banks visited with just one credit card constitutes what the offenders called a "run," a "ride" or a "pass." The total amount of cash withdrawals during a run is the take. The crime wave we will describe in this paper is an integrated sequence of over 50 runs. It may be of interest to point out how official police crime statistics will transform this "real" event. First, crime waves that last for only a few weeks or months (we suspect that a great many crime waves are of this nature) will disappear because official estimates are made on an annual basis. Secondly, official statistics will transform this credit card fraud wave into a set of 900 offences, each cashing withdrawal made during a run being counted as an individual offence. Passers, security bank officials, and police investigators agree, however, that this is a legal nicety. Thirdly, a crime wave, such as the cheque guarantee scheme, is a collective process whereby a number of offenders take advantage of a specific kind of criminal opportunity which structures the way crime is done or practised. Official statistics are not designed, however, to show how crime works and will lump together in abstract, substantive categories any number of criminal practices, whether or not related in fact. Of course, police crime statistics as they are can be useful in many ways. The point is that police archives do provide a set of information that could very well be the basis of a second set of crime statistics, very different from the ones with which we are familiar.

HOW TO RIDE A CARD: GEOGRAPHICAL PATTERNS

Making a run or a pass is carefully worked out. What is crucial is the speed with which it is carried out. One time-constraint depends on how much time the credit card holder or cheque owner takes to report the loss or theft. A second time-constraint, which structures the "ride" because it is tighter, is the time it takes the bank to advertise the fraudulent cashing itself.

All five Canadian chartered banks were not equally vulnerable in this respect. In fact, only two of them suffered from this fraud for a number of reasons, the main one being that the computer security system in Bank A required a 48 hour delay for relaying the alarm process through its domestic branch network, whereas in Bank B it took 24 hours. The other banks either did not invest energy in this kind of personal advance cashing service, or were equipped with a computer security system that inhibited any subsequent fraudulent cashing transaction. Depending on the sort of bank defrauded (A or B), each particular run could not (and did not, in fact) exceed a day or two.

This time-constraint structures much of the geographical ecology of our crime wave. The fraud had to be operated in large cities rather than small ones. The bigger the city, the more the domestic branches are close to each other, and the bigger the take. This is why the passes operated mainly in Montreal, Quebec and Toronto rather than in smaller urban settings. If the fraud could have been operated in still larger cities, such as New York, the aggregate take would have been still more profitable.

The offenders could not repeatedly "visit" the same domestic branches over and over again. The more often a branch is sensibilised to the scheme, the more alert its personnel. The probability of personal and camera identification also increases. This forced offenders to spread out regionally, even though the time devoted to travelling increased the cost of making the score (cost of transportation) and decreased the score itself (since there was less time to cash the cheques). This explains why the crime wave which began in Montreal had to spread out progressively. Whereas most of the rides occurred in Montreal and Quebec in January and February, in March the offenders began to operate simultaneously in Ontario and in Quebec. In April most of the runs occurred in Ontario. If the crime wave could have operated in Europe, for example, where population density is much higher, and where distance between large cities is small (by our standards) the aggregate take of this particular fraud would have been much higher.

This increasing geographical spreading-out required different kinds of adjustments. The offenders participating in this crime wave lived in Montreal and, as we shall see, relied heavily on the local market for stolen wallets. Whereas initially a passer could ride just one credit card at a time, the regional diffusion of the fraud required offenders to go on their "trips" with several stolen credit cards and cheques and to "ride" them simultaneously. One reason for this was that a run can always abort for different unpredictable reasons. The other factor, of course, was that it was the only way to minimize the cost of travelling.

All this explains, then, the geographical ecology of the crime wave: why takes occur more frequently in large cities than in smaller ones; why the smaller urban settings whose domestic branches got scored were located along highways between the nearest big cities around Montreal (rather than the ones which were located on secondary roads); and why, having started in Montreal, the first other city was the closest one (Quebec rather than Toronto, Quebec requiring only three hours and a half driving instead of seven hours for Toronto).

CRIME OPPORTUNITY RECOGNITION

Why was the cheque guarantee service perceived so *quickly* as a crime opportunity? One reason is that the cheque guarantee fraud was only one of many related frauds which occurred in Montreal at the time. All these frauds have one thing in common: their purpose is not to succeed in a few major scores (elaborate con-games or long-term types of fraud) but rather to carry out systematically a large number of small fraudulent transactions. We will call them quantity frauds (compare with Walsh's related study on quantity thieving, 1977). Success and complexity in these frauds depend largely on volume or productivity management. The passers involved are neither isolates, high class "canons" nor slick manipulators of appearances, because much of contemporary credit card and cheque frauds does not require it.

Two criteria appear to be useful in sorting the array of quantity frauds that occurred in Montreal between 1975 and 1981. Our first criterion was whether or not a given fraud relied on a fencing market to channel its proceeds. Much of the current credit card and cheque frauds concentrates on purchasing goods from big and small retailers that will be then resold on the fencing market. Others, however, such as the cheque guarantee fraud, are not so structured. A second criterion was whether or not a given fraud depended on an elaborate market of stolen or forged means of payment. Whereas private (but mostly company) cheques, either stolen or counterfeited, can be bought and sold in large quantities, this cannot be done with credit cards: they cannot be stocked, their value is their "freshness." This does not imply that the life of a hot card cannot be extended for months through an intricate downward process (known as "milking" a card).

The two criteria are sufficient for a preliminary classification of all quantity frauds that got reported and investigated on the research site. The interesting fact is that since 1975, up to the 1981 occurrence of the cheque guarantee crime wave, all possible fraud practices had been extensively experimented in Montreal. Moreover, the cheque guarantee crime wave happens to be a repeat occurrence of a similar scheme which operated in the late 1970s and which was known at the time as the "advance cashing fraud." Our argument, then, is a "crime explains crime" argument: the cheque guarantee programme was perceived immediately as a crime opportunity because active offenders were already for a number of years involved in similar quantity frauds. It was precisely because a new crime opportunity appeared to be a *familiar* one that it was acted upon so rapidly. Since the crimes occurred or started in Montreal, this would imply, given the national scope of the cheque guarantee programme, that there existed no similar quantity fraud "tradition" in Toronto or Quebec, the two closest largest cities. We have not conducted research on this matter, although the possibility of comparative inter-city crime opportunity analysis seems a worthwhile endeavour.

There may be, however, another reason which can explain the immediacy with which the cheque guarantee opportunity was so quickly recognized as worthwhile. A passer can expect from an average run in the cheque guarantee fraud a take of $6,000. If the ride is particularly successful, he can even expect scores of over $15,000. A sample analysis of credit card purchase fraud indicates, however, that the average run in this type of venture varies between $1,000 and $2,000. Furthermore, it requires more time, given the credit withdrawal limits of retail stores. Investigation files also show that many of the suspects or convicted offenders involved in the cheque guarantee scheme had temporarily switched from purchase credit frauds in January and had switched back to their "main line" in May. This, then, could explain why the recognition of the new crime opportunity occurred so rapidly. It also implies that if the main line of passers had been involved in some other quantity fraud (for example, certified cheque schemes), the relative value of engaging in the cheque guarantee venture might have been different. Perhaps there would have been no crime wave as such. Perhaps its occurrence would have happened much later. Therefore the fact that the crime wave was acted out in Montreal does not necessarily indicate that no similar quantity fraud "tradition" exists in Toronto. It may be that, at the time, the relative gains and risks provided by the alternative existing quantity frauds in this latter setting did not induce offenders into engaging in this particular innovation.

THE CRIME WAVE EFFECT

Only a subset of crime fluctuations over time qualify as crime waves. Four distinctive features characterize such waves: a specific initiating factor that triggers a crime increase; an abnormally rapid growth in crime at onset; a saturation process that stabilises the crime rate at a given maximum level; and a terminating factor that induces an abnormally rapid decrease, and a return to the previous "normal" base rate. Crime waves are complex events. How they appear may not explain how they disappear. What triggers the abrupt onset of a crime shift may not be what accounts for its subsequent rapid increase. Crime waves may last a few days, a few months or many years; they may concern a way of doing crime, a specific kind of crime, or many different crime practices; such waves may occur in a given

urban setting, or may spread out regionally, or nationally. Models that explain a given kind of crime wave may be of little relevance in understanding the remaining varieties. In fact, a systematic review of the crime wave literature has yet to be undertaken.

The bank credit card fraud considered in this paper had a short life expectancy of no more than three months. The initiating factor was a new crime opportunity (a cheque cashing procedure with a higher withdrawal margin), and what terminated the crime wave was the bank decision in May 1981 to lower the daily withdrawal limit from $500 to $100. Why, however, didn't the wave last longer? One important feature of Canadian banking is that there are so few banks in the market. Whereas many thousands of different banks operate in the United States, only five nation-wide chartered banks do so in Canada. The target selection process for offenders is therefore extremely restricted. Since the cheque guarantee service was offered on a national basis, offenders could not hope or expect to increase the life expectancy of the fraud by switching from one bank to another. The duration of the crime wave was thus severely constrained by the victimised banks' delay in reacting to it; and since there were so few victims, delay in reacting could be expected to be reasonably swift. Internal memoranda indicate that bank security officials had in fact foreseen the crime opportunity. Marketing strategists had written it off as a built-in additional cost. It was decided, finally, that the "acceptable" level of victimisation had to remain in the aggregate under the $300,000 threshold. This restrained the life expectancy of the cheque guarantee fraud but does not account for the wave effect that was observed.

Participants could theoretically have operated in a leisurely fashion (very few runs per month on a yearly basis) and there would have been no wave effect. The reason offenders did not do so, however, suggests that the venture was a group event. All participants did not, of course, necessarily know each other on a personal basis, but many did in fact know passers who were on the make or were aware that others — "friends of friends," acquaintances of acquaintances — were also involved. This implied that participants were involved in a zero-sum game. If a given offender did not visit as many runs as feasible per month, he could expect that others would do so. In doing so, they would inevitably curtail his future ability to take advantage of the "remaining" opportunity, and lower his overall score. All participants were therefore limited to two alternatives: either getting in on the fraud as quickly as possible, making as many runs per month as feasible, and getting out quickly (low risk preference), or getting in quickly and intensively, and riding the fraud till the banks reacted (high risk preference). The situation was thus structured in such a way as to increase rapidly the participation rate in the scheme and to increase simultaneously the commission rate of individual offenders.

Students of crime waves have developed complex epidemiological models of criminal populations' recruitment processes (Noble, 1977). They have investigated unconscious triggering factors, such as media stories exhibiting suggestive models to potential candidates for suicide and homicide (Philips, 1979, 1983). Others have shown that crime waves may be either manufactured by the media or amplified by social control itself (Ditton, 1979). These approaches appear in this instance to be largely irrelevant. The cheque guarantee fraud did not "make" it either in the papers or in the police statistics. It was not a media event. Although banks created the possibility of a crime wave by offering a new crime opportunity, they did not by themselves trigger the wave effect and were capable, furthermore, of rapidly terminating it. Thus no amplification occurred. Finally, the crime wave did not require a subset of offenders or "missionaries" to recruit "virgins" into crime and increase abnormally a given "criminal population." Instead of an "epidemic" what we have is a given population of "checkmen," already familiar with the workings of quantity cheque or card frauds, who decided to "switch" to a specific scheme in order to take advantage of a new crime opportunity. The situation, however, required that they had to move in quickly, and operate as intensively as possible, in order to maximize their individual gains, creating thereby a "wave" effect.

FUNCTIONAL CONCATENATIONS OF CRIME ACTIVITIES

Tie-ins between criminal activities are numerous, and lead the student of crime to the identification of functional concatenations linking types of crime, such sequences being of variable length and complexity. Whereas police crime statistics are constructed as if crimes were committed independently of one another, police archives files show instead how crime practices are intricately interconnected. The cheque guarantee fraud crime structure (as shown in figure 2) has been analysed in this perspective. Its main features are the following: (a) it could not have been carried out without access to a stable supply of stolen credit cards, cheques and identity kits; (b) thieving itself relied in some cases on prostitutes' routine activities; (c) bank account openings under false pretences, a necessary operation in a great variety of frauds, became an alternative way of obtaining personalized cheques; and (d) many related quantity frauds depended on a complex fencing market, fencing being itself a nexus for still another array of crime practices.

Approximately 90 per cent of stolen credit card victims were not aware, at the time, of having been victimised. Bank officials were those who informed them about it. One reason for this is that wallet theft does not imply that the whole wallet, or the cash that happens to be in it, is appropriated. Nor are all credit cards equally interesting. The more selective the thieving, the less likely that the victims will be immediately aware of their loss. Thus the cheque guarantee fraud is not structured by victims' reaction to the initial theft (complaints) but rather by the banks' security procedures. Moreover, 30 per cent of the victims could not even ascertain the circumstances in which the theft had presumably occurred. Some of these memory losses were probably voluntary, investigation findings showing that in some cases the theft occurred while the victim was engaged in commercial sex gratification. When a crime occurs in the context of a second deviant activity, there is little chance that the first crime will either be reported or reported exactly as it

FIGURE 2
A SAMPLE CRIME OPPORTUNITY STRUCTURE

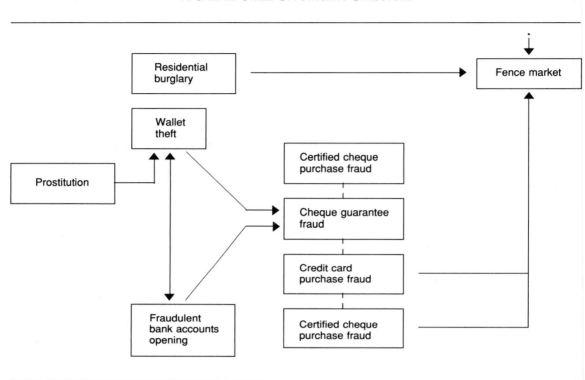

occurred. Furthermore, five of the 50 credit card loss or theft reports that we examined were found to be of a suspicious nature, either because the holder happened to be an active participant in the cheque guarantee fraud or because the victim had in fact sold it to the passer himself. This accounted for some of the most successful runs.

Thefts occurred mainly in hospitals (40 per cent) and in parking lots (30 per cent). The remaining targets were leisure (sporting) clubs and postboxes. Why hospitals? A great number of successful white collar employees work in hospitals. Not only are they excellent credit customers of good standing, but they have the added advantage of having to remove some of their clothing in the course of their work routine, and put on their uniforms. They are thus induced to abandon some of their personal

effects for some time. The same is true of leisure club customers. Parking lots are also a choice target. They are often adjacent to nightlife areas and clients, apparently afraid of being robbed or mugged, prefer to leave their credit cards in their cars. Thus the fear of one kind of crime (mugging or pickpocketing) induces them to resort to preventive measures that encourage another kind of crime (car thieving).

As often occurs in police archives data, what has not happened is just as interesting as what did happen. First, burglary did not provide any of the cards which were used in the cheque guarantee fraud. The main reason for this, one suspects, is that burglary would have precipitated victims into reporting their loss to the banks. Secondly, postboxes were not a preferred target for thieves, as was the case in other quantity frauds investigated on the research site. One possible reason may be that, at the time, security procedures relating to the mailing of new credit cards had changed. Another reason is that since the cheque guarantee fraud insures that credit cards used in the runs will be burned rapidly, there is no point in stealing new credit cards that could be used more profitably, and for a longer time period, in other kinds of credit frauds. Just as Walsh (1977) has shown that certain kinds of fencing require certain kinds of thieving, all quantity frauds do not require the same types of thefts. This brings us to an interesting question: why did the cheque guarantee fraud rely on stolen credit cards? There are more elaborate ways of obtaining fraudulently honourable credit cards. These subtle techniques, however, are most often the preliminary phase of credit card frauds that do not operate on a quantity or volume basis. The argument, then, is that it would have been extravagant to borrow long-term techniques for a fraud that operates on a very short time basis.

The cheque guarantee fraud did not rely only on stolen credit cards but also on an illicit supply of cheques. In fact there must always be two wallets stolen for each given run, two separate thefts concerning two different victims. The cheque of victim A will be cashed with B's credit card (to whom the cheques are made out). One cannot, however, in a first run ride the card of A on B's cheques and then, in a subsequent run, ride B's card on A's cheques, because as soon as the first run is completed, both A's and B's account numbers will be "burned." Thus there was no overlapping between credit and cheque victims. It may happen, however, that when short of cheques, the passer will have to resort to riding two different credit cards on A's cheques. Moreover, whereas credit cards have to be absolutely "fresh" (that is, stolen the night before being run), cheques can be stocked for some time before being used in fraud activities. Thus, although passers face a double demand problem, it is the credit card market that shapes the occurrence of credit card quantity frauds.

Cheques do not necessarily have to be stolen. They can be obtained illicitly by opening up bank accounts. One advantage is that a passer can easily acquire, by this means, booklets of personalized encoded cheques. Obviously, opening accounts requires stolen or forged identity papers, which brings us back to wallet theft. In short, wallet theft has three distinct functions: supplying credit cards, cheques and identity kits. Whereas in credit purchase frauds (the retail market), it is sufficient to steal a single card, in a guarantee fraud either you buy the card of A and the cheques of B, or the card of A and the identity kit of B, depending on whether or not you have anticipated opening an account in B's name. In the guarantee fraud wave, 16 bank accounts were opened. Thus approximately 25 per cent of the passes relied on this less expensive way of obtaining cheques, which had the added advantage of not getting the passer involved in the uncertainties of illicit transactions. Opening accounts did get the passer filmed on closed circuit camera, however. Thus, account "openers" are often not the offenders who will ride the card. This deliberate confusion technique also occurs when cheques cashed on the run are signed: the person who endorses the cheque will often not be the same as the one who has constructed its front. It is also of interest to observe that all account opening occurred at bank C, whereas the runs targeted banks A and B. When asked about it during an interview, the offender replied that bank C had the advantage of supplying personalized cheque booklets the very same day, or the day following, the account opening, and that in choosing C rather than A or B for this purpose he delayed the alarm notification process.

CONCLUSION

The study of crime is not what most criminologists usually do. Whereas nineteenth century criminologists were also crime students, who even participated in criminalistic research, contemporary criminology has not been much interested in the workings of crime, and police or security officials have become the single recognized authority on how crime occurs. As the Katzenbach Commission (1967) pointed out, little research had been done in particular on contemporary "laying paper rackets." Sutherland (1937) considered it as a typical province of happy professionals of crime, with special technical skills learned through personalized differential associations, who operated within certain geographical areas, accomplished lasting careers and avoided conviction by "fix" arrangements. Lemert's (1967) study of systematic "checkmen" presented fraudsters instead as unhappy, migratory isolates, who anxiously eschewed differential associations, with no special skills of their own, repeatedly convicted and somewhat pleased about it. It may or may not be that Lemert's "checkmen" belong to a later and altogether different generation than Sutherland's "paper hangers," operating within a different framework of commercial and banking routines, facing a transformation of policing behaviour. However, neither description allows the reader the possibility of evaluating this, because neither author engaged in analysing minutely just how these offenders operated their frauds, and in uncovering the latent crime opportunity structure that made them possible. They were more interested in offender characterisation than in crime analysis. What this paper suggests is that much offender characterisation produced by criminologists should be attributed instead to the situational circumstances that structure criminal behaviour.

Chapter 14

URBAN CRIME IN CANADA*

Timothy F. Hartnagel and G. Won Lee

INTRODUCTION

An association between urban location and crime has long been recognized both theoretically and empirically in the literature of criminology.

However, a number of aspects of this association remain contentious. First of all, alternative theoretical perspectives for explaining this association have been formulated over the years. Prominent among these are urbanization theory, inequality theory, compositional theory and opportunity theory. Furthermore, only a few attempts (Blau and Blau, 1982; Carroll and Jackson, 1983; Laub, 1983; Sampson, 1986b) have been made to empirically assess several of these perspectives together. In addition, most of the theoretical and empirical literature is specific to the context of the United States and has not been extended to other settings. Finally, a good deal of the research in this area has been descriptive and lacking in an a priori theoretical focus.

The present research is an attempt to contribute to the literature on this topic through the formulation of hypotheses derived from several theoretical perspectives concerned with urban crime, and the testing of these hypotheses using data from cities outside the United States. Specifically, we will formulate hypotheses based on a review of urbanization, inequality, compositional and opportunity theories and test them with data drawn from eighty-eight Canadian cities with a population of 25,000 or more.

THEORY AND RELATED RESEARCH

Urbanization theory is a specific version of the more general notion that social change is disorganizing and disruptive of social relationships. As developed by Wirth (1938), urbanization — the increased size, density and heterogeneity of a population — results in certain characteristically urban social relations. The concentration of a large and heterogeneous population leads to the weakening of interpersonal ties, primary social relations and normative consensus, with the ultimate consequences of individual alienation, anomie and an increased prevalence of deviant behaviors (Fisher, 1975). Each of the ecological characteristics of urbanization has social structural consequences. "Large size lends an impersonal, anonymous, transitory, and utilitarian flavor to relationships among members of a system. Density demands and facilitates the evolution of specialized and segregated economic and social roles, a complex community structure which demands increased formal coordination and regulation. The heterogeneous population assembled in

---

* Edited version of T.F. Hartnagel and G. Won Lee, "Urban Crime in Canada," *Canadian Journal of Criminology* 32 (October 1990):#591-606. Reprinted with permission of authors and of the *Canadian Journal of Criminology*, Volume 32, No. 4, October 1990. Copyright by the Canadian Criminal Justice Association.

urban areas share few common understandings, and friction generated in the competitive hubbub of daily life should find outlet in 'aggrandizement and mutual exploitation,' 'nervous tension,' and 'violent collective behavior'" (Skogan, 1977). Therefore, more urbanized locales should exhibit a weakening of informal mechanisms of social control and higher rates of personal disorganization, crime and disorder.

Fischer (1976) has claimed that compositional theory, derived from Gans (1962), poses the most significant challenge to the Wirthian hypothesis by maintaining that small, primary groups persist undiminished in the city. He pointed out that compositional theory denies that the size, density and heterogeneity of the wider community have any serious, direct consequences for personal social worlds since the dynamics of social life depend largely on the non-ecological factors of social class, ethnicity and stage in the life cycle. Thus, since urban populations are disproportionately young and childless, the behaviors to which they are especially prone — including crime — will be particularly evident in urban areas (Fischer, 1976). Hence the higher urban crime rate may result from the demographic composition of cities rather than from the alleged breakdown of social relations supposedly brought on by their ecological characteristics. However, it is possible to argue that urbanization and at least some compositional characteristics of the population affect crime rates through similar mechanisms. Thus young, unattached males may be less socially integrated (Briar and Piliavan, 1965; Rowe and Tittle, 1977) and therefore less subject to the restraining influence of informal social controls.

Inequality is a third theoretical perspective that can be applied to the relationship between urban location and crime. However, we need to distinguish between the absolute and relative deprivation varieties of this type of explanation. Absolute deprivation explanations focus upon the criminogenic conditions of life experienced by the poor and oppressed. While numerous studies have attributed crime to poverty, the major theoretical elaboration of this theme has come from Marxist writers who argue that crime results from the economic exploitation and alienation of the working class by the capitalist ruling class (Engels, 1969; Spitzer, 1975).

The concept of relative deprivation emphasizes poverty in the midst of wealth or the contrast in the distribution of valued resources as the critical explanatory factor. Merton (1938), who wished to argue against the simple notion that poverty causes crime, claimed that the officially more prevalent rate of lower-class crime results from the deprivation of legitimate means relative to the high material success goals of North American society. Others have argued that relative deprivation or inequality engenders a sense of injustice and hostility which is criminogenic (Blau and Blau, 1982).

While the previously reviewed theories all focus upon social structural variables that allegedly generate higher crime rates, opportunity theory emphasizes the crime-eliciting potential of given circumstances or situations. For example, opportunity theory would argue that certain features of urban settings such as the density of potential targets, increased potential for interaction, greater anonymity, and ease of transportation to avoid detection, are particularly conducive to crime.

Cohen and Felson (1979) have maintained that changes in routine activity patterns can influence crime rates by affecting the convergence in space and time of the three minimal elements required for the commission of direct contact, predatory crimes: (1) motivated offenders, (2) suitable targets, and (3) the absence of capable guardians. A major shift in routine activities in North America, noted by these authors, is the dispersion of activities away from the household and of the population across more households due to such historical changes as the increase in the female labor force, the increase in the percentage of the population enrolled in higher education and changes in leisure activity patterns. These changes in routine activities not only create a greater market for movable and portable goods; they also mean that homes and individuals are move vulnerable to victimization. In short, Cohen and Felson argue that these changes in routine activities increase the opportunity for certain crimes by permitting the criminally motivated to translate their activities into action due to the spatial and temporal organization of these activities.

Based upon this review of four theoretical perspectives and their respective research, we can specify a number of expected relationships. First of all, we expect only weak support for the urbanization perspective. More specifically, while population size is likely to be directly related to crime rates, particularly for property crime, we do not expect such a relation for density or heterogeneity, net of other predictors. Furthermore, an adequate test of the urbanization hypothesis requires measures of change in urban characteristics or urban growth and, based on the work of Lodhi and Tilly (1973) we do not expect urban growth to affect city crime rates. But following Fischer (1976), we will examine possible indirect effects of urbanization via the population composition or urban areas. We also expect to find positive, direct effects of population composition on both property and violent crime rates. With respect to inequality, we expect strong, positive, direct effects of relative income inequality with at best only weak support ofr the absolute deprivation or poverty interpretation of income inequality. And while the literature suggests such positive effects of relative deprivation on both property and violent crime, there is some reason to expect stronger effects on property crime rates. Finally, we also expect to find a positive relationship between opportunity and crime but, based on Carroll and Jackson's (1983) recent research, the effect of such opportunity is likely to be indirect and mediated by income inequality. In addition to testing these hypotheses, this research will also permit some assessment of the relative contribution of these four theoretical perspectives to the explanation of variation in urban crime rates.

MEASUREMENT

The dependent variable of crime rates was derived from the records of offenses known to the police as given in *Crime and Traffic Enforcement Statistics* (Statistics Canada, 1977). Two types of crime were used in the analysis: crimes of violence and crimes against property. The former consisted of murder, attempted murder, manslaughter, rape, other sexual offenses, wounding, assaults (not indecent), and robbery; the latter included breaking and entering, motor vehicle theft, theft over $200, theft under $200, and having stolen goods. While we recognize that using two broad categories may mask important differences for specific offences, it is also likely to increase the reliability of the measurement of crime since a general category is less likely to be as greatly affected by city-specific reporting or recording anomalies of a particular year compared to any single, specific offense. Property crimes constituted about 64% of all Criminal Code offenses during 1977 and crimes of violence approximately 6%. Crime rates were computed with the population base of age 10 and over to include only the population at risk of committing crime.

The demographic, social and economic data to measure the several independent variables were obtained from various census materials published by Statistics Canada (1976). Three components of urbanization were measured: population size, density and heterogeneity. Population size referred to the total number of individuals living in a community. Density was operationally defined as the population per square mile of land area. Heterogeneity was defined in terms of ethnic composition; and since in the Canadian census ethnic identity is differentiated according to mother tongue, the proportion of minority mother tongue (either non-English or non-French, depending on community location) was the indicator chosen for population heterogeneity. In addition to these static urbanization measures, we also included two indicators of urban growth or change — percentage change in population size and in population heterogeneity from 1971 to 1976. Two measures of population composition were selected: the proportion of the male population age 15 to 24 and the proportion of the population unattached or non-family, measured as the proportion of economically one-person families. Measures of both absolute and relative deprivation were included to test the inequality perspective. Relative deprivation or income dispersion was measured by the difference between the median income of the population and the average income of the poorest 20% of the population. Absolute deprivation or poverty was indicated separately for the family and non-family populations using the low income levels established by Statistics Canada. The unemployment rate was also included as an indicator of absolute deprivation. Finally, the measure of opportunity was the household activity ratio presented by Cohen and Felson (1979) as an estimate of households expected to be most at risk for personal or property crime victimization due to the dispersion of their activities away from family and household and/or their likelihood of owning durable goods of high risk. Specifically, this household activity ratio is the proportion of households occupied by non-family and husband-wife families where the wife is in the labor force.

The unit of analysis was cities in Canada with a population of 25,000 and over.

DATA ANALYSIS

To assess the relative contribution of urbanization, demographic composition, inequality and opportunity perspectives to the explanation of urban violent and property crime rates, we regressed the twelve predictor variables on each of the violent and property crime rates.

Table 1 shows the results of these regressions. For violent crime, about 45% of the variation is explained by this set of predictors combined. But only two of these predictors contribute significantly to this explained variation.

The predictor with the largest effect is criminal opportunity: as the opportunity for crime increases so does the rate of urban violence. The proportion of the male population that is age 15 to 24 has the second largest effect, net of other predictors; but surprisingly, its effect is negative. This finding runs counter to our expectations with respect to the direction of the effect of this predictor and we will have to return to a further consideration of it shortly. None of the remaining variables have statistically significant effects, although population size and population change and the change in population heterogeneity have small effects. As population size increases, so does violent crime; but, contrary to urbanization theory, changes in population size and heterogeneity result in a lower violent crime rate. So there is little in these results to support the urbanization thesis, nor is there any evidence for an effect of inequality on violent crime.

Turning to property crime, a slightly larger percentage of its variation is explained (54%) by the same ten predictors. However, the only statistically significant effect is for opportunity: as it increases so does, as expected, the rate of property crime. The other two variables with small, positive effects are population size and unemployment. So again, there is little or no support for the urbanization, population composition or inequality explanations of urban crime.

These regression results emphasize the overwhelming importance of opportunity in the explanation of urban violence and, particularly, property crime. They also demonstrate the absence of any significant contribution of inequality to the explanation of Canadian urban crime rates. Urbanization theory, particularly its strong version emphasizing change, also lacks support in these data. And while the proportion of males age 15 to 24 had a significant effect on violent crime, this result cannot be said to support the population composition perspective since the direction of its effect is opposite to that expected.

Several of the hypotheses noted above specified patterns of indirect, along with direct, effects of predictor variables on the dependent variables. In order to test these possibilities, path coefficients for a succession of reduced-form regression equations were calculated and then decomposed into direct and indirect effects (Alwin and Hauser, 1975). Contrary to the results of Carroll and Jackson (1983), there was no evidence that the effects of opportunity were largely indirect and mediated by the inequality/poverty variables. In fact, virtually all of the effect of opportunity in our data is direct. Furthermore, opportunity exhibited significant and positive total effects on both dependent variables. As for the urbanization variables, the total effect on violent and property crime of population size is significant and positive but it loses significance with the introduction of the population composition/opportunity and

TABLE 1
CANADIAN URBAN CRIME RATES: DECOMPOSITION OF EFFECTS AND MULTIPLE REGRESSION

Dependent Variable	Predetermined Variable	Total Effect	Indirect Effects via Population Composition and Opportunity	Indirect Effects via Poverty and Inequality	Direct Effect
Violent Crime	Population size	.2432*	.0485	.0128	.1820
	Density	.0471	.1742	-.0237	-.1034
	Heterogeneity	.0500	.1995	-.0130	-.1365
	Population Change	-.1754	.0521	-.0448	-.1827
	Heterogeneity Change	-.2034	-.0106	-.0235	-.1693
	Young Male Population	-.3390**	-----	.0101	-.3491**
	Opportunity	.4855***	-----	.0593	.4262***
	Low Income Individuals	-.0953	-----	-----	-.0953
	Unemployment	.0482	-----	-----	.0482
	Inequality	-.1219	-----	-----	-.1219

			ANOVA	DE	SS	MS
$R^2 = .449$	$F = 6.29^{***}$	SE = .186	Regression	10	2.17	.217
			Residual	77	2.66	.035

Dependent Variable	Predetermined Variable	Total Effect	Indirect Effects via Population Composition and Opportunity	Indirect Effects via Poverty and Inequality	Direct Effect
Property Crime	Population size	.2899*	.1106	.0031	.1762
	Density	.0455	.1664	-.0568	-.0641
	Heterogeneity	.2007	.1150	-.0072	.0929
	Population Change	-.1231	-.0813	-.1009	.0591
	Heterogeneity Change	-.1271	-.0479	.0178	-.0970
	Young Male Population	-.1032	-----	.0126	-.1158
	Opportunity	.6016	-----	.0247	.5769***
	Low Income Individuals	-.1240	-----	-----	-.1013
	Unemployment	.1187	-----	-----	.1660
	Inequality	.0045	-----	-----	-.0764

			ANOVA	DE	SS	MS
$R^2 = .538$	$F = 8.97^{***}$	SE = .114	Regression	10	1.16	.116
			Residual	77	.99	.013

* $P < .05$
** $P < .01$
*** $P < .001$

poverty/inequality variables. But none of the remaining urbanization variables have significant total effects on either type of crime. So this is hardly strong support for the argument of compositional theory that urbanization has strong indirect effects mediated by the demographic composition of the population.

DISCUSSION

These results support several, but not all, of our hypotheses. As expected, there is little evidence to support urbanization theory, and particularly its process version, which claims that change in population is disruptive of social relations and therefore criminogenic. Only population size showed any significant effect and, as expected, it was positive: the larger-sized cities have higher crime rates, both violent and property. However, this effect of population size, though somewhat mediated by population composition/opportunity, is not substantial enough to be significant net of other predictors. But it could be argued that population size would exhibit a stronger effect with the inclusion of some larger-sized cities. Furthermore, the five-year time period used to calculate change in population size and heterogeneity may not be sufficient for measuring the process of urbanization and detecting any of the allegedly disorganizing effects of such change. In addition, other aspects of population change, such as migration or residential mobility, should be considered, as well as alternative measures of density such as persons per household.

There is some evidence for the direct effect of compositional variables, though it is far from clear-cut and unambiguous. The proportion of the male population that is between 15 and 24 years of age exhibits a significant net effect on violent buy not property crime. However, this effect of age/sex population composition is negative: as the proportion of young males increases, violent crime declines. While this result is contrary to the individual level evidence which suggests that crime is disproportionately a young, male phenomenon, it is similar to findings reported in ecological studies (Messner and Blau, 1987; Crutchfield et al.,

1982; De Fronzo, 1983). Perhaps this finding results from the different age distributions for violent and property crime. The peak ages for violent crime are somewhat older than those for property crime and thus it could be that a slightly older age category (e.g., 20-30) would be most at risk for violent crime. So it could be that the negative effect present here is at least partly the product of the particular age category chosen for analysis.

Our results provide strong support for the opportunity thesis that the nature of certain routine activity patterns directly affects the level of crime in cities. Those cities with a greater dispersal of activities away from households contain more opportunities for predatory crime and this gets translated into higher rates of both violent and property offences. What is more surprising is the relative importance of opportunity compared to the other predictors. These results strongly suggest the theoretical importance of shifting our focus away from an almost exclusive attention to urban features shaping the motivation to commit crime — be they disorganization, poverty or population demography — toward a greater effort to understand the structure of opportunities for crime of more specifically, the availability of suitable targets for crime in the absence of (informal) guardians capable of preventing the violation.

However, future work along these lines would probably benefit from several extensions to this approach. First, variation in formal guardianship capable of preventing crime should be included in future research and linked to the by now large body of literature concerned with deterrence of crime. Secondly, additional research should attempt to specify some of the conditions under which opportunity is more strongly linked to crime. For example, Jackson (1984) has recently demonstrated that the effect of the dispersion of household activities is a function of city size, having a greater effect on the crime rate in larger cities. Similarly, attention should now be turned to an exploration of other possible interactions between so-called motivational and opportunity variables. In fact, in their statement of the opportunity hypothesis, Cohen and Felson (1979) emphasize the convergence in space and time of motivated offenders, suitable targets and the absence of capable guardians. But the measurement of opportunity in terms of the dispersion of household activities focuses only upon the latter two aspects. So future research should incorporate tests for possible interactions between potential "motivational" factors such as urbanization and inequality on the one hand, and victim proneness on the other (Cantor and Land, 1985).

We are surprised by the absence of any significant effect of the income dispersion or relative deprivation variable, particularly with respect to property crime. This could be at least partly the result of using a general property crime index rather than specific categories of property crime since some research, at least, has observed different results for different types of crime (Cohen, Kluegel, and Land, 1981). It's also possible that Canadian cities exhibit less income inequality than U.S. cities, or perhaps less variability in income inequality than their U.S. counterparts, particularly given the restricted upper range of population size for cities in this sample and the somewhat greater emphasis upon social welfare and income redistribution in Canada, even though Stack's (1982) results for Sweden failed to support such a welfare effect. Furthermore, Cohen, Kluegel and Land (1981), in their elaboration upon the opportunity model, present results which run counter to some conventional criminological wisdom in showing that income — not income dispersion — is inversely related to risk of assault, directly related to risk of personal larceny and parabolically related to risk of burglary victimization. But with controls for several risk factors, the affluent had the highest risk of victimization for each of these three crimes. These results suggest that income level rather than income inequality may be the more critical variable since, given similar exposure to risk and lifestyle patterns, the affluent are the most attractive crime targets. So in explaining urban crime rates perhaps future research should focus upon the proportion in the upper income levels, rather than the more traditional focus upon poverty or income inequality. And somewhat similar to our suggestion above concerning interaction between motivational and opportunity factors, Cohen et al. interpret their results as suggesting that such social power resources as age, income and race relate to criminal victimization only insofar as they are indicative of differences in exposure to risk, guardianship patterns, proximity to potential offenders, and identification of lucrative targets. So perhaps future research attempting to explain urban crime rate variation should follow this lead in focusing upon the combinations and interactions among different types of predictor variables.

PART IV

Crimes and Criminals: Selected Research

READINGS

Desroches's "Tearoom Trade: A Research Update" provides Canadian data on homosexual activities in public washrooms, revealing that the practice continues even though criminal sanctions with sometimes devastating effects can follow. Control theory and the limits of deterrence should be kept in mind as you read about this behaviour.

Gabor and Normandeau in "Armed Robbery: Highlights of a Canadian Study" reveal data on trends in armed robbery, the nature of the crime, the motives of the offenders, and the reactions of the victims. French-Canadian participation in the offence is also discussed.

"Social Economy and Arson in Nova Scotia" represents a social economy analysis by McMullan and Swan. Arson appears to be a response to economic hard times and a way to shift burdens away from individuals to the insurance industry. It is perceived as a victimless crime and appears to know no class boundaries.

"Physician Fraud and Abuse in Canada: A Preliminary Examination" by Wilson, Lincoln, and Chappell illustrates yet another infrequently studied (and thought about) crime. The types and extent of physician fraud and the difficulties in dealing with this white-collar crime are well illustrated. Note the great amount of money involved and compare it with the losses described by Gabor and Normandeau.

A somewhat related crime, which also costs Canadians millions of dollars, is described by Keane in his article "Corporate Crime." Keane describes the extra- and intra-corporate, as well as the individual, factors thought to lie behind these crimes and the difficulties in dealing with corporate criminals.

Finally, Keane, Gillis, and Hagan examine labelling and deterrence theories as they apply to marijuana use and conclude that girls are more likely to be deterred after official reaction, while boys may become more deviant. Differences in risk taking are thought to lie behind the different reactions.

Chapter 15

TEAROOM TRADE: A RESEARCH UPDATE*

Frederick J. Desroches

INTRODUCTION

From 1985 to 1988, the arrests of large numbers of men involved in impersonal sex in public toilets became a major Canadian news story. Sparked by the publication in local newspapers of the accused persons' names, a nationwide debate took place in the media through radio talk shows, letters to the editor, and television interviews. Never before had this covert sexual activity been so publicly exposed. Many citizens were shocked by the detailed descriptions of the behavior, the characteristics of the men involved, police investigative techniques, and the resulting destruction of families, careers, and the death by suicide of one of the accused. The present study examines this deviant activity using information generated by police surveillance of seven public washrooms in five Canadian communities.

This paper attempts to replicate Laud Humphreys' famous study, *Tearoom Trade: Impersonal Sex in Public Places*. Originally published in 1970, his award-winning book describes the activities of men who frequent public washrooms (tearooms) in search of quick anonymous sex. Based on surreptitious

observations of sexual encounters as a voyeur-lookout ("watchqueen"), in-depth interviews with selected players, and disguised interviews with others, Humphreys' research is a detailed sociological analysis of a seldom studied form of deviance common to urban areas. Despite limiting his systematic observations to one city, Humphreys contends that "the basic rules of the game — and the profile of the players — are applicable to any place in the United States" (1970:21). The present research aims to test this assertion by comparing data on tearoom activities — gathered two decades later, using different methodologies, and in a different country — with the behaviors described by Humphreys in his innovative research.

A discussion of the data and research methodology of each study is followed by an analysis and comparison of the following: the location of tearooms, how tearooms are discovered, characteristics of participants, and tearoom behavior. The paper concludes with a sociological analysis of participant motivation. Despite some differences, the overall patterns observed in Canadian communities are remarkably the same.

* Reprinted from F.J. Desroches, "Tearoom Trade: A Research Update," *Qualitatiave Sociology* 13(Spring 1990): 39-61. Reprinted with permission of the author and Human Sciences Press.

The financial support of the Social Science and Humanities Research Council of Canada is Gratefully acknowledged. The author also wishes to thank Michelle Coupal, Augie Fleras, and Des Rowland for helpful comments on earlier drafts of this paper and the police officers whose cooperation made the research possible.

THE DATA AND RESEARCH METHODOLOGY

HUMPHREYS' STUDY

Although the origin of the term "tearoom" is unknown, Humphreys explains that it is generally used in homosexual argot to refer to locales or facilities that are frequented by men for sexual encounters. Public toilets favored for these purposes are isolated structures, infrequently used by other persons, yet easily accessible by car (1970:7).

From April 1966 to April 1967, Humphreys observed 120 sexual acts in 19 different men's washrooms, located in five parks in a city of two million people. In order to gain as representative a sample as possible, he ignored tearooms that because of location attracted specific occupational groups and focused instead on the more accessible and "democratic" restrooms of public parks — i.e., facilities likely to attract a wider cross section of the population (1970:13, 19). He also distributed observations throughout different time periods, parks, and seasons of the year.

Humphreys discovered that the fear and suspicion encountered by tearoom participants produced a lookout role, whereby one man would situate himself at a door or window and alert participants of anyone approaching. By serving as voyeur-lookout ("watchqueen") — "a role superbly suited for sociologists and the only lookout role that is not overtly sexual" (1970:28) — Humphreys was able to observe the action without alarming or disrupting participants.

In addition, Humphreys initiated conversations with several participants outside the toilet and eventually gained the trust and cooperation of twelve men for his research project. He also recorded the license plate numbers of numerous participants whom he identified and visited in their homes a year later. In disguise, Humphreys interviewed a sample of 50 men under the pretense of conducting a social health survey. His varied but controversial (Von Hoffman, 1970) research strategies provided him with detailed, intimate, and comprehensive data on the behavior, lifestyles, and social characteristics of tearoom participants.

THE PRESENT STUDY

This paper examines tearoom activity using data gathered from police case materials and through interviews with law enforcement personnel in five Canadian urban areas ranging in size from 24,000 to 600,000. Based on direct observations of sexual behavior in seven public toilets, police in these communities arrested 190 men, charging them with Committing an Indecent Act (Section 173 of the Canadian Criminal Code) or Gross Indecency (Section 157 C.C. — repealed January 1988). Table 1 shows that the washrooms under surveillance comprise the following: (1) a park washroom, (2) a washroom in the basement of a town theater, (3) three washrooms located in shopping malls, (4) a washroom in a large department store located in a shopping center, and (5) a restaurant washroom located in the basement of a shopping mall. Surveillance was maintained from six days to eight weeks with 190 men arrested and charged. Police in communities 1, 2, and 5 gathered evidence with the use of a video camera, whereas police in communities 3 and 4 made direct observations through air vents installed in the ceiling and wall. Because surveillance was maintained continuously, the sample of men in communities 1, 2, and 5 represents all tearoom participants — except for one man who escaped arrest — using the washroom facilities for sexual purposes during each period of observation. Police in all communities arrested men engaged in sexual encounters, including those who masturbated in front of another. Men who visited the facility to watch were either ignored or cautioned since their behavior did not constitute a criminal offence. Video surveillance in communities 1, 2, and 5 indicates that players visited the tearoom for sexual encounters on average 2.3 times over a six-day period.

The research began when a former student, and Superintendent of Special Forces, informed me that the morality squad in his police department (community 3) had begun arresting men for sexual offences committed in mall washrooms. Permission was granted to interview detectives and examine case materials throughout the ongoing investigation. Detectives were frequently questioned immediately

TABLE 1
POLICE SURVEILLANCE AND TEAROOM LOCATION

	Number Arrested	Surveillance Technique	Tearoom Location	Duration of Investigation
Community 1	27	Videotape	Public Park	6 Days
Community 2	32	Videotape	Basement of Town Theater	18 Days
Community 3	62	Direct Surveillance	Three Shopping Centers	8 Weeks
Community 4	37	Direct Surveillance	Department Store in Shopping Mall	6 Days
Community 5	32	Videotape	Basement of Shopping Mall	6 Days
TOTAL	**190**			

following an arrest and although I was often present when offenders were brought into the office to be issued a summons, no attempt was made to interview tearoom participants.

The data from the remaining four police forces were gathered at the completion of each investigation and were also based upon interviews and case materials. A total of 15 detectives were interviewed, most at least twice. The initial focus of the study was on the police response to this behavior (see Desroches, 1991). Very quickly, however, the descriptions of the tearoom behavior alerted me to the serendipitous possibility of replicating Humphreys' research with police generated data. I carefully re-read his study and began questioning detectives in detail. The interviews and case materials provided in-depth descriptions of the behavior as well as offender characteristics such as age, marital status, place of residence, occupation, and previous criminal record. Police investigators in community 5 were particularly conscientious and recorded numerous details as they viewed the action on video. Each participant was assigned a number, in sequence, to label his file and record information. Repeat offenders were identified by the same number with each separate occurrence recorded by date and alphabetical order. For example, offender 3 was observed in illegal acts on three separate occasions and his actions were recorded as follows: 3a Dec. 13, performed fellatio on 4a; 3b Dec. 14, performed fellatio on 12a; 3c Dec. 16, performed fellatio on 9b. Police notes and reports also describe the behavior and position(s) of the offenders, their appearance, the length of time observed, and other details. Because the data provided sufficient information with which to assess Humphreys' work, an offer by one police force to view the videos was declined.

Given the fact that police surveillance of tearooms generates rich descriptive accounts of the behavior of participants, it appears that some of the observations done by Humphreys, and for which he received severe criticism for intrusiveness, are perhaps unnecessary. It is recognized, however, that his technique allowed him, among other things, to become acquainted with twelve cooperative respondents — the "intensive dozen" — who provided him with some of the richest data in the study. In addition, police generated data do not provide the kinds of information Humphreys uncovered in his covert interviews.

I was initially struck by two differences: (a) the behavior took place in shopping mall washrooms rather than parks, and (b) the voyeur-lookout role Humphreys assumed as participant observer appeared to be absent. It soon became increasingly clear, however, that police observations were largely consistent with Humphreys' data.

THE LOCATION OF TEAROOMS

Although he does not address the issue directly, Humphreys implies that the bulk of tearoom activity occurs in the toilets of public parks. He acknowledges the existence of other tearooms not located in parks — referring to three well-known locales — but nonetheless focuses his observations on 19 different men's rooms in five parks of the city (1970:19).

A significant difference between the two studies is that most tearoom activities in this sample took place in the restrooms of shopping malls. Only in community 1 did tearoom activity take place in a park washroom. Police in this jurisdiction report, however, that several tearooms are active in shopping malls. In addition, police departments in the remaining four communities have no evidence that park washrooms have been systematically used as tearooms.

It appears that shopping malls may have usurped parks as the favorite locale of tearoom participants because malls have the same favorable conditions that Humphreys outlines, with fewer disadvantages:

(1) Shopping centers devote heavily travelled areas to retail ventures and relegate public washrooms to out-of-the-way corridors. Located in basements and other isolated areas of the mall, these facilities are seldom used by shoppers, making them ideal for tearoom play. Humphreys noted that the women's side of park restrooms was seldom used. Similarly, investigating officers in this study noted that women seldom visit these out-of-the-way facilities, preferring to use the washrooms provided by restaurants and taverns located in the malls. They also note that 85%-90% of male visitors to these more remote facilities either participate in tearoom sex or appear to be looking for action.

(2) Humphreys' research took place in the mid 1960s. Shopping plazas have proliferated since then and provide an increasing number of locales that compete favorably against the few park washrooms that exist. In addition, unlike park facilities in Canada, shopping centers are open year round and are more easily accessible.

(3) Individuals who use park toilets for illegitimate sexual activities are at greater risk of detection than men who use the facilities provided in large shopping centers. As Humphreys indicated, active park tearooms are easily identifiable: "If two or more cars remain in front of a relatively isolated restroom for more than ten minutes, one may be reasonably certain that homosexual activity is in progress inside" (1970:7). Participants are conspicuous by the presence of unoccupied cars in the vicinity, by the lone automobile occupant lingering for a participant to arrive, and by the traffic of men to and from their cars and the restroom.

Just as Humphreys recorded the license plate numbers of tearoom participants, the police in community 1 identified offenders by watching and photographing them leave the tearoom and enter their vehicles. Police in this community were initially alerted to the activity by local residents suspicious of the high number of men frequenting the park washroom.

Participants who use the facilities of large shopping malls are less conspicuous because numerous vehicles are parked in the surrounding parking lot. In addition, people have many legitimate reasons for visiting a shopping center — e.g., groceries, clothing, browsing, movies, etc. — and one's presence in a mall, unlike the out-of-the-way park washroom, is not likely to arouse suspicion. Tearoom encounters in shopping centers can be accomplished in the course of everyday activities. One offender accompanied his wife to the mall each Saturday, excused himself for a few minutes while she shopped, and visited the washroom for quick sex without her suspecting anything was amiss.

(4) Many police forces deter sexual encounters in park washrooms by patrolling these areas to protect children who use recreational facilities. In addition, police often maintain a presence in order to reduce incidents of noisy parties, mini-bikers, drug usage, and sexual deviance. Shopping malls, on the other hand, are privately run and plaza owners normally contract security firms to discourage undesirables. Private security is less of a deterrent to tearoom participants than the police, who are better trained, equipped, and legally empowered. Police cannot investigate tearoom activities in shopping malls, however, without being invited by mall owners. Investigating officers in three of these communities report tearoom activities in malls about which owners refuse to complain for fear of adverse publicity. This situation creates an attractive and busy setting for impersonal sexual encounters.

DISCOVERING THE TEAROOM

As noted by Humphreys, certain washrooms gain a reputation in the gay community as places where homosexual encounters occur, attracting men who wish to engage. When asked what brought them to the park washroom, participants in community 1 stated that the park itself is known as a meeting spot for gay men. Two of the investigating officers strolled through the park at separate intervals and reported being propositioned by gays on the make. A month after this research had begun, a member of the local gay community was murdered as he walked through the park alone in the evening.

The park's reputation presumably develops through communication between gay men. This does not explain how tearoom participants learn about the popularity of a washroom, since most do not participate in the gay community. In addition, both Humphreys; research and this study indicate that most players hide their deviance from others, remain silent during sex play, and avoid outside homosexual contacts. Even knowing of their existence, Humphreys initially had difficulty in the early stages of his research discovering active tearooms. How then does the uninitiated discover the existence and location of these facilities?

One possibility is through the media. In community 4, police were curious why men gravitated to the Hudson's Bay Department Store washroom, since there is a more isolated public washroom in the basement of this shopping center. Surprisingly, the majority of men explained that they had interpreted the store's advertisement sexually — "Meet me at the Bay" — and correctly assumed that others would do likewise. Security indicates that stores throughout the country have had similar problems. This suggests that media publicity given to tearoom arrests may deter some men from involvement, but at the same time inform others who were previously unaware that such locales exist. Ironically, media reports on police investigations and arrests can become advertisements for new recruits.

Tearooms are also discovered accidentally and through seduction. Several men report being initiated into tearoom sex inadvertently. One man explained that he had been using the washroom a few months earlier when the occupant in the adjoining stall pushed open the 6" by 8" paper dispenser and began masturbating. The accused reports that he was at first shocked, then curious, then aroused. He returned occasionally to the same washroom for impersonal sex until apprehended and charged.

It can also be hypothesized that some participants discover tearooms through explicit homosexual graffiti as described by Humphreys and evident in all washrooms in this study. In one toilet stall, for example, someone had written the following invitation at the base of the divider: "If you put your hand down here, I know you want a blow job." Police observed that several men responded to this message, thus initiating sexual activities.

Some offenders, in addition, admit to having looked for action in out-of-the-way washrooms. A few men, having been convicted of this activity in their own jurisdiction, searched for tearooms in other communities hoping for a safer place to play.

THE PLAYERS

The age of tearoom participants in the present sample ranges from 14 to 68 with the median at 41 and an average of 41.29 years. Only three teenagers were observed participating in tearoom sex — two of them together. In that particular case, a 14-year-old public school student was observed engaging in fellatio with a 17-year-old secondary school student. In no cases were children involved.

Detailed information on the social characteristics of the players in Humphreys' study is provided on 50 tearoom participants. The median age in his sample is 34 years compared to a median age of 41 years in this study. The seven year age gap between tearoom participants in the two studies may be partly explained by the fact that the median age of the total population in the United States and Canada has increased in the past two decades as the birth rate has dropped and longevity increased.

The occupational status of participants in this sample varies widely and includes the following: one elementary school, seven secondary school, six community college, and two university students; one elementary school teacher, six secondary school teachers, a secondary school principal; two community college administrators; one police officer and one young man recently recruited into the police force; two ministers and a seminarian; a funeral director; a midget professional wrestler; three Revenue Canada tax auditors; five accountants; a medical doctor; a pharmacist; two nurses; a commercial artist; two bank managers; a soldier; two hairdressers; a customs official; a letter carrier; several unskilled laborers; a hotel manager; two real estate salesmen; a fireman; numerous salesmen in a variety of businesses; several men who were retired; many who were unemployed; and a number of self-employed men in such diverse occupations as butcher, cook, caterer, computer consultant, roofer, and appliance repairman.

As Humphreys states, "Like other next door neighbors, the participants in tearoom sex are of no one type. They vary along a number of possible continua of social characteristics" (1970:129). In both samples, tearoom participants appear to be mainly working, lower-middle, or middle-class men whose occupational statuses cover a broad spectrum.

Of the 50 men interviewed by Humphreys, 27 (54%) are married, 19 (38%) single, three (6%) divorced, and one (2%) separated. As indicated in Table 3, 58% in this sample are known to be married and living with their wives, 28.9% are single, 6.3% are separated or divorced, and 3.15% are living common-law. The percentage of single men (28.9%) is 10% less than in Humphrey's group. The significant pattern, however, is the fact that, like Humphreys' sample, the majority of tearoom participants are married, many have children,

TABLE 2
AGE OF TEAROOM PARTICIPANTS

	Number Charged	Average Age	Range
Community 1	27	40.0	21 - 65
Community 2	32	48.1	24 - 68
Community 3	62	38.2	14 - 67
Community 4	37	39.25	16 - 60
Community 5	32	44.31	19 - 68
TOTAL SAMPLE	**190**	**41.29**	**14 - 68**

TABLE 3
MARITAL STATUS

	Sample Size	Married	Single	Separated/ Divorced	Common- Law	Unknown
Community 1	27	15	9	1	2	0
Community 2	32	21	3	5	0	3
Community 3	62	31	21	5	3	2
Community 4	37	19	15	1	1	1
Community 5	32	25	7	0	0	0
TOTAL SAMPLE	**190**	**111**	**55**	**12**	**6**	**6**
Percentage	100 %	58.4%	28.9%	6.3%	3.15%	3.15%
Humphreys' Sample		54 %	38 %	8 %	0 %	0 %

and some even have grandchildren.

Although a few men admit to being gay or bisexual, most present themselves as heterosexual. Of the 27 accused in community 1, for example, only three are professed homosexuals. The majority of men in all communities appear to fall into the category Humphreys refers to as "trade" — married or once married men with dependent occupations, masculine in appearance, and heterosexual in their orientation (1970:111). These men do not seek homosexual contact as such, do not involve themselves in the gay community, and hide their deviance from family and others. They are emotionally devastated at arrest and express extreme concern over the possibility that they may be publicly identified.

With the exception of community 4, the majority of offenders (80% - 90%) reside in the jurisdiction in which they are apprehended. In community 4, 30/37 men live outside the area and visited this tearoom because it is located near an exit ramp on a major highway connecting two large cities. Offenders estimate that their visit would add no more than an average 20 to 40 minutes to their travelling time.

The following case synopses, taken from police files and investigating officers' notes, illustrate the variety of persons involved in the tearoom trade.

1 *Insurance Salesman, Age 35, Single.* This man was observed on 14 separate occasions and was nicknamed "Roger the Dodger" by the police surveillance team. He would spend up to five hours a day in the washroom and typically enter, wait, leave for a coffee, and repeat the pattern, connecting several times a day with different men. While waiting, he would casually masturbate and always take stall 1 from which he could watch the urinals. He had no previous conviction.

2 *Unemployed Laborer, Age 54, Married with Children.* He has a criminal record for possession of an offensive weapon and Break and Enter. This man says that if he receives any flak from people over his offence, he will kill them. The police indicate deep concern about this threat with one officer writing: "He has the appearance of a guy who means what he says." The offender expressed no animosity towards the police and asked the arresting officer to accompany him to his home to help explain his actions to his wife.

3 *Retired, Age 68, Married with Children and Grandchildren.* This man was well known in the community and played on the "Old Timers" hockey team. He was very surveillance conscious but insisted that this was his first offence.

4 *Laborer, Manufacturing Plant, Age 40, Married with Children.* This man cried when arrested and threatened suicide. He left work the next day with the intention of killing himself but decided against this course of action.

5 *Bank Manager, Age 49, Married with Children.* Charged with committing an indecent act, this offender had been arrested on a previous occasion for the same behavior but was released with a caution. He explained that he was

taking counselling but that it had not changed his desires. He was later dismissed from his job when his name appeared in local newspapers.

6 *Gardener, Age 48, Married with Children.* He was observed involved in fellatio on two separate occasions and has a previous conviction for Gross Indecency. He requested to see the video of his offence, and watched up to the point at which his face could be clearly identified. He then said, "That's enough." In response to the officer's comment, "Pretty bad eh?" he replied, "Especially when you're not in the mood."

7 *Automotive Plant Employee, Age 52, Married with Children.* This man is a Croatian who came into the station with his wallet open stating, "I pay." Later he brought his family photograph book expecting sympathy and hoping to have the charges dropped. Eventually he obtained a lawyer and insisted he was innocent. His lawyer watched the video and persuaded the accused to plead guilty.

8 *Nurse, Age 41, Married with Children.* This man had been arrested a month earlier in another washroom. Because his name appeared in the papers, his children aged 9, 10, and 11 were verbally abused by other students at school and engaged in several fights. After the second charge, his wife left with the children stating, "This is not over. I'm getting out."

9 *Doctor, Age 45, Married with Children.* The offender was apprehended in his home community several years earlier but was able to have the charges dropped when his lawyer presented psychiatric evidence that he was suicidal. He was re-arrested in a community 125 miles from his home. Police in the two communities cooperated to ensure that he was convicted the second time around. Local newspapers gave the incident full coverage.

THE BREASTPLATE OF RIGHTEOUSNESS

From interviews conducted in their homes, Humphreys noted a strong tendency of many tearoom participants to maintain an outward appearance of superpropriety. This is particularly true of those men whose lifestyle makes them vulnerable to exposure — married men in dependent occupations. Most of these covert deviants — referred to as "trade" by Humphreys — drive late model automobiles that are clean and polished, maintain exceptionally manicured yards, and are impeccably groomed and dressed. The covert deviant, in physical and moral presentation of self, creates an image of one who is neat, clean, proper, conscientious, moral, conservative, righteous, and religious.

Investigating officers in our samples similarly note the neat and conservative appearance of tearoom participants. As a case in point, a subject who committed suicide shortly after his arrest was an exemplary husband and father. In reporting his death, the local newspaper described him as a "model citizen who was a victim of his secret life":

He had a few more drinks than usual at the neighborhood Christmas party. That was the only indication something was bothering the tall, handsome, 42-year-old sales manager. Not even his wife suspected what was eating away at the normally outgoing, likeable man...On Saturday afternoon, he kissed his wife and two young children goodbye and drove to a nearby village. With his car moving at slow speed, he doused himself with gasoline and flashed his lighter. Hours earlier, he had been summoned to the police station where he was charged with gross indecency in connection with alleged homosexual activity in the public washroom at a local shopping mall...Neighbors and associates of the salesman stated that he was respectable and "normal in every sense of the word"...His friends and family are shocked because he was a model citizen, a dedicated family man married for about 15 years, active in his church and well liked by everyone who knew him. He taught Sunday school and coached children's soccer. On public holidays he flew the Canadian flag on his front lawn.

The meticulous and scrupulous image cultivated by this man was about to be destroyed by his arrest for tearoom activities and he no doubt anticipated the loss of all that was important to him — family, community respect, self-respect, and perhaps even his job. Because he chose to die rather than face such a loss, his death can be viewed as an example of anomic suicide (Durkheim, 1951).

Although the data in this study are insufficient to systematically test Humphreys' findings, detectives apprised of his observations are of the opinion that the "breastplate of righteousness" concept accurately portrays the lifestyle, dress, and appearance of the majority of tearoom participants they encountered.

What accounts for this concern with a squeaky clean image? The motive, Humphreys suggests, is to shield oneself from exposure. He writes:

In donning the breastplate of righteousness, the covert deviant assumes a protective shield of superpropriety...Motivated largely by his own awareness of the discreditable nature of his secret behavior, [he] develops a presentation of self that is respectable to a fault. His whole life style becomes an incarnation of what is proper and orthodox. In manners and taste, religion and art, he strives for an otherwise low resistance to the shock of exposure. (Humphreys, 1970:135-36)

The problem with this strategy is that it does not protect the offender from police surveillance, arrest, and public disgrace. Furthermore, he faces a horrible backlash from persons who view his actions as a form of betrayal and/or hypocrisy. The pillar of the community topples from a great height because he has publicly proclaimed this higher status. Three additional hypotheses are offered for consideration.

1. REACTION FORMATION

Reaction formation is a psychiatric concept used to describe an exaggerated or intense reaction of persons to something that is threatening. The overreaction functions to reassure the subject against the inner and/or external threat. In his theory of delinquency, Albert Cohen suggests that lower-class boys, frustrated over their inability to achieve status in a middle-class world, respond by repudiating middle-class values. Reaction formation occurs because they are unable to conform to standards that are foreign to them (Cohen, 1955:133).

With tearoom participants, the process may be reversed. They conform on the surface but covertly engage in deviant sexual practices. The overreaction — i.e., this excessive concern with neatness and propriety — results form the anxiety brought on by their sexual deviance. The donning of the breastplate of righteousness may have a psychological cleansing effect — an emotional catharsis — in which the "clean" life-style washes away the "stains" that have been picked up at play.

2. SELF-VALIDATION

The public definition of tearoom behavior as "sick" or "perverted" threatens the self-concept of participants. The donning of the breastplate of righteousness may function to validate a view of oneself as "normal" and reassure players that they are not perverted.

The actor encapsulates the deviant activity, forgetting about it for the time being and denying that this is "really him." Instead, he takes seriously the clean image that is fostered and in which he has placed so much effort. He is indeed this person that everyone knows him to be — a husband, a father, a faithful employee, a good neighbor, and an upstanding citizen in the community. Erving Goffman describes the process:

At one extreme, one finds that the performer can be fully taken in by his own act; he can be sincerely convinced that the impression of reality which he stages is the real reality. When his audience is also convinced in this way about the show he puts on — and this seems to be the typical case — then for the moment at least, only the sociologist or the socially disgruntled will have any doubts about the "realness" of what is presented. (1959:17)

The mask of propriety represents the view that these men have or wish to have of themselves. By playing a conforming role, they convince themselves (and others) that this is their true self. The successful performance validates their identity.

3. THE BREASTPLATE OF RIGHTEOUSNESS — CAUSE OR EFFECT?

The donning of the breastplate of righteousness may serve all three functions outlined above: (a) to deflect suspicion away from deviant actions as Humphreys suggests, (b) as a means of cleansing oneself, and (c) as a mechanism for self-validation. Whereas Humphreys' explanation assumes that the performance is intended for the general public, the other two hypotheses imply that the behavior is meant for self-consumption.

Each assumes, however, that tearoom participation precedes the concern with an image or lifestyle that is clean, conservative, and righteous. But neither study has sufficient evidence to indicate which comes first. Was the breastplate of righteousness erected to hide the deviant activity from society and the player himself? Or is the covert deviant behavior a result of a highly constrictive lifestyle?

Consider the lifestyle of the participants for a moment. These men lead lives characterized by conservative, moral ideology and devoted to religious and family responsibilities. Humphreys' tearoom sample included a disproportionately high representation of Roman Catholics and Episcopalians (1970:137). Obviously their religious upbringing precedes tearoom participation. It may be that an overly conservative and sexually repressive childhood influences sexual behavior later in life. Perhaps the breastplate of righteousness is merely their acquiescence to society's definition of how their lives should be led — a home, family, career, church, and all the other trappings of a socially conservative and respectable person. But clearly, participation in this sexual activity indicates that something is lacking in their lives. Unfulfilled but unable or unwilling to reject the values and roles they have acquired, they seek release in the furtive and impersonal sex offered in men's washrooms.

RULES, ROLES, AND STRATEGIES — HUMPHREYS' OBSERVATIONS

From the perspective of watchqueen, Humphreys provides a detailed analysis of the behaviors and roles of participants. Although tactics differ, he suggests that rules and roles remain essentially the same from encounter to encounter. Rules are primarily aimed at minimizing risks and include the following: avoiding the exchange of biographical data, avoiding youths and children, and never forcing one's intentions on anyone.

Tearoom participants avoid the exchange of biographical information to the point where sexual encounters are contracted and performed in silence. This silence also has the important function of keeping the encounters impersonal. As Humphreys suggests, propositioning strangers for sex acts in a public washroom is dangerous, "so much so that it is made possible only by concerted action which pro-

gresses in stages of increasing mutuality" (1970:60). A man who knows nothing of the homosexual game in progress may enter a restroom, spend a minute urinating, and leave. He is recognized as being "straight" by the fact that he "stands close to the fixture, so that his front side may not easily be seen and gazes downward" (1970:62). Straights, Humphreys argues, do not have to be concerned about being propositioned, molested, or otherwise involved in the action.

A man who knows the rules and wishes to play, however, will stand back from the urinal, allowing his gaze to shift from side to side or to the ceiling. (Humphreys, 1970:62).

Besides lingering at the urinals and looking about, participants will signal a willingness to play by openly fondling their penis in "casual masturbation." By means of various bodily movements, the actors achieve through silent communication a sign of willingness to proceed and the role each will play. Most sexual acts that Humphreys observed involved fellatio whereby one man, the insertee, performs oral sex on another, the insertor. One who wishes to be an insertee may take hold of his partner's exposed and erect penis, or take a seat in the stalls and peer out, and/or beckon to another through head or hand motions (1970:66). One who wishes to be an insertor steps into the stall in which his partner is seated. Humphreys notes that most acts of fellatio take place in this manner (71% in the stalls vs. 29% at the urinals) because it is more comfortable for the insertee to sit than to crouch. It also means that only one participant need move if an intrusion takes place (1970:75).

Other roles described by Humphreys include three different lookouts (watchqueens): (a) waiters — men waiting for a particular person or a chance to get in on the action; (b) masturbators — those who are present just to masturbate or who engage in masturbation while being waiters; (c) voyeurs — those who "get their kicks" out of watching others (these men are sometimes also masturbators).

Humphreys describes no instances in which fellatio is reciprocated, although he does state that mutual masturbation at the urinals occurs.

Only two instances of anal intercourse were observed, perhaps because of the danger involved in the removal of clothing. When the sex act is complete, the insertor usually zips up, occasionally expresses his gratitude with a pat on the shoulder, wave of the hand, or whispered "thanks," and departs. The insertee leaves afterward but may remain to participate in further action. Humphreys describes these ongoing and sequential sex acts as "series encounters," whereby sexual activity continues with differing men throughout the day, "each group of participants trading upon the legitimization process of the previous game" (1970:77). He also observes "simultaneous encounters" in which more than one sexual act is in progress at the same time.

RULES, ROLES, AND STRATEGIES — THE PRESENT STUDY

The data in this study largely support Humphreys' assertion that the rules and roles of tearoom sex remain essentially the same from encounter to encounter. Police observations in all five communities reveal that youth and children are not involved in sex play, the action is noncoercive, and silence and impersonality are maintained. Although regular patrons occasionally nod to one another in recognition, no conversations occur within the washrooms.

Police in community 5 made the only observations of participants leaving together and speaking briefly outside the washroom. In one instance, the conversation took place in the mall coffee shop; in the other case, the two sex partners spoke in one man's car before departing in their respective vehicles.

The various roles described by Humphreys — insertor, insertee, straights, waiters, masturbators, voyeurs — are also clearly observed in these five communities. A significant difference, however, is the relative absence of teenagers (chickens) in sex play. Humphreys describes three roles played by teenagers in the tearoom trade: enlisters — youths who want to get into the action; toughs — youths who harass other tearoom participants, sometimes by physical attacks such as "rolling"; and hustlers — enlisters who demand payment for serving as insertors.

Humphreys argues that because involvement with youths is legally dangerous, most tearoom participants avoid them. In addition, enlisters are difficult to distinguish from hustlers and hustlers are potential threats because they demand payment and can turn into toughs if refused. In only three cases were teenagers involved in the tearooms of the five communities in this study. Their absence is perhaps explained by the fact that gang delinquency and teenage prostitution are not large problems in these communities.

The actual behavior or strategies of tearoom participants in this study varied somewhat from washroom to washroom and appears to have been influenced by the physical characteristics of each room. Specifically, sexual encounters usually took place in the area of the washroom hidden from view, allowing participants time to disengage when intruded upon. In community 1, for example, the sexual activity took place mainly at the urinals situated behind a partition and out of view of the entrance. As Humphreys describes, the action typically begins with one man lingering at the urinal until another arrives. He then fondles and displays an erection and looks for a response. Sex play begins by one man reaching over and stroking his neighbor's penis or fellating him. Although mutual masturbation is common, fellatio is not reciprocated. A squeaky door warns participants of intruders, allowing each man sufficient time to zip up and depart. The amount of time spent in sexual encounters is brief and most men leave immediately afterward.

In the other four communities, sexual contact usually took place in the toilet stalls hidden from view. In communities 2 and 4, an opening in the metal divider separating the stalls was strategic in sex play. In the former, a fist-sized "glory hole" had been punctured three feet above the floor; in the latter, the toilet paper dispenser could be opened to allow the occupants to peer in on one another. With the stalls occupied, sex play begins with casual masturbation. This activity is visible through the opening and appears to be the cue for action. Other overtures or gestures that precede sexual encounters involve one man beckoning the other with his finger. Participants were also commonly observed writing and passing notes on toilet paper. The notes contain explicit sexual come-ons and this activity sometimes continues 15 or 20 minutes before sexual contact is initiated. Police observed that some men engage in sex immediately, while others seem to enjoy the flirtation as a type of foreplay. Still others appear shy and nervous, perhaps needing the time to build up their courage before making contact.

On occasion, one of the men will show no interest and depart. Most times, however, one player will reach over and touch the other's penis or thrust his own through the opening. In both communities, masturbation, mutual masturbation, and fellatio result. Most of the activity takes place through the opening or underneath the stalls. Fellatio and mutual masturbation are the most common activities, with the glory hole in community 2 occasionally being used for anal sex. One participant, a bank manager, was observed in anal sex with three different men in a one-hour period. It was later discovered that he was afflicted with syphilis and may have transmitted the disease.

In community 3, sexual activities were observed in three washrooms of two shopping malls with most of the action taking place between adjacent stalls. Normally a player arrives, waits in the stall, engages in casual masturbation, and spends time reading and/or writing messages on the wall. When the adjacent booth becomes occupied, contact begins by one man gradually moving his foot into the other's stall, eventually touching his neighbor's foot. Several men also come equipped with hand mirrors which they use to look up into the adjacent stall.

In most instances, sexual encounters take the form of mutual masturbation or fellatio beneath the partition without either leaving the stall or even viewing one another's faces. Participants do not speak and the role of fellator is assumed by one man kneeling and taking the other man's penis in his mouth. An examination of the notes that are exchanged also indicates that the insertor-insertee role is sometimes determined in this manner.

Similarly, in community 5, sexual activity takes place between the stalls with one man or both men extending their lower torsos (much like limbo dancers) under the partition in order to be masturbated or fellated. Contact is usually initiated through the touching of feet or note passing. As in all communities, the insertor leaves afterward while the insertee waits in his stall for a moment before departing. Thus, participants rarely see one another's faces. In the few instances in which they do leave the stalls at the same time, nothing is spoken and neither will look at the other except for an occasional quick glance. As in community 4, several men were observed using hand mirrors to view the action. Stall occupants also read and wrote graffiti while waiting for someone to enter the washroom.

Humphreys observed that the most common form of sex play involved one man entering a stall in which another was seated in order to be fellated. This tactic was observed in this sample only in community 5 in which the urinals were situated directly in front of the end stall. The proximity of the two allowed the man at the urinal to step into the stall and quickly step back to the urinal at the first sign of intrusion.

In all park washrooms observed by Humphreys, stall doors had been removed. This fact along with the additional benefit of having someone act as lookout allowed participants to move into and out of the stalls without being observed by an intruder.

Next to the physical setting itself, the lookout plays the most important part in maintaining the boundaries of the tearoom encounter. He signals when an intrusion is about to occur and serves to legitimize those who enter. (Humphreys, 1970:54)

Although the roles of waiter, masturbator, and voyeur were observed by police, on only three occasions did anyone appear to act as a lookout for others. By holding the entrance door slightly ajar, these watchqueens could survey the corridor and warn of anyone approaching. Their position, however, did not allow them to watch the action at the same time. This explains in part why the lookout role does not emerge in these toilets to the same degree that Humphreys found. Moreover, since there were no windows, the physical means by which to discreetly play the role were unavailable. A squeaky door was the first sign of an intrusion, giving the participants little time to disengage. This necessitated the use of different strategies and accounts for the fact that most participants committed their acts out of sight of the entrance: at the urinals where they could quickly disengage, or in separate stalls where they could sit up and look innocent. All toilets in this study had doors.

Despite the danger of being caught in the act, men in several communities were occasionally observed entering another's stall or involved in simultaneous sexual encounters in open areas of the washroom. Police in two communities discovered that some participants brought with them brown paper shopping bags in which they stood while being fellated in another's stall. To the casual observer, it would simply appear as though the occupant had placed a bag of groceries at his feet.

Like Humphreys, police observed numerous men masturbate alone and/or attend the washrooms simply to watch others. Participants were charged only if they engaged in sexual acts with one another or in open view of someone. Police also observed numerous men who were unsuccessful in their search for a sexual partner. These men would enter the washroom, linger for long periods, sit in the stall, play with themselves, read and write graffiti, and leave often without using the facilities. Some men are discriminating and will enter the washroom up to a dozen times a day without meeting someone to their liking. Most, however, respond to whoever happens to be willing. Frequent tearoom visitors generally do not have sex with one another, apparently preferring someone new. In both studies, men waited outside the tearoom and watched for others to arrive.

Although tearoom participants do not force themselves on others, some men are brash and persistent in their attempt to engage shy and reluctant partners. In more instances than not, this boldness pays off and sexual contact follows. Occasionally, however, this aggressiveness can lead to a rebuke by someone who is not inclined. In one instance, a subject was kicked in the hand when he reached into another's stall. In another case, a subject ran from the washroom when threatened by a man he attempted to look in upon. These two *faux pas*,

however, represent less than 1% of tearoom encounters observed. Most participants are cautious enough to wait for cues that others are willing before moving into sex play.

THE MOTIVATION

Why do men, many of whom are married and presumably heterosexual, participate in sexual activities with other men in public washrooms? Why do they risk criminal prosecution and serious damage to family relations, reputations, and careers?

Men who are closet gays or bisexual may find this type of sexual activity arousing because they are attracted to other men yet do not wish to be known as homosexual. Because they value their marriages, careers, and reputations, open involvement in the gay community is ruled out. Tearooms allow them to keep their homosexual urges private and lead publicly respectable lives as long as they are not exposed.

An example of such a case involves a 24-year-old man who traveled 200 miles round trip to community 2 for tearoom encounters. He cried when arrested and expressed remorse and shame over his behavior, explaining to the police that he had known since childhood that he was gay. His overwhelming concern was to keep this secret from his mother who he said would be devastated. Consequently, he avoided gay bars, did not have a boyfriend, and stated that he would never marry. He chose to participate in tearoom sex because he considered it relatively safe.

For men who are gay, the attraction to tearoom sex is perhaps easier to understand given their sexual orientation. Yet most gay men avoid tearooms. It can be hypothesized that they do so because they are less concerned about having a gay reputation, thus allowing them the freedom to frequent gay bars, parties, and so forth; gay locales offer personal and impersonal sex if desired in a less dangerous setting; finally, some men are involved in monogamous relationships, spurning impersonal encounters.

For men who are primarily heterosexual, involvement in tearoom sex is theoretically difficult to explain because the behavior conflicts with a heterosexual self-concept.

Humphreys' research indicates that such men are unlikely to take the insertee role in fellatio, telling themselves that they're not "queer" if they're on the receiving end. Other studies similarly note the use of this rationalization in male-to-male sex (Reiss, 1961). Several men in this sample emphasized their limited role in the sexual encounter, stating, "No I'm not gay! I never gave blow jobs."

It appears that the impersonal nature of their contact with other men, in conjunction with the self-imposed restrictions on sexual behavior, allows them to participate in tearoom sex yet still protect their self-concept as heterosexual. There is, after all, minimal physical involvement (participants often do not even see one another) and no emotional commitment.

For some men, tearoom sex may be attractive because it is their only sexual outlet. One participant, a midget professional wrestler, justified his actions by complaining that he has no other means of obtaining sexual gratification: "I go there for sex because I can't get it anywhere else. Who would want to screw me?"

Married men who find their sex lives inadequate may also turn to tearooms as an alternative means of sexual gratification. Humphreys describes the married lives of several of the men that he interviewed as woefully lacking in affect and physical pleasure. Tearoom sex, he argues, is fulfilling a need that is not met in the context of their conjugal relationship.

I find no indication that these men seek homosexual contact as such; rather they want a form of orgasm producing action that is less lonely than masturbation and less involving than a love relationship. (Humphreys, 1970:115)

Police in this sample report that although a few men complain that their wives have put on weight or are no longer interested in sex, many more say that they are happily married family men who do not have serious marital problems. The only explanation given is that they have "this urge." A subject who regularly took his children to play in the park while he visited the tearoom said to the police: "I have a wife and two children and I'm happily married. Why am I doing this? I don't know...I never think of it afterwards; it's as though it didn't happen."

If heterosexual men have an urge for illicit sex, why don't they have an affair or visit a prostitute? Even if they are bisexual or gay, why participate in furtive impersonal sex in a public washroom with so much risk? What are the factors that make tearoom sex attractive?

As Humphreys tells us, tearoom sex is impersonal and anonymous — it does not lead to problem entanglements. Ironically, it may be considered a safer alternative than having an affair. Tearoom sex, unlike an affair, involves minimal effort, commitment, obligation, expectation, resources, or demands on one's time. The fact that tearoom sex is free is also an attraction. Prostitution is impersonal, anonymous, and free of entanglements and obligations but can become expensive if used on a regular basis. This may preclude its use by those who might otherwise be so inclined.

Another feature of tearoom sex is the speed at which encounters can be contracted and completed — some taking no more than five minutes from start to finish. Players do not have to be away from family for extended periods of time or explain lengthy absences.

The variety of partners available adds unknown and exciting elements to the encounters, providing additional incentives for some. Humphreys further argues that kicks are derived from playing the game successfully, that is, making contact with a stranger and following through until the sexual payoff is achieved. Danger itself may be experienced as stimulating, enhancing the game and the sexual pleasure. Readers may recollect instances in which they have been involved in sexual encounters open to discovery (in a car or next door to one's parents' bedroom) and recall the aphrodisiac effect of taking such risks.

For men attracted to other men or for whom heterosexual outlets are unavailable, tearoom sex is attractive because it provides fast, inexpensive, impersonal, relatively safe, exciting sex with a variety of partners.

One final question must still be addressed. Even if one is inclined to participate in tearoom sex, why does the possibility of arrest and exposure not act as a powerful deterrent? Although some men are surveillance conscious, most are not. Given the fact that the majority participate regularly in tearoom sex, they have perhaps been lulled into a false sense of security because they have experienced no problems. After all, they don't force themselves on others, there is no victim to complain, and their behavior is discreet. Consequently, some participants may believe that they are involved in an activity that law enforcement agencies care and/or know little about. Supporting this hypothesis is the fact that in three of these five communities, no police investigation of this type had ever taken place before. In another, police had made arrests four years previously but little publicity was involved and the names of offenders were not made public.

In community 5, however, a highly publicized police investigation had recently occurred. Although tearoom participants in this community were cautious and surveillance conscious, they were obviously undeterred. Many searched for cameras, left quickly if disturbed, and/or took evasive actions when leaving the washroom. These men knowingly took risks, but ignorance of police capabilities perhaps led them to believe that they could detect surveillance and were safe in this criminal conduct.

We can also hypothesize that most offenders simply fail to consider the possibility or consequences of getting caught. Like shoplifters apprehended in a store, many of the tearoom participants are mortified and humiliated at arrest and terrified that their identity may be made public. They involve themselves in a crime failing to consider the possible harm that may result to themselves and their families.

Finally, some men may be naively unaware that their behavior constitutes a criminal offence. Several men who masturbated in front of others expressed surprise at their arrest, stating, for example, that, "I didn't know it was against the law to pull your own wire." It is the public nature of the act that makes it an offence.

CONCLUSION

Like many studies of covert deviance, this paper is based upon a captive sample of persons who have come to the attention of law enforcement agencies. The existence of Laud Humphreys' research, however, makes possible a comparison of police-generated data with data obtained through observations and interviews with "unapprehended" offenders. Because police observations were so detailed, a rare opportunity to replicate a qualitative study presented itself. This research largely substantiates the picture drawn by Humphreys in his classic study, *Tearoom Trade: Impersonal Sex in Public Places*. Consistent with his observations, most tearoom participants (a) communicate through nonverbal gestures and seldom speak, (b) do not associate outside the tearoom or attempt to learn one another's identities or exchange biographical information, (c) do not use force or coercion or attempt to involve youths or children, (d) are primarily heterosexual and married, (e) depart separately with the insertor leaving first, (f) commit their sex acts out of sight of the entrance and accidental exposure, (g) do not undress or engage in anal sex, (h) break off sexual contact when someone enters the washroom, (i) rarely approach straight men, (j) read and write sexually explicit homosexual graffiti, and (k) linger inside and outside the washroom for someone to appear. In addition, (l) fellatio is generally not reciprocated and fellators are usually older men; (m) most offenders are neat in appearance; (n) some engage in series and simultaneous encounters; (o) encounters are brief, usually not exceeding twenty minutes; and (p) few have criminal records, with the exception of those previously convicted of similar offences.

The behavior of players reveals remarkable consistency over time, from community to community, and across national boundaries. Many men, the majority of them married and primarily heterosexual, continue to visit out-of-the-way public washrooms in search of fast, impersonal, and exciting sex despite the risk to family, friends, job, and reputation. Although shopping malls have usurped public parks as the favorite locale of tearoom participants, the basic rules of the game and profiles of the players — as Humphreys contends — remain the same over time and place.

Chapter 16

ARMED ROBBERY:
HIGHLIGHTS OF A CANADIAN STUDY*

Thomas Gabor and André Normandeau

There are many misconceptions about the crime of armed robbery. A major Canadian study conducted at the International Centre of Comparative Criminology at Montreal sheds further light on this offence and hopefully clears up some of these misconceptions. The findings of the five-year study are summarized comprehensively elsewhere (Gabor et al., 1987). This article presents some of the major highlights of the project by focusing on five issues: 1) trends in armed robbery over the last 25-30 years; 2) the nature and dynamics of the crime; 3) the motives and perspectives of offenders; 4) the role and reactions of victims; and 5) the response of the police and judiciary to robbery incidents.

The data for the study were drawn principally from Montreal and Quebec City, although some comparisons were made with other Canadian cities as well as with some urban centres in the United States. The robbery problem in Quebec, although benign by American standards, is serious relative to other provinces. Although Quebec's overall rates of violence have been substantially lower than national rates, its armed robbery rates have been consistently over twice the national rate. Furthermore, Montreal's robbery rates have been

well over those of any other major Canadian city (Gabor et al., 1987). Below, this paper will address some of the socioeconomic factors that appear to have contributed to the disproportionate involvement in armed robbery of groups such as French Quebeckers and black Americans. Although dealing with such disproportionate participation on the part of these groups is a sensitive matter, facing such issues is, we believe, essential to tackling the problem.

TRENDS IN ROBBERY

From 1962 to 1980, there was a four-fold increase in the per capita robbery rate in both Canada and the United States. Since the early 1980s, there has been some decline in both countries; however, it is unlikely that the levels of robbery will approach those low levels prevailing in the early 1960s in the foreseeable future.

What led to the rather dramatic upsurge in robbery over the past 25 years? When we examine the trends in other crimes over the same years we realize that increases in robbery did not occur in a social vacuum. In both Canada and the United States, other violent crimes have

---

* Edited version of T. Gabor and A. Normandeau, "Armed Robbery: Highlights of a Canadian Study," *Canadian Police College Journal* 13(1989): 273–82. Reprinted with permission of the authors, the *Canadian Police College Journal*, and the Minister of Supply and Services Canada, 1990.

This article is the keynote address presented by the first author at the seminar on Armed Robbery at the Australian Institute of Criminology, Canberra, March 22, 1988.

increased at about the same pace and the official rates of various property crimes have also gone up, although not quite so dramatically (Brantingham and Brantingham, 1984). Thus, many of the explanations for the overall increases in crime are probably applicable as well to armed robbery.

Sir Leon Radzinowicz of Cambridge University and his collaborator Joan King have argued that increases in crime since the Second World War, and particularly the 1960s, have been virtually world-wide (Radzinowicz and King, 1977). They allude to the effects of societal changes such as increasing urbanization and modernization. These changes can disrupt family and community life, lessen the controls that keep the young from engaging in crime, raise people's expectations along material lines, and provide environments with greater criminal temptations and opportunities. The extent to which robbery today is an urban crime can be appreciated through a glimpse of the F.B.I.'s Uniform Crime Reports. There is a positive, linear relationship between the size of American cities and their robbery rates. As an example, cities of over one million people collectively have the highest rates, cities between a quarter of a million and a million people have the next highest rates, and this pattern continues through to the smallest cities and rural communities which have the lowest rates (F.B.I., 1985).

Another factor that has undoubtedly accounted for the general increases in crime, including robbery, is demographic change. The low birth rates during the depression and war years yielded a relatively small number of teenagers and young adults in the population during the 1950s. Beginning in 1946, there was a very sharp upturn in births in what has been called the "baby boom." The baby boom continued into the 1950s and resulted in a flooding of the population by young people in the 1960s and 1970s. Some demographers consider this factor as accounting for a substantial proportion of the increases in crime during the 1960s and 1970s; as well, they see the reversal of this trend as responsible for the stabilization and even slight decline of crime in the 1980s (Sagi and Wellford, 1968).

Another factor contributing to increases in robbery and other crimes, in North America, has been the more pervasive use of hard drugs over the last 25 years. Studies in which addicted offenders have been interviewed have revealed an extent of criminal activity that is mind-boggling. Some addicts have confessed to committing thousands of predatory street crimes, such as muggings, in the span of one year (Ball, 1981).

Still another development that might account for the increases in robbery over the period we have discussed has been the changing social situation of groups particularly susceptible to this crime. In Canada, the French Canadian minority is overrepresented in armed robbery in a significant way. The predominantly French province of Quebec accounts for 60 percent of all armed robberies in Canada while having only a quarter of Canada's population. The black minority in the United States is likewise overrepresented in robbery as blacks make up about 67 percent of all robbery suspects even though they only constitute about 12 percent of the U.S. population. In their case, they are overrepresented in other major crime categories as well, but nowhere as much as in the case of robbery.

The overrepresentation of French Canadians and black Americans can be understood perhaps in terms of their historic role in North American society. When one looks at their experience as a group, one finds many analogies. Also, both groups were going through considerable upheaval during the 1960s, a fact that may explain the intensification of their participation in robbery at that time. Both groups have faced political oppression and exclusion from the economic elite. Both have faced the humiliations accorded those considered inferior in status. Both have, in this century, experienced large-scale migrations from repressive and parochial rural communities to large, competitive urban centers.

In the 1960s, the Quiet Revolution was going on in Quebec and the Civil Rights Movement was in full gear in the United States. These movements allowed members of these groups to become socially mobile to an extent they had never experienced and to penetrate the spheres of business, education, and the professions as never before. Many social and economic barriers were being removed, engendering the widespread belief that the time for French Canadians and black Americans had finally come. A very large, unyielding underclass, however, has remained in the case of both groups — an underclass that increasingly appears unable to extricate itself from the bottom of the social ladder. In many American urban ghettos, the unemployment rates of black youth are at 40 to 50 percent. Drugs are prevalent, educational opportunities poor, and a feeling of hopelessness is prevalent. The situation is almost as bad amongst lower class youth in French Canada.

Not only do these young people lack access to opportunities to make a living in a law-abiding way, they also reside in areas where access to professional, organized criminal activity is limited. The disorganized slum in American cities leaves few alternatives to ghetto youth in terms of a criminal orientation other than crude robberies that require no collaborators, no contacts to unload stolen merchandise, and that demand only primitive skills to execute. Armed robbery, because of its potential simplicity,is in a sense an ideal crime for unskilled and unconnected persons who need cash quickly.

THE NATURE OF ARMED ROBBERY

Is armed robbery, in fact, a crudely executed crime? The "Hollywood" image of robbery is one in which professional criminals plan their robberies to the last detail. Earlier investigators focused on the organization of professional gangs. More recent studies suggest that the typical robber is anything but professional. Present-day robbers are portrayed as individuals who possess little sophistication in their methods, do little planning in preparation for their offences, often have a drug or alcohol problem, and even commit offences under their influence. Today's robbers are also viewed as taking little professional pride in their work and as being unconcerned about the consequences of their actions.

We examined 1266 cases of armed robbery in Montreal and Quebec City using police files and found that the evidence supported the more recent depictions of robbery (Gabor et al., 1987). The targets in Quebec are usually convenience stores and other small businesses. The most common type of weapon, by far, was a firearm of some sort.

The perpetrators' lack of professionalism was shown by a number of factors. First of all, the age of suspects, as indicated by victims and witnesses, usually was under 22 years. No disguises were worn in three-quarters of the incidents studied. Almost two-thirds of the robberies brought the offender(s) less than $500. The most typical amount stolen was $100. Even these very modest profits often had to be divided up. The most frequent scenarios, occurring in over 85 percent of the incidents, were those in which there were either one or two offenders.

The means of escape, too, contradict the notion that robbers tend to be a professional lot. By far the most frequent means of escape observed by victims and witnesses was on foot and not with the help of a motor vehicle. We will try to illuminate the issue of professionalism further when we address the results of our interviews with convicted armed robbers.

First, in concluding our discussion of the nature of armed robberies, we shall deal with two additional issues: 1) the level of violence in armed robberies; and 2) the different types of incidents.

Robbery is ordinarily classified as a violent crime. It is usually defined legally as the use of force or threat of force to secure the property of another. The actual deployment of weapons, whether this means the discharging of firearms, pistol-whipping, or other blatant acts of intimidation with weapons, occurred in only about eight percent of the 1266 incidents we examined. If one also includes jostling, punching, and the tying up of victims, then about 30 percent of the robberies involved physical force. Only three percent of the cases caused injuries requiring medical care and only about one and a half percent of the incidents resulted in hospitalization or death. Interestingly, those in this last category were more likely to be suspects than victims. We also found that violence is not merely a function of the offender's inclinations; the level of violence is also dependent on the reactions of victims and bystanders. To say this is not to blame victims for the injuries they may incur. It is merely important to point out that robberies are fluid and dynamic events in which understanding the interaction of all the parties is vital in making sense of the outcome. For example, the resistance of victims to the demands of the perpetrators, or the attempt of victims or other bystanders to otherwise obstruct them, increased the likelihood that violence would occur.

The robberies varied in their sophistication, violence, and profits, according to the nature of the target. Bank robberies tended to be the most sophisticated in terms of the weapons, escape vehicles, and disguises used. They also tended to yield the greatest profits and involved the least violence. On the other end of the spectrum are convenience store and service station robberies as well as those targeting individuals (muggings). These types tend to be the least sophisticated, involve the crudest weapons, and yield the most modest profits. It is paradoxical that robberies committed with inferior weapons, such as knives used in muggings, have the highest incidence of violence. It would appear that crude weapons make resistance by the victim more likely as they do not afford the perpetrator the same credibility as do firearms. Bank robberies and muggings were found to be polar types not only in terms of sophistication, violence, and profits, but also in terms of the seriousness with which they were viewed by the police and prosecutors. The interests of the banks seem to take precedence over the welfare of those unfortunate enough to be mugged.

THE OFFENDER

Now, let us take a closer look at the offender. Most of our material pertaining to offender motives and outlooks was drawn from interviews with convicted armed robbers (39 in all). Some of these men had a large number of armed robbery convictions and others only a few. All but one were still serving sentences in the Montreal area. Most were under 30 years of age, had no more than a secondary school education, and came from a blue collar background. Many of them showed a high degree of residential mobility as adults. Their self-re-

ported criminality was far in excess of that indicated by their files. Interestingly, almost all the subjects mentioned they had, at one time or another, pauses in their criminal activities (from several weeks to several years). They tended to attribute these periods of inactivity to the fact they were working and were not seeing their friends as regularly.

As far as their armed robberies were concerned, the manner in which they went about selecting their targets was quite varied. Target selection could be based on chance, a tip from a reliable source, based on the individual's familiarity with potential targets, on the amount of money thought to be there, and on a target's propitiousness as far as escape is concerned. Although the amount of money was an important factor, a number of subjects mentioned that the minimization of risks was a principal goal. After all, as a few indicated, a great deal of money would do them little good in prison. Finally, a few of the robbers showed they had a code of ethics as they eliminated certain targets from consideration; namely, very small businesses in which the owners themselves were struggling to make a living.

Close to half the subjects either did no planning whatsoever or at most undertook about an hour of preparation. Some, however, did tend to prepare for their offences over several days or weeks. These preparations could consist of identifying a site, observing the target, obtaining arms and disguises, determining the roles of each participant, and planning the "getaway." The major emphasis seemed to be on the selection and surveillance of the site, and the escape.

On the other extreme were events in which offenders decided spontaneously to commit a robbery, in which case their efforts were circumscribed by the weapons, disguises, and vehicles they had at hand, as well as by the particular time and place.

Most of the robbers indicated that, just prior to the offence, they would observe the target for a few minutes to ensure there were no police in the area and only a limited number of passersby. Where two offenders are committing a commercial armed robbery, one usually collects the cash and the other controls people at the scene. The driver of the "get-away" vehicle, when present, does not generally have the same status as those executing the crime. The crime is usually concluded within one minute. Despite the heavy weapons sometimes used in Montreal robberies, the bulk of our subjects conveyed the impression that one of the greatest fears was the possibility they would have to resort to violence.

There were three principal reactions following the robbery. Some experience feelings of relief, euphoria, and satisfaction. Others are nervous and ruminate about the mistakes they may have made. The more experienced tend to go home and relax. There are those who take additional precautions following the offence. As one subject related: "I get rid of my clothes, take a shower, and go see my parole officer to create an alibi."

What are some of the major motives mentioned by our subjects? Many indicated that armed robbery constitutes the fastest and most direct way of getting money. Burglary and fraud were seen as more complicated and less lucrative. The younger robbers, in particular, like the thrills, status, and feelings of power afforded by the crime. The following statement supports this point:

"When I have a gun in my hands nothing can stop me. It makes me feel important and strong. With a revolver you're somebody..."

Another says:

"It's funny to see the expression of people when they have a .38 in their face. Sometimes when I went home at night I thought of it and laughed ...Maybe I was just fascinated..."

Aside from the underlying reasons, we asked the subjects to tell us what triggered or precipitated their robberies. Some of the factors mentioned were unemployment, the need to obtain drugs or other recreational needs, suggestions made by criminal associates, and exceptional circumstances such as provocation by an employer. The younger offenders were more likely to spend their profits purchasing drugs and alcohol, going to clubs, and taking trips, while those with more experience more often used the money acquired from robberies to pay debts and take care of daily expenses.

Most of the subjects began their careers in crime committing burglaries, auto thefts, and drug trafficking before advancing to armed robbery. There were a few, however, who began their criminal careers with armed robbery. The careers of the subjects spanned anywhere from a few weeks to a good number of years. Their persistence in armed robbery cannot be understood by simply looking at their motives for beginning in it.

After the initial success, the offender gains confidence and is encouraged by the ease with which money is obtained and by his ability to evade capture. Some mentioned that robbing becomes an entire lifestyle and that they are driven to commit the crime. Others state that robbery simply becomes their line; it becomes their profession, they develop a set of skills, so why change?

One good reason for changing, of course, is the fairly stiff sentences meted out for robbery in Canada. Several respondents indicated, interestingly, that rather than developing an immunity to prison as they aged, the fear of incarceration exercised a progressively greater deterrent effect after they had already served several sentences inside. They had tired of institutional life and knew that each successive sentence would be longer. They mentioned that in their younger years they were less concerned about punishment.

Some leave armed robbery and take up other offences that carry lighter sentences and involve fewer dangers. They also become disillusioned with armed robbery because they find that the profits are far more modest than they first believed. Some offenders, of course, do abandon a career in crime altogether.

A unique aspect of our armed robbery study was an examination of the factors prompting people to give up a life of crime. We located a sample of armed robbers (17 in all) who had clean records for at least five years at liberty. They revealed that both negative and positive factors could contribute to the decision to leave a life of crime.

On the negative side, these men pointed to the problems and disappointments of a criminal lifestyle: problems with associates in dividing up booty, difficulties with rival gangs, the dangers of being informed on, the constant worry of eluding police, and the pain of incarceration. On the positive side, some indicated that educational and vocational skills learned in prison helped extricate them from a life of crime. Volunteers such as prison chaplains and groups such as Alcoholics Anonymous were also helpful. Finally, the development of stable intimate relationships helped some of them find fulfillment and steered them away from the influence of their former associates.

From our modest sample of 39 robbers, we were able to identify four fairly distinct types. There is the chronic offender who has a career of long duration, commits many other offences, is poorly prepared, and gains moderate amounts from his crime. The professional also has a long career and commits other offences, but is better prepared and makes larger profits. The intensive has a very short career in which he commits poorly planned robberies in quick succession. His gains are very modest. Finally, there is the occasional offender, who also has a fairly short career in armed robbery and commits only a small number of robberies relative to other crimes. The planning tends to be perfunctory and the profits minimal.

THE VICTIM

We interviewed the owners or employees of 182 small businesses in Montreal that had been robbed over a specified two-year period. These interviews supported the impressions about armed robbery we had gained from police files and interviews with robbers. The victims reported that robbers usually work alone or in twos, are quite young, tend to use firearms, only infrequently wear disguises, and emerge from the crime with very modest profits. Furthermore, the victims confirmed the fact that physical force is rarely used. In fact, even explicit threats directed at the victims were absent in about half the incidents.

We distinguished between threats at two points: those issued at the onset of the robbery and those occurring at any other time during the incident. Direct threats were made at the outset of the robbery in 40 percent of the cases. By far the most common first reaction by vic-

tims was immediate compliance with the wishes of the perpetrator(s). The next most likely reaction was one of shock and numbness. A refusal to obey the offender(s) was very unlikely, especially when threats were issued at the beginning.

Threats later in the incident were more likely if the offender(s) issued threats at the beginning. There was thus some consistency in offender behavior throughout an incident. If they made threats at the outset they were far more likely to continue to threaten as the incident progressed than if no initial threat was made. A refusal on the part of the victim to cooperate also increased the likelihood of threats during the event, but such refusal at the outset was rare.

What was somewhat more likely (in a quarter of the cases), at some point during the robbery, was resistance, which we defined as a wholehearted attempt, by verbal, physical, or other means, to foil the crime. Victims, too, showed remarkable consistency in their behavior. Those who refused to obey the perpetrators at the outset resisted fully in all cases, whereas those acquiescing in the beginning rarely resisted. The offender's threats did, however, have some effect as they increased the probability of resistance, although the causal order is unclear. We are not clear as to whether threats tended to lead to resistance or resistance to threats — perhaps both.

Resistance was rarely based on sound logic; that is, a rational calculation of the odds on the part of the victim. Employees were more likely to resist than owners. Victims did not tend to take into account either the number of offenders or the number of witnesses in the decision to resist. Even the type of weapon used had limited impact on their behavior. What seemed to be most influential were the victim's feelings of anger, the presence of threats, and even their prior experiences with robbery.

Resistance did bear fruit in the sense that robbers were almost four times as likely to fail to leave the scene with some money in hand. Resisting the robber(s), however, increased the likelihood of injuries sustained by the victim by a factor of ten.

Armed robbery may leave its victim with residual physical and emotional disorders, and personal difficulties. Two-thirds of the subjects experience one or more of the following physical complaints after a robbery: chronic nervousness, insomnia, nightmares, headaches, loss or gain of appetite. Over 90 percent of the respondents stated that the event shook them up emotionally. The most frequent complaints were a growing fear of hold-ups, a general distrust of others, greater aggressiveness on their part, moodiness, and depression. These emotional disorders tended to last longer than the physical complaints. Both types were more likely to occur when the victim had put up a resistance. Almost a quarter of the respondents also mentioned that the experience with robbery engendered a change in their lifestyle, led them to seek a different job, or produced other personal problems.

THE CRIMINAL JUSTICE SYSTEM RESPONSE

We now turn to the response to armed robbery of the criminal justice system. In Canada, the penalties are stiff; robbery is punishable by life imprisonment. About 90 percent of those convicted for robbery receive a prison sentence; therefore, the certainty of a stiff response by the courts, once one is found guilty, is quite high. The potential of these sentences to deter is, of course, also dependent on the likelihood of achieving a conviction in a given case.

In Quebec, as in most of North America, the solution rate for robbery is about 20 percent. Solution usually means that charges are laid against one suspect (not all) in a reported incident. Victimization surveys in both Canada and the United States indicate that only about half of all robberies are ever brought to the attention of the police (Solicitor General of Canada, 1983). Thus, half never get a chance to be solved, so our solution rate is cut in half to 10 percent. If we also take into account the fact that the laying of charges is no guarantee of a conviction, the clearance rate is even less than 10 percent. Furthermore, if we consider that a case is usually considered solved when one perpetrator is charged and that most armed robberies involve more than one offender, many participants of so-called cleared cases will evade arrest. Thus, for any perpetrator, the chances of conviction for a typical robbery are substantially less than one in ten.

We found that only one-third of those captured are arrested on the day of the offence. Of the 1266 cases we followed up, those captured were arrested an average of 26 days after the incident. Since robbers usually succeed in leaving the scene with some cash and since they often use their booty to achieve short-term goals (e.g., buy drugs), then even some of those who are eventually caught may have already achieved a measure of success. If we apply a very tight definition of failure — robberies in which perpetrators are caught and convicted without achieving even short-term goals, then the failure rate is extremely minuscule, maybe one in twenty or one in thirty. Psychological research on punishment tells us that if it is uncertain and preceded by a more immediate and tangible reinforcer (such as drugs), then the person is more likely to respond to this reinforcer than to the punishment (Watson and Tharp, 1981). This principle applies to human beings in general; it may be even more applicable to the often impulsive people who commit robberies. Our capacity to combat armed robbery through the punishments imposed by the criminal justice system therefore may be seriously limited.

Although the solution of cases is partly a function of good police and prosecutorial work, our research indicates that their work is greatly enhanced by the public's assistance and cooperation. For example, in Montreal and Quebec City, the police respond to the scene of a typical armed robbery in under three minutes after receiving a call. The problem is that it takes almost twice as long for victims or witnesses to place the call after the incident than it does for the police to respond, once they are called. People often call their spouses or employers before phoning the police. Shortening the time that elapses between the incident and the arrival of the police therefore requires a faster reaction by victims and witnesses.

Another indication of the indispensability of the public's help is the manner in which suspects are actually rounded up. The Hollywood image of detective work whereby highly intelligent sleuths slowly unearth and analyze clues until suspects are identified and located, is a distortion. Our study, as others, has found that people are usually arrested in connection with another crime, denounced by other suspects, or captured through information furnished by victims or witnesses. Detective work is not autonomous. Indeed, the more detailed the descriptions of the suspects given by victims and/or bystanders, the more likely it was that a case would be solved.

Just a note on our so-called adversarial system of justice. We found considerable evidence of plea bargaining and of 515 defendants we followed up only 8 were tried in front of judge and jury. Over 80 percent of the sample received a prison term and the average term was two and a half years.

Bank robbers were more likely to be apprehended than those robbing other targets. They were also likely to have more charges laid against them, to be detained before trial, and to receive longer prison sentences. Much of this differential treatment was due to the formation of the Montreal Police Bank Robbery Squad. This squad, in conjunction with a special prosecutorial unit, may have been partly responsible for the 50 percent reduction in the number of bank robberies in the Montreal area over the past ten years.

The Bank Robbery Squad consists of experienced detectives who investigate bank robbery cases only. A special prosecutorial unit has focused on case preparation, attempting to lay the most serious charges possible in bank robbery cases. Both units have superior resources to those available to investigate and prosecute other crimes. They have succeeded in increasing, by about two years, the prison sentences received by bank robbers. Furthermore, solution rates have increased substantially.

At the same time, many banks in Montreal have expanded their security measures. They have added cameras, made physical design changes, and reduced the accessible cash at their branches. The Canadian Bankers' Association also introduced a reward program. The combination of opportunity reduction and tougher penalties have apparently achieved their intended effect, although a number of gangs of armed robbers may have migrated to western Canada. Bank robbery there has risen and some of the increase may have been engineered by offenders from the Province of Quebec, although there is some controversy about this possibility. Such a possibility leaves us with an issue to ponder when we consider prevention. Is a focused program worthwhile if it merely forces offenders to alter their methods or undertake their activities in a more hospitable environment? In other words, to what degree can crime be suppressed through opportunity reduction measures and stiff penalties? The evidence we have accumulated offers more hope for the former than the latter.

Chapter 17

SOCIAL ECONOMY AND ARSON IN NOVA SCOTIA*

John L. McMullan and Peter D. Swan

INTRODUCTION

In the United States and Canada, the incidence of arson has grown tremendously since the end of World War II. In Canada, the arson rate has increased steadily, especially in cities. In 1983, the number of reported or known arsons in Canada was listed at 10,270. Centres such as Montreal, Toronto, and Vancouver, that have large areas of rundown housing, have had to cope with frequent outbreaks of incendiarism in old warehouses, tenement houses and slum dwellings (Arpin, 1982; Cripps, 1982). According to one sociologist who has studied arson extensively, it is the inner city poor who suffer most at the arsonist's hand. Death and injury by fire is largely a "pauper's epitaph" (Brady, 1982).

In the past, arson has often been explained as a crime without rational motive. Traditional sociological paradigms attribute arson to individual deviance. They conjure up the image of the "pyromaniac" — the sick person who derives some perverse satisfaction from setting and observing fires (Battle, 1974; MacDonald,

1977; Witkin, 1979). Explanations attributing wilful vandalism or revenge follow a similar line of reasoning by focussing on the deviance of individual fire-setters, or on the cultural peculiarities of ethnic groups or communities. For example, subcultural theories have alleged that arson is considered to be an irrational and self-destructive pathology based on individual or community impulses (Miller, 1968; Moynihan, 1969). However, the validity of explanations which ignore the structural and socio-economic contexts of arson have been questioned. Criminologists have turned increasingly to the study of *social economy* to understand arson. According to this approach, "arson is essentially a consequence of economic decisions undertaken by the banking, real estate, and insurance industries," as well as by government agencies and policies. The routine profit-making practices of corporations and financial institutions as well as government policies around economic development lead to processes of abandonment, deindustrialization, and decline. In Boston, for example, banks "red line" areas of the city where they refuse loans

* Edited version of J.L. McMullan and P.D. Swan, "Social Economy and Arson in Nova Scotia," *Canadian Journal of Criminology* 31(1989): 281-308. Reprinted with permission of the *Canadian Journal of Criminology* and the authors. Copyright by the Canadian Criminal Justice Association.

An earlier version was presented at the Annual Meeting of The American Society of Criminology, Chicago, November 1988. The authors wish to thank George Smith of the Nova Scotia Police Commission, officials from fire departments, the Fire Marshall's Office, the RCMP and the insurance industry who co-operated with this study; the Solicitor General's Independent Research Program for funding it; and Dr. David Perrier for his help in the early stages of this manuscript.

on housing, thus making it difficult for owners to finance inner-city property. Arson is one way of recouping the anticipated losses by collecting insurance. It becomes both an effective means to increase profits from the cheap investment in rundown apartment buildings and a good way to clear urban land in order to allow for its more profitable use through the construction of new buildings. Much illegality occurs, including organized criminal racketeering (Brady, 1982; Brady, 1983).

This study makes use of some of the insights of the social economy perspective. However, the province of Nova Scotia provides a very different context for its application. Many people still live in towns or rural villages in Nova Scotia. The largest urban communities are considerably smaller than places like Toronto or Montreal. They do not include vast inner-city areas suffering from serious physical decline or substantial indigent populations. The province's largest urban area, Halifax-Dartmouth, has not been subjected to waves of set fires comparable to the ones in the older urban areas of the United States and Canada. Nor do there seem to be visible links between arson, urban renewal and development, and organized crime. Yet despite the difference between arson patterns in Nova Scotia and the larger urban centres of Canada and North America, arson is a major crime in the province. The arson rate is both higher than the national level and higher than in most other provinces of the country.

This paper provides: (1) a summary of the present-day law relating to arson in Canada; (2) a social economy analysis of arson in Nova Scotia from 1970 to 1985; (3) an examination of the social and legal processes that underpin a moral toleration of arson and contribute to an absence of censure and deterrence; and (4) some concluding conjectures about the class patterning of arson in Nova Scotia.[1]

THE CONTEMPORARY LAW OF ARSON AND THE CANADIAN CONTEXT

The contemporary law relating to arson in Canada is contained within the Criminal Code.

It is located within three sections following the Mischief Provisions as set out in Part IX of the Code. Since these Provisions are concerned with "Wilful and Forbidden Acts in Respect of Certain Property," this placement reinforces the contention that arson remains a crime primarily concerned with the protection of property. Arson is defined in section 433 of the Code as follows:

(1) Everyone who wilfully sets fire to
    (a) a building or structure, whether completed or not,
    (b) a stack of vegetable produce or of mineral or vegetable fuel,
    (c) a mine,
    (d) a well or combustible substance,
    (e) a vessel or aircraft, whether completed or not,
    (f) timber or materials placed in a shipyard for building, repairing or fitting out a ship,
    (g) military or public stores or ammunitions of war,
    (h) a crop, whether standing or cut down, or
    (i) any wood, forest, or natural growth, or any lumber, timber, log, float, boom, dam, or slide,

is guilty of an indictable offence and is liable to imprisonment for fourteen years.

(2) Everyone who wilfully and for a fraudulent purpose sets fire to personal property not mentioned in subsection (i) is guilty of an indictable offence and is liable to imprisonment for five years.

Section 433(1) distinguishes arson from the less serious fraudulent burning of personal property by providing a list of specified property that is protected by arson. The list places an emphasis on real property, occupied buildings or structures and on specified materials which were essential to agriculture, commerce and the military in the nineteenth century. With the exception of the addition of aircraft, most of the list relies on the property specified under nineteenth-century statutory provisions which excluded reference to personal property (Law Reform Commission, 1984)

A second arson related offence is established in section 434 of the Code which provides that

Everyone who:

a. wilfully sets fire to anything that is likely to cause anything mentioned in subsection 433(1) to catch fire:

OR

b. wifully and for fraudulent purposes sets fire to anything that is likely to cause personal property not mentioned in subsection 433(1) to catch fire, is guilty of an indictable offence and is liable to imprisonment for five years.

As in section 433, this establishes a hierarchy in terms of property to be protected which is a continuation of the earlier qualified protection of property. Not only does it attribute priority to specific types of property that are regarded as essential to different economic or commercial activity, it also suggests that the main purpose of arson legislation is to protect property owners form vandalism or the vengeful acts of others. Implicitly, the class assumptions underlying early modern definitions of arson persist and in large measure inform the contemporary crime of arson in Canada.

Subsections 433(2) and 434(b), however, do encompass *personal* property provided that fraudulence is demonstrated. The protection afforded by the contemporary definition of arson has been extended to cover the intentional burning of property by their owners. Nevertheless, even with an evidentiary presumption against the holders or beneficiaries of fire insurance policies, the element of fraudulent intent remains very difficult to define and demonstrate, and the penalty is less. Despite this extension of the definition of arson, the main focus of criminal investigation and prosecution in Canada remains the activities of other individuals or groups who resort to vandalism (Arpin, 1982). Arson, for the most part, continues to be thought of as an interclass crime in which the activity of one class (setting fires) is directed against the property of another class.

THE SOCIAL ECONOMY OF ARSON IN NOVA SCOTIA

What do the data on arson show for Nova Scotia? How may we explain the arson situation in the province? What is the class nature of arson in the province?

In a recent study of criminal offences in Atlantic Canada, Kaill and Smith (1984) suggest that arson is the "one major crime category in which overall Atlantic rates exceed the national level." An examination of the crime statistics based on police reported arsons in the period from 1970 to 1985 confirms that finding for the province of Nova Scotia (McMullan and Swan, 1988). There has been a tremendous increase in the number of arsons in Nova Scotia since 1970. This is reflected in both the reported arsons and in the number of confirmed or actual offences. Figure 1 demonstrates, however, that arson rates have fluctuated dramatically over this period reaching a peak in the early years of this decade and declining over the last three years while still remaining considerably above the level of the early 1970s.

Figure 1 also shows that during the early 1970s there were few substantial changes in the arson rate in this province. While there was a rise of over 30% in the number of actual offences in 1971 over that of 1970, by 1973 the number had dropped to a low of 153. By the middle of the decade, however, this figure had doubled to 305. The numbers stayed at this level until 1978 when they reached nearly 400 reported offences. The most dramatic fluctuation in numbers occurred over the next three years. In the years from 1979 to 1982, the number of actual offences rose to over 450 per year and remained at that level. In 1982 the number dropped back to the 1978 level. From 1983 to mid-decade, the numbers declined further to approximately the same level of a decade earlier. Interestingly, as the number of actual arsons have increased so have the number of reported arsons that were classified as unfounded. While in 1973 only 5 out of 158 reported cases of arson proved to be unfounded, in 1982 there were 141 cases that were shown to be incapable of being proven as arson.

It is not just the number of actual arsons that increased but also the arson rate measured in terms of the number per 100,000 population. As indicated in Figure 2, in 1974 the rate of arson in Nova Scotia (28.7 per 100,000) was slightly below the national average (29.5 per 100,000). Relative to the rise in the number of actual arsons in 1975, the Nova Scotia rate (37.1 per 100,000) also rose proportionately while the

Figure 1
Police Reported Arson in Nova Scotia (1970–1985)

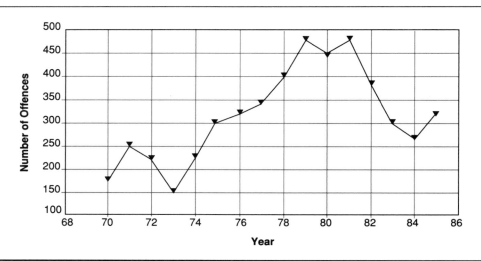

Source: *Crime Statistics*, Canadian Centre for Justice Statistics (Ottawa: Statistics Canada); *Fire Losses in Canada*, Annual Reports, Fire Commissioner of Canada (Ottawa: Department of Supply and Services).

Canadian rate rose only slightly (31.9 per 100,000). There was no substantial difference between the two rates until 1978, however, when the Nova Scotia rate jumped to 47.0 per 100,000 population while the Canadian rate increased only slightly to 32.7 per 100,000 population. In the peak years for the actual numbers of arsons, the Nova Scotia rate per 100,000 population also climbed substantially reaching a high of 55.1 in 1979. During the three peak years from 1979 to 1981, the Canadian arson rate also went up, but at no time did it approach the Nova Scotia rate. After 1982, both the Nova Scotia and Canadian rates declined back to the levels of the middle part of the last decade. By 1985, the Nova Scotia rate was still 5 persons per 100,000 above the national rate.

While the number of arsons and the rate of arson in Nova Scotia increased at the end of the 1970s, there was no significant increase in the number of charges laid relative to the actual number of arsons. From the mid-1970s onward, charges were laid in less than 25% of the cases.

In addition to the *Crime Statistics*, arson data

were also available from the Nova Scotia Fire Marshall's Office.[2] The number of reported arsons in the Fire Marshall's office is generally lower than those produced by police reports. According to Statistics Canada, there were 4421 actual arson offences reported in Nova Scotia between January 1970 and December 31, 1983. The Fire Marshall's statistics indicate that between January 1, 1970, and March 31, 1984, there were 3530 cases of reported arson or suspected incendiary fires.[3]

Both sets of data, however, do show a similar pattern with the peak period being between 1979 and 1982. The arson category may be divided into arson and suspected incendiary. The use of the latter category reflects the difficulty of proving arson as an offence. It generally refers to cases where fire investigators believe a fire was deliberately set but were unable to definitely determine who set the fire, thus undermining the possibility of obtaining a conviction. During the few years when the statistics show these categories by actual numbers, the suspected incendiary category was far

FIGURE 2
ARSON RATE PER 100,000 POPULATION IN NOVA SCOTIA AND CANADA (1971–1985)

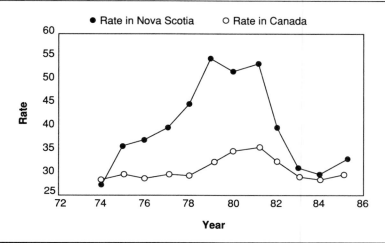

SOURCE: *Crime Statistics*, Canadian Centre for Justice Statistics (Ottawa: Statistics Canada); *Fire Losses in Canada*, Annual Reports, Fire Commissioner of Canada (Ottawa: Department of Supply and Services).

greater than that of confirmed arson. In 1980, the year of the highest recorded number of set fires, only 5 out of 345 were confirmed as arson.

The monetary losses that may be attributed to arson have grown steadily since the early 1970s and reached a high point during the 1979 to 1982 period. Although the growth in monetary loss may, in part, be attributed to inflation, there have been both more arson fires and more expensive arson fires, many of which have occurred in the commercial or industrial sector. During the early to mid-1970s, arson accounted for between 8 percent and 18 percent of the annual fire losses. This percentage grew tremendously toward the end of the last decade to between 20 percent and 30 percent of the annual losses. In 1981, arson fires accounted for $21,666,351 in property damage and 46.3 percent of total fire losses during the years. Although 1980-81 was anomalous, in that one major fire accounted for nearly half the arson loss, the actual monetary loss during the 1979 to 1982 period was much higher than it had been in the late 1970s. In 1979, the monetary losses attributed to arson doubled from the previous

year to over five million dollars. These monetary losses remained at this high level until 1984. Well over 90 percent of property losses attributed to arson have been covered by insurance (Nova Scotia Provincial Fire Marshall's Office, *Annual Report*, 1970-1985).

The statistics also show where the *major* arson or incendiary fires have occurred and what types of economic property were involved. Once again, there has been a rise in both the number of major fires and in the monetary loss attributed to specific fires. In the early 1970s, there were few arson fires where the monetary loss exceeded $50,000; by the early 1980s, there were many more losses where the value exceeded several hundred thousand dollars. Again major fire losses caused by arson were especially high in 1981 and 1982 when 8 fires were reported. Furthermore, while the arson statistics show a decline after 1982, the number of major arson losses continues to increase. While some of the major arson fires and suspected incendiaries were in public institutions, by far the greatest number occurred in the commercial and industrial sectors. Industrial warehouses, apartment buildings, and especially stores, business complexes, and retail outlets were the most common types of property burned. The location of major set fires seems for the most part to have been spread evenly around the province. During the high arson years of 1979-1982, however, Cape Breton was particularly susceptible to major arson fires. In 1982 and 1983, 6 out of 7 major fires were reported to have been on the island (Nova Scotia Provincial Fire Marshall's Office, *Annual Report*, 1970-1985).

The arson statistics from the Fire Marshall's Office also indicate that there were few criminal charges laid in arson cases and even fewer convictions obtained. While the number of arsons increased in the early part of this decade, the number of charges laid remained relatively constant. Charges were generally laid in only 10 percent to 15 percent of cases. Convictions were obtained in less than half of these. Of the 38 major set fires, only 5 were proven to be arson. The other 33 cases were classified as suspected arson or suspected incendiary. In those cases, fire investigators were able to determine that the fires had been set but there was never enough evidence to convict an offender of criminal charges (Nova Scotia Provincial Fire Marshall's Office, *Annual Report*, 1970-1985).

Not only is arson difficult to prove but there also is evidence that it is not always easy to detect. Data from the provincial Fire Marshall's Office indicate that the number of fires by undetermined causes and the total losses have increased from 116 fires valued at $552,928 in 1970 to 637 fires worth $4,984,550 in 1984. In the peak years form 1979-1982, there were 3,224 undetermined fires valued at $28,843,439 (Nova Scotia Provincial Fire Marshall's Office, *Annual Report*, 1970-1985). This reveals the difficulty for fire investigators of determining the exact cause of fires. Often there is a lack of remaining physical evidence or it is impossible to rule out one or more of several possible causes. In such cases, the origin of fire is classified as "suspicious but undetermined." Fire investigators admit that a conservative attitude prevails in this classification. Even if arson is suspected, investigators are reluctant to attach that label. As one experienced investigator

noted, "the basic reason is to avoid legal action." Mentioning the "possibility of arson in public" is regarded by fire officials as risky because it attaches a "stigma to the owner of the property, even where that person is not a suspect because people will blame the owner." Accordingly, the classification of fires as caused by undetermined sources is often taken as "just a matter of protecting yourself. You are not going to put yourself in a spot where you are jeopardizing yourself and your office by saying something that you cannot prove." As a result, the causes of a large number of fires are classified as "suspicious but undetermined." When asked about this classification, fire investigators suggested that it was more applicable to "higher risk cases of fires in businesses or to large fire losses." One officer observed, "no matter how strong the evidence may be that a fire was set, if there was any doubt at all, I would classify the sources of the fire as undetermined." Most fire investigators admitted that their use of classification was cautious and that, on average, about 50 percent of their undetermined cases were probably arson. This suggests that the use of the undetermined category substantially underrepresents the already high rates of arson and suspected arson in Nova Scotia.

The available data on arson do not explain the fluctuations or the peak period of the rates, nor do they provide us with regional profiles for all arsons. In order to try to account for this, we examined general economic characteristics and interviewed the most experienced fire investigators in the province. The results suggest that the period of high arson fires corresponds quite closely with the period in which the regional economy went through a crisis characterized by high interest rates, chronic unemployment, and high business failures.

The prime lending rate of commercial banks was at its lowest during the early part of the 1970s when the numbers and rate of arson were at their lowest levels. More importantly, the lending rate reached its highest point (15-18.25 percent) between 1979-1981, the years when arson was at its highest level. Since 1982, and up until very recently, the prime lending rate like the arson rate has been declining.

This rough correlation suggests that high

interest and mortgage rates are important contributory factors in the high arson rate in Nova Scotia, but they are not the only factors. There has also been a steady growth of the unemployment rate in the Maritimes since 1970. The rate in Nova Scotia has been over 10 percent since 1977 and the rate for the last ten years has been persistently above the national average. Furthermore, between 1979 and 1982 the rate jumped by 3.1 percent. These high unemployment rates reinforced the effects of high mortgage rates and, as we shall see, together they were especially devastating to regional and local economies (Statistics Canada, 1970-1985).

Also relevant to an analysis of arson in Nova Scotia is information with respect to business failures in the province. In the first years of this decade, there was a substantial increase in the number of consumer and business bankruptcies in Nova Scotia. In 1981, there was an increase of nearly 200 bankruptcies from the previous year (665 in 1980 to 839 in 1981). In 1982, the number of bankruptcies rose by almost 300 to 1,102 and stayed at that level increasing slightly to 1,142 in 1983. Thus, in a two-year period, the number of bankruptcies almost doubled (Report of the Superintendent of Bankruptcy, 1970-1985). Although this development took place just when the arson rate was beginning to decline, there was an overlap year in 1981-82 when there were many major fires in business and retail complexes.

The association between the rise in the rate of arson and the severe recession in the provincial economy in the early part of this decade also has been confirmed in interviews with fire officials and arson investigators. While not discounting "pathological fire-setters," revenge fires, and vandalism, most experts attributed the majority of arson fire losses to economic motives. One experienced police officer put it this way, "Arson in Nova Scotia should now be regarded primarily as a money crime."

Changes in the arson rate were seen as tied to fluctuations in the provincial economy. According to one provincial official, "A weak economic climate means that more people will burn for profit." Most agreed that the major factor was interest rates. Another fire investigator noted, "When mortgages were being called in during the downturn in the economy during

the early 80s, the number of set fires increased dramatically." From 1979 to 1982, the arson rate was especially high in residential and in business fires. With respect to the former, a specific pattern emerged. Many arson fires occurred in homes originally purchased when the prime lending rate was much lower. Many home owners were forced to renegotiate their financing at rates ranging from 15 to 18 percent. Some found that they were no longer able to meet their highly inflated mortgage payments. Rather than allow the mortgage to be recalled, they resorted to burning their properties. One fire investigator suggested, "When a guy who has been paying into a house for 15 years knows he is going to lose it, he says to himself, 'These people are not going to take this, I'm going to get some of my equity back out.' He then sets fire to the house, hoping that the insurance company will pay off his mortgage and pay him the other equitable value that is in the building."

This type of logic applies as well to non-residential arsons. For example, in 1984, there were several arson fires in coastal communities in the Shelburne to Meteghan area. According to fire officials, these came about when Federal Fisheries Loans Board announced the foreclosure on unpaid loans on fishing vessels. One investigator recalled, "there was one or two a week... Amazing things! There was an explosion..., or there was a fire at the wharf. The boats were just going out of the harbour and every one of them just happened to be towing a dinghy behind." The string of arsons in fishing communities continued until the Fisheries Loans Board, who were also insuring the boats, announced an end to foreclosures on the loans. "Suddenly, it was as if someone turned off a tap, no more boats were burned."

Arson patterns in Nova Scotia generally seem to be related to the economic stability of the community. Industrial Cape Breton and rural communities that are dependent upon a one resource industry are very susceptible to downturns in the economy, and they also appear to be prone to more arsons than the cities of Halifax and Dartmouth. Between 1971 and 1983, there were only 8 reported *major* fire losses by arson or suspected incendiary in Halifax and Dartmouth. The monetary loss was

$4,326,481 which represents about 13% of the total reported provincial monetary loss of $35,370,391. The bulk of the major arson fires, to say nothing about medium to small losses, were in the rural hinterland or in the deindustrialized region of the province.

Fire officials and police are reluctant to admit that there are closely watched communities, but they do acknowledge that there are predictable 'trouble spots.' According to one senior investigator, "If the economic situation in a community gets worse — the major employer shuts down or whatever — and a hundred or more people are out of work, then we can look to be called to that community on a number of occasions. As the economic situation worsens so go the fires." Pictou County is a case in point. "There have been heavy lay-offs at the Hawker Siddeley rail and car plant in Trenton, and this has been followed by a major arson problem." Investigators now consider the lay-off policy, the unemployment rate, and arson to be connected. In other communities, other economic factors such as local labour unrest may influence the arson rate. During the lengthy strike between bus drivers and the Digby County Board in the early 1980s, arson fires were a common occurrence. Buildings and vehicles were burned regularly during the dispute. However, a number of property owners did attempt to use the instances of "vandal fires" associated with the labour conflict to conceal economic stop loss fires as subsequent investigations and criminal convictions proved.

While residential fires have been linked to problems with mortgage payments, there are other motives for burning for profit associated with the economic decline of communities. For example, when a residential property is located in a community that is undergoing a gradual period of economic decline, property values will fall and become quite low, but the insured value of property may be much higher. If the owner wants to stop the loss or move to another community, it may make more sense to burn the house and recoup losses or even make a profit. In one reported case, the market value of a house declined to $26,000 but it was insured for around $100,000 including contents. As a fire official noted, "In such a case selling to the insurance company was much more profitable than selling at market value."

Within the business and industrial sector, retail stores and complexes seem to be particularly prone to arson or incendiary fires. When a major employer closes down its operations or institutes massive lay-offs, the spending capital in a community is drastically reduced. The retail and commercial sectors are vulnerable because their usual clients no longer have ready cash to spend. In such situations, businesses, including some "that have operated successfully in a community for generations," may find themselves in serious financial difficulties. Arson is regarded as a good business solution to the situation.

Arson, however, is not restricted to communities in decline. Over the last 15 to 20 years, new suburban communities serving the Halifax-Dartmouth area have emerged. Residential arson, while less than the provincial "trouble spots," has been more prevalent in suburbia than in the city centres. This was especially true in the 1970s and early 1980s where rapid suburban growth created populations that were transitory and less secure financially. Over the last few years, the rate of arson has declined as these communities have stabilized, but arson still remains above the levels of established cities like Dartmouth and Halifax.

Fire officials working in suburban communities have also noted the high number of arsons or incendiary fires in the retail sector. As suburbia developed, a proliferation of small retail outlets opened to serve the expanding communities. Competition was often fierce and many small businesses failed. Similarly, small manufacturing enterprises who geared their production to a limited local market suffered when their retail clients closed down or moved away. According to many fire investigators, these small retail outlets and manufacturing units have been the sites of most arson and suspected incendiary fires.

Economic factors have to be seen in the light of social and legal contexts — the main effects of which encourage the perception that arson is both tolerated in certain circumstances and is a crime for which there is little detection, apprehension, or punishment.

Many of the arson officials interviewed

suggested that arson is often used as a "social tool of financial management." When someone runs into difficulty, arson is considered as a legitimate way out. According to one police officer, "bilking the insurance company is not thought to be that great an evil and seems to be a viable way out of financial difficulties." This attitude toward arson was elaborated as follows. "You have hard times. Where can you get the money to get yourself out of them. We have insurance. It's like crop insurance. You have bad weather, the government will pay for your crop insurance. You have a bad economic climate and you have to get rid of a barn or two, you burn the thing down. The insurance will pay for it...I think that this is a really big factor."

In fishing communities, vessels and equipment have often been the primary property burned. If a boat is getting old, needs repair, or is not sufficiently capitalized, it may be burned for the illegal capital which may then be pumped into a new vessel. In some communities, this is a traditional way of cutting economic losses, with a very long history reaching back in memory over generations. It may be part of family and kinship socialization. As one experienced investigator put it, "It seems to go like this — if your grandfather burned and your father burned, it is alright for you to burn." The case of a small truck contractor in the forestry industry is similarly instructive about the intergenerational character of arson and about the widespread community knowledge of arson and arsonists. "I have been investigating a number of truck fires over the last ten years...always the same guy torching some of his trucks...I knew he was doing it but proving it was another matter....anyway in talking to people in the area about all those fires, I learned that the suspected arsonist's father had been doing the same thing 50 years ago...Everyone knew...Why? Because they have to live together in a small place, they know each other's business, but they keep it to themselves..."

This attitude of arson tolerance is especially pronounced when it comes to vehicular arson. Where cash is limited and resale is improbable, a common recourse is to burn the vehicle either by one's own hand or with the help of a hired arsonist. According to one fire marshall, "fires in older, rundown vehicles with me-

chanical problems are fairly frequent...if a guy has an older clunker and the transmission is going, he may decide that the best thing to do will be to set it on fire and collect the insurance." Recruiting a hired arsonist seems to be a relatively easy task. One police officer reported, "You go to the right place or you talk to the right person...it's known...certain taverns or bars...you put your money down, leave your car keys on the table, no questions asked — your car is stolen, driven to an abandoned place and set on fire." Clearly arson practices are common knowledge and to some degree communally tolerated. Few people are actually convicted of arson, especially for vehicular arson, and in some cases the public perception of the 'crime' is such as to minimize its wrongdoing and maximize the harm of official arson control. According to one police officer, "Arson is an acceptable practice within certain community standards."

The community conditions do not mean that everyone engages in or approves of arson, but that people are reluctant to co-operate with police, fire investigators, or agents from insurance companies. In part, this is because suspicion of outsiders is high and also because fear is prevalent. Since everyone knows everyone else in a community, it is difficult to hide co-operation with arson investigation. According to most arson officials, "there always is that fear of retaliation that is very real in people's minds." As a case in point, one investigator referred to the investigation of a series of arson fires in the north of the province. He observed, "the community just closed down to us. No one would talk. The boy at the local gas station was afraid to be seen putting gas in our car. Everyone was afraid that if they were seen talking to us, they would be burned out next."

Whether for reasons of fear, distrust, or sympathy there does seem to be a widespread ambivalence about arson as a crime. Unlike homicide and other forms of property crime, police, insurance investigators, and fire officials report that there is not much stigma attached to arson as a crime. It is by and large a low profile crime generating few law and order concerns. The main reason for this low interest in arson and arson enforcement is said to be because "arson is perceived as victimless crime." Insurance companies are seen as possessing immense capital and thus able to pay out when there is a fire loss. Few people have sympathy for insurance companies in such situations and they easily identify with the alleged arsonist. One police officer suggested that, "Most people at one time or another have had run-ins with insurance companies in terms of delays in collecting on a policy. Often, when someone is charged with arson, people think that this is happening just because the insurance company does not want to pay up." For the most part, sympathy is extended to those who burn in order to avoid financial problems, but it also extends to those who are accused of burning their property in order to defraud the insurance companies.

The apparent lack of sympathy for the insurance companies and the tolerance for those who are alleged to have committed arson not only affects arson investigation but also the prosecution process (McMullan and Swan, 1988). Juries and judges are reluctant to prosecute. It is difficult to prove arson to their satisfaction and many arson suspects are acquitted at trials. One investigator stated bluntly, "judges have little liking or sympathy for arson prosecutions." In combination with the difficult burden of proof for the offense, "it makes it even more difficult to obtain convictions."

The high arson rate in Nova Scotia is undoubtedly encouraged by the low priority accorded it by the public and by the tacit tolerance of the practice in certain communities. Further evidence is found in the fact that there seems to be little deterrence built into the crime of arson itself. Fire investigators confirm the statistics. They maintain that "it is easy to prove that a fire was set, but it is not easy to prove motive or opportunity" (that is that a specific person either set the fire or arranged to have it set). Even in cases associated with insurance fraud where the property owner is the prime suspect, most investigators observed that "you almost have to catch the perpetrator with the match in his hand." In the absence of such evidence or a confession, few charges are laid and fewer cases result in convictions. One veteran investigator related, "in 17 years of fire investigation, I have never given testimony in a court of law." The difficulty in successfully proving arson

is not a secret limited to the fraternity of fire investigators. It is also widely known by sectors of the public. According to police officers, "People know that arson is a crime that can be gotten away with." This is a public perception of arson that is particularly relevant to arson control in small communities. "If in a small community, one car burns," a police officer stated, "in a very short time, others will burn. In such situations, people see others that they know burning their property and getting away with defrauding the insurance company. If people think that arson is an easy crime to get away with , this is going to encourage others to try it as well." There is little social censure and little chance of detection, apprehension, or penalty.

The propensity to commit arson is clearly affected by the rhythms of the economy, both global and local, as the rates between 1979 and 1982 so testify, but the use of arson is supported as well by an enduring moral economy that both tolerates the practice and neutralizes the law.

CONCLUSION

The findings of our social economy analysis of arson in Nova Scotia point to ideological incommensurability in the criminal definition of arson as a form of social censure (Box, 1983; Sumner, 1983). We have argued that most contemporary arsons involve the direct or indirect burning of one's own property rather than that of another. Ordinary citizens burn their cars and property, fishers burn their vessels and equipment, farmers burn their barns, and owners burn their businesses. The continuing high rate of arson and monetary loss is directly attributed to the growing toleration of arson for stop-loss and profit. It has little to do with vandalism or the intentional burning of property by others. Second, arson acts are now committed by individuals from diverse class backgrounds. Of course there continue to be arsons that have 'subcultural' causes and there are those that are linked to rural radicalism and labour struggles, but these are not the major sources of arson fires. Nor does there seem to be much in the way of petit-bourgeois businesses burning out competitors. Most are linked to rational economic plans where persons devise or contract to burn their own property with the intention of having insurance policies cover costs or increase profits. Although those who torch their own vehicles or houses seem to come from a cross section of society, arson is increasingly a crime of capital. Recently, fires in the retail trade, in service industries, and in primary resource industries have accounted for a disproportionate share of monetary losses resulting from incendiary fires. In times when the economic situation has worsened, the number of business and industrial fires has grown. Arson in Nova Scotia has taken on an important *intraclass* dimension. It has been used as a device for shifting the risk of economic investments from the retail, service, or industrial sectors of capital to financial capital as represented by the insurance industry. Rather than go bankrupt, business has chosen "to sell" their enterprises to insurance companies through collecting on fire claims. In this way the insurance industry not only underwrites the damage to property but, as well, underwrites the risk of investment in times of economic crisis.

The definition of arson as a crime in the Criminal Code has not reflected the socio-economic forces at work. Bereft of a clear and separate referent, arson no longer refers to the visible actions of one identifiable social group. The social censure around arson and incendiarism in Nova Scotia is ambivalent and ambiguous. Arson is not seen as a particularly threatening crime either to individuals or communities. Defined by many as a "victimless crime," its harm and social cost remain relatively dispersed. As one lawyer with much experience in insurance law observed, "it can be truly said of arson, it is a crime that pays for everyone." Looking at more general social interests, of course, arson is expensive, wasteful, and at times dangerous to life and limb — but in a strange fashion, it works. It props up a tottering private sector in a province that, outside Halifax and a few mainland centres, is caught in a seemingly endless economic crisis.

Arson has become a part of the way the economic system survives in Nova Scotia. It has deep roots and a future as assured as the province's continued underdevelopment, dependence, and deindustrialization.

NOTES

1. The emphasis in our paper is on an examination of available statistical data. There are, however, gaps in the information that are relevant to the analysis of both the crime of arson and of the process of social censure. As a result of this deficiency in the existing data, we also obtained information through interviews with officials involved in fire investigation from provincial agencies, local fire departments, police, lawyers and representatives of the insurance industry. In total, we conducted 17 intensive interviews.

2. Although there is some duplication in coverage, the Fire Marshall's Office also compiles data with respect to deaths and injuries and monetary loss from damage caused by arson fires. In the case of major fires, these data also specify location, but they do not do so for all arson fires.

3. The discrepancy is difficult to explain. While the reporting periods are different in terms of calendar months and may explain yearly variations, they cannot account for the absolute differences over the long term. This overall discrepancy seems to be due to the nature of the Fire Marshall's reporting system which relies on reports by local fire chiefs. According to officials of the Fire Marshall's Office, some rural fire departments may fail to report arson either because they do not have the training to recognize it or because they may not suspect that someone they know would deliberately set fire to their own property. Furthermore, the failure of local fire department officials to report as many arsons as the police seems to be attributable to their marginal role in the fire investigation process. Their involvement ceases once an investigation has been turned over to the police or to other fire investigators. Frequently, they are not even informed that arson is suspected. This would suggest that local fire departments may not report as much arson to the Fire Marshall's Office because they do not know what has occurred in the subsequent stages of the investigative process.

Chapter 18

PHYSICIAN FRAUD AND ABUSE IN CANADA: A PRELIMINARY EXAMINATION*

Paul R. Wilson, Robyn Lincoln, and Duncan Chappell

Providing universal and relatively inexpensive medical care to all Canadians is an enormous financial undertaking. For example in 1983-84, the federal government spent $9,354 million on programmes to prevent, diagnose and cure illness and disease and that figure is likely to grow considerably in future years. Despite this economic burden, Canada has had a relatively long history of legislative commitment to universal, publicly financed health insurance, the framework of which was established by the Federal Hospital Insurance and Diagnostic Act enacted in 1957 and the Federal Medical Care Act legislated in 1966 (Ministry of National Health and Welfare, 1983).

While federal and provincial governments are obviously concerned with questions of efficiency and effectiveness in the delivery of these programmes, little concern has been expressed publicly by parliament, government agencies, the media or by criminologists about fraud and abuse associated with government funded medical services. This situation can be contrasted with two other industrialized countries — the United States (Pontell, Jesilow and Geis, 1984a, b) and Australia — where widespread attention has recently been given to the commission of fraud and abuse by physicians in regard to public health insurance programmes. Indeed in Australia, a specific term, "medi-

fraud," has become part of public discourse on health care and has, as an activity, been the subject of several commissions of inquiry (Public Accounts Committee, 1982).

The toll extracted by medical abuse is both fiscal and physical. Although no Canadian estimates have been made on the cost to the taxpayer of physician fraud and abuse, careful Australian studies suggest that $AUS200 million is illegally taken annually by practitioners from the national Medicare scheme (Public Accounts Committee, 1982). This dollar figure is equivalent to 7 percent of the total cost of Medicare payments. A crude extrapolation of such an estimate to the Canadian situation would provide a figure between $300 and $400 million that is fraudulently claimed on the nation's Medical Plan. Although in both cases the estimates are tentative, they do give an indication of the scope of the fiscal toll of illegal behaviour by physicians. The physical toll is seen in the results of unnecessary surgery, such as in some appendectomies and hysterectomies, which have severe psychological and physical outcomes for the patient.

Medical fraud and abuse encompass innumerable deviant activities. They range from physicians billing for services never rendered, to billing for services more extensive and expensive than those actually provided, through

* Edited version of P.R. Wilson, R. Lincoln, D. Chappell, "Physician Fraud and Abuse in Canada: A Preliminary Examination" *Canadian Journal of Criminology* 28(1988): 129-46. Reprinted with permission of the *Canadian Journal of Criminology* and the authors. Copyright by the Canadian Criminal Justice Association.

to carrying out medically unnecessary treatments and operations in order to obtain additional fees. Fraud is based on fact — whether a treatment was performed or not. Abuse, on the other hand, is largely a matter of medical judgement and relates to the overutilization of medical services.

With both fraud and abuse, serious practical problems for law enforcers exist in dealing with suspect physicians including those in deciding when an offence has occurred, and in assembling the evidence required to prosecute an offender. In addition, as with much white-collar crime, the power and the prestige of the profession often insulate practitioners against investigation, prosecution and conviction (Sutherland, 1949). In Canada, physicians enjoy a high socio-economic status and exercise substantial power in both their professional relations with patients and in negotiating salaries, fees and conditions (Evans, 1983). The financial resources available to physicians, in association with their political and social power, undoubtedly make investigators more cautious when dealing with allegations of fraud and abuse by members of this professional group than is the case with similar allegations against persons from less prestigious occupations. As one health official commented:

We have to be very careful with physicians because we are taking on a really potent group of people. They can buy the best lawyers, delay the investigation indefinitely and then tell us we don't know what we are talking about and to stop interfering in the privacy between doctors and patients.[1]

In this article two major issues relevant to understanding the nature of medical fraud and abuse are to be addressed: (1) the types of fraud and abuse that physicians engage in; (2) the motivations for committing these abuses.

TYPES OF MEDICAL FRAUD AND ABUSE

This section sets out a classification of common forms of fraud and abuse allegedly engaged in by medical practitioners. Few statistics exist on the Canadian experience with these activities. Materials describing specific cases are generally held by investigating committees and are not available for public perusal. Our sources are therefore, by necessity, gained from other avenues and include interviews with government officials, analyses of professional medical journals and public newspapers, interviews with officers of medical associations and figures obtained from some provincial health departments. [1,2]

The classification is based on the major component in the illegal activity described, e.g., time, money, services or referrals to other professionals. The categories are not exclusive and are comprised of sub-groupings of illegal activities for which specific case examples are given. The form that each category of fraud and abuse takes may differ slightly according to the medical speciality in which it takes place.

1. *EXTRA TIME*

There are numerous ways in which practitioners can manipulate the time-frame of their services to patients in order to achieve the maximum fees redeemable from public health insurance programmes. One form that this type of abuse takes can be called "revolving door consultations," where consultations are conducted quickly and superficially with as many patients as possible in order to maximize income earned.

Another form of manipulating the time-reference of services is a practice which can be designated, "small time, large bill." In some provinces, doctors are able to claim twice the normal rate for their services if they engage in what is generally referred to as an extended consultation or counselling session. According to one official in British Columbia, "this is one of the most abused areas in medical practice today. Sometimes doctors give extended consultations when they don't have to just to get the extra fee. Sometimes they only give a standard consultation and charge for an extended service." [1] Some idea of the size of this abuse can be seen by the fact that, in British Columbia, the number of services paid for under the counselling item number (0120 in the schedule) has expanded almost fivefold during the last ten years. In 1983-84 physicians in the province were paid a total of $19,169,270 for this counselling item alone. This amount compares with the total 1983-84 Medical Services Plan payout for fee-for-service claims by psychiatrists of $21,809,284 (Campbell, 1984).

Commenting recently on this situation, the editor of the *British Columbia Medical Journal* has suggested that media and public concern with the huge increase in the cost of prolonged counselling has been exaggerated, but that some medical practitioners were indeed abusing the system. According to the editor, "the regrettable thing is that perhaps a good deal of this has been engendered by a few bad actors among the profession" (Hardyment, 1984). Just how few, at this stage, can only be a matter of conjecture.

2. *EXTRA MONEY*

A schedule of fees is negotiated between provincial and medical associations and their respective governments to establish the amounts which are claimable for specified services. Physicians can abuse this schedule in order to gain additional income in several ways. One of these methods is termed "medical snowballing." Australian investigators have uncovered numerous examples of claiming for more expensive medical procedures than those actually performed (Gorring and Wilson, 1984). Claims for suturing, for example, are paid for according to the length of the wound and whether subcutaneous tissue is involved. Both of these procedures are open to exaggeration. So too are the number of lesions treated, which is another criterion for payment in the schedule of fees. In surgery, a simple hysterectomy can be claimed as a radical hysterectomy thereby inflating the payment. In other cases, an operation can be described by a single item number or by a combination of fee items. In the latter case, the total of the combined procedures far outweighs the single procedure. Interviews with health officials in Canada suggest that similar "snowballing" exists in this country.[1] In Ottawa, for instance, a physician was jailed for 90 days and fined $25,000 for performing acupuncture on patients being treated for obesity (not claimable under Medicare), and then billing the Plan for a combination of more expensive, orthodox procedures which were claimable (*The Globe and Mail*, 1978a).

Another form of gaining extra money is "double dipping" whereby a practitioner can essentially claim two fees for the provision of one service. This form of abuse is exemplified by the salaried surgeon at a large city hospital who was billing the government health system for private patients he consulted with and operated on while working for the hospital. In effect, this surgeon was collecting extra income for the treatment given, a practice that almost doubled his salary. Health investigators who initially questioned the surgeon by phone on his billing patterns were astonished when the doctor confessed to "double dipping." He claimed that he was required to commit fraud because his hospital salary would not sustain his accustomed affluent lifestyle. RCMP investigation into the case stalled, however, when the surgeon's supervisor stated that permission had been given for "loose working arrangements" for the salaried position enabling the surgeon to work whatever hours he chose at the hospital in addition to performing fee-for-service treatment. Despite the investigators' convictions that the supervisor was 'covering up' for the surgeon, it was not possible to prove the case and the investigation had to be discontinued (Ennais, 1984).

3. *EXTRA TREATMENT*

This category involves the overutilization of medical services. The practices described here are illegal, but of all the forms of physician abuse, they are subject the most to the vagaries of medical judgement and the nebulousness of the definition of quality of care. Many physicians adamantly defend their authority to treat patients as often as necessary and to take whatever measures are needed in the best interests of their patients.[3] But clearly, as is shown in the following examples of extra treatment, there is much room for medical judgement to obscure medical fraud.

"Call-back" is a major form of extra treatment. This occurs when a physician requests that his or her patients return for further consultations, when these are not medically necessary. A case related to the authors by an investigation official concerned a general practitioner in British Columbia whose computer billing profile demonstrated that his practice visits were five standard deviations above those for physicians with comparable patient loads. These profiles provide comparisons with the average billing pattern for the physician speciality and type of practice regarding the number of patients, the number of services, types of services, cost per patient, frequency of repeat visits, frequency of diagnostic tests and so on. Following lengthy investigations on the physician with the "deviant" billing profile, repayment was ordered for the thousands of dollars worth of unnecessary "call-back"consultations that had been paid to him. After two years, only a fraction of this amount was reimbursed to the Medical Services Plan. [1]

Health officials generally believe that the statistical averages they use as guidelines to audit physicians' practices may themselves contain errors. The averages are possibly inflated by widespread overservicing. [1] In this context, recent research has demonstrated that doctors increase the number of "call-backs" with patients in order to sustain a high level of income. Despite increasing numbers of physicians and fewer patients per doctor, physicians' incomes are maintained by "creating their own demand for services" (*The Globe and Mail*, 1984).

Surgical overservicing, when it occurs, is likely to be among the most serious forms of medical fraud and abuse as unnecessary operations can cause great harm and pain. Pontell, Jesilow and Geis, (1982), for example, cite the case of an ophthalmologist who performed cataract surgery on persons with healthy eyes which resulted in blindness in some patients. In Canada, health officials believe that surgical overservicing exists, particularly in the performance of tonsillectomies, hysterectomies, mastectomies, sterilizations, spinal operations and appendectomies. (*The Globe and Mail*, 1984). In this respect, it should be noted that the lowest surgical rates in Canada are found in Newfoundland, a province which has the lowest ratio of physicians per population, and in which about one-third of the doctors are paid by salary (Hatcher, 1981). Elsewhere in Canada, studies demonstrate that salaried surgeons perform less operations than those who work on a fee-for-service basis, suggesting that

many operations are unnecessarily performed in order to obtain monetary rewards (Bunker, 1975; Vayda, 1973).

4. *EXTRA REFERRALS*

The proliferation of medical specialities has radically changed the nature of general practice so that physicians often see themselves as referral services rather than as diagnostic and treatment agents. While there are many legitimate reasons for referring patients to specialists, some unscrupulous practitioners, in concert with specific specialists, enter into arrangements whereby the physician receives a commission for every patient so referred. This is sometimes termed "ping-ponging." Where the payment of a commission is clearly the sole motivation for referral, then abuse of the government health system is obvious. The official told us that, while investigating a dermatologist who was an extremely high income earner, it was found that a large proportion of his patients were referred from two general practitioners. Further investigation revealed that the physicians in question were receiving large annual payments from the dermatologist but linking the payments with deliberate overservicing was difficult to substantiate. No action was taken against either the specialist or the referring physicians. [1]

A specific but costly form of "ping-ponging" is that associated with pathology laboratories. Pathologists are some of the most highly paid of all medical specialists with earnings in some laboratories reaching in excess of $20 million per annum (*Sun*, 1984). It is frequently claimed that these laboratories conduct tests not necessary for the patients' well-being, thus inflating the cost of services for government health schemes. Of particular interest here, however, are the cases of "kickbacks" involving payment by pathologists to general practitioners and other specialists for referrals. Thus in Toronto, a medical laboratory owner was found guilty of defrauding the Ontario Health Insurance Plan of $73,000. Several witnesses testified that bills were "padded" by the laboratory owner in order to make payments to the referring doctors (*The Globe and Mail*, 1978b).

5. *PHANTOM TREATMENT*

The preceding categories are, in the main, instances of abuse. While the activities described are illegal and clearly committed to obtain additional income, they are often so closely aligned with questions of medical judgement and quality of treatment, that fraud is difficult to discern. Fraud is directly evident though, in cases of "phantom treatment." Charging government medical schemes for services that were never performed can range from claims involving non-existent home visits to billing for non-existent patients. Our research has revealed that physicians often rationalize these practices on the grounds that, as there are many services they perform which are not claimable under Medicare, such as telephone consultations or advice and writing up patient record cards, they are justified in charging for occasional phantom services. For example, one doctor we interviewed admitted that he would often record phone calls to patients advising them of the results of pathology tests as consultations and bill the health insurance scheme accordingly. The doctor adamantly defended this practice on the grounds that he was a conscientious, hardworking practitioner who offered a high quality of service and performed many unclaimable duties on behalf of his patients. [3]

In the United States, researchers have found that the medical specialists most frequently charged with acts of fraud and abuse are psychiatrists (Geis et al., 1985). It has yet to be determined whether this situation prevails in Canada but preliminary evidence suggests that fraud in psychiatry is not uncommon in this country. For example, medical insurance plan officials in one jurisdiction related the case of a children's psychiatrist whose billing profile showed that he was seeing more patients for a larger period than there were hours in a day. RCMP investigation involving round-the-clock surveillance found that during many of the periods that the physician claimed to be treating patients, he was in fact at home having dinner with his family, out driving on the freeways, or playing golf. No prosecution followed because law enforcement officials were reluctant to traumatize children with psychiatric problems by using them as witnesses. [1]

These five categories of medical fraud and abuse give some indication of the scope of the problem in Canada. We have no way of knowing how large the size of the problem is in this country as government inquiries and research, of the type that exist in Australia and the United States, have not taken place here. We believe, however, that there is sufficient prima facie evidence to suggest that fraud and abuse by medical practitioners involves significant financial costs.

MOTIVATIONS FOR FRAUD AND ABUSE

Focusing on fraud and abuse perpetrated by medical practitioners allows us to consider a group of well paid and educated persons whose motivations for committing crime do not seem to mesh with traditional explanations of anti-social activity, such as those which centre around economic deprivation for example. Yet the scope and nature of fraud and abuse by medical practitioners does raise some pertinent questions for theorists who seek general explanations of criminal behaviour.

Can we attribute, for instance, fraud and abuse to the results of defective socialization or aberrant personalties? Such explanations of the behaviours described here essentially seek a "cause" for illegal conduct within the individual medical practitioner. Typical of this approach is a recent and frequently referenced text on criminal behaviour which posits that professional crimes carried out by doctors and other professionals "are often committed by marginal figures within the professional groups." Expanding this argument, Don Gibbons (1982) implies that these offences are usually "endeavours of individuals acting alone rather than organizational events involving a collection of fellow deviants." According to Gibbons, occupational offenders are frequently regarded with condemnation within the profession and are sanctioned accordingly.

In contrast to this approach, it has been purported that crimes by doctor and other professionals are not committed by "sick" individuals but rather, have to be seen in the context of the structure of the profession itself. This "political economy" perspective suggests that antecedents of medical fraud and abuse lie within the education of student-physicians, the career expectations and experiences of doctors and the structure of professional medical associations (Wilson and Gorring, 1984). All these factors create an environment which, implicitly at least, encourages some doctors to engage in fraudulent activity in order to maximize their earning potential.

Epitomizing this approach is the theoretical position taken by Thio (1983) who suggests that the more power one has the higher one's aspirations and the greater one's subjective deprivation. The basis of the argument is that professional or managerial persons who have prestige and high incomes, set their standards at the level generated by leaders in their profession or business and feel, in comparison with them, deprived or unfulfilled. Other workers lack such leaders and, therefore, do not set their reference level for prestige or remuneration so high and do not have as great a feeling of subjective deprivation. The doctors, so the argument continues, experience frustration because they are socialized to expect high incomes and they belong to professional associations that are highly motivated and dedicated to raising practitioners' incomes.

Difficulties exist, however, with both of these theoretical approaches. The individualistic orientation often fails to explain adequately the reason why apparently well-trained and highly successful practitioners engage in fraud and abuse.

The political economy perspective, on the other hand, fails to distinguish those doctors who commit fraud and abuse from those who do not. Why is it, for example, that all doctors are subjected to specific training, similar career experiences and belong to the same medical associations yet only some of them indulge in fraud and abuse? This dilemma is not dissimilar to that encountered in discussions of white-collar crime generally where attempts to dissect the symbiosis between organizations and their executive employees have often floundered in uncertainty (Geis et al., 1985). If a

chemical company is responsible for poisonous gas leaking out into the environment, do we blame the company or specific individuals within the organization? Similarly, are we to blame the medical profession generally for pathology laboratories that overservice or only the doctor(s) owning the laboratory?

More modest attempts to explain fraud and abuse amongst practitioners have avoided these contrasting approaches and have concentrated instead on situational features of the environment that push doctors towards fraud. Thus Gorring and Wilson (1984) suggest that some practitioners engage in abuse because their high incomes generate large taxation bills and in order to pay, some physicians commit illegal patterns of practice. Other situational explanations emphasize the regulations placed on billing items (such as the exclusion of telephone consultations) and other treatments (such as acupuncture) which are not redeemable. These are part of the treatments which physicians legitimately supply, yet for which they cannot be paid. This leads to physician frustration and subsequent abuse (Pontell et al., 1984b). In Canada, our interviews with doctors suggest that these reasons together with physicians' perceptions of inadequate levels of reimbursement and general bureaucratic interference in medical affairs motivate much illegal behaviour. [3]

CONCLUSION

In his pioneering study of white-collar crime, Edwin Sutherland (1949) devoted only scant attention to doctors. Sutherland maintained that physicians were probably more honest than other professionals and rarely committed fraud. While the verdict is not yet in on whether medical practitioners are more honest or dishonest than lawyers, accountants or academics, there is substantial evidence to suggest that physicians in Canada, like their counterparts in other industrialized countries, engage in a wide variety of activities that defraud and abuse government medical benefit programmes. What is also apparent is that the policing of fraud and abuse by peer review processes has not worked well with medical practitioners. When doctors dominate tribunals and statutory bodies involved in detecting and investigating medical fraud and over-servicing, few physicians seem to be either prosecuted or punished.

By their very nature, fee-for-service medical delivery systems in Canada offer some physicians the chance to amass considerable amounts of money illegally with little risk of detection. The criminogenic direction of this system could be dramatically altered if more physicians were on salary, or if members of the profession, either individually or collectively, contracted with the provinces to provide medical services at a fixed cost. However, it is unlikely that these directions will be taken in the foreseeable future because basic questions relating to the overall costs of such changes, the quality of health services so delivered, and the political reality of introducing such measures are still open to debate (Evans, 1983).

In the meantime, we would urge Canadian criminologists to direct some attention to the issue of professional crime generally, and crime by physicians specifically. We need to know much more about this neglected area including information concerning the characteristics of medical practitioners who are committing fraud and abuse; the types of abuse; estimates of the magnitude of abuse in terms of cost and frequency; and the effectiveness of particular forms of policing procedures. We suspect that crimes perpetrated by persons of professional occupations cause severe damage to our social values and social institutions. In the case of fraud and abuse by physicians, it is also probable that those who are defrauding the system are providing sub-standard medical services for their patients. Finally, insomuch as medical fraud and abuse contribute to this country's rising health costs, the issue of physician crime relates directly to the question of whether Canada will continue to fund universal, comprehensive and accessible health services in the future, as it has done so well in the past.

NOTES

1. Numerous interviews have been conducted with officials from relevant health agencies across Canada who deal with the implementation, auditing, policing, investigation, and prosecution of fraudulent practices by physicians. Gratitude is expressed to those individuals for the time, comments and documents they have provided. Material from these personal interviews is used extensively in this paper. Each official cannot be identified but the agencies contacted include: Health Departments in Ontario, British Columbia , Manitoba and Nova Scotia; British Columbia Medical Association; College of Physicians and Surgeons; private health funds, Royal Canadian Mounted Police and Health and Welfare Canada. Unless expressly stated to the contrary all research for this paper, including the interviews with officials, was conducted between December, 1984 and February, 1985.

2. Because investigation is still continuing in many of the cases mentioned in this paper, we have carefully avoided referring to names or incidents that would reveal the identity of those involved. The cases given though are representative of forms of fraud and abuse obtained from our interviews and other data sources.

3. In addition to the many interviews conducted with officials in health agencies, quantitative data have also been collected. Survey research focusing on practising physicians' attitudes to public health insurance, medical fraud, investigation practices, professional autonomy and other related issues has been conducted. The results have yet to be fully analyzed and will be published at a later date. However, additional comments and observations made during the collection of data are used in this paper.

Chapter 19

CORPORATE CRIME*

Carl Keane

INTRODUCTION

Every day, middle-class individuals, holding positions of responsibility, and hiding behind veils of corporate bureaucracy, violate the laws of society. Yet few people are aware of the extent of such crime. The few studies that have investigated corporate crime report that it is not uncommon.

It was the ground-breaking work of Sutherland (1949) that first brought corporate crime into the spotlight. Sutherland analyzed the life careers of the seventy largest U.S. manufacturing, mining, and mercantile corporations, examining the following legal violations: restraint of trade; misrepresentation in advertising; infringements of patents, trademarks, and copyrights; labour law violations; illegal rebates; financial fraud and violation of trust; violations of war regulations; and finally some miscellaneous offenses. He found that with an average corporate age of 45 years, a total of 980 decisions had been made against the seventy corporations, an average of 14 decisions per corporation (1949:29). More current research shows that his findings were not unusual. For example, focusing on illegal acts such as price-fixing, overcharging, violation of environmental regulations and antitrust laws, bribes, fraud, patent infringements, and violations of other market regulations, a 1984 survey found that approximately two-thirds of the Fortune 500 largest industrial companies had been in-volved in illegal behaviour since the mid-1970s (Etzioni, 1985).

Perhaps the most extensive examination to date of corporate offending is the study conducted by Clinard and his colleagues (Clinard, et al., 1979; Clinard and Yeager, 1980). This research involved the analysis of federal administrative, civil, and criminal actions either initiated or completed by twenty-five U.S. agencies during 1975-1976 against the 477 largest publicly owned U.S. manufacturing companies and the 105 largest U.S. wholesale, retail and service companies. Six main types of corporate illegal behaviour were discovered: administrative violations such as noncompliance with an order from a court or government agency; environmental violations such as pollution of the air or water; financial violations including bribery, tax violations and accounting malpractices; labour violations involving employment discrimination, occupational safety and health hazards, and unfair labour practices; manufacturing violations such as violations of the Consumer Product Safety Act; and unfair trade practices, involving various abuses of competition such as price-fixing as well as acts such as false advertising (Clinard and Yeager, 1980:113-115). The researchers found that of the 582 corporations, approximately 60% had at least one federal action brought against them, and for those companies that had at least one action brought against them, the average was 4.4 cases (1980:113).

---

* Written for this volume.

Turning closer to home, and focusing on violations of the Combines Act in Canada, Goff and Reasons (1978) reported that between 1952 and 1972 a total of 157 decisions were made against the fifty largest Canadian corporations, an average of 3 decisions per corporation. Taken together, these studies demonstrate the wide extent of corporate offending, and reveal that individuals in the middle and upper socioeconomic classes, contrary to popular stereotypes, quite frequently engage in illegal behaviour.

Reflecting on Sutherland's (1949) point that corporate offenses cannot be explained by conditions of poverty, nor by individual pathology, any search for the causes of corporate crime should begin with an examination of the context within which such crimes occur — the organization. This approach calls for an analysis of the corporation and its impact on the individuals who work there. As such, it is useful to first examine external and internal factors that affect the organization, followed by those factors that affect the employees of the organization. Let us begin with extra-corporate factors of influence.

EXTRA-CORPORATE FACTORS OF INFLUENCE

Any organization both affects, and is affected by, its environment. Organizations are constrained by laws, and at the same time, they may try to influence legislators. Some corporations conduct business in markets with numerous competitors, consumers, and suppliers — others with few. And, organizations operate in economies ranging from capitalist to communist. To help us understand the influence of extra-corporate factors, we can begin with an examination of the economic system.

CAPITALISM

Some criminologists argue that to understand corporate crime we should adopt a macro-perspective in explaining corporate offending and focus on the features of our capitalist economy. They suggest that corporate capitalism, with its primary emphasis on the goals of maximizing profitability and minimizing costs, leads to unsafe products, environmental pollution, employee and consumer deception, and unsafe working conditions (see Henry, 1982:85). At the same time, it is argued that the content and enforcement laws against corporate crime reflect the interests of the economic elite, who through their economic dominance are able to influence the political elite in order to maintain the status quo, that is, either through not passing forceful legislation, or through ineffective enforcement of existing laws (Snider and West, 1985). However, organizational problems are not restricted to capitalist countries. For example, it has been reported that in an effort to meet productivity goals, Soviet workers endure one of the worst records of industrial safety and occupational health in the world (Handelman, 1989). Others have reported the variety of economic crimes such as bribery, fraud, property theft, and "black-market" operations that are widespread in communist countries (Los, 1982). Therefore, the economic system alone cannot provide a comprehensive explanation for organizational deviance. Let us thus look to competition.

COMPETITION

It has been suggested that the predominant ideology of competition, common to both the profit and not-for-profit sectors, is a precipitating factor in the genesis of corporate crime. The case of the Ford Pinto automobile can be cited as an example. Facing increasing competition from foreign small-car imports, the Ford Motor Company attempted to speed up the production process of the Pinto in order to meet the competition. When it was determined that a faulty fuel system could cause the car to explode on impact, Ford executives conducted a cost-benefit analysis weighing the estimated number of injuries and deaths and resulting lawsuits that would occur against the cost of recalling all the defective cars. In accordance with the results of the cost-benefit analysis, the company decided against recalling the Ford Pinto, a decision that ultimately resulted in numerous deaths and injuries (Cullen et al., 1987; Dowie, 1977). This example is but one manifestation of a "culture of competition" which exists in all industrialized countries but is particularly strong in capitalist countries. It is related to corporate crime in that it motivates individuals to succeed at virtually any cost (Coleman, 1987, 1989). According to earlier work by Merton (1938) on anomie, this emphasis on success is reinforced by instilling into members of society three cultural axioms:

1. Everyone must strive for success, since success is equally available to all persons.
2. Failure is just a temporary detour to ultimate success.
3. The real failure is the person who reduces or withdraws his or her ambition for success.

Thus the quest for success is framed within a competitive milieu.

Competition, however, is a necessary but not sufficient cause of corporate crime. For example, although competition exists in every industry, some industries are more crime prone than others. Also, even within the same industry, some firms violate the law more than others. As students of corporate crime we must ask, what is there about particular industries, and particular firms, that produces a higher rate of corporate crime? This question calls for a closer examination of other aspects of the external environment of modern organizations.

ENVIRONMENTAL UNCERTAINTY

In examining the external structure of organizations we can identify certain factors that vary between firms and industries. For example, all organizations are goal oriented and an organizational priority is goal attainment (Finney and Lesieur, 1982). Further, an organization may have a variety of goals, and goals will differ between organizations. Although profitability is often the primary goal, organizations may strive to maximize revenue, earnings per share, market share, growth, and production quotas; or the primary goal may be survival. The organization, however, is not operating in a vacuum. Goals are pursued within an environment of uncertainty. The external environment of an organization comprises political, socio-cultural, economic, physical, and technological factors, and perhaps most importantly, other organizations. The political environment may affect the organization through government legislation; the socio-cultural environment through changing tastes and values; the economic environment through economic changes such as a recession or rampant growth of the economy; the physical environment through pollution levels; the technological environment through changes in technology used by the company or others; and other organizations may have an impact through their actions as competitors, suppliers, or consumers. These various elements of what has been referred to as an organization's "task environment" (Dill, 1958) produce a high degree of uncertainty. In order to meet corporate goals an organization operating within an uncertain environment may attempt to reduce that uncertainty through illegal behaviour (see Aldrich, 1979). For example, to reduce uncertainty concerning pricing vis-à-vis competitors, as well as to reduce the uncertainty of profitability, an organization may collude with other firms in the same industry to set and maintain prices (see Simpson, 1986). This price-fixing conspiracy serves to reduce uncertainty by providing the company with some control over an important element of its external environment. Braithwaite (1984:172) provides an example of this when he describes a conversation he had with an executive of a pharmaceutical company who admitted:

...just recently we got together about 30 of us, all of the accountants and finance directors...to sit around the table together and work out prices that we could all agree on in the submissions that we make to the Health Department...

In general, as environmental uncertainty increases, thus threatening goal attainment, illegal behaviour may increase in attempts to control or minimize the uncertainty, and to increase the likelihood of goal achievement.

MARKET STRUCTURE

The admission reported above reveals that price-fixing reduces uncertainty about profitability and competitive behaviour. The statement quoted also shows that for a price-fixing conspiracy to be successful there must be agreement amongst the firms that prices will be maintained. Hence, the greater the number of firms in a particular industry, the harder it may be to coordinate a collusion, and thus the harder it will be for all to agree to maintain prices. Therefore, price-fixing may be more prevalent in concentrated, oligopolistic industries dominated by a small number of firms. More specifically, Coleman (1989:225) suggested, "it would seem that industries with many small, highly competitive firms would be characterized by a high rate of crimes that are intended to improve competitive performance, such as fraud, false advertising, and espionage, and that collusion and antitrust activities are most common in more concentrated industries." So, the market structure of the industry is important with respect to the type of illegal activity most likely to occur. In addition, some situations may be particularly conducive to criminal behaviour in that there is an increased opportunity to violate the law. This leads us to a discussion of what can be termed opportunity theory.

OPPORTUNITY THEORY

The notion of "opportunity" differs slightly from the preceding discussion of industry concentration and corporate deviance by focusing on the increased likelihood of a firm to violate a *specific* type of law. For example, oil companies in the course of producing and/or shipping oil have a greater likelihood of polluting the environment (Clinard and Yeager, 1980: 250-251), while firms that are labour-intensive, placing a heavy reliance upon workers as opposed to equipment, are more likely to violate labour laws (Clinard and Yeager, 1980:131-132). Thus, some industries, and the firms and employees within them, may be more prone to committing certain offenses than others.

At the same time, some industries more than others may find themselves the target of various regulatory agencies. That is, some industries such as the pharmaceutical industry, the automobile industry, and the chemical and petroleum industries, because of the potential harm their products can cause, are more regulated than others (Coleman, 1989), and in turn, they have higher crime rates than others (Clinard and Yeager, 1980), if only because of the greater regulation imposed upon them. Also, because some industries may be more stringently regulated than others, it follows that those organizations that are diversified into a number of stringently regulated industries are more likely to face "opportunities" to deviate and/or are more likely to attract regulatory attention (Clinard and Yeager, 1980:131).

To summarize briefly, companies are goal oriented, and with factors such as globalization of business and rapid social change, they may find themselves operating in uncertain environments. And, in the process of minimizing uncertainty and maximizing goal attainment, they may violate regulations peculiar to the industry. Nevertheless, differences in the rates of violation exist between companies in the same industry. That is, although some industries tend to violate the law more than others, there is still variation within industries with some firms more deviant than others (Clinard and Yeager, 1980:58). This being the case, we must ask what characteristics distinguish criminal from non-criminal firms? Or, put another way, what are the characteristics of those firms that come to the attention of regulatory bodies? An examination of the internal environment of the corporation may provide an answer to these questions.

INTRA-CORPORATE FACTORS OF INFLUENCE

INTERNAL CONTROL

The modern corporation is a large, diffuse, hierarchical system, oriented towards goal(s) attainment through effective use of available resources in an uncertain environment. Employees of the corporation are one resource deployed to meet organizational goals. And, just as an organization will attempt to have some influence over its external environment, it must also manage its internal resources, including its employees. However, the internal structure of the corporation may make it difficult to control corporate illegality. For example, although the research is contradictory concerning corporate size as a factor in organizational corruption (Clinard and Yeager, 1980), conditions associated with larger size may be conducive to corrupt behaviour. That is, as companies grow along such dimensions as number of product lines, number of employees, and number of geographically dispersed locations, they become more difficult to manage, more difficult to control, and in short, more complex. The complexity of the modern corporation has been documented by Woodsmansee in his description of the General Electric Corporation (cited in Clinard and Yeager, 1980: 24-25) paraphrased below.

GE's employees are organized into separate layers of authority. The corporation is like a pyramid. The majority of the company's workers (over 300,000) form the base of the pyramid where working in small groups of 5 to 50 people they take orders from a supervisor on the second level of the pyramid. The supervisor takes orders from a department General Manager. There are about 180 department General Managers, each heading a department with one or two thousand employees. The department General Managers are supervised by a division Vice President/General Manager of which there are 50. The division Vice Presidents/General Managers report to one of 10 group Vice Presidents/Group Executives. At about the same level of authority are the executives of GE's Corporate Staff, concerned with accounting, planning, legal affairs, and employee relations. The next level above in the pyramid consists of three Vice Chairmen of the Board of Directors, and at the top of the pyramid sits GE's Chief Executive.

This description reflects the size and structure of the modern corporation, and points to the potential for deviant activities to remain hidden in this complex structure. In attempts to control the internal environment in the midst of this complexity, lines of authority may become decentralized. Stated differently, complexity and diversification, resulting from corporate growth, may call for a decentralized corporate structure as a means of coping with the vast numbers of people and information. And, it can be argued that a decentralized corporate structure in turn may be actually more conducive to corruption, rather than less, because visibility

is decreased and responsibility is diffused (Finney and Lesieur, 1982). That is, when an individual is geographically distant, such as in a branch plant in another country, and/or shielded from senior management by several levels of staff, communication may suffer. So, in a decentralized system it is easier to withhold information. In turn, senior management can distance themselves from wrongdoing occurring at the divisional level and/or at a distant location and deny accountability, a tactic referred to by Sutherland (1949:226) as "obfuscation as to responsibility."

On the subject of accountability, Braithwaite (1984) has argued that corporations may intentionally create an impression of a diffusion of responsibility. He writes:

All corporate actors benefit from the protection afforded by presenting to outsiders an appearance of greatly diffused accountability. Yet when companies for their own purposes want accountability, they can generally get it... (Braithwaite, 1984:138-39)

To briefly summarize once more, previously we argued that the organization's external environment is a contributing factor to corporate crime. Now we see that internal corporate factors are also important. But the picture is still incomplete. Although the form of the corporation may provide the setting where control is difficult and the potential for criminal activity is increased, certain individual variables may also be necessary for crime to occur, and we examine these in turn.

INDIVIDUAL LEVEL FACTORS

CONTROL THEORY

Theorists advocating control theories of crime argue that individuals who have weak ties to the norms of conventional society are more likely to deviate than those who are (1) emotionally attached to conventional others and therefore reluctant to deviate for fear of displeasing these others; (2) committed to conventional goals acquired through conventional means; (3) involved in conventional/legal activities; and (4) believe in the validity of the laws of society and the need to obey those laws

(Hirschi, 1969). In essence, control theorists argue that the more the individual is integrated into a legal, as opposed to an illegal, culture, the less likely is the individual to violate society's laws. Thus, at first glance, it appears that social control theory is deficient in explaining crimes of the privileged, since unlike the stereotypical "street" criminal, the corporate executive appears to be strongly connected to the social bond of conventional society. If we modify control theory, however, to use it from a narrower perspective, such as the subculture of the organization, we can hypothesize that corporate offenders may be tightly bonded to the culture of the organization. This again suggests a socialization process whereby the individual comes to identify closely with the organization and its goals. That is, through work-related activities and social interaction with other company employees, the individual intensifies his/her bond of loyalty to the organization. This bond to the organization may be intensified through social mobility via promotions, and/or geographic mobility via transfers (Coleman, 1989:220), both of which may make it difficult for individuals to develop long-term social ties outside the organization. Thus, individuals may come to associate predominantly with other members of the organization for whom they come to care, and from whom they learn the behaviour required to attain corporate goals with which they come to strongly identify.

Recalling that one goal of the corporation is profit maximization, we can see that not meeting this goal is an indication of corporate failure, or more specifically, management failure. This emphasis on the failure of the individual to meet corporate goals leads again to Merton's (1938) strain theory.

STRAIN THEORY

When discussing extra-corporate factors of corporation crime we saw how companies are pitted against each other in a "culture of competition" which produces a situation of interfirm rivalry wherein some firms might violate the law to gain advantage over a competitor. What we have described is a setting where the industry culture promotes competition as a means of attaining corporate goals, but the market structure limits the opportunity for all companies to achieve success. This discrepancy between culture and structure produces a situation of strain which increases the possibility of corporate corruption. A similar process can be seen at the individual level. That is, in the planning and budgeting process, companies regularly set internal corporate goals. In this situation competition may exist between two divisions, between plants, and/or between time periods such as when a company budgets to decrease costs, or forecasts to increase sales, over the previous year. Again we have a situation where the corporate culture emphasizes competition, but the corporate structure may not provide the opportunity to achieve the corporate goal. According to Merton (1938) this type of situation may lead to illegal behaviour. Merton postulated that if individuals are thwarted in their quest to attain their desired goals, such as the culturally prescribed goal of success, they will become frustrated. This frustration, caused by a disjuncture between legal means and desired goals, will produce a situation of strain, and individuals will adapt to alleviate the strain. Some individuals, whom Merton called "innovators," while accepting the goal will reject conventional means and embrace illegal means of attaining the goal. With respect to strain, Clinard (1983) has reported on the pressure exerted on middle managers from top management to increase profitability, decrease costs, and meet production and sales quotas, pressure which may result in illegal behaviour. Simply stated, some individuals faced with a discrepancy between goals and the legal means to achieve them will become corporate criminals. But still this statement does not tell us which individuals will deviate. Opportunity theory and learning theory may help answer this question.

Expanding on Merton, Cloward and Ohlin (1960) asserted that in order to become criminal not only must individuals experience strain, but they must also be exposed to the opportunity to learn from a subculture how to become delinquent. This emphasis on the relevance of a subculture, while still concerned with intracorporate forces, continues the focus on the individual and allows us to examine the theory of "differential association."

DIFFERENTIAL ASSOCIATION

Continuing with individual level explanations of wrongdoing, Sutherland's (1949) interactionist theory of "differential association" makes a contribution to research in the area of corporate corruption. A form of learning theory, differential association postulates that deviant behaviour is learned, just like any other type of behaviour. Essentially, differential association theory asserts that "criminal behaviour is learned in association with those who define such behaviour favorably and in isolation from those who define it unfavorably, and that a person in an appropriate situation engages in such criminal behaviour if, and only if, the weight of the favorable definitions exceeds the weight of the unfavorable definitions" (Sutherland, 1949:234).

Clinard and Yeager (1980:58) have confirmed the validity of differential association theory in explaining economic crimes, arguing that although the corporation is influenced by its external environment, the behaviour of a firm is also a product of cultural norms operating within a given corporation. With respect to corporate crimes, the theory suggests that executives become enmeshed in a corporate or professional subculture, and through association with deviant peers learn illegal behaviour. Two essential components of this theory are that (1) the individual must be exposed to an excess of definitions favorable to crime, and (2) the individual must be isolated from definitions unfavorable to crime. Given the loyalty and feelings of identification with the corporation that some organizations are able to instill in their employees, it is easy to see how an individual could be socialized to commit an unlawful act. Or, on the other hand, the cultural environment may discourage corrupt behaviour.

Finney and Lesieur (1982:277) wrote that internal organizational constraints against crime will vary along a continuum, "one end representing moral commitment against law violation, the middle representing a state of neutral receptivity, and the other end representing positive attitudes towards law violation." Accordingly, illegal behaviour is more likely if corporations selectively hire, selectively promote, and socialize a significant number of employees who adopt a stance on the continuum near the neutral or deviant end. Thus, the presence of internal cultural constraints, or their absence, will have an influence on organizational members, and in turn the level of organizational deviance.

Differential association thus points to the importance of learning both the illegal methods as well as the beliefs supporting the use of the methods.

TECHNIQUES OF NEUTRALIZATION

Finally, how does the corporate criminal justify his or her deviant behaviour? After all, the corporate offender is not deviant twenty-four hours per day; rather the crime is situation specific. The rest of the time the individual is a law-abiding citizen constrained by the norms of conventional society. Again we need to examine the individual. Sykes and Matza (1957:664-70) argued that individuals who periodically "drift" into illegal behaviour will rationalize their guilty behaviour using various "techniques of neutralization." These techniques are:

1. Denial of responsibility

    Vandivier (1987:114-115) relates a conversation he had with a senior executive at the B.F. Goodrich Co., who when asked why he was not going to report to senior management that a faulty aircraft brake was being developed replied: "Because it's none of my business, and it's none of yours. I learned a long time ago not to worry about things over which I had no control. I have no control over this." Not satisfied with this answer, Vandivier asked him if his conscience wouldn't bother him if during test flights on the brake, something should happen resulting in death or injury to the test pilot. To this the executive replied: "I have no control over this thing. Why should my conscience bother me?"

2. Denial of injury

An example of this technique is the occupational crime of Brian Molony, who began his fraudulent activities at the Canadian Imperial Bank of Commerce with the rationalization that he was simply borrowing money from various accounts and the money would be immediately repaid after an expected gambling win (see Ross, 1988).

3. Denial of the victim

Testifying before the Senate Subcommittee on Antitrust and Monopoly, a Westinghouse executive testified as follows:

Committee Attorney: Did you know that these meetings with competitors were illegal?

Witness: Illegal? Yes, but not criminal. I didn't find that out until I read the indictment....I assumed that criminal action meant damaging someone, and we did not do that...(Gies, 1977:122)

4. Condemnation of the condemners

An example of this technique is cited by Vaughan (1983). Charged with fraudulently billing the Ohio Department of Public Welfare over $500,000 by falsifying prescriptions, Revco Drug Stores, Inc., assumed the role of victim, blaming the inefficiencies of the state welfare department for the company's illegal actions.

5. Appeal to higher loyalties

The same Westinghouse executive cited in (3) above, justified his illegal behaviour by claiming: "I thought that we were more or less working on a survival basis in order to try to make enough to keep our plant and employees."

To this point we have seen that at the macro-level, extra-corporate factors impact on the organization and have some influence on the structure of the organization. Further, these macro-level factors, as well as micro-level influences, are felt at the individual level. Let us now attempt to synthesize these findings.

THEORETICAL INTEGRATION

In order to gain a clearer picture of corporate crime a theoretical integration of extra-corporate, intra-corporate, and individual factors related to corporate offending may be useful. To begin with, the economic condition of the industry and the extent of task-environment uncertainty is important, as is the degree of industry competition which may lead to behaviour to reduce uncertainty. Also, the likelihood of a firm violating a particular law varies with the type of industry and the level of industry regulation. Further, large firms may be more likely to be deviant because the concomitants of size, such as diversity and complexity, may be conducive to corrupt behaviour because of the diffusion of responsibility and diminished control. And, if the firm is not performing well, the potential for illegal behaviour increases.

So, to this point we can speculate that large firms operating in regulated industries, experiencing economic strain and environmental uncertainty, may be more at risk of corporate crime. However, although this setting may be conducive to illegal behaviour, individuals must also be exposed to a socialization process whereby they come to identify with the company and its goals, learn the illegal behaviour required to meet the objectives perceived to be unattainable through legal means, and rationalize their actions through various techniques. Hence, the extra-corporate culture and the intra-corporate culture interact to either promote or inhibit law violation. An element of strain exists in both cultures of an offending corporation. At the extra-corporate level the strain may be caused by external forces such as competitors, suppliers, or government legislation, posing a threat to the corporation's objectives. At the intra-corporate level the strain may also be caused by the potential failure to meet corporate objectives, but the pressure is imposed by internal rather than external factors. And, if cultural restraints such as values and regulations opposing and thus inhibiting corporate criminal behaviour are lacking or weak, both externally, in society in general, and internally, within the organization, corruption is more likely to occur. This being the case, can we control corporate crime?

CONTROLLING CORPORATE OFFENDING

Braithwaite (1989:40) has argued that "In modern capitalist societies there are many more statutes that criminalize the behaviour of corporations (anti-pollution laws, occupational health and safety laws, consumer protection laws, antitrust laws, laws to enforce compliance with standards) than there are laws that criminalize the behaviour of the poor." However, application of the law is another matter. That is, evidence suggests that crimes of the powerful are punished differently from crimes of the powerless. For example, focusing on Canadian securities violations, Hagan (1989; Hagan and Parker, 1985) examined all cases referred for prosecution under the Criminal Code or the Securities Act from 1966 to 1983. After categorizing offenders in terms of their class position, the researchers found that those offenders in positions of power committed crimes larger in scope than those with less power, but they received proportionately less severe sanctions. It is argued that one reason for this is because the powerful were less likely to be charged under the Criminal Code, and more likely to be charged under the Securities Act which carries lesser sanctions.

Also considering the element of power is research by Goff and Reasons (1978). Their research involved an investigation of the major Canadian corporations which have violated the Combines Act and have been investigated by the Combines Branch from 1952 to 1973. Concentrating on the illegal acts of combinations, mergers, monopolies, resale price maintenance, misleading price advertising, predatory pricing, price discrimination, and violations of patents, they concluded that the "Combines Branch has centered its attentions upon the investigation, prosecution, and conviction of small- and medium-sized companies and corporations leaving the very largest corporations free to engage in their monopolistic practices" (Goff and Reasons, 1978:86). Again, they suggested that this is because large corporations operating in oligopolistic industries have the ability to obscure their illegal practices.

Snider (1982) compared the punishments given to those offenders who commit traditional non-violent economic offenses with those offenders who commit what she terms "upperworld" non-violent economic offenses. Examples of upperworld non-violent economic offenses are acts such as false advertising, misleading price representation, and violations of acts such as the Food and Drug Act, the Packaging and Labelling Act, the Weights and Measures Act, the Hazardous Products Act, and the Combines Investigation Act. Examples of traditional non-violent economic offenses are: theft, possession of stolen goods, breaking and entering, and taking a motor vehicle without consent. In brief, she found that over a considerable period of time more traditional offenders were charged, and the sanctions for the traditional economic crimes were much heavier than for the upperworld economic crimes. Others have similarly argued that corporate criminals enjoy a legal advantage because of the types and combinations of legal sanctions that they experience (see Hagan and Nagel, 1982). As an example, in 1980 a $148 million lawsuit was filed by Revenue Canada against Amway Canada Ltd. for unpaid custom duties and sales tax. If the lawsuit had gone to trial, and the government had won, the government would have had the right to seize Amway's Canadian assets. However, Amway had been disposing of some of its Canadian assets, and was able to negotiate an out-of-court settlement in 1989 for $45 million (Miller, 1989).

In summary, corporate criminals have been spared the stigma of criminalization often imposed on those less privileged. Furthermore, given the evidence of recidivism reported by researchers such as Goff and Reasons (1978) and Clinard and Yeager (1980), the existing sanctions appear to have little deterrent effect. This being the case, to control corporate corruption perhaps we should recall that the roots of unethical behaviour are embedded in the organizational and cultural contexts.

Extra-corporate sanctions which have been

suggested to inhibit organizational deviance include stiffer penalties for corporations and executives, negative publicity, nationalization of firms that are habitual offenders, and forced deconcentration and divestiture of offending firms, to name a few (Braithwaite, 1984; Clinard and Yeager, 1980; Coleman, 1989). These sanctions are similar in that they are imposed by others external to the organization, and they are punishment imposed after the criminal act. It may also be possible to control corporate crime at the intra-corporate level.

Intra-corporate control can be increased by actions such as improving and strengthening the firm's self-regulatory systems (Braithwaite, 1984) and providing for public and/or union representation on corporate boards of directors (Clinard and Yeager, 1980). These intra-corporate mechanisms would serve to control the actions of executives prior to any offense. Another method of controlling corporate crime which has received increased attention is the development of a stronger business ethic (Clinard and Yeager, 1980; Coleman, 1989). This proposal is directed at the culture of the organization and is preventive in its orientation. An increasing number of companies are finding that "good ethics is good business"(Etzioni, 1989). Unethical corporate behaviour may destroy a company's reputation, and given the increase in foreign competition experienced by many industries, a loss of customers may accompany the loss of reputation. In addition, failure to follow ethical business practices may result not only in consumer protest, but also in government intervention (Hilts, 1989). Many companies are taking steps to avoid this possibility. A survey conducted in 1984 of the Fortune 500 industrial and 500 service companies found that 80% of those responding were incorporating an ethics program into their organizations (Hoffman, 1986).

Whether the institutionalization of ethics is successful in decreasing corporate crime remains to be seen. However, it will be a step in creating a culture in which corporate crime is, at least publicly, not tolerated. On a broader scale, Braithwaite (1989) has argued that what society needs "is punishment for organizational crime that maximizes the sense of shame and sends a message to executives that corporate crime is as despicable to society as street crime." He has further asserted that "once members of the organization internalize this abhorrence of corporate wrongdoing, then the self-regulation of executive consciences and corporate ethics and compliance policies will do most of the work for the government" (1989:143).

SUMMARY

This article has sought to provide an integrated explanation of corporate crime from an extra-corporate and intra-corporate perspective. In addition, it has sought to suggest possible remedies for this form of deviant behaviour. It has also implicitly argued that the recognition by those both inside and outside the organization that corporate crime is a contemptible form of deviant behaviour is the first step in its eradication.

Chapter 20

DETERRENCE AND AMPLIFICATION OF JUVENILE DELINQUENCY BY POLICE CONTACT: THE IMPORTANCE OF GENDER AND RISK-ORIENTATION*

Carl Keane, A.R. Gillis, and John Hagan

The nature of the relationship between contact with police and deviant behaviour is an unresolved issue for students of crime and delinquency. Deterrence theory suggests that apprehension by the police will deter subsequent deviant behaviour. Reaction arguments suggest that contact with police will not only fail to deter subsequent deviance, but, by increasing exposure to deviant subcultures, may actually amplify the likelihood of its reoccurrence (see Wilkins, 1967). Thus, theories of delinquency seem to provide two mutually exclusive predictions on the impact of policing. This paper argues that both, argues that both may be accurate, depending on the gender of the individual experiencing contact with the police. In other words, we suggest that gender is an important scope restriction on deterrence and amplification arguments (Walker and Cohen, 1985).

With this in mind, we examine the reciprocal relationship between police contact and deviant behaviour among male and female juveniles. The specific behaviour on which we focus is the use of marijuana, because of its strong subcultural component (Becker, 1963; Hinde-lang, 1976). In addition, because marijuana use is a less serious crime than, say, car theft, female participation is likely to more closely approximate male participation.

CONTROL, DETERRENCE, AND RISK-TAKING

Control theory basically posits that society has norms and values that are generally shared by its members, and that if individuals transgress social norms, societal constraints or "social bonds" (Hirschi, 1969) are too weak to offset the pleasures of deviance. Social integration and/or the likelihood or severity of punishment are too low.

To elaborate on this in relation to juvenile delinquency, we suggest that the family is the first agent of socialization and control, but as children grow older and autonomous, familial influence decreases and formal mechanisms of control in the wider community, such as churches, schools and the police, become more salient (see Hagan, Simpson, and Gillis,

* Edited version of Carl Keane, A.R. Gillis, John Hagan, "Deterrence and Amplification of Juvenile Delinquency by Police Contact: The Importance of Gender and Risk-Orientation." *British Journal of Criminology* 29(1989): 336-52. Reprinted by permission of Oxford University Press.

This research was made possible by a grant from the Social Science and Humanities Research Council of Canada. An earlier version of this paper was presented at the Annual Meetings of the Canadian Sociology and Anthropology Association, Winnipeg, Manitoba, 1986.

1979; Agnew, 1984a, and also Linden and Fillmore, 1981; Segrave and Hastad, 1985; Elliott, Huizinga, and Ageton, 1985).

The link between social control and adolescent marijuana use was noted by Jessor and Jessor (1978:68), who reported that adolescents who are likely to be involved with marijuana show a "concern with personal autonomy, a lack of interest in the goals of conventional institutions like church and school, a jaundiced view of the larger society and a more tolerant view of transgression" (see also Kandel, Kessler, and Margulies, 1978). This finding reflects a shift of focus from conventional to non-conventional beliefs and activities concomitant with a striving for autonomy which we suggest is manifested through risk-taking behaviour. That is, adolescents who are risk-takers will be more inclined to use marijuana than are those who are more risk-averse. This is similar to the position taken by Hagan, Simpson, and Gillis (1979), who posited that delinquency involves the opportunity to take risks and is a liberating experience (1979:29). Hagan and his associates (1979, and also 1985, 1987) have also observed that because of structural factors and differences in socialization, male and females differ in their "taste for risk," and that this leads them towards or away from deviance and accounts for large gender differences in rates. A link between risk-taking and drugs was reported by Zuckerman (1978), who termed risk-taking behaviour "sensation seeking" and found that sensation seekers were more likely to experiment with stimulating kinds of drugs such as marijuana. This link between the willingness to take risks or chances and deviant behaviour is similar to Hirschi's description of drug use and delinquency being manifestations of the "tendency or propensity of the individual to seek short-term immediate pleasure" (Hirschi, 1984:51). Therefore, if delinquency is perceived as an activity rationally undertaken to provide some benefit, such as pleasure and/or status, at the expense (risk) of certain costs (apprehension and punishment), then the implication is that to reduce delinquency we should increase the costs (controls). This is similar to the suggestion by Wilson (1975), who writes that "criminals may be willing to run greater risks (or they may have a weaker sense of morality) than the average citizen, but if the expected cost of crime goes up without a corresponding increase in the expected benefits then the would-be criminal... engages in less crime" (Wilson, 1975:197).

To summarize, as adolescents mature, their primary normative reference group shifts from family to peers and the wider community. The greater the degree of this shift, the more adolescents identify with peers and their values and behaviours. Accompanying this shift away from the family as the sole reference group is a striving for autonomy; Erickson (1963) has called this process a search for a "sense of identity." Risk-taking behaviour is one element of this process that provides immediate feedback (amplified if performed in a group setting) concerning personal limitations (e.g., physical capability) as well as societal limitations (e.g., norms, laws) and the extent to which these limitations can be "stretched." As such, risk-taking behaviour may be placed on a continuum wherein some adolescents will be able to satisfy their search for autonomy with mild and legal forms of risk-taking behaviour (e.g., surfing, skate-boarding), while others push for different and/or greater thrills, which may include activities that derive part of their excitement from the fact that they defy the law and community control (e.g., shoplifting). We suggest that those adolescents who are risk-takers will be more resistant to familial and formal control, and more inclined to engage in deviant behaviour such as marijuana use. We further suggest that because females are more risk-averse than males, they are more susceptible to deterrence.

DIFFERENTIAL ASSOCIATION AND AMPLIFICATION

Differential association theory (Sutherland and Cressey, 1970) asserts that the major factor in delinquent behaviour is the presence of deviant role models in the adolescent peer group. This emphasis on a delinquent peer group implies the existence of a subculture with which individuals identify, and wherein certain behaviours and attitudes are learned. The relevance of social learning theory in explaining delinquent behaviour within a subcultural domain has been shown by Akers (1973), and more recently by Segrave and Hastad, (1985), who after examining a variety of delinquent behaviour report that in a comparison of subcultural theory, control theory, and strain theory, subcultural theory was the most robust in terms of explaining the most unique variance in both male and female delinquency (see also Matsueda and Heimer, 1987).

Looking at adolescent marijuana use, Akers et al. (1979) stated that the major explanatory variables from social learning theory — differential association, differential reinforcement, definitions, and imitation — combine to account for 68 per cent of the variance in marijuana use and 39 per cent of the variance in marijuana abuse. These results echo the work of Kandel (1978) and her finding that a similarity of attributes between friends is an essential component in predicting adolescent marijuana use. She writes that both socialization and selection are important, that is, adolescents may provocatively seek friends with attitudes similar to their own. Once enmeshed in the friendship group, behaviour patterns are shared and learned. (See also Kandel, Kessler, and Margulies, 1978; Glynn, 1981; Krohn et al., 1982; Meier, Burkett, and Hickman, 1984).

Although many delinquent acts are performed without accomplices (Hindelang, 1971), some are conducted in a group context. Hindelang found that out of a selection of eighteen delinquent activities, using marijuana was more often cited as being a collective rather than an individual activity (see also Becker, 1963).

Further research by Hindelang found that adolescent offenders "who engage in delinquent behaviour in groups are more likely to have been picked up by the police than are offenders who tend to engage in illegal behaviour in isolation, even when the seriousness and frequency of the offenses in which the two groups have engaged are comparable" (Hindelang, 1976: 123). Hence, the social context of the act, coupled with the inherent risk involved in breaking the law, may serve to reinforce and perpetuate this behaviour.

This points to the relevance of amplification theory, Wilkins (1967:91-92) suggested that a positive feedback system which may unintentionally promote additional deviance is often created. The system he proposes is the following: the action taken by society and the resulting self-perception of the individuals defined as deviant leads to their isolation and alienation. This provides the basis of a deviation-amplifying system. The definition of society leads to the development of the self-perception as "deviant" on the part of the "outliers" (outlaws), and it is hardly to be expected that people who are excluded by a system will continue to regard themselves as part of it. So deviant groups will tend to develop their own values, which may run counter to the values of the parent system which defined them as "outliers." The increased deviance demonstrated by the deviant groups (resulting from the deviation-amplifying effect of the self-perception, which in turn may have derived from the defining acts of society) results in more forceful action by the conforming groups against the non-conformists. Information about the behaviour of the non-conformists received by the conforming groups leads to more acts being defined as deviant, or to more stringent action against the "outliers." Thus, the whole system can continue round and round in an amplifying circuit. (See also Cohen, 1955 and Lemert, 1962; and more recently Farrington, Osborn, and West, 1978; Gove, 1980; and Tittle, 1988 on the continuing question of the impact of labelling.)

So differential association theory posits that adolescents are more likely to engage in delinquency in general, and in some delinquent behaviours in particular, such as the use of marijuana, if peers do so as well. Further, contact with formal agents of control, such as the police, may increase alienation and result in further acts of deviance rather than conformity. Thus, counter to deterrence arguments, the impact of efforts at control may inflate rather than deflate rates of delinquency.

GENDER AND RISK-TAKING AS INTERACTING VARIABLES

Whether the result of adolescents' encounters with formal control is amplification or deterrence may depend on the gender of the juvenile. As noted earlier, gender is an important correlate of delinquency. Females are more often the objects of informal than formal social control, more risk-aversive, and less inclined to engage in deviant behaviour than are males. This suggests that females may be more susceptible to deterrence than are males, who are more likely to take risks, including deviant behaviour, and are more often in contact with the police (see, e.g., Hagan et al., 1979, 1985, 1987). Together with the recent research reporting that among males differential association is a better predictor of delinquency than is control theory (Matsueda and Hiemer, 1987), this suggests that contact with police is more likely to amplify the deviant behaviour of males than females. In view of this, then, gender is not only important in its interaction with other variables as a predictor of deviance, but may operate as a critical scope restriction on theories of deviance. Specifically, deterrence theory may hold for females, who are more risk-aversive, while amplification arguments may be more credible for males, who are more risk-oriented and likely to see a brush with the police as a challenge rather than an inhibition.

POPULATION, SAMPLE, AND PROCEDURES

The population for this research was the student body of four secondary schools in metropolitan Toronto. One school serves an upper middle-class area, another a middle-class neighbourhood, a third serves a working-class area, while the fourth is a vocational school with a student body drawn primarily from a working-class population. This selection procedure guaranteed a wide variation in socioeconomic status (SES) and related factors. School board lists were the sampling frame, and a stratified random sample was drawn resulting in a sample of 835 respondents. This represented a response rate of 83.5 per cent.

The questionnaire was administered to groups of respondents in classrooms after school. One of the investigators read the questionnaire aloud, with the respondents following along filling out their own questionnaires.

This procedure was used to increase comprehension of the questions and hence reliability, in light of the possibility that delinquency may be related to reading comprehension (see Hirschi and Hindelang, 1977). List-wise deletion for this analysis (see Gillis and Hagan, 1982) resulted in a final sample of 665, comprised of 360 males and 305 females.

Measurement was as follows:

Exogenous variables:

1. *Orientation to risk-taking.* We measured this attitude by asking respondents to rank themselves on the statement "I like to take chances," with the scale ranging from "strongly agree" to "strongly disagree."
2. *Age.* In actual years.
3. *Neighbourhood susceptibility.* The presence of a delinquent milieu was ascertained by having respondents answer the statement "Most young people around my neighbourhood are always getting into trouble." The scale ranged from "strongly agree" to "strongly disagree."
4. *Differential association.* The existence of a delinquent peer group was determined by asking respondents whether any of their close friends had ever been picked up by the police. The scale ranged from "none" to "most close friends."

Endogenous variables:

5. *Police contact.* We used responses to the question "Have you ever been picked up by the police." Answers ranged from "never" to "four or more times."
6. *Marijuana use.* This was determined by asking how often a respondent had used cannabis products during the last year.

Control variables:

7. *Gender.* Coded male 1, female 2.
8. *Socio-economic status.* We used Blishen's (1961) scale, based on father's occupation.

RESULTS

We began by testing the relative predictive power of the two theories under consideration. Figure 1 (omitted) is a path model where age, gender, SES, risk-taking and the existence of a delinquent milieu are exogenous variables, and marijuana use and police contact are endogenous variables. We analysed the model using LISREL VI (Jöreskog and Sörbom, 1983; Saris and Stronkhurst, 1984) and allowed for the possibility of reciprocal causation between the endogenous variables.

The model shows that gender, SES, and neighbourhood susceptibility are significant predictors of police contact, with $\gamma = -0.32$, -0.13, and 0.10 respectively. Thus, males, individuals of lower SES, and those experiencing the presence in the neighbourhood of delinquent others are more likely to report that they have been picked up by the police. However, these exogenous variables are not significant predictors of marijuana use, whereas age and a positive attitude towards risk-taking are ($\gamma = 0.21$ and 0.16, respectively). The data also show that using marijuana is a positive predictor of

being picked up by the police ($\beta = 0.23$) with significant feedback effect ($\beta = 0.22$). This reciprocal effect suggests that using marijuana attracts police attention, which in turn leads to marijuana use, which attracts police attention, and so on.

This model also suggests that neighbourhood affects police contact, either through a subcultural influence or a selective policing phenomenon. That is, being part of a delinquent subculture may lead to increased police contact and/or to activities that attract police attention. In order to further examine this empirically, we entered differential association (having close friends who have had contact with the police) as an additional exogenous variable. Figure 2 shows the path model with the introduction of this variable.

Differential association is the best predictor of both marijuana use and police contact, with $\gamma = 0.51$ and 0.35, respectively. Further, the γ coefficient for the path from neighbourhood susceptibility to police contact is attenuated to insignificance, and the feedback path from police contact to marijuana use disappears completely. The inclusion of contact with a

FIGURE 2

EXPANDED PATH MODEL TESTING DETERRENCE VERSUS AMPLIFICATION (BOTH GENDERS)

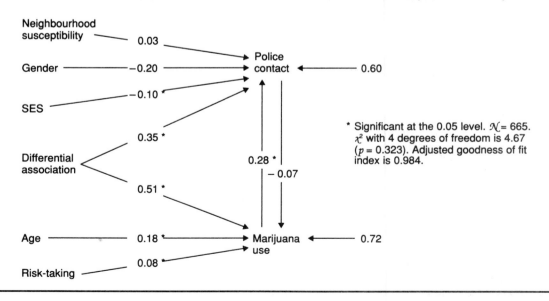

* Significant at the 0.05 level. $N = 665$.
x^2 with 4 degrees of freedom is 4.67 ($p = 0.323$). Adjusted goodness of fit index is 0.984.

deviant subculture improves the explained variance for both endogenous variables.

The next step in this analysis was to examine the impact of gender as a scope restriction. To do this, we examined gender as an interacting variable by splitting the sample into males and females, and then examining the model again. Of course, this procedure eliminated gender as an exogenous variable. Further, since the two samples were now half the size of the original, we used the 0.10 level of statistical significance instead of the 0.05 level as the minimal level. As shown in Figures 3 and 4, gender does not profoundly affect the relationships among the exogenous variables. However, differential association is a relatively weak predictor of police contact for females (0.20 vs. 0.49), but a relatively strong predictor of marijuana use (0.47 vs. 0.38). Further, for females, using marijuana is a predictor of police contact, while being picked up by the police is negatively related to marijuana use ($\beta=-0.25$). In contrast, males who have been picked up by the police report increased marijuana use ($\beta=0.21$). Figures 3 and 4 also show that the model explains more of the variance in deviance for males than for females, explaining 34 per cent vs. 13 per cent of the variance for police contact and 40 per cent vs. 7 per cent for marijuana use.

The principal reason we examined the fit of the original model for males and females separately is that they tend to differ in their orientations to risk, and this could reflect differences in susceptibility to deterrence and an amplification reaction. To see whether the variables in the model indeed interact with orientation to risk, we split the sample on this variable and ran the structural equations within each subsample of risk-takers and risk-aversives (Fig. 5).

Risk-takers (Fig. 5) resemble males (Fig. 4) in that both subsamples show the same small but significant amplification effect of police contact on marijuana use ($\beta=0.19$ and 0.21, respectively). Also, the use of marijuana does not lead to contact with the police in either subsample ($\beta=0.06$ and 0.09). Neighbourhood susceptibility is a relatively insignificant predictor in both subsamples, although the substantial impact of differential association and the smaller effects of SES and age are almost identical in both risk-takers and males.

Figure 3
Path Model Testing Deterrence versus Amplification (Females)

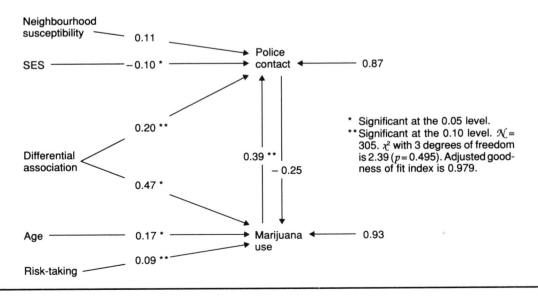

* Significant at the 0.05 level.
** Significant at the 0.10 level. $\mathcal{N}=$ 305. x^2 with 3 degrees of freedom is 2.39 ($p=0.495$). Adjusted goodness of fit index is 0.979.

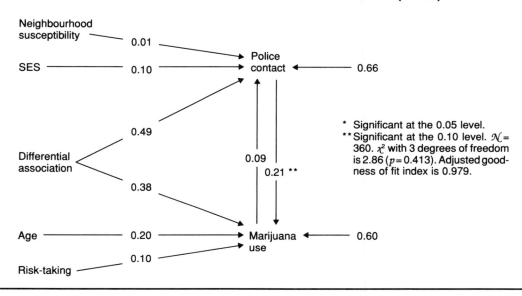

FIGURE 4
PATH MODEL TESTING DETERRENCE VERSUS AMPLIFICATION (MALES)

* Significant at the 0.05 level.
** Significant at the 0.10 level. $\mathcal{N} =$ 360. x^2 with 3 degrees of freedom is 2.86 ($p = 0.413$). Adjusted goodness of fit index is 0.979.

In some respects, the risk-takers do not differ from the subsample of risk-aversive juveniles (Fig. 6). Neighbourhood susceptibility and SES are inconsequential predictors of the endogenous variables, and age is a significant but weak predictor of marijuana use in both subsamples. However, in other respects, the two subsamples differ dramatically. Differential association increases the chances of risk-takers using marijuana ($\gamma = 0.37$) as well as coming into contact with the police ($\gamma = 0.49$). On the other hand, among risk-aversive juveniles, differential association does not increase chances of encountering the police ($\gamma = 0.05$), but chances of using marijuana are greatly enhanced ($\gamma = 0.71$). Also, risk-aversive marijuana smokers are much more likely to report that they have had contact with the police ($\beta = 0.59$) than are risk-takers ($\beta = 0.06$). Finally, among risk-aversive juveniles, contact with the police is a strong negative predictor of marijuana use ($\beta = 0.43$), suggesting a deterrent effect; while a β value of 0.59 indicates that risk-aversive marijuana users have a substantially greater likelihood of encountering the police than have their risk-taking counterparts. In these respects the risk-aversive subsample is similar to the subsample of females (Fig. 3).

The more extreme values of the correlations in Figures 5 and 6 suggests that orientation to risk has a greater impact on the relationship between the endogenous variables than has gender. This, the argument presented earlier, and the fact that the relationship between gender and orientation to risk is significant ($r = 0.26$), suggests that orientation to risk intervenes between gender and its impact on the relationship between marijuana use and policing.

DISCUSSION AND CONCLUSIONS

We began our study with an examination of two competing perspectives on the relationship between deviance and control: deterrence and amplification. We suggested that gender may act as a scope restrictor and determine the nature of the relationship. The data support this reasoning. Generally, the effects of the exogenous variables in Figures 3 and 4 do not

FIGURE 5

PATH MODEL TESTING DETERRENCE VERSUS AMPLIFICATION (RISK-TAKERS, BOTH GENDERS)

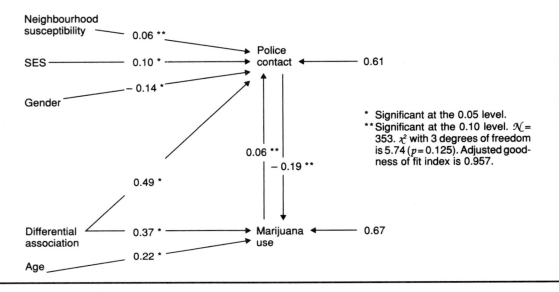

* Significant at the 0.05 level.
** Significant at the 0.10 level. $\mathcal{N} =$ 353. x^2 with 3 degrees of freedom is 5.74 ($p = 0.125$). Adjusted goodness of fit index is 0.957.

FIGURE 6

PATH MODEL TESTING DETERRENCE VERSUS AMPLIFICATION (RISK-TAKERS, BOTH GENDERS)

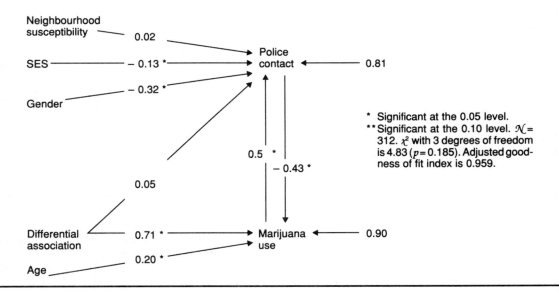

* Significant at the 0.05 level.
** Significant at the 0.10 level. $\mathcal{N} =$ 312. x^2 with 3 degrees of freedom is 4.83 ($p = 0.185$). Adjusted goodness of fit index is 0.959.

differ greatly between males and females. However, the most significant finding is that female adolescents may be deterred from some delinquent behaviour because of contact with the police, whereas male delinquency may be amplified because of this experience. As suggested earlier, males may use this experience to expand their network of delinquent peers (subculture) with which future association will lead to additional delinquency. However, female adolescents who have been picked up by the police may find parental restrictions (control) will limit opportunities for future deviance.

Subsequent controls (omitted) suggest that the reason for these gender effects is orientation to risk. Males are more likely to take risks, while females tend to be risk-aversive. Because of this, females are more likely to be deterred from delinquency as a result of police contact while male delinquent behaviour is likely to be amplified.

These findings support both deterrence and amplification arguments in explaining the presence or absence of adolescent deviance, and highlight the importance of specifying the scope of theories. That is, deterrence theory and amplification theory are both useful in explaining deviant behaviour; what is necessary is to specify the conditions under which each will apply. This research points to orientation to risk as the key scope restriction.

With respect to differential association theory in general, we suggest that it can explain the relationship between having delinquent peers and both police contact and marijuana use. That is, those adolescents who have friends who have been picked up by the police are more likely to have been picked up by the police themselves, and those with friends who have ben picked up by the police are more likely to report using marijuana. In addition, for risk-takers there is a positive relationship between being picked up by the police and reporting the use of marijuana. We suggest that whereas for risk-aversive juveniles police contact acts as a deterrent and generates an increase in control, for risk-takers it provides an opportunity for involvement and interaction with delinquent others which may lead to further delinquent behaviour, such as using marijuana. There is also the possibility of reciprocity (although the path coefficient is not statistically significant) between police contact and marijuana use for males. This implies that police contact leads to marijuana use which leads to further police contact, resulting in "deviance amplification" (Wilkins, 1967), again supporting a differential association and/or selective policing perspective. On the other side, among risk-aversive juveniles, there is a significant reciprocal relationship between police contact and marijuana use, supporting deterrence arguments. Marijuana use increases the likelihood of police contact, which reduces the use of marijuana.

FUTURE RESEARCH

The patterns shown by these data suggest causality, but do not conclusively demonstrate it. Longitudinal data derived through panel studies would be useful in testing further the causal sequences suggested here. For example, Osgood et al., (1988:91) report that "marijuana use during the high school senior year had significant impact on use of other illicit drugs one to two years later. Further, use of illicit drugs became increasingly tied to general involvement in deviance." The patterns in our data may reflect evolving careers in drug use as well as contact with the police, so that the causal relationships estimated may need to be more fully specified. It may also be important in future research to bear in mind that experiences with the police may vary for girls and boys (see e.g., Chesney-Lind, 1986).

Finally, self-reported marijuana use in high school students does not represent all deviant behaviour, or even "common deviance" (Hagan, Gillis, and Simpson, 1985). So whether the patterns shown in this research hold for more serious delinquents than those who attend high school, or for more serious delinquencies than marijuana use, is unknown, and should be examined by further research. Research on differences between males and females on rates of recidivism for more serious offences could shed important light on how far the model introduced in this study can be extended.

APPENDIX

Crime in Canada, 1988*

---

*   Edited version of Table 2, *Canadian Crime Statistics*, 1988, Catalogue 85-205 (Statistics Canada: Minister of Supply and Services, 1989). Reproduced with the permission of the Minister of Supply and Services Canada, 1990.

POLICE REPORTED CRIME BY OFFENCE CANADA AND THE PROVINCES/TERRITORIES, 1988

No	Offences	Reported or known	Unfoun-ded	Actual offences	Offences cleared	
					By charge	Otherwise
	CANADA					
	Homicide					
1	First degree murder	323	32	291	201	44
2	Second degree murder	254	8	246	203	17
3	Manslaughter	38	3	35	37	2
4	Infanticide	8	5	3	3	—
5	**Total**	**623**	**48**	**575**	**444**	**63**
6	Attempted murder	861	25	836	668	38
	Assault					
7	Aggravated sexual assault	415	45	370	222	39
8	Sexual assault with weapon	1,041	74	967	539	72
9	Sexual assault	27,655	4,106	23,549	11,337	4,975
10	Assault level 1	140,265	10,156	130,109	55,995	48,994
11	Assault with weapon or causing bodily harm level 2	32,084	1,104	30,980	19,435	5,486
12	Aggravated assault level 3	2,912	88	2,824	1,873	314
13	Unlawfully causing bodily harm	3,936	201	3,735	2,372	696
14	Discharge firearm with intent	185	30	155	97	22
15	Police	5,577	9	5,568	5,283	220
16	Other peace-public officers	626	5	621	554	40
17	Other assaults	4,561	599	3,962	1,744	1,342
18	**Total**	**219,257**	**16,417**	**202,840**	**99,451**	**62,200**
19	Other sexual offences	3,362	220	3,142	1,659	434
	Abduction					
20	Abduction of person under 14	625	263	362	98	99
21	Abduction of person under 16	88	31	57	19	16
22	Abduction contravening custody order	487	98	389	129	182
23	Abduction no custody order	369	120	249	75	120
24	**Total**	**1,569**	**512**	**1,057**	**321**	**417**
	Robbery					
25	Firearms	6,200	114	6,086	2,124	200
26	Other offensive weapons	6,838	133	6,705	2,097	191
27	Other robbery	11,949	491	11,458	3,094	495
28	**Total**	**24,987**	**738**	**24,249**	**7,315**	**886**
29	**CRIMES OF VIOLENCE — TOTAL**	**250,659**	**17,960**	**232,699**	**109,858**	**64,038**

POLICE REPORTED CRIME BY OFFENCE CANADA AND THE PROVINCES/TERRITORIES, 1988

Adults charged		Young Offenders		% Unfounded	Actual offences		% offences cleared	
Male	Female				Rate per 100,000 population	% of offences Canada	By charge	Otherwise
207	17	27		9.9	1	100.0	69.1	15.1
174	33	18		3.1	1	100.0	82.5	6.9
28	7	5		7.9	–	100.0	105.7	5.7
–	3	–		62.5	–	100.0	100.0	0.0
409	**60**	**50**		**7.7**	**2**	**100.0**	**77.2**	**11.0**
598	92	65		2.9	3	100.0	79.9	4.5
194	8	30		10.8	1	100.0	60.0	10.5
435	17	50		7.1	4	100.0	55.7	7.4
7,640	111	1,772		14.8	91	100.0	48.1	21.1
43,710	5,324	9,215		7.2	502	100.0	43.0	37.7
15,149	1,751	2,698		3.4	120	100.0	62.7	17.7
1,508	239	199		3.0	11	100.0	66.3	11.1
2,043	167	285		5.1	14	100.0	63.5	18.6
74	3	28		16.2	1	100.0	62.6	14.2
3,458	582	289		0.2	21	100.0	94.9	4.0
416	36	57		0.8	2	100.0	89.2	6.4
1,294	134	268		13.1	15	100.0	44.0	33.9
75,921	**8,372**	**14,891**		**7.5**	**783**	**100.0**	**49.0**	**30.7**
943	27	180		6.5	12	100.0	52.8	13.8
58	25	6		42.1	1	100.0	27.1	27.3
20	-	3		35.2	–	100.0	33.3	28.1
80	47	1		20.1	2	100.0	33.2	46.8
46	19	5		32.5	1	100.0	30.1	48.2
204	**91**	**15**		**32.6**	**4**	**100.0**	**30.4**	**39.5**
1,502	92	179		1.8	23	100.0	34.9	3.3
1,543	141	562		1.9	26	100.0	31.3	2.8
2,397	302	975		4.1	44	100.0	27.0	4.3
5,442	**535**	**1,716**		**3.0**	**94**	**100.0**	**30.2**	**3.7**
83,517	**9,177**	**16,917**		**7.2**	**896**	**100.0**	**47.2**	**27.6**

Police Reported Crime by Offence Canada and The Provinces/Territories, 1988

No	Offences	Reported or known	Unfoun-ded	Actual offences	Offences cleared	
					By charge	Otherwise
	CANADA — Continued					
	Breaking and entering					
30	Business premises	103,752	3,119	100,633	16,664	5,829
31	Residence	225,790	11,551	214,239	29,117	14,720
32	Other break and enter	45,944	1,569	44,375	4,931	2,271
33	**Total**	**375,486**	**16,239**	**359,247**	**50,712**	**22,820**
	Theft/motor vehicles					
34	Automobiles	63,387	7,374	56,013	8,633	4,594
35	Trucks	21,703	2,084	19,619	3,141	1,437
36	Motorcycles	7,880	350	7,530	1,003	405
37	Other motor vehicles	6,567	504	6,063	1,142	544
38	**Total**	**99,537**	**10,312**	**89,225**	**13,919**	**6,980**
	Theft-over $1,000					
39	Bicycles	1,713	62	1,651	75	97
40	From motor vehicles	32,700	209	32,491	1,086	1,121
41	Shoplifting	2,655	26	2,629	533	125
42	Other thefts over $1,000	46,240	3,005	43,235	5,552	2,560
43	**Total**	**83,308**	**3,302**	**80,006**	**7,246**	**3,903**
	Theft $1,000 and under					
44	Bicycles	106,384	2,118	104,226	2,417	4,478
45	From motor vehicles	292,677	2,926	289,751	11,970	11,488
46	Shoplifting	100,282	716	99,566	70,661	17,344
47	Other thefts $1,000 and under	300,164	16,374	283,790	26,803	25,365
48	**Total**	**799,507**	**22,134**	**777,373**	**111,851**	**58,675**
49	Have stolen goods	28,539	1,033	27,506	23,813	2,200
	Fraud					
50	Cheques	77,002	3,671	73,331	37,008	14,857
51	Credit cards	13,738	487	13,251	7,449	1,085
52	Other frauds	42,023	3,141	38,882	22,126	6,070
53	**Total**	**132,763**	**7,299**	**125,464**	**66,583**	**22,012**
54	**PROPERTY CRIMES — TOTAL**	**1,519,140**	**60,319**	**1,458,821**	**274,124**	**116,590**

POLICE REPORTED CRIME BY OFFENCE CANADA AND THE PROVINCES/TERRITORIES, 1988

Adults charged		Young Offenders		Actual offences		% offences cleared	
Male	**Female**		**% Unfounded**	**Rate per 100,000 population**	**% of offences Canada**	**By charge**	**Otherwise**
12,988	469	10,032	3.0	388	100.0	16.6	5.8
18,676	1,094	15,450	5.1	827	100.0	13.6	6.9
3,941	138	5,210	3.4	171	100.0	11.1	5.1
35,696	**1,781**	**30,692**	**4.3**	**1,386**	**100.0**	**14.1**	**6.4**
5,416	459	4,647	11.6	216	100.0	15.4	8.2
2,187	109	1,421	9.6	76	100.0	16.0	7.3
539	8	821	4.4	29	100.0	13.3	5.4
768	20	963	7.7	23	100.0	18.8	9.0
8,910	**596**	**7,852**	**10.4**	**344**	**100.0**	**15.6**	**7.8**
51	3	46	3.6	6	100.0	4.5	5.9
820	25	436	0.6	125	100.0	3.3	3.5
326	158	155	1.0	10	100.0	20.3	4.8
4,308	838	1,115	6.5	167	100.0	12.8	5.9
5,505	**1,024**	**1,752**	**4.0**	**309**	**100.0**	**9.1**	**4.9**
903	74	2,680	2.0	402	100.0	2.3	4.3
7,294	297	6,825	1.0	1,118	100.0	4.1	4.0
30,433	24,237	31,986	0.7	384	100.0	71.0	17.4
17,465	3,685	13,910	5.5	1,095	100.0	9.4	8.9
56,095	**28,293**	**55,401**	**2.8**	**3,000**	**100.0**	**14.4**	**7.5**
12,100	1,635	5,826	3.6	106	100.0	86.6	8.0
14,959	5,886	1,215	4.8	283	100.0	50.5	20.3
2,771	714	662	3.5	51	100.0	56.2	8.2
9,773	3,388	1,440	7.5	150	100.0	56.9	15.6
27,503	**9,988**	**3,317**	**5.5**	**484**	**100.0**	**53.1**	**17.6**
145,809	**43,237**	**104,840**	**4.0**	**5,630**	**100.0**	**18.8**	**8.0**

POLICE REPORTED CRIME BY OFFENCE CANADA AND THE PROVINCES/TERRITORIES, 1988

No	Offences	Reported or known	Unfounded	Actual offences	Offences cleared	
					By charge	Otherwise
	CANADA — Continued					
	Prostitution					
55	Bawdy house	307	13	294	268	7
56	Procuring	463	4	459	417	9
57	Other prostitution	9,909	7	9,902	9,801	32
58	**Total**	**10,679**	**24**	**10,655**	**10,486**	**48**
	Gaming and betting					
59	Betting house	218	1	217	205	6
60	Gaming house	505	8	497	460	99
61	Other gaming and betting offences	684	24	660	483	81
62	**Total**	**1,407**	**33**	**1,374**	**1,148**	**186**
	Offensive weapons					
63	Explosives	740	292	448	120	105
64	Prohibited weapons	3,507	143	3,364	2,372	655
65	Restricted weapons	2,706	316	2,390	1,660	422
66	Other offensive weapons	11,855	1,064	10,791	7,359	1,836
67	**Total**	**18,808**	**1,815**	**16,993**	**11,511**	**3,018**
	Other Criminal Code offences					
68	Arson	10,460	2,246	8,214	1,210	760
69	Bail violations	48,384	287	48,097	47,946	1,675
70	Counterfeiting currency	1,995	404	1,591	158	136
71	Disturbing the peace	59,019	7,107	51,912	8,890	28,684
72	Escape custody	3,817	63	3,754	3,173	345
73	Indecent acts	11,478	252	11,226	3,144	1,659
74	Kidnapping	900	252	648	364	68
75	Public morals	675	67	608	212	126
76	Obstruct public peace officer	7,922	31	7,891	7,351	370
77	Prisoner unlawfully at large	5,479	148	5,331	4,361	431
78	Trespass at night	10,314	16,31	8,683	1,288	1,747
79	Mischief (prop. damage) over $1,000	59,703	1,093	58,610	6,588	3,889
80	Mischief (prop. damage) $1,000 & under	314,470	8,457	306,013	24,537	24,303
81	Other Criminal Code offences	169,284	9,985	159,299	58,554	45,604
82	**Total**	**703,900**	**32,023**	**671,877**	**167,776**	**109,797**
83	**OTHER CRIMES — TOTAL**	**734,794**	**33,895**	**700,899**	**190,921**	**113,049**
84	**CRIMINAL CODE — TOTAL**	**2,504,593**	**112,174**	**2,392,419**	**574,903**	**293,677**

POLICE REPORTED CRIME BY OFFENCE CANADA AND THE PROVINCES/TERRITORIES, 1988

Adults charged		Young Offenders	% Unfounded	Actual offences		% offences cleared	
Male	Female			Rate per 100,000 population	% of offences Canada	By charge	Otherwise
214	373	27	4.2	1	100.0	91.2	2.4
130	162	13	0.9	2	100.0	90.8	2.0
4,835	4,910	539	0.1	38	100.0	99.0	0.3
5,179	**5,445**	**579**	**0.2**	**41**	**100.0**	**98.4**	**0.5**
25	2	—	0.5	1	100.0	94.6	2.8
791	77	2	1.6	2	100.0	92.6	19.9
397	105	3	3.5	3	100.0	73.2	12.3
1,213	**184**	**5**	**2.3**	**5**	**100.0**	**83.6**	**13.5**
65	8	92	39.5	2	100.0	26.8	23.4
1,397	71	522	4.1	13	100.0	70.5	19.5
1,169	84	77	11.7	9	100.0	69.5	17.7
4,479	379	1,604	9.0	42	100.0	68.2	17.0
7,110	**542**	**2,295**	**9.7**	**66**	**100.0**	**67.7**	**17.8**
773	141	803	21.5	32	100.0	14.7	9.3
26,793	3,967	3,750	0.6	186	100.0	99.7	3.5
94	17	28	20.3	6	100.0	9.9	8.5
8,082	1,122	3,035	12.0	200	100.0	17.1	55.3
1,424	117	1,748	1.7	14	100.0	84.5	9.2
2,740	227	299	2.2	43	100.0	28.0	14.8
299	22	52	28.0	3	100.0	56.2	10.5
107	9	11	9.9	2	100.0	34.9	20.7
4,932	845	509	0.4	30	100.0	93.2	4.7
3,202	251	1,002	2.7	21	100.0	81.8	8.1
988	20	804	15.8	334	100.0	14.8	20.1
3,923	356	2,188	1.8	226	100.0	11.2	6.6
16,191	**1,680**	**15,265**	**2.7**	**1,181**	**100.0**	**8.0**	**7.9**
34,702	**4,821**	**8,596**	**5.9**	**615**	**100.0**	**36.8**	**28.6**
104,250	**13,595**	**38,090**	**4.5**	**2,593**	**100.0**	**25.0**	**16.3**
117,752	**19,766**	**40,969**	**4.6**	**2,705**	**100.0**	**27.2**	**16.1**
347,078	**72,180**	**162,726**	**4.5**	**9,233**	**100.0**	**24.0**	**12.3**

POLICE REPORTED CRIME BY OFFENCE CANADA AND THE PROVINCES/TERRITORIES, 1988

No	Offences	Reported or known	Unfoun-ded	Actual offences	Offences cleared	
					By charge	Otherwise
	CANADA — Continued					
	Heroin					
85	Possession	402	16	386	286	40
86	Trafficking	478	21	457	352	55
87	Importation	127	27	100	34	5
88	**Total**	**1,007**	**64**	**943**	**672**	**100**
	Cocaine					
89	Possession	5,120	127	4,993	4,271	392
90	Trafficking	6,164	277	5,887	4,150	251
91	Importation	342	45	297	78	31
92	**Total**	**11,626**	**449**	**11,177**	**8,499**	**674**
	Other drugs					
93	Possession	4,466	190	4,276	2,655	759
94	Trafficking	1,014	59	955	728	35
95	Importation	82	38	44	6	3
96	**Total**	**5,562**	**287**	**5,275**	**3,389**	**797**
	Cannabis					
97	Possession	30,260	623	29,637	21,951	5,600
98	Trafficking	9,723	448	9,275	7,157	472
99	Importation	500	46	454	159	138
100	Cultivation	1,345	227	1,118	445	147
101	**Total**	**41,828**	**1,344**	**40,484**	**29,712**	**6,357**
102	Controlled drugs (Trafficking)	725	57	668	388	178
	Restricted drugs					
103	Possession	778	40	738	594	71
104	Trafficking	1,124	52	1,072	839	105
105	**Total**	**1,902**	**92**	**1,810**	**1,433**	**176**
106	**Drugs — Total**	**62,650**	**2,293**	**60,357**	**44,093**	**8,282**
	Other federal statutes					
107	Bankruptcy Act	724	138	586	508	156
108	Canada Shipping Act	7,661	52	7,609	2,789	4,871
109	Customs Act	3,791	1,164	2,627	248	1,392
110	Excise Act	333	62	271	74	71
111	Immigration Act	8,806	1,324	7,482	797	5,412
112	Other federal statute offences	19,873	1,183	18,690	11,601	7,122
113	**Total**	**41,188**	**3,923**	**37,265**	**16,017**	**19,024**
114	**Federal statutes — Total**	**103,838**	**6,216**	**97,622**	**60,110**	**27,306**
	Provincial statutes					
115	Liquor Acts	241,997	3,167	238,830	206,442	25,009
116	Securities Act	103	3	100	74	17
117	Other provincial statutes	131,838	4,630	127,208	62,629	48,000
118	**Total**	**373,938**	**7,800**	**366,138**	**269,145**	**73,026**
119	**Municipal by-laws**	**109,592**	**7,964**	**101,628**	**33,776**	**47,924**
120	**ALL OFFENCES — TOTAL**	**3,091,961**	**134,154**	**2,957,807**	**937,934**	**441,933**

POLICE REPORTED CRIME BY OFFENCE CANADA AND THE PROVINCES/TERRITORIES, 1988

Adults charged		Young Offenders		Actual offences		% offences cleared	
Male	Female		% Unfounded	Rate per 100,000 population	% of offences Canada	By charge	Otherwise
185	82	6	4.0	1	100.0	74.1	10.4
237	46	10	4.4	2	100.0	77.0	12.0
30	12	–	21.3	–	100.0	34.0	5.0
452	**140**	**16**	**6.4**	**4**	**100.0**	**71.3**	**10.6**
3,582	662	105	2.5	19	100.0	85.5	7.9
3,071	546	81	4.5	23	100.0	70.5	4.3
82	20	1	13.2	1	100.0	26.3	10.4
6,735	**1,228**	**187**	**3.9**	**43**	**100.0**	**76.0**	**6.0**
793	270	97	4.3	17	100.0	62.1	17.8
377	108	25	5.8	4	100.0	76.2	3.7
4	–	2	46.3	–	100.0	13.6	6.8
1,174	**378**	**124**	**5.2**	**20**	**100.0**	**64.2**	**15.1**
18,737	1,928	2,922	2.1	114	100.0	74.1	18.9
5,519	801	648	4.6	36	100.0	77.2	5.1
142	44	5	9.2	2	100.0	35.0	30.4
458	128	12	16.9	4	100.0	39.8	13.1
24,856	**2,901**	**3,587**	**3.2**	**156**	**100.0**	**73.4**	**15.7**
166	42	10	7.9	3	100.0	58.1	26.6
424	58	87	5.1	3	100.0	80.5	9.6
649	73	101	4.6	4	100.0	78.3	9.8
1,073	**131**	**188**	**4.8**	**7**	**100.0**	**79.2**	**9.7**
34,456	**4,820**	**4,112**	**3.7**	**233**	**100.0**	**73.1**	**13.7**
129	15	4	19.1	2	100.0	86.7	26.6
2,432	109	83	0.7	29	100.0	36.7	64.0
201	29	3	30.7	10	100.0	9.4	53.0
48	4	3	18.6	1	100.0	27.3	26.2
612	112	12	15.0	29	100.0	10.7	72.3
4,281	666	2,028	6.0	72	100.0	62.1	38.1
7,703	**935**	**2,133**	**9.5**	**144**	**100.0**	**43.0**	**51.1**
42,159	**5,755**	**6,245**	**6.0**	**377**	**100.0**	**61.6**	**28.0**
173,062	19,161	23,886	1.3	922	100.0	86.4	10.5
54	13	8	2.9	–	100.0	74.0	17.0
46,293	6,277	6,609	3.5	491	100.0	49.2	37.7
219,409	**25,451**	**30,503**	**2.1**	**1,413**	**100.0**	**73.5**	**19.9**
25,606	**5,230**	**3,742**	**7.3**	**392**	**100.0**	**33.2**	**47.2**
634,252	**108,616**	**203,216**	**4.3**	**11,415**	**100.0**	**31.7**	**14.9**

Bibliography

Adams, S. G.
  1978   *The Female Offender: A Statistical Perspective.* Ottawa: Ministry of the Solicitor General.

Adelberg, E., and C. Currie (eds.)
  1987   *Too Few to Count: Canadian Women in Conflict with the Law.* Vancouver: Press Gang Publishers.

Adler, F.
  1975   *Sisters in Crime.* New York: McGraw-Hill.

Adler, P. A. and P. Adler
  1983   "Shifts and Oscillations in Deviant Careers: The Case of Upper-Level Drug Dealers and Smugglers." *Social Problems* 31(2): 195-207.

Agnew, R.
  1984a   "Autonomy and Delinquency." *Sociological Perspectives* 27(2): 219-40.
  1984b   "Goal Achievement and Delinquency." *Sociology and Social Research* 68:435-51.
  1985   "A Revised Strain Theory of Delinquency." *Social Forces* 64 (September): 151-67.

Akers, R. L.
  1973   *Deviant Behavior: A Social Learning Approach.* Belmont, Calif.: Wadsworth Publishing Co.
  1985   *Deviant Behavior: A Social Learning Approach.* 3d. ed. Belmont, Calif.: Wadsworth Publishing Co.

Akers, R. L., M. D. Krohn, L. Lanza-Kaduce, and M. Radosevich
  1979   "Social Learning and Deviant Behavior: A Specific Test of a General Theory." *American Sociological Review* 44:636-55.

Akman, D. D., and A. Normandeau
  1967   "The Measurement of Crime and Delinquency in Canada: A Replication Study." *British Journal of Criminology* 7:129-49.

Aldrich, H. E.
  1979   *Organizations and Environments.* Englewood Cliffs, N.J.: Prentice-Hall.

Alexander, B. K., and G. S. Dibb
  1975   "Optiate Addicts and Their Parents." *Family Process* 14.

Allen, H. T.
  1981   *Forty Years Journey: The Temperance Movement in British Columbia to 1900.* Victoria: B.C. Historical Society.

Althusser, L.
  1971   "Ideology and the Ideological State Apparatuses." *Lenin and Philosophy.* London: New Left Books.

Alwin, D. F., and R. M. Hauser
  1975   "The Decomposition of Effects in Path Analysis." *American Sociological Review* 40:37-47.

Archambault, O.
  1983   "Young Offenders Act: Philosophy and Principles." *Provincial Judges Journal* 7(2): 1-7.

Arnold, B.
  1984   "Criminal Justice Education in B.C.: A Political Perspective." *Canadian Criminology Forum* 7(Fall): 21-40.

Arpin, C.
  1982   *The Gazette* (Montreal) May 29.

Atrens, J.
  1989   *The Charter and Criminal Procedure: The Application of Sections 7 and 11.* Toronto: Butterworths.

Bakalar, J. B., and L. Grinspoon
  1984   *Drug Control in a Free Society.* Cambridge: Cambridge University Press.

Bala, N.
  1987   "Annotation to *R. v. Robert C.*" *Young Offenders Service,* 7353-3 to 7353-6.

Bala, N., and R. Corrado
  1985   *Juvenile Justice in Canada: A Comparative Study.* Ottawa: Ministry of the Solicitor General of Canada.

Balbus, I. D.
  1973   *Dialectics of Legal Repression.* New York: Russell Sage Foundation.
  1977   "Commodity Form and Legal Form: An Essay on the Relative Autonomy of the Law." *Law and Society Review* 7(Winter): 571-88.

Ball, J. C.
  1981   "The Criminality of Heroin Addicts When Addicted and When Off Opiates." In J. Inciardi (ed.), *The Drugs-Crime Connection.* Beverly Hills, Calif.: Sage Publications.

Battle, B.
  1974   *A Handbook for Selection and Investigation.* New York: Arco Publishing.

Beccaria, C.
  1764   *Essays on Crime and Punishment.* Translated in 1963 by H. Paolucci. Indianapolis, Ind.: Bobbs-Merrill Co.

Becker, H. S.
  1963   *Outsiders: Studies in the Sociology of Deviance.* New York: Free Press.

Bennett, W. L.
  1983   *News: The Politics of Illusion.* New York: Longman.

Bentham, J.
  1843   "Principles of Penal Law." In J. Bowing, (ed.), *The Works of Jeremy Bentham.* Edinburgh: W. Tait.

Bernard, T. J.
  1981   "The Distinction between Conflict and Radical Criminology." *Journal of Criminal Law and Criminology* 72:362-79.

Berridge, V., and G. Edwards
  1981   *Opium and the People: Opiate Use in Nineteenth Century England.* London: Allen Lane.

Bertrand, M.-A.
  1969   "Self-Image and Delinquency: A Contribution to the Study of Female Criminality and Woman's Image." *Acta Criminologica* 2:71-144.

Biderman, A. D., L. A. Johnson, J. McIntyre, and A. W. Weir
  1967   *Report on a Pilot Study in the District of Columbia on Victimization and Attitudes towards Law Enforcement.* In United States President's Commission on Law Enforcement and the Administration of Justice, Field Survey I. Washington, D.C.: U.S. Government Printing Office.

Bittner, E.
  1967   "The Police on Skid-Row: A Study of Peace Keeping." *American Sociological Review* 32:699-715.

Black, D. J.
  1970   "Production of Crime Rates." *American Sociological Review* 35:733-47.
  1971   "The Social Organization of Arrest." *Stanford Law Review* 23:1087-1111.
  1976   *The Behavior of Law.* New York: Academic Press.

Black, D. J., and A. J. Reiss
    1967   "Patterns of Behavior in Police and Citizen Transactions." In President's Commission on Law
            Enforcement and the Administration of Justice, *Studies in Crime and Law Enforcement in Major
            Metropolitan Areas*, Field Surveys III. vol. 2. Washington, D.C.: U.S. Government Printing Office.
    1970   "Police Control of Juveniles." *American Sociological Review* 35:63-77.

Blau, J. R., and P. M. Blau
    1982   "The Cost of Inequality: Metropolitan Structure and Violent Crime." *American Sociological Review*
            47(February): 114-29.

Blishen, B. R.
    1961   "The Construction and Use of an Occupational Class Scale." In B. R. Blishen, F. E. Jones, K. D.
            Naegele, and J. Porter (eds.), *Canadian Society: Sociological Perspectives*. New York: Free Press.

Bordua, D.
    1961   "Delinquent Subcultures: Sociological Interpretations of Gang Delinquency." *Annals of the
            American Academy of Political and Social Science* 338:119-38.

Bowker, L. (ed.)
    1981   *Women and Crime in America*. New York: Macmillan Publishing Co.

Box, S.
    1983   *Power, Crime, and Mystification*. London: Tavistock.

Box, S., and C. Hale
    1982   "Economic Crisis and the Rising Prisoner Population in England and Wales." *Crime and Social
            Justice* 17:20-25.
    1985   "Unemployment, Imprisonment and Prison Overcrowding." *Contemporary Crisis* 9:209-28.
    1986   "Unemployment, Crime and Imprisonment, and the Enduring Problem of Prison Overcrowd-
            ing." In R. Matthews and J. Young (eds.), *Confronting Crime*. London: Sage.

Boyd, N.
    1983   "The Supreme Court on Drugs: Masters of Reason in Disarray?" *Canadian Lawyer* 7:6-10.
    1984   "The Origins of Canadian Narcotics Legislation: The Process of Criminalization in Historical
            Context." *Dalhousie Law Journal* 8.

Boyd, S., and E. A. Sheehy
    1989   "Feminism and the Law in Canada: An Overview." In T.C. Caputo et al. (eds.), *Law and Society:
            A Critical Perspective*. Toronto: Harcourt Brace Jovanovitch.

Boydell, C.
    1985   "Rural Justice: A Systems Analysis of Property Crimes." *Canadian Journal of Criminology* 27(3).

Boydell, C., P. Whitehead, and C. Grindstaff (eds.)
    1974   *The Administration of Criminal Justice in Canada*. Toronto: Holt, Rinehart & Winston.

Boyle, C., M.-A. Bertrand, C. Lacerte-Lamontagne, and R. Shamai
    1985   *A Feminist Review of Criminal Law*. Ottawa: Ministry of Supply and Services Canada.

Brady, J.
    1982   "Arson, Fiscal Crisis, and Community Action: Dialectics of Urban Crime and Popular Re-
            sponse." *Crime and Delinquency* 28(2): 247-70.
    1983   "Arson, Urban Economy, and Organized Crime: The Case of Boston." *Social Problems* 31(1): 1-27.

Braithwaite, J. B.
    1979   *Inequality, Crime and Public Policy*. London: Routledge and Kegan Paul.

Braithwaite, J.
    1981   "The Myth of Social Class and Criminality Reconsidered." *American Sociological Review* 46:36-
            57.
    1984   *Corporate Crime in the Pharmaceutical Industry*. London: Routledge.
    1989   *Crime, Shame, and Reintegration*. Cambridge: Cambridge University Press.

Brantingham, P., and P. Brantingham
    1984   *Patterns in Crime*. New York: Macmillan Publishing Co.

Braucht, G. N., D. Brakarsh, D. Follingstad, and K. L. Berry
    1973   "Deviant Drug Use in Adolescence: A Review of the Psychosocial Correlates." *Psychological Bulletin* 79.

Brecher, E. M.
    1972   *Licit and Illicit Drugs*. Boston: Little, Brown & Co.

Brett, P.
    1963   *An Enquiry into Criminal Guilt*. Sydney: Law Book Co. of Australia.

Briar, S., and I. Piliavin
    1965   "Delinquency, Situational Inducements and Commitment to Conformity." *Social Problems* 13:35-45.

Brickey, S., and E. Comack
    1986   *The Social Basis of Law: Critical Readings in the Sociology of Law*. Toronto: Garamond Press.

Browne, A.
    1987   *When Battered Women Kill*. New York: Free Press.

Browne, A., and D. Finkelhor
    1986   "Impact of Child Sexual Abuse: A Review of the Research." *Psychological Bulletin* 99.

Brownmiller, S.
    1975   *Against Our Will: Men, Women, and Rape*. New York: Simon and Schuster.

Bunker, J.
    1975   "Surgical Manpower — Comparison of Operations and Surgeons in the U.S., England and Wales." *New England Journal of Medicine* 282:135.

Burgess, E.W.
    1923   "The Growth of the City." Paper prepared for the meetings of the American Sociological Society. Reprinted in R. Park, *The City*. Chicago: University of Chicago Press.

Burgess, R. L., and R. L. Akers
    1966   "A Differential Association-Reinforcement Theory of Criminal Behavior." *Social Problems* 14(Fall): 128-47.

Burris, C., and P. Jaffe
    1983   "Wife Abuse as a Crime: The Impact of Police Laying Charges." *Canadian Journal of Criminology* 25:309-18.

Byrne, J. M., and R. J. Sampson
    1986   "Key Issues in the Social Ecology of Crime." In J. M. Byrne and R. J. Sampson (eds.), *The Social Ecology of Crime*. New York: Springer-Verlag.

Campbell, D.
    1984   "President's Newsletter for the General Practice Section of B. C. Medical Association." Vancouver: BCMA.

Canada
    1982   *The Criminal Law in Canadian Society*. Ottawa: Canadian Centre for Justice Statistics.

Canadian Centre for Justice Statistics
    1987a   *Youth Court Statistics: Preliminary Tables 1984-85*. Ottawa: C.C.J.S.
    1987b   *Youth Court Statistics: Preliminary Tables 1985-86*. Ottawa: C.C.J.S.
    1988   *Youth Court Statistics: Preliminary Tables 1986-87*. Ottawa: C.C.J.S.
    1989   *Youth Court Statistics: Preliminary Tables 1988-89*. Ottawa: C.C.J.S.
    1990   *The Development of Data Quality Assessment Procedures for the Uniform Crime Reporting Survey: A Case Study of Calgary - Edmonton*. Ottawa: C.C.J.S.

Canadian Charter of Rights and Freedoms
    1982   Part I of the Constitution Act, 1982, being Schedule B of the Canada Act 1982 (U.K.), c. 11.

Canadian Urban Victimization Survey. *See* Solicitor General of Canada.

Cantor, D., and K. C. Land
1985   "Unemployment and Crime Rates in the Post-World War II United States." *American Sociological Review* 50:317-32.

Carey, J. T.
1978   *An Introduction to Criminology*. Englewood Cliffs, N.J.: Prentice-Hall.

Carlen, P., and A. Worall (eds.)
1980   *Gender, Crime and Justice*. Milton Keynes, England: Open University Press.

Carr-Hill, R. A., and N. H. Stern
1983   "Unemployment and Crime: A Comment." *Journal of Social Policy* 12(3): 387-94.

Carrier, J. G.
1986   *Learning Disability: Social Class and the Construction of Inequality in American Education*. New York: Greenwood Press.

Carroll, L., and P. I. Jackson
1983   "Inequality, Opportunity, and Crime Rates in Central Cities." *Criminology* 21:178-94.

Cartwright, D. S.
1975   "The Nature of Gangs." In D. S. Cartwright et al. (eds.), *Gang Delinquency*. Belmont, Calif.: Wadsworth Publishing Co.

Centers for Disease Control
1986   *Homicide Surveillance: High-Risk Racial and Ethnic Groups — Blacks and Hispanics, 1970 to 1983*. Atlanta: Centers for Disease Control.

Chambliss, W. J.
1973   "The Saints and the Roughnecks." *Society* 11:24-31.
1975   "Toward a Political Economy of Crime." *Theory and Society* 2(Summer): 152-53.
1979   "On Lawmaking." *British Journal of Law and Society* 6(2): 149-71.

Chambliss, W. J., and R. Nagasawa
1969   "On the Validity of Official Statistics: A Comparative Study of White, Black, and Japanese High School Boys." *Journal of Research in Crime and Delinquency* 6(1): 71-77.

Chapman, J.
1980   *Economic Realities and the Female Offender*. Lexington, Mass.: D. C. Heath Co.

Chappell, D., and L. P. Graham
1985   *Police Use of Deadly Force: Canadian Perspectives*. Toronto: Centre for Criminology, University of Toronto.

Chein, I., D. L. Gerard, R. S. Lee, and E. Rosenfeld
1964   *The Road to H: Narcotics, Delinquency, and Social Policy*. New York: Basic Books.

Chesney-Lind, M.
1973   "Judicial Enforcement of the Female Sex Role: The Family Court and the Female Delinquent." *Issues in Criminology* 8(2): 51-59.
1982   "Guilty by Reason of Sex: Young Women and the Juvenile Justice System." In B. R. Price and N. J. Sokoloff (eds.), *The Criminal Justice System and Women*. New York: Clark Boardman Co.
1986   "Women and Crime: The Female Offender." *Signs: Journal of Women in Culture and Society* 12:78-96.

Chiniquy, C.
1847   *Manual of the Temperance Society*. Montreal: Lovell and Gibson.

Chng, C. L.
1981   "The Goal of Abstinence: Implications for Drug Education." *Journal of Drug Education* 11:13-18.

Clark, L., and D. Lewis
1977   *Rape: The Price of Coercive Sexuality*. Toronto: Women's Press.

Clark, R. D.,
1988   "Celerity and Specific Deterrence: A Look at the Evidence." *Canadian Journal of Criminology* 30:109-20.

Clarke, A. M.
 1986 *Summary-Public Hearing Proceedings: Background Report, Royal Commission on Employment and Unemployment.* St. John's, Newfoundland: Queen's Printer.

Clarke, R. V. and D. B. Cornish
 1985 "Modelling Offenders' Decisions: A Framework for Research and Policy." In M. Tonry and N. Morris (eds.), *Crime and Justice.* Chicago: University of Chicago Press.

Clement, W.
 1975 *The Corporate Elite.* Toronto: McClelland and Stewart.
 1979 *Continental Corporate Power.* Toronto: McClelland and Stewart.

Clinard, M. B.
 1983 *Corporate Ethics and Crime: The Role of Middle Management.* Beverly Hills, Calif.: Sage Publications.

Clinard, M. B., and P. C. Yeager
 1980 *Corporate Crime.* New York: Free Press.

Clinard, M. B., et al.
 1979 *Illegal Corporate Behavior.* Washington, D.C.: U.S. Department of Justice.

Cloward, R. A., and L. E. Ohlin
 1960 *Delinquency and Opportunity: A Theory of Delinquent Gangs.* New York: Free Press.

Cloyd, J. W.
 1982 *Drugs and Information Control: The Role of Men and Manipulation in the Control of Drug Trafficking.* Westport, Conn.: Greenwood Press.

Cohen, A. K.
 1955 *Delinquent Boys: The Culture of the Gang.* Glencoe, Ill.: Free Press.

Cohen, L. E., and D. Cantor
 1980 "The Determinants of Larceny: An Empirical and Theoretical Study." *Journal of Research in Crime and Delinquency* 17:140-59.

Cohen, L. E., and M. Felson
 1979 "Social Change and Crime Rate Trends: A Routine Activity Approach." *American Sociological Review* 44:588-608.

Cohen, L. E., D. Cantor, and J. R. Kluegel
 1981 "Robbery Victimization in the U.S.: An Analysis of a Nonrandom Event." *Social Science Quarterly* 62: 644-57.

Cohen, L. E., J. R. Kluegel, and K. C. Land
 1981 "Social Inequality and Predatory Criminal Victimization: An Exposition and Test of a Formal Theory." *American Sociological Review* 46:505-24.

Cohen, S.
 1973 *Folk Devils and Moral Panics.* London: Paladin.
 1985 "Adverse Effects of Cocaine." *Consumers Research Magazine* 68:14-16.

Coleman, J.
 1986 "Social Theory, Social Research and a Theory of Action." *American Journal of Sociology* 91:1309-35.

Coleman, J. W.
 1987 "Toward an Integrated Theory of White-Collar Crime." *American Journal of Sociology* 93(2): 406-39.
 1989 *The Criminal Elite: The Sociology of White Collar Crime.* 2d ed. New York: St. Martin's Press.

Collins, J. J., B. G. Cox, and P. A. Langan
 1987 "Job Activities and Personal Crime Victimization: Implications for Theory." *Social Science Research* 16:345-60.

Comack, A. E.
1985   "The Origins of Canadian Drug Legislation: Labelling Versus Analysis." In T. Fleming (ed.), *The New Criminologies in Canada*. Toronto: Oxford University Press.

Comack, E.
1987   "Theorizing on the Canadian State and Social Formation." In R. Ratner and J. McMullan (eds.), *State Control*, Vancouver: University of British Columbia Press.
1988   "Law and Order Issues in the Canadian Context." Paper presented at The American Society of Criminology Meetings, Chicago, Ill., November.

Comack-Antony, A. E.
1980   "Radical Criminology" In R. A. Silverman and J. Teevan (eds.), *Crime in Canadian Society*. 2d ed. Toronto: Butterworths.

Committee on Trauma Research
1985   *Injury in America*. Washington, D.C.: National Academy Press.

Conklin, J. E.
1986   *Criminology*. New York: Macmillan Publishing Co.

Connidis, I.
1982   *Rethinking Criminal Justice Research: A Systems Perspective*. Toronto: Holt, Rinehart & Winston.

Constitution Act
1982   R.S.C. 1985. Appendix II, No. 44, *Canadian Charter of Rights and Freedoms*.

Cook, S.
1969   "Canadian Narcotics Legislation: A Conflict Model Interpretation." *Canadian Review of Sociology and Anthropology* 6(1): 34-46.

Coons, W.
1982   "Learning Disabilities and Criminality." *Canadian Journal of Criminology* 24:251-66.

Copeland, A.
1986   "Homicide among the Elderly: The Metro Dade County Experience 1979-1983." *Medical Science and Law* 28(4): 259-62.

Corrado, R., R. Roesch, W. Glackman, J. L. Evans, and G. J. Leger
1980   "Lifestyles and Victimization: A Test of the Model with Canadian Survey Data." *Journal of Crime and Justice* 3:129-39.

Coser, R.
1985   "Power Lost and Status Gained: The American Middle Class Husband." Paper presented at the American Sociological Association Meetings, Washington, D.C.

Crealock, C. M.
1987   *The LD/JD Link: Causation or Correlation*. Ottawa: Solicitor General of Canada.

Criminal Code
1985   *An Act Respecting The Criminal Law*. Revised Statutes of Canada, 1985. Chapter C-46 and Amendments.

Cripps, R.
1982   "Arson Takes Economic Toll." *The Canadian Fire Fighter* 8 (May-June): 29.

Crites, L.
1976   *The Female Offender*. Lexington, Mass.: D.C. Heath Co.

Cruickshank, J.
1986   "PM Promises Tax Reforms, Drug Controls." *The Globe and Mail* (Toronto) September 15:A1.

Crutchfield, R. K., M. R. Geerken, and W. R. Gove
1982   "Crime Rate and Social Integration." *Criminology* 20:467-78.

Cullen, F. T., W.J. Maakestad, and G. Cavender
1987   *Corporate Crime under Attack: The Ford Pinto Case and Beyond*. Cincinnati, Ohio: Anderson.

Curtis, R.
  1986   "Household and Family in Theory on Equality." *American Sociological Review* 51:168-83.

Daly, K.
  1987   "Structure and Practice of Familial Based Justice in a Criminal Court." *Law and Society Review* 21(2): 268-89.
  1989   "Criminal Justice Ideologies and Practices in Different Voices: Some Feminist Questions about Criminal Justice." *International Journal of Sociology of Law.*

Decker, S. H.
  1983   "Comparing Victimization and Official Estimates of Crime: A Re-Examination of the Validity of Police Statistics." *American Journal of Police* 2(2): 193-201.

De Fronzo, J.
  1983   "Economic Assistance to Impoverished Americans." *Criminology* 21:119-36.

Department of Justice (Canada). Special Committee on Juvenile Delinquency
  1965   *Juvenile Delinquency in Canada.*

Department of Justice, Newfoundland and Labrador.
  1985   *Annual Report of the Adult Corrections Division.*

Desroches, F.
  n.a.   "Tearoom Trade: A Law Enforcement Problem." *Canadian Journal of Criminology.* Forthcoming.

De Vos, G., and K. Abbott
  1966   *The Chinese Family in San Francisco.* Master's thesis, University of California.

Dill, W. R.
  1958   "Environment as an Influence on Managerial Autonomy." *Administrative Science Quarterly* 2:409-43.

Ditton, J.
  1979   *Controlology: Beyond the New Criminology.* London: Macmillan.

Dobash, R. E., and R. Dobash
  1975   *Violence against Wives: A Case against Patriarchy.* New York: Free Press.

Dobash, R. P., R. E. Dobash, and S. Gutteridge
  1986   *The Imprisonment of Women.* Oxford: Basil Blackwell.

Doob, A., and J. Chan
  1982   "Factors Affecting Police Decisions to Take Children to Court." *Canadian Journal of Criminology* 24:25-38.

Doob, A. N.
  1979a   "The Canadian Trial Judges View of the Criminal Jury Trial." In Law Reform Commission of Canada, *Background Studies on the Jury.* Ottawa.
  1979b   "The Public's View of the Criminal Jury Trial." In Law Reform Commission of Canada, *Background Studies on the Jury.* Ottawa.

Dowie, M.
  1977   "Pinto Madness." *Mother Jones* September-October: 18-32.

Downes, D., and P. Rock
  1988   *Understanding Deviance.* 2d ed. Oxford: Clarendon Press.

Dunivant, N.
  1982   *A Causal Analysis of the Relationship between Learning Disabilities and Juvenile Delinquency.* Williamsburg, Va.: National Center for State Courts.

Durkheim, E.
  1951   *Suicide.* New York: Free Press.
  1964   *The Rules of Sociological Method.* New York: Free Press.

Dussich, J., and C. Eichman
  1976   "The Elderly Victim: Vulnerability to the Criminal Act." In J. Goldsmith and S. Goldsmith (eds.), *Crime and the Elderly.* Lexington, Mass.: D. C. Heath Co.

Dutton, D.
  1984   *The Criminal Justice System's Response to Wife Assault.* Ottawa: Program Branch User Report #26. Ministry of the Solicitor General.

Eck, J. E., and L. J. Riccio
  1979   "Relationship between Reported Crime Rates and Victimization Survey Results: An Empirical and Analytic Study." *Journal of Criminal Justice* 7(4): 293-308.

Eisenstadt, S. N.
  1959   "Delinquent Group Formation among Immigrant Youth." In S. Glueck (ed.), *The Problem of Delinquency.* Boston: Houghton Mifflin Co.

Ekland-Olson, S., and S. Martin
  1988   "Organizational Compliance with Court Ordered Reform." *Law and Society Review* 22(2):359-83.

Elias, R.
  1986   *The Politics of Victimization.* New York: Oxford University Press.

Elliott, D. S., and S. Ageton
  1980   "Reconciling Race and Class Differences in Self-Reported and Official Estimates of Delinquency." *American Sociological Review* 45:95-110.

Elliott, D. S., and D. Huizinga
  1983   "Social Class and Delinquent Behavior in a National Youth Panel: 1976-1980." *Criminology* 21: 149-77.

Elliott, D. S., D. Huizinga, and S. S. Ageton
  1985   *Explaining Delinquency and Drug Use.* Beverly Hills, Calif.: Sage Publications.

Emerson, R.
  1969   *Judging Delinquents: Context and Process in Juvenile Court.* Chicago: Aldine.

Empey, L. T.
  1978   *American Delinquency: Its Meaning and Construction.* Homewood, Ill.: Richard D. Irwin.

Empey, L., and M. Erickson
  1966   "Hidden Delinquency and Social Status." *Social Forces* 44:46-54.

Engels, F.
  1969   *The Condition of the Working Class in England in 1844.* Harmondsworth: Penguin Books.

English Law Commission
  1968   *Working Paper on the Mental Element in Crime.* London.

Engstad, P.
  1980   "Environmental Opportunities and the Ecology of Crime." In R. Silverman and J. Teevan (eds.), *Crime in Canadian Society.* 2d ed. Toronto: Butterworths.

Ennals, C.
  1984   "Winds of Change in Patterns of Practice." *British Columbia Medical Journal* 26:31.

Ennis, P. H.
  1967   *Criminal Victimization in the United States: A Report of National Survey.* In President's Commission on Law Enforcement and the Administration of Justice, Field Survey II. Washington, D.C.: U.S. Government Printing Office.

Erickson, P. G. and B. K. Alexander
  n.d.   "Cocaine and Addictive Liability: A Critical Review." Manuscript.

Erickson, P. G., E. M. Adlaf, G. G. Murray and R. G. Smart
  1987   *The Steel Drug: Cocaine in Perspective.* Lexington, Mass.: Lexington Books.

Ericson, R. V.
    1981   *Making Crime: A Study of Detective Work.* Toronto: Butterworths.
    1982   *Reproducing Order.* Toronto: University of Toronto Press.
    1987   "The State and Criminal Justice Reform." In R. Ratner and J. McMullan (eds.), *State Control: Criminal Justice Politics in Canada.* Vancouver: University of British Columbia Press.

Ericson, R. and P. M. Baranek
    1982   *The Ordering of Justice: A Study of Accused Persons as Dependents in the Criminal Process.* Toronto: University of Toronto Press.

Ericson, R., P. Baranek, and J. Chan
    1987   *Visualizing Deviance: A Study of News Organizations.* Toronto: University of Toronto Press.

Erikson, E. H.
    1963   *Childhood and Society.* 2d ed. New York: W.W. Norton and Co.

Esbensen, F.
    1982   "Measurement Error and Self-Reported Delinquency: An Examination of Interviewer Bias." In G. Waldo, *Measurement Issues in Criminal Justice.* Beverly Hills, Calif.: Sage Publications.

Etzioni, A.
    1985   "Will A Few Bad Apples Spoil the Core of Big Business?" *Business and Society Review* 55(Fall):4-5.
    1989   "Good Ethics is Good Business — Really." *The New York Times* February 12:F2.

Evans, R. G.
    1983   "The Welfare Economics of Public Health Insurance: Theory and Canadian Practice." In L. Sodeston (ed.), *Social Insurance.* Amsterdam: North Holland.

Eve, S. B.
    1985   "Criminal Victimization and Fear of Crime among the Non-Institutionalized Elderly in the United States: A Critique of the Empirical Research Literature." *Victimology* 10(1-4): 397-408.

F. B. I.
    1985   *Uniform Crime Reports.* Washington, D. C.: U. S. Department of Justice.

Faith, K.
    1989   "Justice Where Art Thou? And Do We Care?" *Journal of Human Justice* 1(Autumn): 77-99.

Farrington, D. P.
    1977   "The Effects of Public Labelling." *British Journal of Criminology* 17(April): 12-25.

Farrington, D., S. Osborn, and D. J. West
    1978   "The Persistence of Labelling Effects." *British Journal of Criminology* 18:277-84.

Fattah, E. A.
    1979   "Some Recent Theoretical Developments in Victimology." *Victimology* 4.
    1983   "A Critique of Deterrence Research with Particular Reference to the Economic Approach." *Canadian Journal of Criminology* 25:79-90.
    n.d.   "The Elasticity of Terrorism." Department of Criminology, Simon Fraser University. Manuscript.

Fattah, E. A., and V. F. Sacco
    1989   *Crime and Victimization of the Elderly.* New York: Springer-Verlag.

Fejer, D., R. G. Smart, P. C. Whitehead, and L. Laforest
    1971   "Sources of Information about Drugs among High School Students." *Public Opinion Quarterly* 35:235-41.

Felson, M. and L. Cohen
    1980   "Human Ecology and Crime: A Routine Activity Approach." *Human Ecology* 4:389-406.

Felson, R. B., and H. J. Steadman
    1983   "Situational Factors in Disputes Leading to Criminal Violence." *Criminology* 21(1): 59-74.

Ferraro, K. R., and R. L. LaGrange
    1988   "Are Older People Afraid of Crime?" *Journal of Aging Studies* 2(3): 277-87.

Ferraro, K. J., and J. M. Johnson
    1983   "How Women Experience Battering: The Process of Victimization." *Social Problems* 30:325-35.

Feyerherm, W.
    1981   "Measuring Gender Differences in Delinquency: Self-Reports versus Police Contact." In M. Q. Warren (ed.), *Comparing Female and Male Offenders*. Beverly Hills, Calif.: Sage Publications.

Figlio, R. M., S. Hakim, and G. F. Rengert
    1986   *Metropolitan Crime Patterns*. Monsey, N.Y.: Criminal Justice Press.

Fine, R., et al. (eds.)
    1979   *Capitalism and the Rule of Law*. London: Hutchinson.

Fink, A.
    1938   *Causes of Crime: Biological Theories in the United States 1800-1915*. Philadelphia: University of Pennsylvania Press.

Finney, H. C., and H. R. Lesieur
    1982   "A Contingency Theory of Organizational Crime." In S. B. Bachrach (ed.), *Research in the Sociology of Organizations*, vol. 1. Greenwich, Conn.: JAI Press.

Fishcer, C. S.
    1975   "Toward a Subcultural Theory of Urbanism." *American Journal of Sociology* 80(6): 1319-41.
    1976   *The Urban Experience*. New York: Harcourt Brace Jovanovich.

Fishbein, D. H.
    1990   "Biological Perspectives in Criminology." *Criminology* 28(1): 27-72.

Fishman, M.
    1978   "Crime Waves as Ideology." *Social Problems* 25(May): 531-43.

Fleming T. (ed.)
    1985   *The New Criminologies in Canada: State, Crime and Control*. Toronto: Oxford University Press.

Fors, S. W.
    1980   "On the Ethics of Selective Omission and/or Inclusion of Relevant Information in School Drug Education Programs." *Journal of Drug Education* 10:111-17.

Freedman, E. B.
    1981   *Their Sisters' Keepers: Women's Prison Reform in America, 1830-1930*. Ann Arbor: University of Michigan Press.

Gabor, T., and E. Gotteil
    1984   "Offender Characteristics and Spatial Mobility: An Empirical Study and Some Policy Implications." *Canadian Journal of Criminology* 26:276-81.

Gabor, T., M. Baril, M. Cusson, D. Elie, M. LeBlanc, and A. Normandeau
    1987   *Armed Robbery: Cops, Robbers, and Victims*. Springfield, Ill.: Charles C. Thomas.

Gans, H.,
    1962   *The Urban Villagers*. New York: Free Press.

Garofalo, J.
    1986   "Lifestyles and Victimization: An Update." In E.A. Fattah (ed.), *From Crime Policy to Victim Policy: Reorienting the Justice System*. London: Macmillan.

Garofalo, J., L. Siegel, and J. Laub
    1987   "School-Related Victimizations among Adolescents: An Analysis of National Crime Survey (NCS) Narratives." *Journal of Quantitative Criminology* 3(4): 321-38.

Gaucher, B.
    1987   "Canadian Civil Society, the Canadian State, and Criminal Justice Institutions: Theoretical Considerations." In R. Ratner and J. McMullan (eds.), *State Control*. Vancouver: University of British Columbia Press.

Geis, G., P. Jesilow, H. Pontell, and M. J. O'Brien
 1985 "Fraud and Abuse by Psychiatrists against Government Medical Benefit Programs." *American Journal of Psychiatry* February.

Geis, G.
 1977 "The Heavy Electrical Equipment Antitrust Cases of 1961." In G. Geis and R. F. Meier (eds.), *White Collar Crime*. rev. ed. New York: Free Press.

Geller, G.
 1987 "Young Women in Conflict with the Law." In E. Adelberg and C. Currie (eds.), *Too Few to Count*. Vancouver: Press Gang.

Gervais, C. H.
 1980 *The Rumrunners: A Prohibition Scrapbook*. Thornhill, Ont.: Firefly Books.

Gibbens, T. C., and R. H. Ahrenfeldt
 1966 *Cultural Factors in Delinquency*. London: Tavistock Publications.

Gibbons, D. C.
 1979 *The Criminology Enterprise*. Englewood Cliffs, N.J.: Prentice-Hall.
 1982 *Society, Crime and Criminal Behavior*. Englewood Cliffs, N.J.: Prentice-Hall.

Gibbs, J. P.
 1975 *Crime, Punishment and Deterrence*. New York: Elseview.

Gillin, J.
 1945 *Criminology and Penology*. 3d ed. New York: Appleton-Century-Crofts.

Gillis, A. R., and J. Hagan
 1982 "Density, Delinquency and Design: Formal and Informal Control and the Built Environment." *Criminology* 19(4): 514-29.

Ginsberg, B.
 1986 *The Captive Public: How Mass Opinion Promotes State Power*. New York: Basic Books.

Glaser, D.
 1956 "Criminality Theories and Behavioral Images." *American Journal of Sociology* 61(March): 433-44.

The Globe and Mail (Toronto)
 1978a "MD Jailed 90 Days and Fined $25,000." May 13.
 1978b "Padded Bills, Laboratory Owner Guilty of $73,000 OHIP Fraud." October 5.
 1984 "Third of Family Doctors Unneeded: Study." Toronto, April 17.

Glynn, T. J.
 1981 "From Family to Peer: Transitions of Influence among Drug-Using Youth." In D. J. Lettieri and J. P. Ladford (eds.), *Drug Abuse and the American Adolescent*. NIDA Research Monograph 38. Rockville, Md.: Dept. of Health and Human Services.

Goff, C., and C. Reasons
 1978 *Corporate Crime in Canada*. Toronto: Prentice-Hall.

Goffman, E.
 1959 *The Presentation of Self in Everyday Life*. New York: Doubleday & Co.
 1963 *Stigma: Notes on the Management of Spoiled Identity*. Englewood Cliffs, N.J.: Prentice-Hall.

Gold, M. S.
 1984 *800—Cocaine*. Toronto: Bantam Books.

Goldberg, M. A., and J. Mercer
 1986 *The Myth of the North American City*. Vancouver: University of British Columbia Press.

Goldsmith, J., and S. Goldsmith
 1976 *Crime and the Elderly*. Lexington, Mass.: D. C. Heath Co.

Goodstadt, M.
 1980 "Drug Education — A Turn On or a Turn Off?" *Journal of Drug Education* 10:89-99.

Gordon, R., A. Hatch, and C. Griffiths
    n.a.   *Young Offenders and Youth Justice in Canada*. Toronto: Prentice-Hall. Forthcoming.

Goring, C.
    1913   *The English Convict*. London: His Majesty's Stationery Office.

Gorring, P., and P. R. Wilson
    1984   "The Structure of Medical Fraud and Overservicing: How Doctors Commit Crime." Paper presented to the American Society of Criminology Meetings, Cincinnati, November.

Gottfredson, M. R., and M. J. Hindlelang
    1981   "Sociological Aspects of Criminal Victimization." *Annual Review of Sociology* 7:107-28.

Gove, W.
    1980   *"The Labelling Perspective: An Overview and Postscript."* In W. Gove (ed.), *The Labelling of Deviance*. 2d ed. Beverly Hills, Calif.: Sage Publications.

Gove, W. R. (ed.)
    1975   *The Labelling of Deviance: Evaluating a Perspective*. New York: Sage Publications.

Graham, D.
    1987   "Methadone Treatment in British Columbia: Bad Medicine?" *Canadian Medical Association Journal* 136:564-66.

Gramsci, A.
    1971   *Prison Notebooks*. London: Laurence and Wishart.

Green, M.
    1979   "A History of Canadian Narcotics Legislation: The Formative Years." *University of Toronto Faculty of Law Review* 37:42-79.

Greenberg, D.
    1981   *Crime and Capitalism*. Palo Alto, Calif.: Mayfield Publishing Co.

Griffiths, C., J. Klein, and S. Verdun-Jones
    1980   *Criminal Justice in Canada*. Toronto: Butterworths.

Grinspoon, L., and J. B. Bakalar
    1976   *Cocaine: A Drug and Its Social Evolution*. New York: Basic Books.

Grosman, B.
    1975   *Police Command*. Toronto: Macmillan Publishing Co.

Guest, A.
    1969   "The Applicability of the Burgess Zonal Hypothesis to Urban Canada." *Demography* 6:271-77.

Guillet, E. C.
    1933   *Pioneer Days in Upper Canada*. Toronto: University of Toronto Press.

Gusfield, J. J.
    1963   *Symbolic Crusade: Status Politics and the American Temperance Movement*. Urbana: University of Illinois Press.

Hackler, J.
    1988   *The Reduction of Violent Crime and Equality for Women*. Edmonton: Centre for Criminological Research, University of Alberta.

Hackler, J., and W. Paranjape
    1983   "Juvenile Justice Statistics: Mythmaking or Measure of System Response." *Canadian Journal of Criminology* 25:209-26.

Hadaway, P. F., and B. L. Beyerstein.
    1987   "Then They Came for the Smokers but I Didn't Speak Up Because I Wasn't a Smoker: Legislation and Tobacco Use." *Canadian Psychology* 28:259-65.

Hagan, J.
    1980   "The Legislation of Crime and Delinquency: A Review of Theory, Research and Method." *Law and Society Review* 14(3): 603-28.

1984   *The Disreputable Pleasures: Crime and Deviance in Canada*. 2d ed. Toronto: McGraw-Hill Ryerson.
1985a   *Modern Criminology*. New York: McGraw-Hill.
1985b   "Toward a Structural Theory of Crime, Race, and Gender: The Canadian Case." *Crime and Delinquency* 31(1): 129-46.
1989   *Structural Criminology*. New Brunswick, N.J.: Rutgers University Press.

Hagan, J., and I. Nagel
1982   "White Collar Crime, White Collar Time: The Sentencing of White Collar Criminals in the Southern District of New York." *American Criminal Law Review* 20(2): 259-301.

Hagan, J., and P. Parker
1985   "White-Collar Crime and Punishment: The Class Structure and Legal Sanctioning of Security Violations." *American Sociological Review* 50:302-16.

Hagan, J., A. R. Gillis, and J. Chan
1978   "Explaining Official Delinquency: A Spatial Study of Class, Conflict and Control." *Sociological Quarterly* 19(Summer): 386-98.

Hagan, J., A. R. Gillis, and J. Simpson
1985   "The Class Structure of Gender and Delinquency: Toward a Power-Control Theory of Common Delinquent Behavior." *American Journal of Sociology* 90(6): 1151-78.

Hagan, J., J. H. Simpson, and A. R. Gillis
1979   "The Sexual Stratification of Social Control: A Gender-Based Perspective." *British Journal of Sociology* 30:25-38.
1987   "Class in the Household: Deprivation, Liberation and a Power-Control Theory of Gender and Delinquency." *American Journal of Sociology* 92(4): 788-816.
1988   "Feminist Scholarship, Relational and Instrumental Control, and a Power-Control Theory of Gender and Delinquency." *British Journal of Sociology* 39(3): 301-36.

Hall, J.
1982   *General Principles of the Criminal Law*. Toronto.

Hall, S., et al.
1978   *Policing the Crisis: Mugging, the State, and Law and Order*. London: Macmillan.

Hallowell, G. A.
1972   *Prohibition in Ontario 1919-1923*. Toronto: Ontario Historical Society.

Handelman, S.
1989   "Fighting to Put People Before Production." *The Toronto Star* July 16:H1-H2.

Hardyment, A. F.
1984   "Counselling Confusion." *British Columbia Medical Journal* 20:11.

Harlow, L. L., M. D. Newcomb, and P. M. Bentler
1986   "Depression, Self-Derogation, Substance Use, and Suicide Ideation: Lack of Purpose in Life as a Mediational Factor." *Journal of Clinical Psychology* 421.

Hartnagel, T. F.
1978   "The Effect of Age and Sex Composition of Provincial Populations on Provincial Crime Rates." *Canadian Journal of Criminology* 20:28-33.

Haskell, M., and L. Yablonsky
1974   *Crime and Delinquency*. Skokie, Ill.: Rand McNally.

Hastings, R., and R. P. Saunders
1987   "State Control, State Autonomy and Legal Reform: The Law Reform Commission of Canada." In R. Ratner and J. McMullen (eds.), *State Control*. Vancouver: University of British Columbia Press.

Hatcher, G.
1981   *Universal Free Health Care in Canada* 1947-77. Washington, D. C.: U.S. Department of Health and Human Services.

Hatt, K., T. C. Caputo, and B. Perry
1989   "Managing the Crisis: The New Right, the Media, and Criminal Justice Policy in Canada." Paper presented at the Annual Meetings of the Canadian Law and Society Association, Quebec City, June.

Heindensohn, F.
1985   *Women and Crime*. London: Macmillan.
1990   *Crime and Society*. New York: New York University Press.

Helzer, J. E., L. N. Robins, and D. H. Davis
1975-76 "Antecedents of Narcotic Use and Addiction: A Study of 898 Vietnam Veterans." *Drug and Alcohol Dependence* 1.

Henry, F.
1982   "Capitalism, Capital Accumulation, and Crime." *Crime and Social Justice* 18:79-87.

Hepburn, J.
1977   "Social Control and the Legal Order: Legitimated Repression in a Capitalist State." *Contemporary Crises* 1(1): 77-90.

Hiller, H.
1980   "Paradigmatic Shifts, Indigenization, and the Development of Sociology in Canada." *Journal of the History of Behavioral Sciences* 16:263-74.

Hilts, P. J.
1989   "Wave of Protests Developing on Profits from AIDS Drug." *The New York Times* September 16: 1.

Hinch, R.
1988   "Inconsistencies and Contradictions in Canada's Sexual Assault Laws." *Canadian Public Policy* 14:282-94.

Hindelang, M. J.
1971   "The Social versus Solitary Nature of Delinquent Involvements." *British Journal of Criminology* 11:167-75.
1976   "With a Little Help from Their Friends: Group Participation in Reported Delinquent Behaviour." *British Journal of Criminology* 16(2): 109-25.

Hindelang, M. J., M. R. Gottfredson, and J. Garofalo
1978   *Victims of Personal Crime: An Empirical Foundation for a Theory of Personal Victimization*. Cambridge, Mass.: Ballinger Publishing Co.

Hindelang, M., T. Hirschi, and J. Weis
1981   *Measuring Delinquency*. Beverly Hills, Calif.: Sage Publications.

Hirschi, T.
1969   *Causes of Delinquency*. Berkeley: University of California Press.
1984   "A Brief Commentary on Akers' Delinquent Behavior, Drugs, and Alcohol: What Is the Relationship?" *Today's Delinquent* 3:49-52.

Hirschi, T., and M. J. Hindelang
1977   "Intelligence and Delinquency: A Revisionist Review." *American Sociological Review* 42:571-87.

Hoffman, W. M.
1986   "Developing the Moral Corporation." *Bell Atlantic Quarterly*, 1(Spring): 31-41.

Hogarth, J.
1971   *Sentencing as a Human Process*. Toronto: University of Toronto Press.

Holloway, J., and S. Picciotto
1978   *State and Capital: A Marxist Debate*. London: Edward Arnold.

Horton, J.
1981   "The Rise of the Right: A Global View." *Crime and Social Justice* 15(Summer): 7-17.

Hudson, J., et al.
    1988   *Justice and the Young Offender in Canada.* Toronto: Wall & Thompson.

Humphreys, L.
    1970   *Tearoom Trade: Impersonal Sex in Public Places.* New York: Aldine Publishing Co.

Hunt, A.
    1985   "The Ideology of Law: Advances and Problems in Recent Applications of the Concept of Ideology to the Analysis of Law." *Law and Society Review* 19:11.

Jackson, M.
    1983   *Prisoners of Isolation: Solitary Confinement in Canada.* Toronto: University of Toronto Press.
    1986   "Prisoners of Isolation: Solitary Confinement in Canada." In N. Boyd (ed.), *The Social Dimensions of Law.* Scarborough, Ont.: Prentice-Hall.

Jackson, P.
    1977   "City Psychiatrist Feels Criminals Are Brain Damaged." *The Edmonton Journal* July 5:14.

Jackson, P. I.
    1984   "Opportunity and Crime: A Function of City Size." *Sociology and Social Research* 68:172-93.

Jarvis, G., and S. Messinger
    1975   "Ecological Correlates of Juvenile Delinquency Rates." In R. A. Silverman and J. J. Teevan (eds.), *Crime in Canadian Society.* 1st ed. Toronto: Butterworths.

Jeffrey, C. R.
    1990   *Criminology: An Interdisciplinary Approach.* Englewood Cliffs, N.J.: Prentice-Hall.

Jensen, G. F.
    1972   "Delinquency and Adolescent Self-Conceptions: A Study of the Personal Relevance of Infraction." *Social Problems* 20:84-102.

Jessor, R., and S. L. Jessor
    1978   "Theory Testing in Longitudinal Research on Marijuana Use." In D. B. Kandel (ed.), *Longitudinal Research on Drug Use.* Toronto: John Wiley & Sons.

Johnson, Hollis
    1988   *Media and the Creation of Myth: The Role of the Print Media in the Popularization of Stranger-Danger Child Abduction.* Master's thesis, School of Criminology, Simon Fraser University.

Johnson, Holly
    1986   *Women and Crime in Canada.* Ottawa: Programs Branch, Solicitor General Canada.

Jörsekog, K. G. and D. Sörbom
    1983   *LISREL: Analysis of Linear Structural Relationships by the Method of Maximum Likelihood.* 2d ed. Uppsala, Sweden: University of Uppsala.

Josephson, E.
    1981   "Marijuana Decriminalization: The Processes and Prospects of Change." *Contemporary Drug Problems* 10.

Juvenile Delinquents Act
    1970   *Revised Statutes of Canada 1970,* c. C-34

Kaill, R., and P. Smith
    1984   *Atlantic Crime Profile.* Halifax: Atlantic Institute of Criminology.

Kandel, D. B.
    1978   "Homophily, Selection, and Socialization in Adolescent Friendships." *American Journal of Sociology* 84(2): 427-36.

Kandel, D. B., R. C. Kessler, and R. Z. Margulies
    1978   "Antecedents of Adolescent Initiation into Stages of Drug Use: A Developmental Analysis." in D. B. Kandel (ed.), *Longitudinal Research on Drug Use.* Toronto: John Wiley & Sons.

Karmen, A.
    1984   *Crime Victims: An Introduction to Criminology.* Monterey, Calif.: Brooks/Cole Publishing Co.

Katzenback Commission. *See* United States.

Kelly, W., and N. Kelly
1976 *Policing in Canada*. Toronto: Macmillan Publishing Co.

Kennedy, L. W., and D. G. Dutton
1989 "The Incidence of Wife Assault in Alberta." *Canadian Journal of Behavioural Science* 2(1): 40-54.

Kennedy, L. W., and D. Forde
1990 "Routine Activities and Crime: An Analysis of Victimization in Canada." *Criminology* 28:137-52.

Kinsey, R., and J. Young
1986 *Losing the Fight against Crime*. London: Basil Blackwell.

Kitsuse, J., and A. Cicourel
1963 "A Note on the Use of Official Statistics." *Social Problems* 29:131-39.

Klein, D., and J. Kress.
1976 "Any Woman's Blues: A Critical Overview of Women, Crime and the Criminal Justice System." *Crime and Social Justice* 5:34-49.

Knox, R. A.
1984 "Powerfully Addictive Cocaine." *Winnipeg Free Press* December 27:23.

Kornhauser, R.
1978 *Social Sources of Delinquency*. Chicago: University of Chicago Press.

Kosberg, J.
1985 "Victimization of the Elderly: Causation and Prevention." *Victimology*, 10(1-4): 376-96.

Krohn, M. D., R. L. Akers, M. J. Radosevich, and L. Lanza-Kaduce
1982 "Norm Qualities and Adolescent Drinking and Drug Behavior: The Effects of Norm Quality and Reference Group on Using and Abusing Alcohol and Marijuana." *Journal of Drug Issues* 12(4): 343.

Kunkle, S., and J. Humphrey
1982-83 "Murder of the Elderly: An Analysis of Increased Vulnerability." *Omega* 13(1): 927-34.

Lab, S. P., and R. B. Allen
1984 "Self Report and Official Measures: A Further Examination of the Validity Issue." *Journal of Criminal Justice* 12(15): 445-55.

Lander, B.
1954 *Toward an Understanding of Juvenile Delinquency*. New York: Columbia University Press.

Laub, J. H.
1983 "Urbanism, Race and Crime." *Journal of Research in Crime and Delinquency* 20:183-98.

Law Reform Commission of Canada
1974 *The Meaning of Guilt: Strict Liability* (Working Paper 2). Ottawa: Information Canada.
1977 *Report: Our Criminal Law*. Ottawa: The Commission.
1984 *Damage to Property: Arson*. Ottawa: Minister of Supply and Services.

Lea, J., and J. Young
1984 *What Is to Be Done about Law and Order: Crisis in the Eighties*. Harmondsworth: Penguin Books, in association with the Socialist Society.

LeBlanc, M.
1975 "Upper Class vs. Working Class Delinquency." In R. A. Silverman and J. Teevan (eds.), *Crime in Canadian Society*. 1st ed. Toronto: Butterworths.

LeDain, G.
1971 "Interim Report of the Commission of Inquiry into the Non-Medical Use of Drugs." Ottawa: Information Canada.

Lee, G. W.
1984 "Are Crime Rates Increasing? A Study of the Impact of Demographic Shifts on Crime Rates in Canada." *Canadian Journal of Criminology* 26:29-42.

Lemert, E. M.,
    1951   *Social Pathology*. New York: McGraw-Hill.
    1962   "Paranoia and the Dynamics of Exclusion," *Sociometry* 25:2-20.
    1967   *Human Deviance, Social Problems and Social Control*. Englewood Cliffs, N.J.: Prentice-Hall.

Leonard, E.
    1982   *Women, Crime and Society: A Critique of Theoretical Criminology*. New York: Longman.

Leschied, A., and P. Jaffe
    1987   "Impact of the Young Offenders Act on Court Dispositions: A Comparative Analysis." *Canadian Journal of Criminology* 30:421-30.

Levine, H. G.
    1978   "The Discovery of Addiction: Changing Conceptions of Habitual Drunkenness in America." *Journal of Studies on Alcohol* 39:144.

Levine, J.
    1976   "The Potential for Crime over Reporting in Criminal Victimization Surveys." *Criminology* 14:307-30.

Linden, R., and C. Fillmore
    1981   "A Comparative Study of Delinquency Involvement." *The Canadian Review of Sociology and Anthropology* 18(3): 343-61.

Liska, A. E.
    1981   *Perspectives on Deviance*. Englewood Cliffs, N.J.: Prentice-Hall.

Lodhi, A. Q., and C. Tilly
    1973   "Urbanization, Crime, and Collective Violence in 19th-Century France." *American Journal of Sociology* 79:296-318.

Loftin, C., and R. H. Hill
    1974   "Regional Subculture and Homicide: An Examination of the Gastil-Hackney Thesis." *American Sociological Review* 39:714-24.

Lombroso, C.
    1876   *L'Uomo Delinquente [The Criminal Man]*. Milano: Hoepli.

Los, M.
    1982   "Crime and Economy in the Communist Countries." In P. Wickman and T. Dailey (eds.), *White Collar and Economic Crime*. Toronto: D. C. Heath Co.

Lowman, J.
    1985   "From Pillar to Post: The Contradictions in the Regulating of Prostitution Should Be Resolved, Not Enshrined in Ineffective Legislation." *Policy Options* 6(8): 4-6.

Lowman, J.
    1989   "The Geography of Social Control: Clarifying Some Themes." In D. Evans and D. Herbert (eds.), *The Geography of Crime*. London: Routledge.

Luckenbill, D. F.
    1977   "Criminal Homicide as a Situated Transaction." *Social Problems* 25:176-86.
    1984   "Murder and Assault." In R. F. Meier (ed.), *Major Forms of Crime*. Beverly Hills, Calif.: Sage Publications.

Lynch, J. P.
    1987   "Routine Activity and Victimization at Work." *Journal of Quantitative Criminology* 3(4): 283-300.

Macdonald, D.
    1982a   *Sexual Offenses — A Comparative Study of the Present Law, Bill C-127, and the Report of the Law Reform Commission*. Ottawa: Law and Government Division, Research Branch, Library of Parliament.
    1982b   *The Doctrine of Recent Complaint*. Ottawa: Law and Government Division, Research Branch, Library of Parliament.

MacDonald, J.
    1977   *Bombers and Fire Setters*. Springfield., Ill.: Charles C. Thomas.

MacLean, B.
 1989 "Framing the Law and Order Debate: Left Realism, Local Crime Surveys and Police Accountability." Paper presented at the annual meetings of the American Society of Criminology, Reno,
  Nevada.

Maclean's
 1988 "Sermon from the Mount." January 11, 38-39.

Maclennan, A.
 1986 "'Crack' Threat to Canada Being Overplayed." *The Journal* 15:8.

Macleod, L.
 1980 *Wife Battering in Canada: The Vicious Cycle.* Ottawa: Ministry of Supply and Services.

Magnet, J. E.
 1985 *Constitutional Law of Canada,* vol. 2. 2d ed. Toronto: Carswell.

Maloff, D.
 1981 "A Review of the Effects of Decriminalization of Marijuana." *Contemporary Drug Problems* 10.

Mandel, M.
 1986a "Democracy, Class, and Canadian Sentencing Law." In S. Brickey and E. Comack (eds.), *The
  Social Basis of Law.* Toronto: Garamond Press.
 1986b "Democracy, Class, and the National Parole Board." In N. Boyd (ed.), *The Social Dimensions of
  Law.* Scarborough, Ont.: Prentice-Hall.
 1986c "Legalization of Prison Discipline." *Crime and Social Justice* 26:79-94.
 1987 "'Relative Autonomy' and the Criminal Justice Apparatus." In R. Ratner and J. McMullan (eds.),
  State Control. Vancouver: University of British Columbia Press.

Marchak, P.
 1981 *Ideological Perspectives on Canada.* 2d ed. Toronto: McGraw-Hill Ryerson.
 1985 "Canadian Political Economy." *Canadian Review of Sociology and Anthropology* 22(5): 673-709.

Martin, F. E., and G. White
 1988 "West Indian Adolescent Offenders." *Canadian Journal of Criminology* 30:367-79.

Marx, G. T.
 1981 "Ironies of Social Control: Authorities as Contributors to Deviance through Escalation, Nonen-
  forcement and Covert Facilitation." *Social Problems* 28 (February): 221-46.

Matsueda, R. L., and K. Heimer
 1987 "Race, Family Structure, and Delinquency: A Test of Differential Association and Social Control
  Theories." *American Sociological Review* 52 (December): 826-40.

Matthews, R., and J. Young
 1986 *Confronting Crime.* London: Sage Publications.

Matza, D.
 1964 *Delinquency and Drift.* New York: John Wiley & Sons.

Maxfield, M. G.
 1987a "Household Composition, Routine Activity and Victimization: A Comparative Analysis."
  Journal of Quantitative Criminology 3(4): 301-20.
 1987b "Lifestyle and Routine Activity Theories of Crime: Empirical Studies of Victimization, Delinquency and Offender Decision-Making." *Journal of Quantitative Criminology* 3(4): 275-82.
 1989 "Circumstances in Supplementary Homicide Reports: Variety and Validity." *Criminology* 27(4):
  671-95.

Maxim, P.
 1985 "Cohort Size and Juvenile Delinquency: A Test of the Easterlin Hypothesis." *Social Forces* 63(3):
  661-81.

McCandless, P.
 1984 "Curses of Civilization: Insanity and Drunkenness in Victorian Britain." *British Journal of
  Addiction* 79.

McClintock, F. H.
    1970   "The Dark Figures." *In Collected Studies in Criminological Research*, vol. 5. Strasbourg: Council of
              Europe.

McClung, N.
    1915   *In Times Like These*. Toronto: McLeod and Allen.

McCormack, D.
    1984   "Beware of Cocaine Doctor Warns." *The Toronto Star*, May 5:F3.

McDonald, M.
    1986   "A War on Cocaine." *Maclean's* August 4:20.

McGahan, P.
    1984   *Police Images of a City*. New York: Peter Lang Publishing.

McGrath, W. T. (ed.)
    1976   *Crime and its Treatment in Canada*. Toronto: Macmillan Publishing Co.

McMahon, M. W., and R. V. Ericson
    1987   "Reforming the Police and Policing Reform." In R. Ratner and J. McMullan (eds.), *State Control*.
              Vancouver: University of British Columbia Press.

McMullan, J.
    1986   "Socialist Criminology." *Studies in Political Economy* 21(Autumn): 175-92.
    1987   "Crime, Law and Order in Early Modern England." *British Journal of Criminology* 27(3): 252-74.

McMullan, J. and P. Swan
    1988   *The Social Economy of Arson and Arson Control in Nova Scotia (1970-1985): A Preliminary Report*.
              Ottawa: Department of Solicitor General.

Medea, A., and K. Thompson
    1974   *Against Rape*. New York: Farrar, Straus & Giroux.

Meier, R. F., J. R. Burkett, and C. A. Hickman
    1984   "Sanctions, Peers, and Deviance: Preliminary Models of a Social Control Process." *Sociological
              Quarterly* 25:67-82.

Merton, R. K.
    1938   "Social Structure and Anomie." *American Sociological Review* 3:672-82.
    1957   *Social Theory and Social Structure*. New York: Free Press.

Messerschmidt, J.
    1986   *Capitalism, Patriarchy and Crime: Toward a Socialist Feminist Criminology*. Totowa, N.J.: Rowman
              and Littlefield.

Messner S., and K. Tardiff
    1985   "The Social Ecology of Urban Homicide: An Application of the 'Routine Activities' Approach."
              Criminology 23(2): 241-67.

Messner, S. F., and J. R. Blau
    1987   "Routine Leisure Activities and Rates of Crime." *Social Forces* 65:1035-52.

Michalowski, R., and E. Bohlander
    1976   "Repression and Criminal Justice in Capitalist America." *Sociological Inquiry* 46(2): 95-106.

Miethe, T. D., M. C. Stafford, and J. S. Long
    1987   "Social Differentiation in Criminal Victimization: A Test of Routine Activities/Lifestyle Theo-
              ries." *American Sociological Review* 52 (April): 184-94.

Miller, D.
    1989   "Dispute Costs Amway $45 Million." *The London Free Press* September 23:B8.

Miller, W.
    1968   "Lower Class Culture as a Generating Milieu of Gang Delinquency." *Journal of Social Issues* 14:5-
              19.

1975   *Violence by Youth Gangs as a Crime Problem in Major American Cities.* Washington, D.C.: U.S. Government Printing Office.

1977   "The Rumble This Time." *Psychology Today* 10: 52-59.

Miliband, R.

1969   *The State in Capitalist Society.* New York: Basic Books.

Millett, K.

1970   *Sexual Politics.* Garden City, N.Y.: Doubleday.

Mills, C. W.

1943   "The Professional Ideology of Social Pathologists." *American Journal of Sociology* 49:165-80.

Ministry of National Health and Welfare

1983   *Preserving Universal Medicare.* Ottawa: Ministry of Supply and Services.

Mitchell, C. N.

1986   "A Justice-Based Argument for the Uniform Regulation of Psychoactive Drugs." *McGill Law Journal* 31.

Mitchell, R. G., Jr.

1984   "Alienation and Deviance: Strain Theory Reconsidered." *Sociological Inquiry* 54(Summer): 330-45.

Monyihan, D.

1969   *On Understanding Poverty.* New York: Basic Books.

Morris, A.

1987   *Women, Crime and Criminal Justice.* Oxford: Basil Blackwell.

Morton, F. L., et al.

1989   "Justice Nullification and Statutes under the Charter of Rights and Freedoms, 1982-1988." Occasional Paper 4.3. Calgary: Research Unit for Socio-Legal Studies.

Moskowitz, J. M., J. H. Malvin, G. A. Schaeffer, and E. Schaps.

1984   "An Experimental Evaluation of a Drug Education Course." *Journal of Drug Education* 14:9-22.

Moyer, S.

1980   *Diversion from the Juvenile Justice System and Its Impact on Children: A Review of the Literature.* Ottawa: Ministry of the Solicitor General of Canada.

Mungham, G.

1982   "Workless Youth as a 'Moral Panic.'" In T. L. Rees and P. Atkinson (eds.), *Youth Unemployment and State Intervention.* London: Routledge and Kegan Paul.

Murray, C.

1976   *The Link between Learning Disabilities and Juvenile Delinquency: Current Theory and Knowledge.* Washington, D.C.: U.S. Government Printing Office.

Needham, P.

1986   "RCMP Drug Plot Called Scandalous." *Sun* (Vancouver) July 3:A12.

Neilsen, M.

1979   *R.C.M.P. Policing: A Question of Style.* Master's thesis, University of Alberta, Edmonton.

Nettler, G.

1984   *Explaining Crime.* 3d ed. New York: McGraw-Hill.

Noble, J. V.

1977   "Feedback, Instability, and Crime Waves." *Journal of Research in Crime and Delinquency* 14(1): 107-28.

Nova Scotia Provincial Fire Marshall's Office

1970-85 *Annual Report.* Halifax: Department of Labour.

O'Brien, R. M.

1985   *Crime and Victimization Data.* Beverly Hills, Calif.: Sage Publications.

O'Connor, J.
 1973   *The Fiscal Crisis of the State*. New York: St. Martin's Press.

Osborne, J.
 1983   "The Prosecutor's Discretion to Withdraw Criminal Cases in the Lower Courts." *Canadian Journal of Criminology* 25:55-78.

Osgood, D. W., L. D. Johnston, P. M. O'Malley, and J. G. Bachman
 1988   "The Generality of Deviance in Late Adolescence and Early Adulthood." *American Sociological Review* 53 (February): 81-93.

Ouimet, R. (Chair)
 1969   *Report of the Canadian Committee on Corrections: Toward Unity — Criminal Justice and Corrections*. Ottawa: Information Canada.

Overton, J.
 1988   "Beyond the Counting of Costs: A Critique of Efforts to Politicize the Unemployment Problem." Working Paper, Department of Sociology, Memorial University of Newfoundland, St. John's.

Overton, J., and B. O'Grady
 1987   "Popular Anxiety, Armed Robbery and Sentencing in Newfoundland." Department of Sociology, Memorial University, St. John's, Newfoundland. Unpublished paper.

Panitch, L., and D. Swartz
 1985   *From Consent to Coercion: The Assault on Trade Union Freedoms*. Toronto: Garamond Press.

Parker, R. N.
 1985   "Poverty, Subculture of Violence, and Type of Homicide." *Social Forces* 67(4): 983-1007.

Parkin, F.
 1979   *Marxism and Class Theory: A Bourgeois Critique*. New York: Columbia University Press.

Pashukanis, E. B.
 1978   *Law and Marxism*. London: Ink Links.

Patterson, E. J.
 1979   "How the Legal System Responds to Battered Women." In E. M. Moore (ed.), *Battered Women*. Beverly Hills, Calif.: Sage Publications.

Peele, S.
 1985   *The Meaning of Addiction: Compulsive Experience and Its Interpretation*. Lexington, Mass.: D. C. Heath.

Peterson, R.
 1985   "Seniors Gain Rights as Alberta Follows Charter." *The Edmonton Journal* May 11.

Pfohl, S. J.
 1985   *Images of Deviance and Social Control*. New York: McGraw-Hill.

Philips, D. P.
 1979   "Suicide, Motor Vehicle Fatalities, and the Mass Media: Evidence toward a Theory of Suggestion." *American Journal of Sociology* 84(5): 1150-74.
 1983   "The Impact of Mass Media Violence on U.S. Homicides." *American Sociological Review* 48(August): 560-68.

Phipps, A.
 1986   "Radical Criminology and Victimization: Proposals for the Development of Theory and Intervention." In R. Matthews and J. Young (eds.), *Confronting Crime*. London: Sage.

Piliavin, I., and S. Briar
 1965   "Police Encounters with Juveniles." *American Journal of Sociology* 70:206-14.

Pocket Criminal Code
 1989   *Criminal Code of Canada*. Agincourt, Ont.: Carswell.

Poirier, P.
 1986   "PM's War on Drug 'Epidemic' Baffles Experts." *The Globe and Mail* (Toronto) September 16:A1.

Pollak, O.
1950   *The Criminality of Women*. Philadelphia: University of Pennsylvania Press.

Pontell, H., P. Jesilow, and G. Geis
1982   "Policing Physicians: Practitioner Fraud and Abuse in a Government Medical Program." *Social Problems* 30:117-25.
1984a   "Medical Criminals: Physicians and White-Collar Offenses." Unpublished paper, Irvine: University of California.
1984b   "Practitioner Fraud and Abuse in Medical Benefits Programs." *Law and Policy* October.

Poulantzas, N.
1973   *Political Power and Social Classes*. London: New Left Books.

Pound, R.
1943   "A Survey of Social Interest." *Harvard Law Review* 57:1-39.

Public Accounts Committee
1982   *Medical Fraud and Overservicing (Report 212)*. Canberra: Australian Government Publishing Services.

Quetelet, A.
1842   *Treatise on Man*. Paris: Bachelier.

Quinney, R.
1974   *Critique of Legal Order*. Boston: Little, Brown & Co.

Rabinovitch, P.
1986   "Diversion under Section 4: Is There a Future for It in Ontario?" *Young Offenders Service* 7533-42.

Radzinowicz, L., and J. King
1977   *The Growth of Crime: The International Experience*. London: Cox and Wyman.

Rafter, N. H.
1985   *Partial Justice: Women in State Prisons*, 1800-1935. Boston: Northeastern University Press.

Rahav, G.
1981   "Culture Conflict, Urbanism, and Delinquency." *Criminology* 18(4): 523-30.

Rapport, N.
1987   *Talking Violence: An Anthropological Interpretation of Conversations in the City*. St. John's: Institute of Social and Economic Research.

Ratner, R. S.
1984   "Inside the Liberal Boot: The Criminological Enterprise in Canada." *Studies in Political Economy: A Socialist Review* 13 (Spring): 145-64.
1986   "Capital, State and Criminal Justice." In B. D. MacLean (ed.), *The Political Economy of Crime*. Scarborough, Ont.: Prentice-Hall.

Ratner, R., and J. McMullan
1983   "Social Control and the Rise of the Exceptional State in Britain, United States and Canada." *Crime and Social Justice* Summer.

Ratner, R. S., J. L. McMullan, and B. E. Burtch
1987   "The Problem of Relative Automony and Criminal Justice in the Canadian State." In R. Ratner and J. McMullan (eds.), *State Control*. Vancouver: University of British Columbia Press.

Reasons, C., L. Ross, and C. Paterson
1981   *Assault on the Worker: Occupational Health and Safety in Canada*. Toronto: Butterworths.

Reiman, J.
1982   *The Rich Get Richer and the Poor Get Prison*. Toronto: J. Wiley & Sons.

Reiss, A. J., Jr.
1961   "The Social Integration of Queers and Peers." *Social Problems* 9(2).
1980   "Understanding Changes in Crime Rates." In S. E. Reinberg and A. J. Reiss (eds.), *Indicators of Crime and Criminal Justice: Quantitative Studies*. Washington, D. C.: U.S. Department of Justice.

1986   "Why are Communities Important in Understanding Crime?" In A. J. Reiss, Jr., and M. Tonry (eds.), *Communities and Crime*. Chicago: University of Chicago Press.

Reiss, A. J., Jr., and M. Tonry
1986   *Communities and Crime*. Chicago: University of Chicago Press.

Report of the Superintendent of Bankruptcy
1970-85 Canada Corporations Bulletin, Insolvency Bulletin.

Reppetto, T. J.
1974   *Residential Crime*. Cambridge, Mass.: Ballinger Publishing Co.

Ribordy, F.
1980   "Culture Conflict and Crime among Italian Immigrants." In R. A. Silvermen and J. Teevan (eds.), *Crime in Canadian Society*. 2d ed. Toronto: Butterworths.

Rice, B.
1977   "The New Gangs of Chinatown." *Psychology Today* 10:68-69.

Robinson, M.
1977   "Innocent Couple Manhandled." *Sun* (Vancouver) July 14:2.

Roffman, R. A.
1977   "Marijuana and Its Control in the Late 1970's." *Contemporary Drug Problems* 6.
1980   "Interstate Marijuana Law Enforcement — An Analysis of Local Attitudes and Criminal Justice System Accommodations." *Contemporary Drug Problems* 9.

Rojek, D. G.
1982   "Social Status and Delinquency: Do Reports and Official Reports Match?" In G. Waldo, *Measurement Issues in Criminal Justice*. Beverly Hills, Calif.: Sage Publications.

Rokeach, M.
1974   "Some Reflections about the Place of Values in Canadian Social Science." In T. Guinsberg and G. Reuber (eds.), *Perspectives on the Social Sciences in Canada*. Toronto: University of Toronto Press.

Rosenblatt, E., and C. Greenland
1974   "Female Crimes of Violence." *Canadian Journal of Criminology and Corrections* 16(2): 173-80.

Rosenfield, R.
1986   "Urban Crime Rates: Effects of Inequality, Welfare Dependency, Region, and Race." In J. M. Byrne and R. J. Sampson (eds.), *The Social Ecology of Crime*. New York: Springer-Verlag.

Ross, G.
1988   *Stung: The Incredible Obsession of Brian Molony*. Toronto: General.

Ross, R.
1977   "Reading Disability and Crime: In Search of a Link." *Crime and/et Justice May*.

Rowe, A. R., and C. R. Tittle
1977   "Life Cycle Changes and Criminal Propensity." *The Sociological Quarterly* 18:233-36.

Royal Newfoundland Constabulary.
1985   1985 *Annual Statistical Report*. St. John's, Nfld.: R.N.C.

Sacco, V. F.
1985   "City Size and Perceptions of Crime." *Canadian Journal of Sociology* 10:277-93.

Sacco, V. F., and H. Johnson
1990   *Patterns of Criminal Victimization in Canada*. Ottawa: Minister of Supply and Services.

Sagarin, E.
1975   *Deviants and Deviance*. New York: Praeger.

Sagi, P., and C. Wellford
1968   "Age Composition and Patterns of Change in Criminal Statistics." *Journal of Criminal Law, Criminology, and Police Science* 59(1): 29-36.

St. John's Board of Trade
    1985   "A Case Study of Retail Crime." St. John's, Newfoundland.

Sampson, R. J.
    1986a   "Crime in Cities: The Effects of Formal and Informal Social Control." In A. J. Reiss, Jr., and M. Tonry (eds.), *Communities and Crime*. Chicago: University of Chicago Press.
    1986b   "The Effects of Urbanization and Neighborhood Characteristics on Criminal Victimization." In R. M. Figlio et al. (eds.), *Metropolitan Crime Patterns*. Monsey, N. Y.: Willow Tree Press.
    1986c   "Neighborhood Family Structure and the Risk of Personal Victimization." In J. M. Byrne and R. J. Sampson (eds.), *The Social Ecology of Crime*. New York: Springer-Verlag.
    1987   "Personal Violence by Strangers: An Extension and Test of the Opportunity Model of Predatory Victimization." *Journal of Criminal Law and Criminology* 78(2): 327-56.

Sampson, R. J., and J. D. Wooldredge
    1987   "Linking the Micro- and Macro-level Dimensions of Lifestyle/Routine Activity and Opportunity Models of Predatory Victimization." *Journal of Quantitative Criminology* 3(4): 371-93.

Saris, W., and H. Stronkhurst
    1984   *Causal Modelling in Nonexperimental Research*. Amsterdam: Sociometric Research Foundation.

Saveland, W., and D. F. Bray
    1981   "Trends in Cannibis Use among American States with Different and Changing Legal Regimes, 1972-1977." *Contemporary Drug Problems* 10:335-61.

Schaps, E., R. DiBartolo, J. Moskowitz, C. S. Palley, and S. Churgin
    1981   "A Review of 127 Drug Abuse Prevention Program Evaluations." *Journal of Drug Issues* 11:17-44.

Schneider, A. L.
    1977   *The Portland Forward Record's Check of Crime Victims: Final Report*. Eugene, Oreg.: Institute for Policy Analysis.

Schneider, A. L., and D. Sumi
    1981   "Patterns of Forgetting and Telescoping: An Analysis of LEAA Survey Victimization Data." *Criminology* 19(3): 400-410.

Schwartz, R. D., and J. H. Skolnick
    1962   "Two Studies of Legal Stigma." *Social Problems* 10: 133-43.

Scull, A.
    1977   "Madness and Segregative Controls: The Rise of the Insane Asylum." *Social Problems* 24:346.

Scully, D., and J. Marolla
    1985   "Riding the Bull at Gilley's: Convicted Rapists Describe the Rewards of Rape." *Social Problems* 32:251-64.

Segrave, J. O., and D. N. Hastad
    1985   "Evaluating Three Models of Delinquency Causation for Males and Females: Strain Theory, Subculture Theory and Control Theory." *Sociological Focus* 18(1): 1-17.

Select Committee of the Legislative Assembly of Canada
    1849   Cited by R. E. Spence, *Prohibition in Canada*. Toronto: The Ontario Branch of the Dominion Alliance, 1919.

Sellin, T., and M. E. Wolfgang
    1963   *Constructing an Index of Delinquency*. Philadelphia: Center for Criminology Research.

Sellin, T.
    1932   "The Basis of a Crime Index." *Journal of Criminal Law and Criminology* 23:335-56.
    1938   *Culture Conflict and Crime*. New York: Social Science Research Council.

Sewell, J.
    1985   *Police: Urban Policing in Canada*. Toronto: James Lorimer & Co.,

Shaw, C., and H. McKay
    1942   *Juvenile Delinquency and Urban Areas*. Chicago: University of Chicago Press.

Shearing, C., (ed.)
1981 *Organizational Police Deviance*. Toronto: Butterworths.

Shelley, J. F.
1980 "Crime Seriousness Rating: The Impact of Survey Questionnaire Form and Item Content." *British Journal of Criminology* 20(2): 123-35.

Sheppard, M. A.
1980 "Sources of Information about Drugs." *Journal of Drug Education* 10.

Sheppard, M. A., M. S. Goodstadt, and G. Chan
1981 "Drug Education in Ontario Schools: Content and Process." *Journal of Drug Education* 11:317-26.

Sheppard, M. A., M. S. Goodstadt, and B. Williamson
1985 "Drug Education: Why We Have So Little Impact." *Journal of Drug Education* 15:1-5.

Sherman, L., and E. Cohen
1989 "The Impact of Research on Legal Policy: The Minneapolis Domestic Violence Experiment." *Law and Society Review* 23:117-44.

Sherman, L. W., P. Gartin, and M. E. Buerger
1989 "Hot Spots of Predatory Crime: Routine Activities and the Sociology of Place." *Criminology* 27(1): 27-55.

Short, J., and F. Nye
1958 "Extent of Unrecorded Juvenile Delinquency: Tentative Conclusions." *Journal of Criminal Law, Criminology and Police Science* 49:296-302.

Siegel, R. K.
1984 "Cocaine and the Privileged Class: A Review of Historical and Contemporary Images." *Advances in Alcohol and Substance Abuse* 4:37-49.

Silver, G., and M. Aldrich (eds.).
1979 *The Dope Chronicles 1850-1950*. San Francisco: Harper and Row.

Silverman, R. A.
1974 "Victim Precipitation: An Examination of the Concept." In I. Drapkin and E. Viano (eds.), *Victimology: A New Focus*. Lexington, Mass.: D.C. Heath Co.
1977 "Criminal Statistics: A Comparison of Two Cities." *Report to the Solicitor General of Alberta*. Mimeographed.
1980 "Measuring Crime: A Tale of Two Cities." In R. A. Silverman and J. J. Teevan (eds.), *Crime in Canadian Society*. 2d ed. Toronto: Butterworths.

Silverman, R. A., and L. W. Kennedy
1987a *The Female Perpetrator of Homicide in Canada*. Edmonton: Centre for Criminological Research, University of Alberta.
1987b "Relational Distance and Homicide: The Role of the Stranger." *Journal of Criminal Law and Criminology* 78(2): 272-308.

Silverman R. A., and J. J. Teevan, Jr.
1975 *Crime in Canadian Society*. 1st ed. Toronto: Butterworths.
1980 *Crime in Canadian Society*. 2d ed. Toronto: Butterworths.
1986 *Crime in Canadian Society*. 3d ed. Toronto: Butterworths.

Simmons, J. L.
1969 *Deviants*. Berkeley, Calif.: Glendessary Press.

Simpson, S.
1986 "The Decomposition of Antitrust: Testing A Multi-Level, Longitudinal Model of Profit Squeeze." *American Sociological Review* 51:859-75.

Skogan, W. G.
1977 "The Changing Distribution of Big-City Crime: A Multi-City Time-Series Analysis." *Urban Affairs Quarterly* 13:33-48.
1981 *Issues in the Measurement of Victimization*. Washington, D.C.: U. S. Government Printing Office.

| 1984 | "Reporting Crimes to the Police: The Status of World Research." *Journal of Research in Crime and Delinquency* 21:113-37. |

1984   "Reporting Crimes to the Police: The Status of World Research." *Journal of Research in Crime and Delinquency* 21:113-37.

1986   "Methodological Issues in the Study of Victimization." In E. Fattah (ed.), *From Crime Policy to Victim Policy*. London: Macmillan.

Skogan, W. G., and M. G. Maxfield
1981   *Coping with Crime: Individual and Neighborhood Reactions*. Beverly Hills, Calif.: Sage Publications.

Small, S. J.
1978   "Canadian Narcotics Legislation, 1908-1923: A Conflict Model Interpretation." In W. K. Greenaway and S. L. Brickey (eds.), *Law and Social Control in Canada*. Scarborough, Ont.: Prentice-Hall.

Smart, C.
1976   *Women, Crime and Criminology: A Feminist Critique*. London: Routledge and Kegan Paul.

Smart, R. G.
1983   *Forbidden Highs: The Nature, Treatment and Prevention of Illicit Drug Abuse*. Toronto: Addiction Research Foundation.

Smart, R. G., and D. Fejer
1972   "Credibility of Sources of Drug Information for High School Students." *Journal of Drug Issues* 2:8-18.

1974   "The Effect of High and Low Fear Messages about Drugs." *Journal of Drug Education* 4:225-35.

Smart, R. G., and A. C. Ogborne
1986   *Northern Spirits: Drinking in Canada Then and Now*. Toronto: Addiction Research Foundation.

Smith, D. A., and C. A. Visher
1981   "Street-level Justice: Situational Determinants of Police Arrest Decisions." *Social Problems* 29:167-77.

Snider, D. L.
1978   "Corporate Crime in Canada: A Preliminary Report." *Canadian Journal of Criminology* 29(2).

1982   "Traditional and Corporate Theft: A Comparison of Sanctions." In P. Wickman and T. Dailey (eds.), *White Collar and Economic Crime*. Toronto: D. C. Heath Co.

1985   "Legal Reform and Social Control: The Dangers of Abolishing Rape." *International Journal of the Sociology of Law* 13.

1986   "Legal Aid Reform and the Welfare State." *Crime and Social Justice* 24:210-42.

1987   "Towards a Political Economy of Reform, Regulation and Corporate Crime." *Law and Policy* 9(1): 37-68.

1988a   "Commercial Crime." In V. F. Sacco (ed.), *Deviance: Control and Conformity in Canadian Society*. Scarborough, Ont.: Prentice-Hall.

1988b   "The Criminal Justice System in Canada." In D. Forcese and S. Richer (eds.), *Social Issues*. 2d ed. Scarborough, Ont.: Prentice-Hall.

1990   "The Potential of the Criminal Justice System to Promote Feminist Concerns." *Studies in Law, Politics, and Society*. 10.

Snider, D. L., and W. G. West
1985   "A Critical Perspective on Law in the Canadian State: Delinquency and Corporate Crime." In T. Fleming (ed.), *The New Criminologies in Canada: Crime, State, and Control*. New York: Oxford University Press.

Solicitor General of Canada *Canadian Urban Victimization Survey*
1983   *Bulletin 1. Victims of Crime.*
1984   *Bulletin 2. Reported and Unreported Crimes.*
1984   *Bulletin 3. Crime Prevention: Awareness and Practice.*
1985   *Bulletin 4: Female Victims of Crime.*
1985   *Bulletin 5: Cost of Crime to Victims.*
1985   *Bulletin 6. Criminal Victimization of Elderly Canadians.*
1986   *Bulletin 7. Household Property Crimes.*
1987   *Bulletin 8. Patterns in Violent Crime.*
1988   *Bulletin 9. Patterns in Property Crime.*

1988   *Bulletin 10. Multiple Victimization.*
          Ottawa: Research and Statistics Group, Solicitor General of Canada.

Solicitor General
1985   *A Statistical Profile of Female Offenders in Canada.* Ottawa: Statistics Division, Solicitor General
          Canada.

Solomon, R. R., and M. Green
1988   "The First Century: The History of Non-Medical Opiate Use and Control Policies in Canada,
          1870-1970." In J. C. Blackwell and P. G. Erickson (eds.), *Illicit Drugs in Canada: A Risky Business.*
          Toronto: Methuen Publications.

Solomon, R., T. Hammond, and S. Langdon
1986   *Drug and Alcohol Law for Canadians.* 2d ed. Toronto: Addiction Research Foundation.

Special Committee on Pornography and Prostitution (Paul Fraser, Chair)
1985   *Pornography and Prostitution in Canada: Report of the Special Committee on Pornography and
          Prostitution.* Ottawa: Minister of Supply and Services Canada.

Spergel, I.
1964   *Racketville, Slumtown, and Haulbrug: An Exploratory Study of Delinquent Subcultures.* Chicago:
          University of Chicago Press.

Spitzer, S.
1975   "Toward a Marxian Theory of Deviance." *Social Problems* 22:638-51.

Stack, S.
1982   "Social Structure and Swedish Crime Rates." *Criminology* 20:499-513.

Stark, R.
1987   "Deviant Places: A Theory of the Ecology of Crime." *Criminology* 25(4): 893-909.

Statistics Canada
1970-85   *Canada Year Book.* Ottawa: Minister of Supply and Services Canada.
1975   *Crime and Traffic Enforcement Statistics, 1974.* Ottawa: Supply and Services Canada.
1976   *1976 Census.* Ottawa: Government of Canada.
1977   *Crime and Traffic Enforcement Statistics.* Ottawa: Government of Canada.
1983   *Juvenile Delinquents, 1982.* Ottawa: Minister of Supply and Services Canada.
1984   *The Elderly in Canada.* Cat. 99-932. Ottawa: Statistics Canada.
1986   *Canadian Crime Statistics 1985.* Ottawa: Minister of Supply and Services.
1988a   "Break and Enter in Canada." *Juristat Service Bulletin* 8(1): 1- 12.
1988b   *Canadian Crime Statistics, 1987.* Ottawa: Canadian Centre for Justice Statistics.
1989   *Canadian Crime Statistics 1988.* Ottawa: Minister of Supply and Services.

Steffensmeier, D.
1980   "Sex Differences in Patterns of Adult Crime, 1965-77: A Review and Assessment." *Social Forces*
          58(4): 1080-1107.
1981   "Patterns of Female Property Crime 1960-1978: A Postscript." In L. H. Bowker (ed.), *Women and
          Crime in America.* New York: Macmillan Publishing Co.
1983   "Organizational Properties and Sex-Segregation in the Underworld: Building a Sociological
          Theory of Sex Differences in Crime." *Social Forces* 61:1010-32.

Stevenson, G. H., L. R. Lingley, G. E. Trasov, and H. Stansfield
1956   *Drug Addiction in British Columbia.* Vancouver: University of British Columbia Press.

Stoddart, K.
1968   *Drug Transactions: The Social Organization of a Deviant Activity.* Master's thesis, Department of
          Sociology and Anthropology, University of British Columbia.
1974a   "The Facts of Life about Dope: Observations of a Local Pharmacology." *Urban Life and Culture*
          3:179-204.
1974b   "Pinched: Notes on the Ethnographer's Location of Argot." In R. Turner (ed.), *Ethnomethodology.*
          Harmondsworth: Penguin Books.

1980 "Membership by Sign: Essential Insignia and Passing as Deviant." In K. Stoddart (ed.), *Sociology of Deviance*. Book 1. Richmond: Open Learning Institute.

1981 "As Long As I Can't See You Do It: A Case Study of Drug-Related Activities in Public Places." *Canadian Journal of Criminology* 23:391-406.

1983 "Enforcement of Narcotics Violations in a Canadian City: Heroin Users' Perspectives on the Production of Official Statistics." *Canadian Journal of Criminology* 24:425-38.

Stuart, D.
1987 "Annotation to R. *v.* R. C." *Criminal Reports* (3d), 56:185-86.

Sumner, C.
1978 *Reading Ideologies: An Investigation into the Marxist Theory of Ideology and Law*. New York: Academic Press.

1983 "Rethinking Deviance: Towards a Sociology of Censures." *Research in Law, Deviance, and Social Control* 5.

Sun (Vancouver)
1984 "Pay Figures Mask Lab's Reality." October 24.

Sung, B. L.
1967 *Mountain of Gold: The Story of the Chinese in America*. New York: Macmillan Publishing Co.

Sutherland, E.
1937 *The Professional Thief*. Chicago: University of Chicago Press.

1939 *Criminology*. Philadelphia: J. B. Lippincott.

1949 *White Collar Crime*. New York: Holt, Rinehart & Winston.

Sutherland, E. H., and D. R. Cressey
1955 *Principles of Criminology*. Philadelphia: J. B. Lippincott.

1970 *Criminology*. 8th ed. New York: J. B. Lippincott.

1978 *Criminology*. 10th ed. Philadelphia: J. B. Lippincott.

Skyes, G., and D. Matza
1957 "Techniques of Neutralization: A Theory of Delinquency." *American Sociological Review* 22:664-70.

Szasz, T.
1975 *Ceremonial Chemistry: The Ritual Persecution of Drugs, Addicts and Pushers*. Garden City, N.J.: Anchor Press.

Tannenbaum, F.
1938 *Crime and the Community*. Boston: Ginn.

Tanner, J., G. S. Lowe, and H. Krahn
1984 "Youth Unemployment and Moral Panics." *Perception* 7(5): 27-29.

Tappan, P.
1947 "Who Is the Criminal?" *American Sociological Review* 12:96-112.

Taylor, I.
1983a *Crime, Capitalism and Canadian Society: Three Essays in Socialist Criminology*. Toronto: Butterworths.

1983b "Justice Expenditure, Welfare Expenditure and the Restructuring of the Canadian State." In I. Taylor, *Crime, Capitalism and Community: Three Essays in Socialist Criminology*. Toronto: Butterworths.

1984 "Criminology, the Unemployment Crisis and the Liberal Tradition in Canada." Paper delivered at the Atlantic Institute of Criminology Meetings, St. John's, April.

1985 "Criminology, the Unemployment Crisis and the Liberal Tradition." In T. Fleming (ed.), *The New Criminologies in Canada*. Toronto: Oxford University Press.

1986 "Martyrdom and Surveillance: Ideological and Social Practices of Police in Canada in 1980's." *Crime and Social Justice* 26:60-94.

1987 "Theorizing the Crisis in Canada." In R. Ratner and J. McMullan (eds.), *State Control*. Vancouver: University of British Columbia Press.

Taylor, I., P. Walton, and J. Young
    1973   *The New Criminology: For a Social Theory of Deviance.* London: Routledge and Kegan Paul.

Thio, A.
    1983   *Deviant Behavior.* Boston: Houghton Mifflin Co.
    1988   *Deviant Behavior.* 3d ed. Cambridge: Harper and Row.

Thompson, J. H.
    1972   "The Beginning of our Regeneration: The Great War and Western Canadian Reform Movements." In R. D. Francis and D. B. Smith, *Readings in Canadian History.* Toronto: Holt, Rinehart & Winston.

Thomson, G.
    1983   "Commentary on the Young Offenders Act." *Provincial Judges Journal* 7(2): 27-29, 34.

Thornberry, T. P.
    1967   "Delinquency and Social Class: A Critique of Self-Reported Studies." Manuscript. Philadelphia: University of Pennsylvania.

Thrasher, F. M.
    1963   [1927] *The Gang.* Chicago: University of Chicago Press.

Tigar, M., and M. Levy
    1977   *Law and the Rise of Capitalism.* New York: Monthly Review Press.

Timberlake, J. H.
    1963   *Prohibition and the Progressive Movement 1900-1920.* Cambridge: Harvard University Press.

Tisshaw, K.
    1976   "Recently Immigrated Chinese Youth and Strathcona Experience: A Report to the Strathcona Youth Service Advisory Committee." Mimeographed.

Tittle, C. R.
    1983   "Social Class and Criminal Behavior: A Critique of the Theoretical Foundation." *Social Forces* 62:334-58.
    1988   "Two Empirical Regularities (Maybe) in Search of an Explanation: Commentary on the Age/Crime Debate." *Criminology* 26:75-86.
    1989   "Urbanness and Unconventional Behavior: A Partial Test of Claude Fischer's Subcultural Theory." *Criminology* 27(2): 273-306.

Tjaden, P. G., and C. D. Tjaden
    1981   "Differential Treatment of the Female Felon: Myth or Reality?" In M. Q. Warren (ed.), *Comparing Female and Male Offenders.* Beverly Hills, Calif.: Sage Publications.

Trebach, A. S.
    1987   *The Great Drug War.* New York: Macmillan Publishing Co.

Tribble, S.
    1975   "Socioeconomic Status and Self-Reported Juvenile Delinquency." In R. A. Silverman and J. Teevan (eds.), *Crime in Canadian Society.* 1st ed. Toronto: Butterworths.

Turk, A.
    1976a   "Law as a Weapon in Social Conflict." *Social Problems* 23:276-92.
    1976b   "Law, Conflict, and Order: From Theorizing toward Theories." *Canadian Review of Sociology and Anthropology* 13:282-94.
    1986   "Class, Conflict and Criminalization." In R. A. Silverman and J. Teevan (eds.), *Crime In Canadian Society.* 3d ed. Toronto: Butterworths.

Tversky, A., and D. Kahneman
    1974   "Judgement under Uncertainty: Heuristics and Biases." *Science* 185:1124-31.

United States
    1967   *Crime and Its Impact: An Assessment.* Task Force Report of the President's Commission on Law Enforcement and Administration of Justice. Washington, D.C.: U. S. Government Printing Office. (Katzenbach Commission).

University of Montreal
    1981   "Group Research on Attitudes toward Criminality." Pilot Study. University of Montreal School of Criminology.

Vandivier, K.
    1987   "Why Should My Conscience Bother Me?" In M. D. Ermann and R. J. Lundman (eds.), *Corporate and Governmental Deviance*. New York: Oxford University Press.

Vaughan, D.
    1983   *Controlling Unlawful Organizational Behavior: Social Structure and Corporate Misconduct*. Chicago: University of Chicago Press.

Vayda, E.
    1973   "A Comparison of Operations and Surgeons in Canada and England and Wales." *New England Journal of Medicine* 282:1224.

Veblen, T.
    1967   [1899]. *The Theory of the Leisure Class*. New York: Viking Press.

Vogel, L.
    1983   *Marxism and the Oppression of Women: Toward a Unifying Theory*. New Brunswick, N.J.: Rutgers University Press.

Vogt, I.
    1984   "Defining Alcohol Problems as a Repressive Mechanism: Its Formative Phase in Imperial Germany and Its Strength Today." *The International Journal of Addictions* 19.

Vold, G. B.
    1958   *Theoretical Criminology*. New York: Oxford University Press.

Vold, G. B., and T. J. Bernard
    1986   *Theoretical Criminology*. 3d ed. New York: Oxford University Press.

Von Hoffman, N.
    1970   "Sociological Snoopers and Journalistic Moralizers." In L. Humphreys (ed.), *Tearoom Sex: Impersonal Sex in Public Places*. New York: Aldine.

Waddington, P. A. J.
    1986   "Mugging as a Moral Panic: A Question of Proportion." *The British Journal of Sociology* 37(2): 245-59.

Waldorf, D., S. Murphy, C. Reinarman, and C. Joyce
    1977   *Doing Coke: An Ethnography of Cocaine Users and Sellers*. Washington, D. C.: Drug Abuse Council.

Walker, H. A., and B. P. Cohen
    1985   "Scope Statements: Imperatives for Evaluating Theory." *American Sociological Review* 50(3): 288-301.

Walsh, M.
    1977   *The Fence*. Westport, Conn.: Greenwood Press.

Walters, G. D., and T. W. White
    1989   "Heredity and Crime: Bad Genes or Bad Research." *Criminology* 27(3): 455-85.

Ward, D.
    1988   "Kelleher Favours U.S. Get-Tough Drug Policy." Sun (Vancouver) May 3: B1.

Wardell, W.
    1987   "The Young Offenders Act: A Report Card 1984-86." *Journal of Law and Social Policy* 2:39-72.

Warner, Q. and A. G. N. Bradshaw
    1925   *Report of the Juvenile Court of London and Middlesex, June to December, 1925*. London: City of London.

Warr, M.
    1988   "Rape, Burglary, and Opportunity." *Journal of Quantitative Criminology* 4(3): 275-88.

Watson, D., and R. Tharp
    1981   *Self-Directed Behavior: Self Modification for Personal Adjustment.* Monterey, Calif.: Brooks/Cole Publishing Co.

Weber, M.
    1947   *The Theory of Social and Economic Organization.* Glencoe, Ill.: Free Press.

Weil, A., and W. Rosen
    1983   *Chocolates to Morphine: Understanding Mind-Active Drugs.* Boston: Houghton Mifflin Co.

Wellford, C.
    1975   "Labelling Theory and Criminology: An Assessment." *Social Problems* 22:332-45.

Welter, B.
    1966   "The Cult of Womanhood, 1820-1860." *American Quarterly* 18:151-74.

Whittingham, M.
    1981   "Vandalism — The Urge to Change Property." *Canadian Journal of Criminology* 23:69-74.

Whyte, W. F.
    1955   *Street Corner Society: The Social Structure of an Italian Slum.* Chicago: University of Chicago Press.

Wilbanks, W.
    1981-82 "Trends in Violent Death among the Elderly." *International Journal of Aging and Human Development* 14(3): 167-75.

Wilkins, L. T.
    1967   *Social Policy, Action, and Research: Studies in Social Deviance.* London: Associated Book Publishers.

Williams, G.
    1961   *Criminal Law: The General Part.* 2d ed. London: Stevens.

Williams, F. P., and M. D. McShane
    1988   *Criminological Theory.* Englewood Cliffs, N. J.: Prentice-Hall.

Wilson, J. Q.
    1968   *Varieties of Police Behavior: The Management of Law and Order in Eight Communities.* Cambridge: Harvard University Press.
    1975   *Thinking about Crime.* New York: Basic Books.

Wilson, J. Q., and R. J. Herrnstein
    1985   *Crime and Human Nature.* New York: Simon and Schuster.

Wilson, P. R., and P. Gorring
    1984   "Social Antecedents of Medical Fraud and Overservicing: Why Doctors Commit Fraud." Paper presented to the American Society of Criminology Meetings, Cincinnati, November.

Wirth, L.
    1938   "Urbanism as a Way of Life." *American Journal of Sociology* 44:3-24.

Witkin, G.
    1979   "All Pyros Are Psychos." *Fire and Arson Investigation* 32(2).

Wolfgang, M. E.
    1958   *Patterns in Criminal Homicide.* New York: John Wiley & Sons.

Wolfgang, M. E., and F. Ferracuti
    1967   *The Subculture of Violence.* London: Tavistock Publications.

Wolfgang, M. E., R. Figlio, and T. Sellin
    1972   *Delinquency in a Birth Cohort.* Chicago: University of Chicago Press.

Wright, K. N.,
    1981   "Economic Adversity, Reindustrialization, and Criminality." In K. N. Wright (ed.), *Crime and Criminal Justice in a Declining Economy.* Cambridge, Mass.: Oelgeschlager, Gunn and Hain Publishers.

Wurmser, L.
1978   *The Hidden Dimension: Psychodynamics in Compulsive Drug Use*. New York: Jason Aronson Publishers.

Yeary, J.
1982   "Incest and Chemical Dependency." *Journal of Psychoactive Drugs* 14.

Yeudall, L.
1977   "Neuropsychological Correlates of Criminal Psychopathy Part I: Differential Diagnosis." Paper presented at the Fifth International Seminar in Comparative Clinical Criminology, Montreal.

Yin, P.
1985   *Victimization and the Aged*. Springfield, Ill.: Charles C. Thomas.

Young Offenders Act, R.S.C.
1985   C.Y-1. *An Act Respecting Young Offenders*.

Zimmerman, J., and P. K. Broder
1980   "A Comparison of Different Delinquent Measures Derived from Self-Report Data." *Journal of Criminal Justice* 8(3): 147-62.

Zimring, F. E., and G. J. Hawkins
1973   *Deterrence: The Legal Threat in Crime Control*. Chicago: University of Chicago Press.

Zinbreg, N. E.
1984   *Drug Set and Setting: The Basis for Controlled Intoxicant Use*. New Haven: Yale University Press.

Zinberg, N. E., and J. A. Robertson
1972   *Drugs and the Public*. New York: Simon and Schuster.

Zuckerman, M.
1978   "The Search for High Sensation." *Psychology Today* 11:38.